D'Apocalypse™ Now!

The Doomsday Cycle

The Federal Reserve Trilogy
Volume III

By: Robert L. Kelly

A   PUBLICATION
JACK ASSBANKER ™

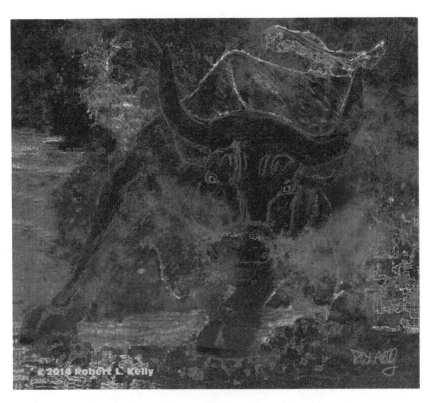

D'Apocalypse™ Now!
The Doomsday Cycle
By: Robert L. Kelly

Library of Congress Control Number: 2014901895
All Rights Reserved. Printed in the U.S.A.
© 2014 Robert L. Kelly

Jack Assbanker™ Publications
Attention: Robert Kelly
1732 1st Avenue #24739
New York, New York 10128

A   PUBLICATION
JACK ASSBANKER ™

Acknowledgements

I would like to thank every person who has continued to believe in me throughout my life. Each of you provides me with inspiration and hope to help everyone live better lives---it is what drives me forward, no matter what. I love you all, always and forever. Without your kindness, love and support this book and The Federal Reserve Trilogy would not have been possible to write.

I also want to thank God for putting Jesus in my life and giving me inspiration to write the trilogy and expose the evil which exists throughout the system. With Him, I have no fear and look forward to His powerful and triumphant return when evil shall be defeated and thrown into the gates of Hell, forever.

With best wishes and prayers for you and your loved ones, always!

Robert L. Kelly
aka:
Dad, Uncle Bob, Bob & Kel
XOXOXOXOXOXOXOXOXOXOXOXOXOXOXOXOXOXO

About The Federal Reserve Trilogy:

Mr. Kelly's warnings relating to the approaching credit crisis in 2007 and 2008 helped some people avoid devastating losses in their portfolios, because they took action *before* the crisis erupted. As everyone knows, ultimately, there was a complete stock-market meltdown and difficulty! In a "Déjà vu, all-over again" moment, Mr. Kelly is sounding the alarm bells EVEN LOUDER, yet another time.

The Federal Reserve Trilogy issues an urgent warning to all people and documents the causes, the motivations and the outcome of a devastating economic firestorm, called "D'Apocalypse™." It is swiftly approaching and set to strike nations all over the world. The trilogy unveils the secret plans of the bankers and global elite to collapse the financial system and seize control of the world's monetary policy and money supply systems. Mr. Kelly sleuths out the facts, figures, history, charts and patterns, revealing their master strategy, while compellingly providing nations, corporations and all wealth classes, specific recommendations to avoid disaster during this upcoming grab for power. The end result of D'Apocalypse™ will be social devastation and a severe economic meltdown, purposely caused by the bankers and the elite. It will rain ruin on hundreds of millions of people—with the onset of a dangerous and real global war, the likely result!

There are very few people, or organizations, with the ability to analyze and distill sets of complex information into understandable, tactical and easy-to-implement action plans. Mr. Kelly amply demonstrates these abilities, with the writing of The Federal Reserve Trilogy.

The $30 Trillion Heist—Scene Of The Crime?, and The $30 Trillion Heist—Follow The Money!, spell out how the banks, the Federal Reserve and the elite heisted nearly $30 Trillion from U.S. taxpayers—without the knowledge, or consent of Congress. Importantly, the books uncover what they are doing with this heist money. D'Apocalypse™ Now! unveils the logical conclusion and aftermath of the great heist. Reading it will help families, hedge funds, companies, and nations, avoid the worst of this purposely engineered, financial catastrophe.

Fortunes will be made and lost during the Great D'Apocalypse™ and The Federal Reserve Trilogy empowers you to assess the facts and compelling evidence, allowing you to make powerful and intelligent decisions during the course of the next several years. It is a set of books you will want to have in digital format because of their robust links, marvelous images, graphics and artwork. You may also want a hard copy for backup, just in case the lights go out and things really get bad!

A **Jack Assbanker**™ **Publication**

TABLE OF CONTENTS

"And the kings of the earth, and the great men, and the rich men, and the chief captains, and the mighty men, and every bondman, and every free man, hid themselves in the dens and in the rocks of the mountains;

And said to the mountains and rocks, Fall on us, and hide us from the face of Him that sitteth on the throne, and from the wrath of the Lamb:

For the great day of his wrath is come; and who shall be able to stand?"
(Source: The Bible, <u>Revelation 6:15-17</u>, King James Version).

WORKING THE PRESS

©2014 Robert L. Kelly

"WORKING THE PRESS," and other art of the author published in the Federal Reserve Trilogy, is available at http://www.jackassbanker.com. This cartoon was adapted from an 1862 Abraham Lincoln-era cartoon, titled, "Lincoln Spins the News." It may be retrieved at http://commons.wikimedia.org/wiki/File:1862_political_cartoon_(%22Lincoln_spins_the_news%22).JPG).

Introduction

D'Apocalypse™ Now! --- The Doomsday Cycle is the last book of The Federal Reserve Trilogy which also includes The $30 Trillion Heist in its Volume I, Scene Of The Crime? and its Volume II, Follow The Money!

Collectively, the trilogy distills a logical, yet complex investigation into simple, undeniable truths to warn people what is coming to the Western banking system and Western economies, worldwide:

A virtual holocaust and economic firestorm
caused by the collapse of debt and the
bursting of an astounding derivatives bubble.

The trilogy labels this the
"Doomsday Cycle of the Great "D'Apocalypse™!"

By reading D'Apocalypse™ Now! you will learn how to protect yourself, your company and your country (if you are in government around the world). You will also learn why this disaster is inevitable and heading our way, faster than just about anyone thinks it will, or should.

Even if you are an expert in derivatives, or the markets, this book will be extremely helpful to you. Yes, a novice will learn what a derivative is---in simple language virtually anyone can understand---but all readers will learn WHY this market is ready to collapse at ANY moment.

You will become informed, or better informed, of the overwhelming forces piling up against the American people and indebted world because of the monstrous plans and actions of the bankers, the elite, the Federal Reserve and their co-conspirators.

The author unveils the truth and intentions of their plans which are nothing short of shocking and should cause everyone to stagger in fear.

As any reader of either of the two previous books of The Federal Reserve Trilogy knows, this author is not a fear monger. He is an experienced Chief Executive Officer calling them as he sees them---with facts to back up the logical conclusions these works reach and present to the reader.

Globally, these modern-day banking pirates have a pre-determined strategy seeking world-wide control of monetary policy and the money supply. The elite know this is the key to controlling and taking the world's wealth—particularly from the merely "well-to-do," the "poor" and the "middle class." They also know this is the key to allowing them to operate without accountability to government of any kind—anywhere in the world.

The breakthrough work documenting the actions of the Federal Reserve, the gorillas of the global banking system and their owners in the first two books of the trilogy (The $30 Trillion Heist---Scene Of The Crime? and The $30 Trillion Heist---Follow The Money!) provides the reader with direct evidence a heist has taken place against the American People---which totals an amount approaching a stunning $30 Trillion.

D'Apocalypse™ Now!, the "Heist's" companion work in the trilogy, documents and predicts the logical outcome of these nefarious activities upon the entire world---and this outcome will and should cause you to take immediate action to protect yourself, your company and your nation from this coming Doomsday Cycle. It is better to look at the facts of the situation objectively, forming a game plan to survive and potentially thrive, than to bury your head in the sand and hope nothing bad happens.

This particular book provides bold governments and bold thinkers, alike, all over the globe, with very specific defensive and offensive plans and strategies to counteract the elite's grab for power which will bring the financial system to its knees, once again.

No reader will want to miss Chapter 9 of this book, "What To Do Now."

The elite's plan is well staged and brilliant in its deviance. Using trillions of dollars taken from the American people, they are driving up asset prices in their preferred sectors (bonds—which already had their historic bull run---, stocks---which are going to scream higher in 2015 and high-end luxury items, including real estate, jewelry, etc.). At the very peak expected during 2015, they will have unloaded their liquid and now highly profitable securities positions, they will be holding their $30 Trillion in heist money and ***they will be prepared*** for the greatest crash of all time----the great D'Apocalypse™!

The question is---will you, the reader, who may not be part of the elite, be prepared? Alternatively, the question is---will you, the reader, who *is* part of the elite, be comfortable with your actions and implicit support of this evil plan to continue pillaging of trillions of dollars from innocent people when you have to meet your maker? These are the big questions this book poses.

The D'Apocalypse™ is a planned event designed to pick up where the credit crisis left off. The bankers will use this pre-planned and elite-manufactured crisis to dramatically increase interest rates and mark down asset prices, causing a derivatives' betting pyramid in the U.S., and world, to collapse. The U.S. derivatives market is 93% owned and controlled by only four major banks, the 4 Horsemen of the D'Apocalypse™---JP Morgan Chase, Citigroup, Bank of America and Goldman Sachs. They will be aided and abetted by ten additional banks from around the world, which are also members of the "G14."

The reader will read much more about derivatives and gain a good understanding of the dangers they pose, due to the leverage being used in them.

A derivative is simply a contract between multiple parties (typically a bank and a counter party) which involves interest rates, commodities, equities, debt, credit default swaps, futures, options, swaps, currencies, or other underlying assets, conditions, products, or items. Over 90% of the derivatives market is not even traded on an exchange, and is transacted in secret, with no transparency, leaving a small number of banks in a position of monopoly power over this enormous market.

Globally and nominally, the derivatives market is estimated at over $700 TRILLION dollars, with some insiders saying its true size approaches $1.5 QUADRILLION DOLLARS!

With the U.S. Gross Domestic Product "only" at a total of about $16 Trillion, anyone reading these few sentences can see the system is leveraged to the hilt, in a reckless and shameless manner. Disaster is inevitable.

Because of this recklessness and planned collapse of these markets by the 4 Horsemen and the G14, they shall rain havoc upon nearly every single nation and company on earth.

They intentionally will torch, set ablaze and create the firestorm of D'Apocalypse™ with the ***intentional collapse*** of an "official" $692 Trillion derivatives gaming table controlled uniquely by them.

To put this into perspective, the size of this market is approximately 40 times the size of the United States' Gross Domestic Product ("GDP").

As you will see and learn in this book, 14 banks form an elite club which has a singular, ultimate goal of making money at all costs, have armed themselves with an attitude of:

"Damn the torpedoes and full speed ahead!"

Their plan is to carve up territories and petrify nations, which will be accomplished through a complete heart attack of the financial system. This attack will prevent governments from financing themselves and leave millions to starve and millions and millions more unemployed.

Their goal has been hundreds of years in the making and they pursue it with steadfast rigor, with an objective of ceded control of the global monetary system---with little, or no, government interference. Readers of The $30 Trillion Heist,---Follow The Money! (which has detailed spread sheets and tables detailing the ownership of the New York Federal Reserve Bank---the key to the operations of the Fed), *already know* there are only a very few families who own and control the U.S. banks and the Federal Reserve. Internationally, the situation is eerily similar, with very few powerful families ultimately pulling the strings at the major banks of the G14.

D'Apocalypse™ Now! reveals how they will accomplish their goal, <u>when</u> to expect them to make their move and what, exactly, to do to prepare yourself for this upcoming debacle. Governments, around the world, have an amazing opportunity to turn the tables on these greedy and diabolical organizations and improve, dramatically, the situation for millions of citizens.

The author, as documented in The $30 Trillion Heist, has a strong track record of predicting not only the mortgage and credit crisis, but also predicted a war would start just two weeks before 911 happened (although he had no idea it would start in New York, where he resides!), when war wasn't on anyone's radar screen. He also predicted the NASDAQ and market crash of 2000. He is a Christian technologist and inventor who has spent much of a lifetime studying financial markets and the Federal Reserve.

Chapter 9 of this book provides specific action plans for governments, corporations, pension funds, hedge funds and individuals to help them prepare, prosper and defend themselves from the egregious activities planned by this cabal of bankers and elite.

As readers of $The 30 Trillion Heist know, particularly from the Introduction in Volume I which provides a summary of the author's background, the author is a capitalist who has taken three companies public. He has no problem with wealth when it is accumulated honestly. He believes the best system is one which is based upon God, with a strong sense of community toward others---in short, "live by the golden rule."

As he reported in Volume I of <u>The $30 Trillion Heist</u>---<u>Scene Of The Crime?</u>, he knows The Federal Reserve Trilogy would have never been published, if he hadn't been given the time to research, think and write during the last year. These works document, definitively, the suspected high crimes and egregious activities of the banks, the Federal Reserve System and the elite behind them. It also explains why the government will not prosecute the bankers responsible for any of their suspected crimes. This, despite a mountain of evidence pointing to a nearly $30 Trillion heist, which resulted in economic destruction far greater than the United States' Gross Domestic Product of $16 Trillion in 2013.

And make no mistake—the destruction was caused directly by the banks' and elites' fraudulent behavior, as supported by the Federal Reserve System, during and through their pre-planned, self-engineered, mortgage and credit crisis. Their manufactured crisis allowed them to gobble up competitors and foreclose on most of the once bustling real estate industry, bringing under control the mortgage companies and banks which had gotten too big for the liking of the 4 Horsemen.

In the process, in collaboration with the Federal Reserve, they have put nearly 50 million people on food stamps, with true unemployment towering over 30%. Jobs, in America and in the EU, are non-existent for youth and the middle-aged, who are being fired to avoid pension obligations and replaced with cheap outsourcing overseas. Of course, part-time work is available at fast food restaurants, which pays well below poverty-level wages in the United States and Europe.

As bad as this is currently, it will get much worse. <u>D'Apocalypse™ Now!</u> documents an enormous catastrophe coming to the Western financial markets, particularly, which will cause economic ruin for retirees, pension funds, wealthy individuals, corporations and unprepared hedge funds---AS WELL AS ENTIRE GOVERNMENTS!

During D'Apocalypse™, governments are the
key target of the bankers and their elite owners.
Governments, especially, need to prepare.

If you benefit from this research, advice and prognostications, the author only asks you help others when the dreadful firestorm of D'Apocalypse™ arrives. It is inevitable. So, pray to God you are prepared and when you are saved from its devastation, please remember to help others who are less fortunate. To do nothing will bring disaster on you and your family.

God Bless You!

Robert L. Kelly

Chapter 1
The Debt—Catalyst for D'Apocalypse™

Nearly everyone is familiar with the "real time" debt clock at http://www.usdebtclock.org. It is referenced frequently by the main stream media. What most people DON'T realize is the politicians and the bankers have run up debt and derivatives in such a staggering manner, they have placed nearly $3 Million of exposure on every man, woman and child in the United States! There is no way the debt will ever be repaid and the derivatives situation is beyond macabre. They will be the main cause of an enormous economic collapse coming to the western world.

U.S Debt Clock December 7, 2013

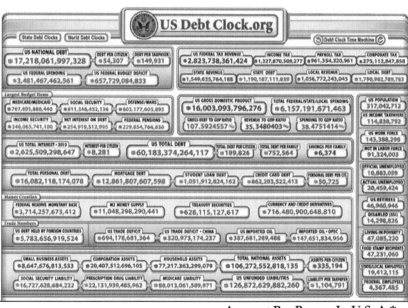

	Amount Per Person In U.S. A.*
U.S. 2013 Gross Domestic Product of $16.0 Trillion	$ 50,592
U.S. National Debt at $17.2 Trillion	$ 53,199
Personal Citizen's Debt of $16 Trillion	$ 50,592
U.S. Unfunded Liabilities of $126.9 Trillion	$ 401,259
Subtotal Debt Per Person	$ 505,050
Currency and Credit Derivatives of over $716 Trillion	$2,265,523
Exposure Per Citizen	$2,770,573

* Based upon 316,254,000 people as of December 2013—see Chapter 7, "A Word on Unemployment," subsection "True Unemployment Picture." Above calculation ignores local debt. (Source: U.S. Debt Clock, as retrieved from http://www.usdebtclock.org).

We all know out-of-control spending ultimately can cause great problems of currency, balance of trade, deflation, inflation, economic turmoil and an enormous debt burden for the future. Depending on how debt is dealt with will determine the resulting impact on the financial markets. When the problem is completely ignored and then combined with wild speculation and incredible leverage, the result is a poisonous cocktail which can completely wipe out any economy—especially if it is too highly leveraged.

America, Western Europe and Japan, particularly, have been able to blithely go about their business and generally ignore the debt burden politicians and the central banks have brought upon the people. This has only been possible because during the last forty years, politicians in nearly all nations have been permitted by the markets to borrow off of the hard work and ingenuity of previous generations of hard-working families. They are the ones who contributed to building vibrant, largely debt-free, nations.

Unfortunately, through a series of abominable strategies deployed by the Federal Reserve System, the elite and the member banks, nearly every single government has been suckered into borrowing trillions of dollars at extremely low interest rates. This has allowed our politicians to spend money wildly---like a drunk on a binge---in their zest for power and desire to be reelected. Now governments are pregnant with debt, with no apparent way out. As the reader will learn, the bankers' trap is ready to be sprung.

The bankers know how to compromise and have planned on compromising governments from day one. Today, governments at all levels are up to their eyeballs in debt and the bankers are setting the stage to raise interest rates. This will cause tremendous economic calamity for every borrower and nearly every derivatives trader in the world.

The bankers and elite know, at the end of the day, the debt ultimately must be settled---and all the trading accounts must be cleared. When the bankers, historically, have ever had a population of people or governments in such a vulnerable position and situation---they have shown no mercy. They just squeeze and go for the jugular! This time will be no different.

Interest rates are going to go sky high in 2015 and will be the major factor which causes D'Apocalypse™. IF the Federal Reserve chooses to buy up every single government auction to keep rates low, artificially, via the Quantitative Easing ("QE") programs, there will be tremendous infrastructure and inflation problems for the majority of people in America, Europe and Japan. Ultimately, however, the bankers' plans are to abruptly halt the supply of credit and send those interest rates to the moon! This will cause an earthquake for every indebted government on earth and result in huge opportunities for the elite.

Just by looking once again at figures under the debt clock, any school child can quickly see the debt per person figures and realize there is something terribly wrong. Today, every baby born into an American family has a debt burden of approximately $500,000 hanging around its head!

Additionally, a more advanced student in junior high, or high school, will immediately see from the debt clock, the derivatives market *is enormous* at $716 Trillion on the clock and wildly out of proportion to the U.S. GDP, which stood at $16 Trillion at the end of 2013, with the world's GDP at $71.8 Trillion in 2012 (CIA estimate) and estimated by the IMF at $74 Trillion in 2013. (see Chapter 2, "Derivatives---the Ticking Time Bomb!," subsection, "Derivatives---$716 TRILLION Unregulated Marketplace").

Everyone understands debt and we shall deal with derivatives in the next chapter. As we all know, debt must be eliminated in one of the following ways:

1) It must be defaulted upon and foreclosed upon; or
2) It must be hyper-inflated away via outright printing of money; or
3) It must be exchanged for a new currency; or
4) It must be repaid.

The collective debt is enormous, as is obvious, because no baby should have to come into life in any country which has placed a ½ million dollar burden on its life!

Most Americans shouldn't have to be repaying these debts, either, because as the facts will reveal, the debts were accumulated at the will and whim of politicians and elite bankers, eager to take the prosperity away from the majority of Americans---in favor of an elite few who benefitted and benefit from their actions.

The preceding discusses the details of the U.S.A's debt clock. But a staggering debt burden has befallen nearly every single government on earth and has unleashed a powerful deflationary force which has caused tremendous unemployment, economic chaos and pain for hundreds of millions of people around the globe. This is also why, given the Federal Reserve's gigantic heist of money and their multi-trillion dollar "QE" programs, there has not been hyper-inflation, as many gold bugs expected to occur by now.

Even though The Federal Reserve has printed, created and iniquitously given away trillions of dollars to the elite, the sheer destructive force of the mortgage and credit crisis meant their money printing scheme and secret heist was merely offset by the loss of wealth throughout the economic system.

Furthermore, the egregious and unfair manner in which the Fed heisted the money for the sole benefit of the elite and the banks is creating a "politonomy" condition reminiscent of the 1600s, 1700s and early 1800s. This is when the Spanish robbed the wealth from nearly everyone in South America, stealing the wealth of nations for the sole favor of their own elite. Instead of sharing those national treasures with the people at large, they plundered the entire continent. We know what the legacy of these actions was and a similar fate is in store for America unless the wrongs committed by the elite are righted.

It is simply impossible to argue the actions by the Fed, the banks and the elite have done anything to help the masses. These people are 21st century conquistadors masquerading as bankers. They have only enriched themselves and their elite handlers---at everyone else's expense.

When D'Apocalypse™ arrives, there will be a tremendous economic calamity and depending on how much money is printed, inflation will ULTIMATELY rear its ugly head and ravage everyone in its path.

D'Apocalypse™ Now!---The Doomsday Cycle believes the Fed or a newly empowered Global Reserve Bank, set up by the elite after empowerment by governments, will eventually print its way out of the fire of collapse (or will entirely replace the currencies, effectively devaluing the dollar, pound, yen, euro, etc.) and wipe out millions of peoples' savings and investment accounts in the process.

Before this happens, however, the world will experience the debacle of D'Apocalypse™ and certain deflation of targeted assets, companies and national treasures the banks and their elite owners want to own and acquire for pennies on the dollar. This will only be possible by yet another banker- and elite-engineered crisis, causing the panic of the ages.

Underlying Problem with the Debt is Interest Rates

Aside from the sheer magnitude and size of the existing debt, the most serious underlying problem lies with interest rates. Interest rates are the napalm which will cause the raging fire of D'Apocalypse™.

As the world continues to collapse around America in the next couple of years, it will turn to the American dollar as the last great "safe haven." The cracks in the European Union, Japan, China and the developing world have now emerged and become well published in the world's press.

As the banks tighten monetary policy, in their quest to obtain control of the system globally, interest rates will rise and the U.S. Dollar will undergo a tremendous rally because of rising interest rates.

The staggering amount of debt held around the world---virtually all of which is denominated in U.S. Dollars---will cause the demand for the dollar to soar, because people will be scrambling to pay off the debt--- demanding dollars to do so.

The U.S. dollar rally---driven by rising interest rates, the debt and scramble for dollars, as well as the fatal attraction to the U.S. being mistakenly thought of as a "safe haven," will ultimately further destroy the U.S. economy---sort of like plunging a stake through the heart of a vampire!

High interest rates will hammer the budget deficit, cripple spending plans and destroy, even further, the economies of America, Europe and Japan.

And VERY unfortunately, rising interest rates are directly and materially tied to the derivatives market where the largest betting sectors deal in---- you guessed it, interest rates and debt securities! These are the Achilles Heel of the entire system and will cause, ultimately, the Doomsday Cycle of the Great D'Apocalypse™--the derivatives and debt collapse which shall wreak havoc on all mankind.

Ultimately, if a "new" currency is foisted upon the world, it will undoubtedly be worth far less than any currency you have in your pocket today. If the bankers are successful in implementing their plan to take control of monetary policy and the global money supply, there could indeed be a one-world currency which will digitally clear all transactions through an elite-controlled, banker-controlled super bank (as outlined in The $30 Trillion Heist---Scene Of The Crime?, Chapter 9 "The $30 Trillion Heist," as well as in The $30 Trillion Heist---Follow The Money!, Chapter 1 "The $30 Trillion Heist---How the Scam Worked").

If this comes to pass, you can count on these Satanic maestros of intellect to emphatically pronounce, with pompous arrogance, a "new," "better" banking system which will prevent another collapse from occurring in the future. This pronouncement and establishment of the super bank will be on the heels of what will be the most horrific crash and shut down in history, the result of the D'Apocalypse™.

Debt---Bargaining Chip for Global Control of Monetary Policy

As the debt has increased astronomically, there is a natural conflict between the bankers, Wall Street and the federal government. The problem is the federal government in the United States, Europe and Japan owes its lenders too much money and can't pay these vast sums back without crushing their economies---one way, or another.

This fact and reality will ultimately allow the bankers and elite to further turn the tables on governments and make additional demands upon nations, worldwide, for the bankers' and elites' direct control over monetary authority. Their plan is to seize this control with complete, or near complete, independence from government.

The bankers, once they start pushing interest rates dramatically higher, will use and blame a phony "recovery" as their cover story. This ratcheting up of rates will cause governments to squeal from here to kingdom come! The interest payments due on governments' accumulated debt will destroy nearly every government budget on earth and make it impossible for them to borrow more money.

This is how bankers will squeeze and it is how they will play hardball in the coming years. Forewarned, is forearmed.

It is also how they will achieve their hundreds-of-years-old objective of seizing control of the monetary apparatus of the world—through the cooperation and acquiescence of corrupt and irresponsible government officials. The bankers and elite *know* this is how they can maintain their super-owner control over the banks, thus guaranteeing their families' power for centuries into the future.

This is their end game---this is why they could care less who they hurt when they torch the economy under the firestorm of D'Apocalypse™!

Increasing Interest Rates Planned---Cause the Firestorm of D'Apocalypse™

The strategy deployed in their conquest of international monetary policy and control of the money supply will entail a rapid, seemingly uncontrollable INCREASE in interest rates, across all marketplaces. By design, this will catastrophically impact governments' abilities to raise capital to continue their gigantic, nonsensical spending policies.

From a practical perspective in the next couple of years, we will see the debt continue to skyrocket and at least into 2015, the stock market will go on a tear, and could nearly DOUBLE (see Chapter 9, "What To Do Now," subsection, "Buy the Dow") in value from current levels (e.g. 16,000 as of December 2013).

This rally will provide the smokescreen needed for the bankers to claim rates only dramatically escalated because of the "recovery." This is a recovery, of course, which is all smoke and mirrors. In reality, it is non-existent. Any appearance of recovery will be strictly limited to the classes of assets serving the elite---and no one else. This event of asset price inflation across only certain asset sectors primarily serving the elite, is coined by the author as Assflation™, which is an intentionally manipulated rise in asset prices across certain, targeted asset sectors for the benefit of the elite (and is more precisely defined in Chapter 2, "Derivatives---the Ticking Time Bomb!," subsection, "When the Bubble Bursts,").

Nonetheless, for most people who know nothing about banking and economics, the bankers will roll out the same old lame excuse they have always used---"it's the business cycle..." to explain why interest rates jumped as dramatically as they will in 2015. Without question, they will point to the crescendo and exuberant rise of the stock market as the falsetto of hope and false evidence of a "recovery," despite its non-existence for the common man.

It is simply incredible these people and institutions will have the chutzpah to claim such an Assflation™-driven market recovery as the "evidence" of genuine economic recovery! Their feigned innocence with respect to their manipulation and rise of interest rates, which are required to kick off D'Apocalypse™, will be an acting job which will be the envy of Hollywood!

Banks and Elite Go for the Jugular Against Governments

Unfortunately, it will also be a vicious, premeditated attack on the financial system of the United States and the West, particularly, since they are under the direct control of the Federal Reserve and the other elite, family-controlled central banks. As most readers understand, the attack will be designed to seize control of monetary authority and steal additional trillions of dollars in assets from seemingly healthy companies and individuals, for pennies on the dollar. The stakes will also be enormous, essentially for control of the world. One thing is for certain---these Barbary Pirates will stop at nothing to make this conquest a reality.

Their offensive will eerily remind many readers and people of the takedown of Lehman Brothers and Bear Stearns and they will be shrewdly correct. Bear Stearns, Lehman Brothers, Countrywide Financial, Merrill Lynch, Washington Mutual, AIG, etc. were the warm up acts for these hungry vultures.

Their legions of attorneys and accountants will come prepared to D'Apocalypse™ and acquire hundreds of other companies rich with assets and shall bankrupt millions of people---most of which were once wealthy. They will also make an art form out of devouring some of the most precious national assets on the planet---acquiring islands, park land, drilling rights, shorelines, water rights…you name it.

This is the time when the banks and the elite will go for the jugular against government.

Does this sound impossible?

The Unprepared Will be Skewered
It is not impossible, particularly when only four banks control 93% of the derivatives market in the United States (and only 14 banks control over 80% of the derivatives market in the world). This gives a handful of men and women iron-grip control over the valuations of the contracts and transactions being traded in this marketplace. When the balloon goes up and the elite decide to turn off the credit spigot, once again, values will collapse and forced margin calls will proliferate throughout the system like wildfire. The unprepared will be skewered as the firestorm of D'Apocalypse™ passes overhead. Not even the blood of the lamb on your door will save you, this time, if you are caught unprepared!

Since the derivatives market, which nominally is measured at $692 TRILLION (nearly 10 times the size of the world's GDP and over 40 times the size of the U.S. GDP), is dominated by transactions involving debt securities and interest rates, the bankers fully plan on *increasing* the rates, extraordinarily and quickly, to effect defaults on thousands of counter parties throughout the system---including and especially, governments. This will create a corresponding economic and social collapse of the system---causing extreme urgency for politicians all over the world to quickly resolve it---or get voted out of office (likely hung, as well!) because of the chaos on the economic front.

Despite many pundits merely decrying the size of the debt and derivatives market, they have generally failed to connect the dots. Size doesn't matter *when the system is working*. In fact, derivatives markets are important. The problem is the *leverage* involved in the derivatives marketplace.

Everything goes along swimmingly well when there are no unexpected changes to a leveraged system, especially when it is controlled by an oligopoly. It is only when a catalyst of extraordinary change is introduced, will the system seize up and fail. Today, there isn't urgency in government to do <u>anything</u> about their debts, or the derivatives market, because government can seemingly print money at will and the public and bankers all go along with it—at least for now.

This will change during the next two years when the bankers, in yet another self-engineered crisis, spring D'Apocalypse™ on the world and interest rates go sky high. The bankers will claim it is because of economic recovery. However, because the entire banking industry and derivatives market is controlled by exactly 4 major banks in this oligopoly, this crisis will, once again, be done on a <u>premeditated basis</u>, allowing them to crash the system and execute their grand plan. The credit crisis was, quite literally, a warm up act to train the bankers' and elites' attorneys, accountants, executives and sales people on how to gobble up competitors and take down industries.

The Satanic Bargain—Politicians, the Elite and the Bankers
Naturally, there will be a quid pro quo---the politicians will be in a helpless state due to the utter impoverishment and distress among the people. The cacophony shall be so great from the populous, the politicians will be SCREAMING, CRYING AND BEGGING the bankers and elite to turn on the supply of money and credit to get the markets moving again.

This time, political blustering will fall on deaf ears until the politicians, together in one room, cede authority to the elite and the major banks to implement the new global currency and monetary policy system planned by the elite, which will be run by their family-controlled banks.

15

These clever and shrewdly brilliant people will even offer an exchange of debt "forgiveness" for the target governments, in exchange for complete control over the reins of monetary policy, worldwide. Once this is accomplished, the bankers and elite will once again re-inflate the system via the implementation of their usury and derivatives trading systems. The big difference this time is they will control the supply of money for all nations in the Western financial world.

This is how they will also force all governments to come through their window to borrow any monies, thereby ensuring the elite and bankers will be guaranteed the payment of their principal and interest, forever. This will virtually guarantee their families' dynasties live forever; at least, this is their hope.

As part of this grand, satanic bargain, the banking elite will promise and guarantee to governments the capability to track and trace all transactions through the system, thereby allowing tax collections to be maximized. This will make the system become more severe, more efficient and create far greater revenues for the politicians, which will be music to the ears of spend-crazy politicos, worldwide.

With this coup-d'état of global monetary authority, the bankers will then have complete control over their ability to LEVERAGE the entire world's money supply into their monopoly-controlled, derivatives trading schemes—without government interference. This will provide the elite with a monopoly to control transactions, profits, and prices, worldwide, across the derivatives and credit markets, as well as, over all real economies on earth.

A new digital currency will also likely emerge and be quickly implemented, acting as the exchange platform for the old dollar, old yen and old euro denominated debt (provided the euro even survives in its current form, which is highly unlikely---as much as the author loves Europe, the EU will fall apart due to debt, unemployment and wild spending).

Government "wins" because it will probably survive and the system will crack down on taxes because all transactions will be tracked, with the added bonus of economic recovery. This will allow the politicians to spend themselves, once again, into oblivion.

The bankers and elite "win" because they have now expanded their power to control virtually all of the world's money supply, as well as the monetary authority over it. They will have succeeded in forcing every government to come to their window to borrow money and will, again, print mounds of money out of thin air. This will mark truly, a centuries-old dream of the elite families who own, or otherwise control, the Federal Reserve System of the United States of America (see The $30 Trillion Heist, Volume II, Follow The Money!, Chapter 16, "OWNERSHIP OF THE FEDERAL RESERVE" for details and the FACTS on this subject) and the major banks around the world.

The new Global Reserve Bank will use a nearly identical system utilized by the Federal Reserve to effect the $30 Trillion heist against the American people. Unfortunately, their solution is only a cancer which merely layers another set of taxes and cost increases upon the working class of the world. It will be important for all of us to remember their plan was only made possible as a direct result of the politicians' overspending and the disastrous decision to allow the Federal Reserve to be owned and controlled by the commercial banks and elite---the private, 3rd parties who maintain control of the Fed through their direct ownership of the 12 Regional Federal Reserve Banks.

Media Will Falsely Trumpet the Bankers' Horn Announcing Their "Rescue" of Governments

The public will be snowed once again by the bankers, Wall Street and the politicians. The regular guy on the street will see on TV and read in banker- and elite-controlled media, mountains of propaganda proclaiming how the 4 Horsemen of the D'Apocalypse™ (e.g. JP Morgan Chase, Goldman Sachs, Bank of America and Citigroup) "road to the rescue" of federal governments all around the world during the great D'Apocalypse™. These headlines are undoubtedly already preplanned and we can expect to hear a veritable symphony of orchestrated press and headlines announcing the salvation of one and all from economic devastation through the banks' and elites' forgiveness of debt and largess.

The public received a little taste of these future headlines when a recent article from the New York Post empathized with JP Morgan Chase because of a pending $13 Billion fine for mortgage fraud (it ultimately became a $20 Billion fine) they committed during the credit crisis (see the article, "How the U.S. thanked Jamie Dimon," which follows).

It is a laughable article because anyone who read The $30 Trillion Heist---Follow The Money, Chapter 11 "The Crystal Ball and the Acquisition of Giants" will know JP Morgan Chase *was paid* $30 Billion to BUY BEAR STEARNS and they picked up over *$13 Trillion* in derivatives transactions from this acquisition alone---without paying a penny out of its own pocket to do so! Additionally, JP Morgan Chase has used the toxic securities sitting in their mortgage operations and their Washington Mutual and Bear Stearns acquisitions to exchange them at the Fed window and participate in the secret heist of nearly $30 Trillion!

This is an excerpt from The $30 Trillion Heist---Follow The Money:

The Crystal Ball and the Acquisition of Giants

"JP Morgan Chase stole the company based on true value, as Bear Stearns was sitting on extremely valuable assets---it owned the Street's most prestigious clearing-firm business, it had over $300 Billion in assets on its balance sheet *and it had $13.4 TRILLION in derivatives* transactions on its books! The lesson here is ANY company with tremendous assets can FAIL—especially if you cannot renew your credit lines." (Source: The $30 Trillion Heist---Follow The Money, Chapter 11 "The Crystal Ball and the Acquisition of Giants", Robert L. Kelly, 2013 Jack Assbanker™ Publications, http://www.jackassbanker.com).

The following is from the New York Post article and a good example of how the bankers' PR machine will work when future headlines proclaim they saved the world after D'Apocalypse™ strikes:

How the US thanked Jamie Dimon

"JPMorgan just got its first thank-you note for helping save the financial system five years ago. It's a strong-armed "settlement" that forces it to pony up $13 billion — $5.1 billion of which goes to Fannie Mae and Freddie Mac, it was announced late Friday — to the same government that asked for its help. And that just covers the civil end of things; the possibility of criminal charges remain…

…CEO Jamie Dimon and JPMorgan's board of directors went above and beyond the call of duty when the phone rang on two Saturdays during the 2008 financial crisis. The shotgun acquisitions of Bear Stearns and Washington Mutual that the feds orchestrated were massive and risky."
(Source: New York Post, "How the US thanked Jamie Dimon," Jonathan Trugman, October 26, 2013, as retrieved from http://nypost.com/2013/10/26/what-works-for-jpmorgan-is-good-for-america/).

It is remarkable isn't it? The spinning of the supposedly free press to try to hoodwink the public and convince them JP Morgan Chase did the United States Government *a favor* in acquiring Bear Stearns and Washington Mutual? How ridiculous and outrageous can you get?

JP Morgan Chase even cut off Bear Stearns' credit line, causing them to become bankrupt---literally overnight, forcing the "shotgun wedding" described in the New York Post article!!

This is called predatory lending at its finest! Between Bank of America gobbling up Countrywide and JP Morgan Chase grabbing Washington Mutual, they took control of the entire mortgage industry and armed themselves with TRILLIONS of dollars of toxic securities these elite banks knew they could exchange with the Fed for good-as-gold, U.S. taxpayer-backed, Federal Reserve Credits and U.S. taxpayer-backed securities!

It is the height of naiveté, ignorance and even possibly conspiracy to even insinuate JP Morgan Chase did the United States a favor in acquiring Bear Stearns and Washington Mutual! It is quite literally, astonishing and insulting.

Unlike the above article from the Post, the time of D'Apocalypse™ will herald a new era where politicians will join the banks, hand in hand at the press conference. They will not be in an adversarial position because both will be responsible for the collapse. The politicians will be profusely praising and thanking the 4 Horsemen for saving the world via their "forgiveness" of the debt of nations, while the bankers and elite assume the new mantle of authority over a new, ever more powerful, "Global Reserve Bank" (or some other name they might give it).

The politicians will have no choice because they have already spent the ENTIRE WORLD into the grave of debt and will be buried by the downfall of the collapsing derivatives markets. There is no way either of these groups of cowards, either the politicians or the bankers, will admit they brought the devastating impact of D'Apocalypse™ upon all nations.

We will all have to sit back and listen to them heap praise and thanks upon the "magnanimous" bankers and their elite owners behind the curtains.

In the process, the elected officials will have also just made a deal with the devil himself. They will be forced to publicly support and *thank* the banking cabal for coming to the rescue and instituting an "incredible" new system of control, which promises to prevent such a collapse from "ever happening again." ***This, despite the fact*** the bankers and the elite purposely caused the system to fail and economy to collapse in the first place!

Some bright readers may wonder why the bankers and elite didn't collapse the markets sooner, e.g., why not 2013? Why not 2014? The system certainly is and obviously will be, highly vulnerable due to the stunning size of the mountain of debt, along with the reckless leveraging and Las Vegas-style betting taking place in the derivatives markets.
It is a fair and very good question.

The Elite Nearly Lost Everything in the Credit Crisis
The answer to this question is really quite simple. The bankers and elite were unprepared to do it sooner than 2015. They ALL NEARLY LOST EVERYTHING during the credit crisis, because they UNDERESTIMATED the impact their engineered collapse would have on them and others with whom they do business.

As you will know from reading this book and perhaps reading the amazing details in the other two books of The Federal Reserve Trilogy, the impact of the crisis was severe. Ben Bernanke, Chairman of the Federal Reserve, secretly bailed out the entire banking industry in North America AND Europe through the $30 Trillion heist. These facts are detailed like no other publication known to this author in both Volumes I and II of The $30 Trillion Heist.

Essentially, during this "Heist," the bankers and elite secretly exchanged MONOPOLY MONEY for $30 Trillion of U.S. taxpayer-backed Federal Reserve Bank credits, cash, U.S. Treasury securities and/or other U.S. cash-equivalents, without the consent of Congress, or anyone else. "Monopoly money," as used in this book and in The Federal Reserve Trilogy, are securities which were literally worthless, had no street value, and were likely worth only a fraction of what the Federal Reserve paid for them. The evidence seems to strongly indicate these securities may have been fraudulently valued at inflated prices, greatly above fair market value, with the premeditated intent of exchanging these fraudulently valued securities for U.S. taxpayer-backed cash, and cash equivalents, from the Federal Reserve System.

Only a full, unabridged audit of the Federal Reserve System and all Regional Federal Reserve Banks will tell the tale on this theory and these presumptions, however. The evidence is quite scary in its strong support of the author's contention that this is exactly what happened.

As most know, the credit crisis and mortgage debacle had a crippling impact on the bankers' and elites' balance sheets. They were devastated by their own greed, their self-engineered credit crisis and their self-promulgated mortgage fraud collapse, as they completely underestimated the impact the destruction would have on them, directly.

Until they cried to the government and Federal Reserve to bail them out, they were on the road to ruin and bankruptcy, which is where they should have gone, allowing other successful business people and investors to take them over, with the government guaranteeing the depositors' monies. Unfortunately, as we all know, this did not occur.

What did occur, however, is the bankers and the elite used the $30 Trillion to recover their balance sheets, create Assflation™ and set up the game board to try and obtain their TRUE DREAM. This will be made possible via their planned D'Apocalypse™ and the economic devastation it will create upon nearly every nation on earth.

To achieve this dream, or nightmare, for most Americans, the elite and the bankers MUST CRASH THE SYSTEM AND BRING GOVERNMENTS TO THEIR KNEES. $30 Trillion, plus all the profits they will have made from Assflation™ (directly caused by Mr. Bernanke secretly bailing them out) in the equity and debt markets, is a tidy sum for them to have in their pockets during the upcoming crash. They will mercilessly use those funds to go on another asset acquisition, company-raiding and government-held-hostage binge, which will only be possible with a purposeful collapse of the system.

The collapse of the debt and derivatives markets will cause thousands of bankruptcies, literally overnight, and create economic ruin for hundreds of millions of additional people. This will place extreme stress on governments, worldwide (with an extremely high probability people AND nations will be revolting and going to war because of starvation, unemployment and destruction throughout the system). In turn, this will stampede the politicians into a virtual bull run (i.e., a mindless stampede), not dissimilar to what you see on TV in Pamplona, Spain, forcing them down a narrow path until they are corralled and cornered by the bankers and elite.

This will allow these fiendish band of pirates to achieve their objective of global monetary control through political acquiescence---albeit, with quite a bit of arm twisting and pain in the process.

The politicians will be frightened, as in few other times in history, by the surrounding economic devastation and firestorm of the D'Apocalypse™. They will be BEGGING the bankers to turn on the printing presses, allowing them to retain power and thereby make an evil bargain with Satan himself.

Ultimately, their plan will be accomplished through one central bank, controlled by the wealthy elite, who will have cut deals with all the other prominent nations, peoples and religions to become part of the "family," with a seat at the table. Expect to hear nothing but GOOD NEWS over the television set, even if the sky is falling. The talking heads on TV are merely reading a tightly controlled corporate script edited by the owners of the banks and Federal Reserve (i.e., the media companies are controlled by other major institutions, all of which lead back to the banks, as documented and detailed in The $30 Trillion Heist, Volume II, Follow The Money!, Chapter 14, "Media Control").

How Much Money Does the U.S. Really Owe?

OK, this sounds frightening, but is it real? How much money does the U.S. really owe, certainly the bankers and elite don't have the power, or ability to crash the system, do they?

Well, to start with, the real answer to this question is, YES, THEY DO HAVE THE POWER! The publicly available information from the debt clock reveals some frightening facts. The grave exposure placed on us by our bankers and politicians should be obvious to one and all. Let's add up the damage:

$126.9 Trillion dollars is the amount of money the U.S. Government knows it does not have to fully fund the Medicare, Medicare Prescription Drug (Medicare Part D) and Social Security programs.

Unfunded liabilities amount to $1,109,382 PER TAXPAYER!

Combined with the outstanding U.S. Debt (which includes household, personal, mortgage, student loan, business, State & Local Governments, financial institutions and The Federal Government) of $60,183,374,264,117 (another $60 TRILLION DOLLARS!), then the **ACTUAL TOTAL DEBT**, NOT INCLUDING DERIVATIVES, is $187.08 TRILLION DOLLARS.

Together, these debts amount to $1,635,486 PER TAXPAYER and is the equivalent of $591,550 FOR EVERY MAN, WOMAN AND CHILD IN AMERICA!

If you include currency and credit derivatives subject to destruction in an economic meltdown, they add up to a whopping $716,480,900,648,810 ($716 TRILLION!!!), or 44.77 TIMES AS BIG AS THE U.S. GDP!!!

> **The derivatives exposure equals a staggering $2,265,523**
> **FOR EVERY MAN WOMAN AND CHILD IN AMERICA.**
> **Combined with total debt and unfunded liabilities, America's people**
> **are at risk for a grand total of $2,857,073 PER**
> **PERSON, the equivalent of $7,899,088 PER TAXPAYER!!!**

This is truly the mother of all bubbles---just ready to pop.

Without going into details in this chapter about derivatives (see Chapter 2, "Derivatives---the Ticking Time Bomb!,"), most pension funds, state and local governments, federal governments, Fortune 1000 companies, hedge funds, etc. use Interest Rate and Credit Default Swap ("CDS") derivatives to "hedge" and/or speculate in debt positions (e.g., when a hedge fund, or bank, purchases a pool of mortgages which has an expected interest rate return, it may purchase "insurance" against default, and/or other credit risks including interest rate increases, etc.).

These markets are enormous and unsurprisingly, Wall Street has once again successfully bamboozled the ratings agencies into assigning high-quality debt ratings to these kinds of contracts. This has allowed the size, scale and leverage associated with the derivatives markets to grow out of control, monstrously. As you have already read and will learn, only a small number of super banks "control" these markets---making these markets vulnerable to manipulation and a potential collapse.

High ratings (obtained in a very similar manner which allowed the banks to fraudulently obtain AAA ratings on junk-mortgage pools causing the credit crisis) allow the funds, banks and major Wall Street firms sell these securities with the auspicious (if not now notorious) "AAA" investment grade ratings.

The ratings are highly likely to be found fraudulent when D'Apocalypse™ arrives, because JP Morgan Chase, Citigroup, Bank of America and Goldman Sachs control over 90% of the derivatives market in the United States and DO NOT HAVE THE ASSETS, INCOME, OR CASH FLOW to properly collateralize the bets they made in this "notional" global market totaling $692 Trillion (please read Chapter 2, "Derivatives---the Ticking Time Bomb!").

By the way, many insiders believe the size of the derivatives market is **double** the "notional" amount. Ultimately, the derivatives market will prove to be one of the biggest schemes and farces in bubble history.

Deliberate Manipulation of Interest Rates and Debt Markets Assure Doom

It will be called a farce because the banks, Federal Reserve and elites in the near future will make further, deliberate manipulations to the interest rate and debt markets (the banks have already been found guilty of fraudulently manipulating the London Interbank Rate "LIBOR," which has an enormous impact on the derivatives market), causing interest rates to escalate, dramatically.

With a derivatives system controlled by just a few banks and those banks in complete control of pricing, settlement and interest rates, the parties on the opposite side of the table from the big banks will be crushed--- especially when rates abruptly and swiftly rise through the roof!

The banks' greed will NOT permit them to <u>NOT</u> manipulate prices and artificially create chaos, allowing the banks to force margin calls on the parties in a derivatives transaction. Overnight, the banks can and will cause thinly traded securities to be quoted "no bid," while normally "liquid" securities' position prices will fall off a cliff---with no explanation, other than "credit conditions have changed!"

In this way, the 4 Horsemen of the D'Apocalypse™, JP Morgan Chase, Bank of America, Citigroup, Goldman Sachs and their co-conspirators, will steal assets and take over cherished corporate targets at will, for pennies on the dollar. After reading this book, it will be difficult to come to any other conclusion than they will be doing this on an orchestrated basis with the other banks. Their premeditated actions will contribute directly to the systemic default of the system and cause a complete meltdown in the economy and market—affecting the world's economies dramatically.

When the firestorm of D'Apocalypse™ arrives, it will become known as the great destroyer all around the world. The least affected economies will be the <u>poorest</u> nations on earth and if you find a safe one which will take you in, it would be an excellent place to ride out this storm!

Minor tremors, just like the buildup to a major earthquake, are sending signals the upcoming collapse is imminent. Economies throughout the developed and developing world are succumbing to debt implosion and spending exhaustion. Italy, France, Greece, Ireland, Spain, Portugal, Brazil, Argentina and Japan are in deep trouble and the EU has its head on a chopping block---all because of excessive debt and too much spending---leaving them vulnerable to a wicked cabal just waiting to attack.

Japan recently saw its interest rates double, overnight, when the government announced it would vastly increase the money supply and go down the sordid path of quantitative easing in an attempt to revive the economy.

Europe will tumble and the EU will likely collapse before 2015, but between now and then, a great deal of capital will flow *into* the U.S. market. The capital will arrive on these shores because of fear and rising interest rates in the U.S., causing a major dollar rally and tremendous additional Assflation™ in the liquid, equity markets which will likely double between now and the fall elections of 2016---with D'Apocalypse™ scheduled to hit the United States before, or during that time frame. See Chapter 9 of this book for specific timing, as well as entry and exit points from the markets.

The U.S. will be the last major Western-trading-nation to go down the tubes, as the elite and bankers will want to ride the tide of rising equity markets and grab every dollar of profit they can prior to the collapse. It will take this kind of robust, bull market in equities to drive every single sucker back into stocks. This way, the bankers and the elite can unload their $30 Trillion heist-money hoard (plus profits), illicitly received from the Federal Reserve, back onto an unsuspecting public---as well as pension funds, governments, companies, mutual funds and the rest of an unprepared marketplace.

Ironically, because the U.S. has issued mountains of debt AND the U.S. Dollar is held as the reserve currency, there will *also* be a bull market in the U.S. Dollar through 2015 (at least until the D'Apocalypse™). The Dollar's bull market will be caused by rising interest rates and loans being called in by the bankers. There will be a mad scramble for U.S. cash which will cause a short squeeze on the dollar in 2015 and further contribute to an enormous equity bull market in major U.S. stocks, particularly.

Ultimately, the Dollar bull market will cripple U.S. exports even further, contributing significantly to the collapse of the economy, which will be a shambles throughout, with 32% of the people currently out of work (see Chapter 7, "A Word on Unemployment").

When the U.S. goes, it will experience exactly what France and other countries are experiencing today, due to the overwhelming debt load left by the socialists in those countries.

Every second, young Frenchmen would prefer to emigrate
"The displeasure of a young Frenchwoman, due to the current policies of the country, recently brought "Clara G," a 20-year-old student, to express in an open letter to Francois Hollande why her generation wants to leave their country:

'Because I do not want to work all my life to pay taxes to simply exist, taxes only serve to pay the €1.9 trillion Euro debt your generation kindly donated to us. If these loans would have at least served to make investments and plan for the future of the country, even if I only had a small benefit from this, I would not have a problem in helping to repay this debt.'" (Source: Deutsche-Wirtschafts-Nachrichten.de, "Every second young Frenchman would prefer to emigrate", May 12, 2013, as retrieved from http://deutsche-wirtschafts-nachrichten.de/2013/05/12/jeder-zweite-junge-franzose-wuerde-am-liebsten-auswandern/. **Note: translation may not be exact).**

The debt, driven by liberal government pension plans for the entrenched politicians and bureaucrats, liberal immigration laws, liberal labor laws and liberal social spending programs---all designed to gain incumbent politicians' reelection, has caused over half of all working-age young people in France TO WANT TO LEAVE THEIR COUNTRY!

What this poor woman and millions of others like her probably don't realize is the politicians' next step will be to attempt to inflate the debt away---FURTHER increasing taxes and hardships on people of all ages because inflation is a direct TAX on the masses.

The elite don't worry about it because they control all the hard assets which keep pace with an inflation environment!

	DEBT CAUSED BY FEDERAL RESERVE & AN OUT OF CONTROL CONGRESS					
U.S. POPULATION 2013	NUMBER TRULY UNEMPLOYED (@12.1%)	BASELINE FEDERAL GOV'T DEBT	DEBTS OF HOUSEHOLDS, BUSINESS, FINANCIAL INSTITUTIONS, STATE & LOCAL GOV'T	UNFUNDED DEBTS OF MEDICARE, PRESCRIPTION DRUG & SOCIAL SECURITY PLANS	TOTAL U.S. INDEBTEDNESS	TOTAL DEBT PER PERSON FOR EVERY MAN, WOMAN & CHILD IN AMERICA!
316,254,000	101,792,000	$17,218,061,997,328	$42,965,312,266,789	$126,872,629,882,260	$187,056,004,146,377	$591,474

DEBT BROKEN DOWN BY THE UNEMPLOYED AND FOR EACH FOOD STAMP RECIPIENT

TOTAL U.S. INDEBTEDNESS/ PERSON UNEMPLOYED	FEDERAL GOVERNMENT DEBT/PERSON UNEMPLOYED	FEDERAL GOVERNMENT DEBT/PERSON ON FOOD STAMPS	FEDERAL GOVERNMENT DEBT/PERSON OF U.S. POPULATION	DEBT OF HOUSEHOLDS, BUSINESSES, FIN'L INSTITUTIONS, STATE & LOCAL GOV'T/PERSON	UNFUNDED DEBTS OF MEDICARE, PRESCRIPTION DRUG & SOCIAL SECURITY PLANS/PERSON	WHAT DOES THIS MEAN?
$1,837,630	$169,149	$360,211	$54,444	$133,857	$401,173	TROUBLE, DEAD AHEAD!

© 2013 Robert L. Kelly. Information as of December 2013.

Source: U.S. Debt Clock, as retrieved from http://www.usdebtclock.org and United States Bureau of Labor Statistics, as retrieved from: http://data.bls.gov/cgi-bin/surveymost?ce

Debt Caused By Federal Reserve & an Out-of-Control Congress

The following table analyzes the debt and how it relates to every single person in America. As you can see, *every baby born* on its first day in America, as of December 2013, OWES $591,474!

This does not include the leverage and debt structure of the derivatives tower. When these figures are included, it totals over a staggering $2,000,000 PER PERSON and $2 MILLION PER PERSON should be a terrifying number because it is REAL. When the derivatives' system breaks, it will be systemic, and every single person will pay the price. *To sum it up: we are looking out over a precipice and down into the abyss of a very dark and very evil disaster designed to only benefit the wealthy elite owners of the banks and their key trading partners.*

27

Wealth of most Americans down 55% since recession
Further exacerbating the debt problem is the reduction in income and employment gripping the United States and Europe. Assflation™, courtesy of the Fed's secret bailouts, only helps the rich and does nothing to help the poor and middle class---traditionally, the backbone of America, particularly.

> **Wealth of Most Americans Down 55%**
> "Increasing housing prices and the stock market's posting all-time highs haven't helped the plight of most Americans. The average U.S. household has recovered only 45 percent of the wealth they lost during the recession, according to a report released yesterday from the Federal Reserve Bank of St. Louis." (Source: MoneyWatch, by Constantine Von Hoffman, May 31, 2013, CBS News, retrieved from http://www.cbsnews.com/8301-505123_162-57587033/wealth-of-most-americans-down-55-since-recession/).

Ignoring the Tiger in the Corner---The Bottom Line on Debt
Debt is the Achilles Heel of every politician on earth and every single person in America, Europe and Japan. It is not something we can just turn our backs on because the major banks are bailed out and the stock market is on the rise. Often times when you ignore the tiger sitting in the corner, you wind up being eaten for lunch!

This is exactly what is about to happen to America, Japan and Western Europe and anyone relying on the derivatives and debt markets to do their business.

Chapter 2
Derivatives---the Ticking Time Bomb!

CURRENCY AND DERIVATIVES EXPOSURE
"DERIVATIVES ARE FINANCIAL WEAPONS OF MASS DESTRUCTION"
----WARREN BUFFETT

U.S. POPULATION December 2013	TOTAL CURRENCY & DERIVATIVES CONTRACTS	TOTAL CURRENCY & DERIVATIVES CONTRACT EXPOSURE/PERSON UNEMPLOYED	TOTAL CURRENCY & DERIVATIVES CONTRACT EXPOSURE/U.S. PERSON	WHAT DOES THIS MEAN?
316,254,000	$716,480,900,648,810	$7,038,675.93	$2,265,523.60	BIG TROUBLE, DEAD AHEAD!!

(Source: Bureau of Labor Statistics, U.S. Debt Clock population growth estimated from 2012 Census).   © 2013 Robert L. Kelly Information as of December 2013.

$2,265,675 in Derivatives Exposure Per Person In U.S.A.!
For every person <u>unemployed in America</u>, the bankers and Wall Street have exposure to over $7,000,000/person in derivatives' contracts. As the table, above indicates, they have $2,265,675 in exposure FOR <u>EVERY MAN, WOMAN AND CHILD IN AMERICA.</u>

"The buildup of leverage during a market expansion and the rush to reduce leverage, or "deleverage," when market conditions deteriorated was common to this and other financial crises. Leverage traditionally has referred to the use of debt, instead of equity, to fund an asset and has been measured by the ratio of total assets to equity on the balance sheet. But as witnessed in the current crisis, leverage also can be used to increase an exposure to a financial asset without using debt, such as by using derivatives.[1] In that regard, leverage can be defined broadly as the ratio between some measure of risk exposure and capital that can be used to absorb unexpected losses from the exposure.[2]"

[1] Derivatives are financial products whose value is determined from an underlying reference rate (interest rates, foreign currency exchange rates); an index (that reflects the collective value of various financial products); or an asset (stocks, bonds, and commodities). Derivatives can be traded through central locations, called exchanges, where buyers and sellers, or their representatives, meet to determine prices; or privately negotiated by the parties off the exchanges or over the counter (OTC). 2Capital generally is defined as a firm's long-term source of funding, contributed largely by a firm's equity stockholders and its own returns in the form of retained earnings. One important function of capital is to absorb losses. (Source: GAO Report to Congressional Committees, July 27, 2009, "FINANCIAL MARKETS REGULATION, Financial Crisis Highlights Need to Improve Oversight of Leverage at Financial Institutions and across System" page 1, GAO-09-739, as retrieved from http://www.gao.gov/new.items/d09739.pdf). Author's emphasis bold.

WHAT COULD POSSIBLY GO WRONG?

> *The Doomsday Cycle heading our way because of the irresponsible and reprehensible use of debt and derivatives will be absolutely horrifying. There are no other words to describe the guillotine hanging over society's head because of banking and elitist greed, combined with the sheer lust for power by the politicians.*

Throughout this chapter there are a number of charts and tables which the reader can QUICKLY scan. If you do so, you will walk away with a good understanding of the gravity of the problem we are facing when it comes to debt and derivatives. This book has done the work to show you, directly, where the trouble lies, so it should be fairly easy to breeze through it. As you peruse the various charts and tables, look for the "red" (or, if you are reading in black & white, the slightly darkened) highlights, they should make the hair on the back of your neck stand up!

You will find several of the key source documents used to create the tables and charts, are from the U.S. Government. This information provides the basis for many of the conclusions the author has reached---causing him to write this book (as well as <u>The $30 Trillion Heist,</u> Volumes I <u>Scene Of The Crime?</u> and Volume II, <u>Follow The Money!</u>), in an effort to warn as many people as possible and expose the truth for what it is, while empowering justice in the future.

> **Even a cursory peak at the tables, graphs, charts and percentages will convince ANYONE (except those earning huge bonus money on Wall Street) derivatives' instruments are TIME BOMBS—just waiting for either the clock to countdown to "zero," or someone to simply just pull the trigger and detonate an explosion waiting to happen).**

Unfortunately, we are not dealing with gun powder. In this case, we are dealing with the weapons of greed which have enveloped every transaction in society. They include credit, swaps, futures, options, equities, interest rate, foreign exchange and many others. Without them, of course, the underlying activities associated with derivatives contracts would not have grown as fast as they have during the last one hundred years. But, like anything else done to excess, it usually leads to pain, or trouble, in one form or another. Having experienced what happened to the markets when even a part of this bubble burst (thanks to the insight the mortgage and credit crisis provided everyone), a very clear path of destruction can be plotted. As the wise man once said---

"The pathway to Hell is paved with good intentions!"
(Source: ---believed originated from Virgil's *Aeneid, written in 29 to 19 BC*:
"facilis descensus Averni"--It is easy to go to Hell).

Top 25 Commercial Banks Derivatives Contract Holdings

The top 25 U.S. commercial banks via their U.S. operations, alone, account for $240 TRILLION of the world's total derivatives contracts. JP Morgan Chase, Citigroup, Bank of America, Goldman Sachs, HSBC, Wells Fargo, Morgan Stanley and Bank of New York Mellon—all members of the "club," dominate the action here in the U.S.A. The 4 Horsemen---JP Morgan Chase, Citigroup, Bank of America and Goldman Sachs control over 93% of the U.S. market!

In the WORLD MARKET for derivatives, the 4 Horsemen control over 40% of this $716 Trillion+ casino (as of June 2013, the "official" size of the "notional" derivatives market was $692 Trillion, according to Bank for International Settlement figures). Under the Fed's leadership, this monstrous market has grown even more staggeringly high during the year, as the total contracts, globally, were $632.579 Trillion at year-end 2012. Please see the following tables which show Office of Comptroller and BIS data on derivatives. The BIS table is printed in the section of this chapter titled, "Interest Rate Derivatives a $561 Trillion Casino".

Distribution of Derivatives Contracts

---

*96% Of All Derivatives Trade On An Unregulated Basis
For The Top 25 Commercial Banks.*

*2013 Year-End U.S. Derivatives Trading Market Is 15 Times The
Size Of The United States ENTIRE Gross Domestic Product!!!*

*The U.S. Derivatives Market Makes Up Approximately
1/3 Of The Entire World's Derivatives Trading.*

*U.S. Bankers Are Trading Derivatives Worth Over 3
Times The Entire World's GDP With NO TRANSPARENCY!!*

*This Is A Recipe For Disaster And Is The
Reason D'Apocalypse™ Is Coming!!!*

©2014 Robert L. Kelly

DISTRIBUTION OF DERIVATIVES CONTRACTS
TOP 25 COMMERCIAL BANKS, SAVINGS ASSOCIATIONS AND TRUST COMPANIES
September 30, 2013*

RANK	BANK NAME	CASH & CASH EQUIVALENTS	DERIVATIVES TO TOTAL CASH EXPOSURE RATIO	DERIVATIVES TO TOTAL ASSETS EXPOSURE RATIO	TOTAL ASSETS	TOTAL DERIVATIVES	% EXCHANGE TRADED CONTRACTS	% UNREGULATED WITH NO EXCHANGE TRADED CONTRACTS
1	JPMORGAN CHASE BANK NA	$638,025,000,000	112.55	36.09	$1,989,875,000,000	$71,810,058,000,000	3.65	96.35
2	CITIBANK NATIONAL ASSN	$479,148,000,000	131.41	46.82	$1,344,751,000,000	$62,963,116,000,000	2.63	97.37
3	GOLDMAN SACHS BANK USA	$289,221,000,000	164.12	427.18	$111,117,000,000	$47,467,154,000,000	4.03	95.97
4	BANK OF AMERICA NA	$603,544,000,000	68.57	28.76	$1,438,859,000,000	$41,386,713,000,000	4.71	95.29
5	HSBC BANK USA NATIONAL ASSN	$170,206,000,000	30.70	29.05	$179,860,546,000	$5,224,907,518,000	4.46	95.54
6	WELLS FARGO BANK NA	$520,566,000,000	8.32	3.26	$1,328,010,000,000	$4,332,672,000,000	4.52	95.48
7	MORGAN STANLEY BANK NA	$191,769,000,000	13.35	25.66	$99,782,000,000	$2,560,224,000,000	5.53	94.47
8	BANK OF NEW YORK MELLON	$153,404,000,000	7.80	4.11	$291,475,000,000	$1,196,907,000,000	2.56	97.44
9	STATE STREET BANK&TRUST CO	$165,955,000,000	6.76	5.27	$212,689,010,000	$1,121,876,568,000	0.46	99.54
10	PNC BANK NATIONAL ASSN	$83,032,000,000	4.59	1.28	$298,485,621,000	$381,329,085,000	27.66	72.34
11	NORTHERN TRUST CO	$59,626,800,000	4.09	2.55	$95,631,363,000	$243,907,399,000	0.00	100.00
12	SUNTRUST BANK	$32,643,000,000	7.30	1.42	$167,525,054,000	$238,201,548,000	14.29	85.71
13	TD BANK NATIONAL ASSN	$29,841,120,000	4.03	0.56	$215,433,360,000	$120,240,152,000	0.00	100.00
14	U S BANK NATIONAL ASSN	$87,826,000,000	1.19	0.29	$356,590,456,000	$104,411,152,000	3.17	96.83
15	REGIONS BANK	$27,996,000,000	2.90	0.70	$116,068,082,000	$81,263,522,000	2.72	97.28
16	BRANCH BANKING&TRUST CO	$39,384,000,000	1.70	0.38	$175,616,476,000	$66,782,582,000	0.15	99.85
17	KEYBANK NATIONAL ASSN	$18,995,000,000	0.75	0.75	$88,092,809,000	$65,874,104,000	8.02	91.98
18	FIFTH THIRD BANK	$21,748,000,000	2.91	0.51	$123,338,495,000	$63,206,777,000	0.90	99.10
19	UNION BANK NATIONAL ASSN	$7,312,000,000	8.44	0.59	$104,956,215,000	$61,693,446,000	9.96	90.04
20	CAPITAL ONE NATIONAL ASSN	$67,126,000,000	0.59	0.17	$234,771,390,000	$39,749,927,000	0.00	100.00
21	RBS CITIZENS NATIONAL ASSN	$115,272,000,000	0.34	0.40	$98,282,921,000	$39,429,226,000	0.00	100.00
22	BOKF NATIONAL BANK	$11,684,775,000	2.80	1.22	$26,911,962,000	$32,765,427,000	4.29	95.71
23	HUNTINGTON NATIONAL BANK	$9,927,727,000	2.43	0.43	$56,434,306,000	$24,113,543,000	0.01	99.99
24	COMERICA BANK	$16,576,000,000	1.36	0.35	$64,590,524,000	$22,509,163,000	0.00	100.00
25	MANUFACTURERS&TRADERS TR (	$12,666,707,000	1.59	0.24	$83,615,586,000	$20,091,666,000	0.00	100.00
	TOP 25 COMMERCIAL BANKS, SAs & TCs WITH DERIVATIVES				$9,302,762,176,000	$239,669,196,805,000	$8,904,185,657,000	$230,765,011,148,000
	OTHER COMMERCIAL BANKS, SAs & TCs WITH DERIVATIVES				$3,592,621,825,000	$369,416,536,000	$16,145,470,000	$353,271,066,000
	TOTAL FOR COMMERCIAL BANKS, SAs & TCs WITH DERIVATIVES				$12,895,384,001,000	$240,038,613,341,000	$8,920,331,127,000	$231,118,282,214,000

U.S. GROSS DOMESTIC PRODUCT (AS OF DEC. 7, 2013, PER U.S. DEBT CLOCK)	$16,003,093,796,276	# TIMES DERIVATIVES BIGGER THAN USA	% TRADED UNREGULATED
		15.00	96.28%

* TD BANK IS AS OF OCTOBER 31, 2013 (Source for data: Office of Comptroller of the Currency, OCC's Quarterly Report on Bank Trading and Derivatives Activities Third Quarter 2013 ; as sourced from http://www.occ.gov/topics/capital-markets/financial-markets/trading/derivatives/dq313.pdf and Yahoo! Finance)

The derivatives market is beyond material and is intertwined with each and every transaction of daily life on earth for the civilized world. Once it blows up, a meltdown will arrive which is so swift, so powerful and so frightening it will blister fire, spit thunder and storm across oceans and nations---sweeping the entire planet.

Its economic destructive power will be worse than a nuclear weapon going off because it will infect the entire earth---literally overnight, causing economic collapse. Among man-made destructive events, only a global solar event or world-wide nuclear, biological and/or chemical war would do more damage, economically speaking.

With the power to destroy nearly every single financial institution and company in the Western world, D'Apocalypse™ promises to steal the future away from those who are unprepared and left in the aftermath of its wake. Once this Pandora's Box is opened and the defaults begin, wave, after powerful wave of firestorm-like destruction will be wrought upon thousands of companies. These companies will lie in ashes and will be just as devoid of life as the smoldering ruins seen vividly on CNN of the out-of-control blazes plaguing the American West.

Derivatives---$716 Trillion Unregulated Marketplace
According to the Bank for International Settlements, at the end of 2012, the total "notional" global derivatives market totaled approximately $633 Trillion. By mid-year 2013 the BIS measured its growth to $692 Trillion and by the end of 2013, it is screaming along at over $716 Trillion! As was seen on the Debt Clock in Chapter 1, the total U.S. GDP as of December 2013 was $16 Trillion, making the nominal and "official" global derivatives market over 40 TIMES larger than the U.S. GDP and nearly 10 TIMES (approximately) larger than the world's GDP, which was measured at approximately $71.8 Trillion in 2012 by the CIA, and according to the IMF, grew another 3% in 2013 (to approximately $74 Trillion. (Source: CIA Fact Book, as retrieved from https://www.cia.gov/library/publications /the-world-factbook/fields/2195.html and as retrieved from the IMF http://www.imf.org/external/pubs/ft/weo/2013/update/02/).

The top 25 commercial banks in the U.S. have approximately $240 Trillion in notional exposure for their U.S. activities, or about 15 TIMES THE SIZE OF THE U.S. GDP, with the top 8 U.S. commercial banks holding $236 TRILLION of the entire notional derivatives exposure.

As any reasonable person would surmise, such a high concentration of leveraged transactions in the hands of a small number of banks (and board rooms) puts the entire nation at risk.

This means 8 companies think they are smart enough to control over 3 times the world's GDP and 15 times the entire United States' GDP---ON AN UNREGULATED BASIS!

Additionally, this is JUST THEIR DERIVATIVES POSITIONS IN THE UNITED STATES; GLOBALLY, THE TOP FOUR U.S. BANKS LEAD THAT MARKET, ALSO!

Who are these banks, really, you might ask? Well, it will come as no surprise these are the key members and owners of the Federal Reserve and are the legacy of the founding fathers of the Federal Reserve System. They include, JP Morgan Chase, Citigroup, Bank of America and Goldman Sachs who control over 90% of the U.S. market. They, along with HSBC, Wells Fargo, Morgan Stanley and Bank of New York Mellon (see subsection, "96% Of All Derivatives Trade On An Unregulated Basis For The Top 25 Commercial Banks," as seen previously in this chapter) enjoy a stranglehold over derivatives trading.

The largest derivatives' market is the interest rate market, with U.S. Dollar transactions dominating the action. It will experience serious, serious problems when interest rates skyrocket and the bankers and elite exploit the radically high leverage used in this derivatives' market sector. They will use the Fed's printing of money, the monetization of U.S. debt and the U.S. Government's out-of-control debt and spending problems to cause interest rates to rise like a rocket ship.

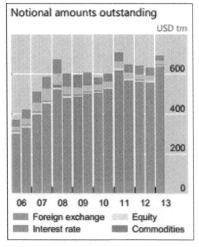

(Source: BIS semiannual OTC derivatives statistics, Table 1 in Section 4, as retrieved from http://www.bis.org/publ/otc_hy1311.pdf).

It will be "bombs away" for this market, as the world loses confidence in the U.S. government and the bond market goes into seizure.

It will be and is scary stuff indeed.

Interest Rate Derivatives a $561 Trillion Casino

"Amounts outstanding for single-currency interest rate derivatives reported by the semiannual reporting sample grew 15% in the first half of 2013 to stand at $561 trillion at end-June 2013…The increase was driven by strong growth (21%) in FRAs to $86 trillion. Notional amounts outstanding in interest rate swaps increased by 15% to $426 trillion, after having declined 2% in the second half of 2012. Interest rate options were little changed." (Source: Bank For International Settlements, June 2013, "Statistical release OTC derivatives statistics at end-June 2013, page 7, as retrieved from http://www.bis.org/publ/otc_hy1311.pdf).

Table 19: Amounts outstanding of over-the-counter (OTC) derivatives
By risk category and instrument
In billions of US dollars

Risk Category / Instrument	Notional amounts outstanding					Gross market values				
	Jun 2011	Dec 2011	Jun 2012	Dec 2012	Jun 2013	Jun 2011	Dec 2011	Jun 2012	Dec 2012	Jun 2013
Total contracts	706,884	647,811	639,396	632,579	692,908	19,518	27,307	25,417	24,740	20,158
Foreign exchange contracts	64,698	63,381	66,672	67,358	73,121	2,336	2,582	2,240	2,304	2,424
Forwards and forex swaps	31,113	30,526	31,395	31,718	34,421	777	919	771	803	953
Currency swaps	22,228	22,791	24,156	25,420	24,654	1,227	1,318	1,184	1,247	1,131
Options	11,358	10,065	11,122	10,220	14,046	332	345	285	254	339
Interest rate contracts	553,240	504,117	494,427	489,703	561,299	13,244	20,001	19,113	18,833	15,155
Forward rate agreements	55,747	50,596	64,711	71,353	86,334	59	67	51	47	168
Interest rate swaps	441,201	402,611	379,401	369,999	425,569	11,861	18,046	17,214	17,080	13,663
Options	56,291	50,911	50,314	48,351	49,396	1,324	1,888	1,848	1,706	1,325
Equity-linked contracts	6,841	5,982	6,313	6,251	6,821	708	679	645	605	693
Forwards and swaps	2,029	1,738	1,880	2,045	2,321	176	156	147	157	206
Options	4,813	4,244	4,434	4,207	4,501	532	523	497	448	487
Commodity contracts	3,197	3,091	2,994	2,587	2,458	471	481	390	358	386
Gold	468	521	523	486	461	50	75	61	53	80
Other commodities	2,729	2,570	2,471	2,101	1,997	421	405	328	306	306
Forwards and swaps	1,846	1,745	1,659	1,363	1,327					
Options	883	824	812	739	670					
Credit default swaps	32,409	28,626	26,931	25,069	24,349	1,345	1,586	1,187	848	725
Single-name instruments	18,105	16,865	15,566	14,309	13,135	854	958	715	527	430
Multi-name instruments	14,305	11,761	11,364	10,760	11,214	490	628	472	321	295
of which index products	12,473	10,514	9,731	9,663	10,170					
Unallocated	46,498	42,613	42,059	41,611	24,860	1,414	1,978	1,842	1,792	775
Memorandum item:										
Gross Credit Exposure						2,971	3,939	3,691	3,609	3,900

(Source: BIS Quarterly Review, December 2013, as retrieved from http://www.bis.org/statistics/dt1920a.pdf).

$561.299 Trillion was bet on interest rate movements---with banks, municipalities, pension funds, insurance companies, corporations and individuals engaging in contracts and transactions with a "party" and a "counter-party" to either hedge, or otherwise speculate on interest rate movements. The staggering number of transactions and quantities of monies involved will become a serious problem when VOLATILITY rises in interest rates and the market prices for the real risk of owning government and corporate bonds (e.g., default risk, inflation risk—after a massive collapse, etc.) is priced into the market.

When this occurs, there will be large numbers of "counter-parties" who default. In fact, as the rates increase, sweeping changes could be made to credit ratings and grades of many governments, municipalities, corporations and other entities which will require an immediate infusion of additional capital and margin to maintain control of derivatives' positions. Because this market is controlled by the 4 Horsemen of the D'Apocalypse™ (JP Morgan Chase, Citigroup, Bank of America and Goldman Sachs) they can easily manipulate and control pricing, contractual terms and even events which could affect the value of the contracts which are underlying the derivatives positions. These banks, for example, can create margin calls "unexpectedly" at a time when it is IMPOSSIBLE for governments, municipalities and corporations to sell bonds, or otherwise raise capital, or alternatively, since there are only a few "market makers," they could easily conspire to lower bid prices and blame an "illiquid or "thin" market on poor execution prices for position liquidation events.

Wise managers in governments and in companies might consider if the banks have it within their capability to manufacture a crisis, which the author knows is not only possible, but will occur. Banks have the ability to squeeze and contract credit and tighten the money supply, thereby having the ability to cause potentially, a massive and sudden downgrade in credit and economic conditions.

If it is realized the banks can do exactly this, then wise managers will know this would allow the banks to astronomically raise margin requirements on derivatives contracts and positions (or drop asset values related to the position), with the full knowledge many counter parties cannot come up with the "call" money required on the contract. Because of the massive leverage involved with these contracts, **bankruptcy** will be the counter party's likely option, or at a minimum, a forced **"shotgun" wedding** will occur, where the bank seizes assets for pennies on the dollar, in exchange for freeing the counter-party target from its obligations under the derivatives' bet.

$561,000,000,000,000 has been bet on the movement of interest rates--- controlled by the 4 Horsemen in the U.S. and only a total of 14 banks worldwide----what do you think they will do with this kind of power and control...and the kind of greed and avarice which flows through their veins?

During the last five years, the Fed has kept interest rates artificially low by monetizing the debt (i.e., buying up all the debt issued by the U.S. Government no one else purchases). Now many governments are shunning U.S. debt and the Fed's <u>KNOWN</u> balance sheet is becoming bloated with "assets" consisting of government paper which carry yields with very low interest rates, not to mention the likely burden of trillions of dollars in toxic assets as a result of the $30 Trillion heist.. The Fed will, sooner, or later, <u>stop buying U.S. Government paper</u>. This will cause interest rates to spike, in a hurry, and create a swift collapse. This book is predicting the collapse to occur in the fall of 2015 and no later than after the Presidential election in 2016, as described in detail in Chapter 9, "What To Do Now."

All of these actions are being orchestrated and engineered to ensure there is enough fear in the marketplace to empower the banking cabal, Federal Reserve and other elite, family-controlled central banks to grasp control of the world's monetary policy and money supply systems. Skyrocketing interest rates will cause and create havoc for thousands of "counter-party" entities and they will not be able to

Probability Density Function

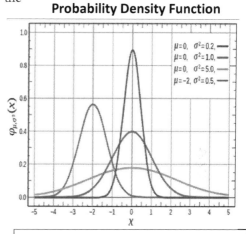

(Source of images: Wikipedia, as retrieved from http://en.wikipedia.org/wiki/Normal_distribution; arrows and -2.5 standard deviation highlight author's additions)

Mathematicians and Wall Street gurus utilize graphs and other tools to analyze risk. "Population distributions" of an asset's price can be modeled differently by varying assumptions (e.g., changes in risk, time, interest rates, etc.). The wizards of Wall Street develop a curve allowing them to price risk and show how prices, rates, etc., are expected to move, given certain conditions.

Major problems occur when "black-swan" events force unexpected changes outside of "worst case" scenarios. "Worst case" scenarios are modeled at a number of "standard deviations" (identified by the symbol sigma, "σ," or **square root of the variance, "σ^2," as shown above**) away from the expected results of the wizard's models. The "arrows" above identify standard deviation movements away from the expected behavior of whatever the math wizard is trying to price.

meet their margin calls, while governments will beg to sell their bonds---with no takers.

Wall Street Wizards

As discussed in the author's sleuthing documentary and truth-shattering book, The $30 Trillion Heist in its Volume II, Follow The Money!, chapter 7 "When Will the Bubble Burst?," (as well as this book in Chapter 9 "What To Do Now," subsection, "If You Are a Corporation Seeking to Survive the Derivatives Debacle ---The Banks Could Go Broke Overnight"), the math wizards on Wall Street who created the algorithms and equations for the derivatives markets, primarily use the Black-Scholes pricing model, or a version of it. None of the models designed by these "geniuses" properly price risk when a firestorm the size and impact of D'Apocalypse™ strikes.

The wizards' models typically only price risk into markets they have been able to historically analyze—with perhaps some of the most daring conservatives among them providing themselves with a little buffer (perhaps a few extra standard deviations of risk tolerance) to ensure they are covered if unexpected events occur which fall in the outer tails of their models. They refer to these kinds of events as "black-swan" events.

Most wizards, who write the equations and set the credit policy for SELLING risk, do not account for very large movements of change which are perhaps many, many multiples above, or below, an asset class's historic "norm." They refer to expected change in a measurement via the term, "standard deviation" (which is just a fancy way of saying an average change of "X" has occurred over the life of an asset, or security). Upon these wizards' usually reliable models, nearly every bank on Wall Street has sold risk and Wall Street has made hundreds of billions of dollars off of the derivatives' markets, controlled by the oligopoly of the 4 Horsemen. What the wizards say has a great impact on decision-making at all firms.

This is a direct quote out of Bank of America's annual report for 2012:

"A VaR model simulates the value of a portfolio under a range of hypothetical scenarios in order to generate a distribution of potential gains and losses. VaR represents the loss the portfolio is expected to experience within a given confidence level based on historical data…the accuracy of a VaR model depends on the availability and quality of historical data for each of the positions in the portfolio…Our VaR model utilizes three years of historical data. This time period was chosen to ensure that VaR reflects both a broad range of market movements as well as being sensitive to recent changes in market volatility. In addition, certain types of risks associated with positions that are illiquid and/or unobservable are not included in VaR. If these risks are determined to be material, the VaR model results will be supplemented." (Source: Bank of America Corporation 2012 Annual Report, page 111).

This is directly from JP Morgan Chase's annual report for 2012:

"The Firm has one overarching VaR model framework used for risk management purposes across the Firm, which utilizes historical simulation based on data for the previous 12 months. The framework's approach assumes that historical changes in market values are representative of the distribution of potential outcomes in the immediate future." (Source: JP Morgan Chase & Co. Annual Report 2012, page 163).

This is directly from Citigroup's annual report for 2012:

"Citi believes its VAR model is conservatively calibrated to incorporate the greater of short-term (most recent month) and long-term (three years) market volatility." (Source: Citigroup, Inc. 2012 Annual Report, page 104).

Finally, this is directly from Goldman Sachs' annual report for 2012:

"We sample from 5 years of historical data to generate the scenarios for our VaR calculation. The historical data is weighted so that the relative importance of the data reduces over time. This gives greater importance to more recent observations and reflects current asset volatilities, which improves the accuracy of our estimates of potential loss...VaR excludes the impact of changes in counterparty and our own credit spreads on derivatives as well as changes in our own credit spreads on unsecured borrowings for which the fair value option was elected." (Source: Goldman Sachs' 2012 Annual Report, page 89 & 93).

What is mind-boggling is no one says anything about these limited, flawed and galactically stupid risk assumptions, which collectively and individually, put our nation and the entire Western financial world in jeopardy! Invariably, these models and calculations do not take into account the real risk associated with major counter-party failures and the ENORMOUS leverage which is packed into the system. This is why these models will ultimately fail.

Banker-Engineered Rate Explosion Pushes Derivatives Market Over the Cliff

Unfortunately, as the elite and upper crust of the banking system knows, realizes and is planning on, when an entire population of investors experiences interest rates rising dramatically and abruptly because of unilateral Federal Reserve and banking actions, they, too, will demand significant, immediate higher risk returns in exchange for their investment dollars. The combination of this poisonous brew will send the wizards' existing models over the precipice and into the abyss, causing the derivatives market to blow up in the face of Wall Street and anyone else who is selling risk in the interest rate and credit markets game.

This blow up will include nearly everyone, particularly any bank, fund, insurance company, corporation, or individual attempting to increase their yields over the last five years by selling risk premiums! It is another perfect storm caused directly by the manipulation of the markets by the U.S. Government and the Federal Reserve System of the United States. Their unsuccessful attempt to supposedly stimulate the economy by artificially keeping interest rates low is the root cause of this tragedy. Anyone playing in this tar pit will be lit on fire as the lightning storm of D'Apocalypse™ sweeps over the land.

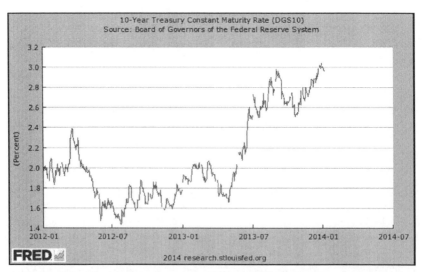

Source: This chart is made available from the St. Louis Federal Reserve Bank, as retrieved from http://research.stlouisfed.org/fred2/graph/?s[1][id]=DGS10

Providing some timely and amazing corroboration to the author's conclusions and predictions is the action in the U.S. Treasury Bond market when the Fed indicated it would halt quantitative easing programs.

The yield on 10-year U.S. Treasury bonds rocketed up to 2.66% after being held artificially below 2% for years by the Fed. This happened immediately and nearly overnight and is a DRAMATIC warning of what is to come!

This provides us with a mere glimpse of what happens to markets when they realize the Fed is going to intentionally STOP PUMPING money (e.g., buying all the government paper up).

By the fall of 2015 (and absolutely no later than 2016), when the Fed really stops pumping in conjunction with the bankers' and elites' preconceived and engineered plan to halt the supply of credit, while simultaneously boosting interest rates---chaos will reign. This one-two punch by the Fed and the banks will cause interest rates, across the board, to skyrocket and absolutely crush the bond market.

The banks will immediately <u>stop</u> lending and <u>increase</u> the margin requirements on active and new positions in the derivatives markets. Their fatal blow, however, will be the direct manipulation of prices in the thinly traded contract markets for derivatives, as the contracts typically are between the bank and another entity. That entity has no control over the pricing of the transaction and the banks can automatically and artificially drop asset prices and/or increase margin requirements, dramatically, causing complete turmoil for those participating in these markets. This is especially true when the banks can point their fingers and claim the "market" interest rates went up---even if the banks surreptitiously caused the changes to begin with! The bankers' and elites' actions and dramatic rise in rates will crush unsuspecting counter parties across countries, worldwide.

It will also manufacture, through a cold, calculating and evil plan, devastating economic collapse on America and the Western world, particularly (Japan included in this devastation). As bad as things have been for the majority since the credit crisis began, things will get MUCH WORSE.

Ultimately, the combination and results of these actions produces the "big scare" required to induce the politicians to plea for the pumping of money and infusion of credit into the system by the bankers and elite, thus allowing them to take control of the global monetary system.....thus....mission accomplished!

Many governments, supposedly brilliant hedge funds, thousands of corporations and millions of people have gone "bust" by not appropriately pricing risk. We will experience, in the next few years, a tremendous groaning from the capital system which will utterly collapse and shut down due to uncontrolled systemic risk ignored by every single executive in the banks, the elite, the Federal Reserve, the Administration, as well as the vast majority of the politicians in the halls of Congress.

The difference between them is the fact Congress and the Administration are oblivious, while the bankers, elite and Fed ***knew exactly*** what they were doing. ***They knew*** by building the destructive and towering derivatives' markets, it would provide them the keys to the kingdom. ***They knew*** when the system was leveraged and their targets were locked in, ***they had the power*** to pull the rug out from under everyone, ***whenever they wanted. They knew!***

This time, their desire will not be only to gobble up assets and taxpayer money, but they will insist upon <u>global</u> control of monetary policy and the money supply---the keys to this earthly kingdom if your god is money, power and avarice, which for them, it is.

Now we have covered interest rate increases, let's dig a little bit deeper into the Credit Default Swap ("CDS") market. What will happen to these contracts and transactions when the balloon goes up and D'Apocalypse™ arrives? This market is also LARGER than the U.S. GDP and even though the interest rate market dwarfs it, the CDS market is another important sector for derivatives trading.

By itself, the CDS marketplace could cause devastation and ruin to the Western world.

Credit Default Swaps a $25 Trillion Casino with $10 Trillion in Very Bad Bets

Credit Default Swaps are a large component of the derivatives marketplace and will also create havoc. When a very large number of these derivatives securities and settlements come due in the coming years (see subsection "When the Bubble Bursts" and the table within "Credit Default Swaps by Category and Maturity" of this chapter), there will be HUGE problems.

The combination of the debt default, skyrocketing interest rates and overall economic disaster will also rain ruin upon those "selling risk" in this market. Selling risk involves institutions receiving a premium payment and IF the underlying security does not default, or stays within certain parameters, the selling institution keeps the premium. In today's low-interest rate environment, this kind of transaction helps improve yields—particularly for governments, pension plans, municipalities, hedge funds and a variety of financial institutions.

However, if there is a debt default (or, in the case of interest rate derivatives, if rates go UP dramatically) the party selling premium LOSES money---and the loss could be catastrophic, as most of the VaR models (see "Var-Value at Risk," in this chapter) do not accommodate the kind of disaster this book is predicting for these markets.

If this doesn't frighten you, look (hopefully, aghast!) at the ENORMOUS positions taken by the financial institutions and marketplace in ***BELOW-INVESTMENT GRADE AND NON-INVESTMENT GRADE SECURITIES*!!** When the economy blows, the counter party who guessed wrong will default and the 4 Horsemen will eat their remains!

See the chart, later in this chapter "Credit Default Swaps by Category and Maturity."

When the Bubble Bursts

When they burst the bubble, likely in the latter part of 2015, the end result over the following several years will be the elite's and banks' seizure of global monetary policy and authority, thus effectively controlling the money supply for all markets. In this way, a basis for a system of global control can be put in place, as is warned about in the Book of Revelation.

Equity markets should continue shooting vertically upwards, until mid-to-late fall 2015, a year before the Presidential elections of 2016 in America. With this rise and froth in the markets, the 4 Horsemen and their elite owners will be ***EXITING*** their long equity positions and unloading their securities onto an unsuspecting public, building a cash hoard to cherry pick off the best assets which will go on the auction block during the crash of D'Apocalypse™.

Any of the banks trading in the derivatives markets, however, have some potentially dynamite liability---even if they are right and their bets go their way and they unload their equity positions at the top of the bubble's crest. This is because many, if not most, of the underlying counter parties to their transactions in the derivatives markets will *go bankrupt* when the pre-planned collapse occurs. This can happen among any of the institutions who are playing the derivatives game when a counter party goes belly up due to their risky bets. Thus, any banks who are NOT MEMBERS of the inner circle of the original founders of the Federal Reserve, will become targets for the 4 Horsemen of the D'Apocalypse™, particularly.

As you can imagine, many derivatives' positions the banks could not, or did not wish to liquidate for "cash" during the great Assflation™, will likely be hedged with a counter party the banking cabal **desires to OWN**. They can force the targeted counter party very quickly into a bankruptcy and inexpensive takeover in this way.

Through the power of the $30 Trillion heist, the economy has witnessed what this book (and its sister publications, The $30 Trillion Heist, Volumes I and II) coins and defines, for the first time ever, the word *"Assflation™"* (pronunciation [as-fley-shuhn]—with the accent on the second syllable). Assflation™ means an intentionally manipulated increase in prices across certain asset classes benefitting, primarily, the elite, causing significant price increases across those assets sectors.

We will see a marked increase in Assflation™ across most liquid equity markets into 2015, as the elite pivot from the overbought bond market, while putting their repaired balance sheets to work in high-quality equity securities. With up to $30 Trillion pivoting in this direction, equity markets will skyrocket in an unsustainable bubble, ultimately creating a massive collapse---all orchestrated with the birth of D'Apocalypse™.

Many of the counter-party targets in the derivatives market will blow up from the extreme volatility arising from interest rate changes, extreme price movements, reductions in credit ratings and defaults which will devastate one and all in late 2015 and beyond. The targets will be asked "out of the blue," to commit greater capital to cover their derivatives' bet(s). It is vital all participants understand the banks control this market and generally have control over the *conditions and terms* of the derivatives' contracts, as well as the credit required to back the trade.

This means the banks can orchestrate a squeeze on the credit markets at will and cause a massive and negative impact on otherwise healthy companies and individuals using derivatives. Many derivatives contracts suffer severe reductions in "fair market value" if a counter party quickly needs to bail out of a   position when a market goes awry. This is because only a few major banks control the transactions and set the terms of the derivatives contracts. Ultimately, these banks have supreme control and monopoly power over these markets. At the right moment during D'Apocalypse™, the 4 Horsemen (and, worldwide, 10 additional banks from the G14) will low-ball fair market values, by using their monopoly control and extremely thin markets---all accomplished through a limited number of market makers, employed by the banks!

This makes it easy for the 4 Horsemen and the ten other banks to lower (or raise) prices and allows them to immediately demand higher margins and call money to cover a bet they decide to "call in." This market is over 96% UNREGULATED, the only way such a scheme could take place. The banks plan to implement a tremendous, unexpected squeeze on thousands of companies, hedge funds and people during D'Apocalypse™! Do not get caught unprepared and do not get caught in their trap!

In the following chart, the lower graph line is the actual Dow Jones Industrial Average. The two graphical plot lines above it represent the Dow Jones, adjusted by inflation---given different inflation assumptions.

The "middle" line is adjusted for the "official" CPI figures, while the "top" graph line is adjusted with higher inflation numbers estimated by the author.

The reader can see, the Dow Jones COULD go quite a bit higher, based upon past performance, when adjusted for inflation.

Prior to D'Apocalypse™, the Federal Reserve will continue to create a great Assflation™ on the assets owned by the elite. This was done with the sole intention of reimbursing them for losses they incurred during the mortgage crisis and to ensure they were restocked with attack capital when the collapse occurs. They will use the $30 Trillion injected by Mr. Bernanke's and Ms. Yellen's Fed to run the markets up, sell at the top, and then use the capital and profits from the run-up to acquire additional trillions of dollars in assets during D'Apocalypse™---for pennies on the dollar! Millions of people will be robbed in the process.

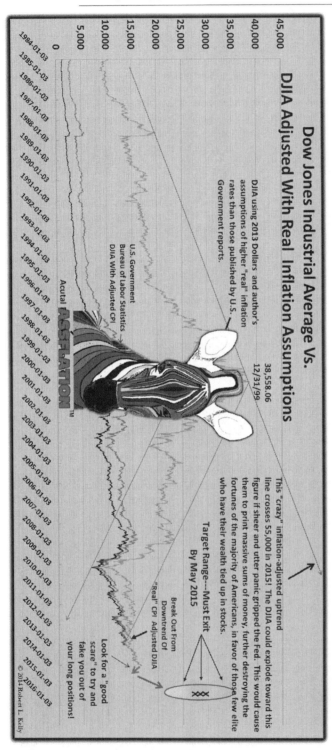

Dow Jones Industrial Average Vs.
DJIA Adjusted With Real Inflation Assumptions

DJIA using 2013 Dollars and author's assumptions of higher "real" inflation rates than those published by U.S. Government reports.

38,558.06
12/31/99

U.S. Government
Bureau of Labor Statistics
DJIA With Adjusted CPI

Acutal **ASSFLATION**™

This "crazy" inflation-adjusted uptrend line crosses 55,000 in 2015! The DJIA could explode toward this figure if sheer and utter panic gripped the Fed. This would cause them to print massive sums of money, further destroying the fortunes of the majority of Americans, in favor of those few elite who have their wealth tied up in stocks.

Target Range---Must Exit
By May 2015

Break Out From
Downtrend Of
"Real" CPI Adjusted DJIA

Look for a "good scare" to try and fake you out of your long positions!

© 2014 Robert L. Kelly

46

The author has created and would like to introduce to the world:

"Jack Assbanker ™ *"*

Jack commemorates and iconizes the Fed's and the banks' greedy, abominable and self-centered exercise in wealth creation for the elite.

They believe their actions, clever language and camouflaged financial statements can hide their egregious and nefarious activities from discovery---but exactly the opposite is true!

Jack Assbanker™   Jack Assbanker™

Standing out like glowing zebras, the elites' movements and attempts to manipulate the masses is being captured, recorded and commemorated for all time, enabling the world to see the truth of their corruption and heist of nearly $30 Trillion from the American people.

The rapacity, materialism and avarice by the bankers, elite and the Federal Reserve shall not go unrewarded---in time. Justice SHALL prevail in the end. Those who wear the colors of Jack send the signal:

WE KNOW WHO YOU ARE AND WE KNOW WHAT YOU'RE UP TO!!

Let one picture speak a thousand words and make Jack Assbanker™ an icon to remember in this battle against powers and principalities!

Please visit **www.jackassbanker.com** for more information.

NO company should be playing in the derivatives game during the next several years. Instead, companies should be LOWERING their profit goals and using their capital to OWN their positions---outright. They should not be taking on risks which can threaten the survival of entire organizations---regardless of how unlikely a scenario might seem. Many derivatives transactions are structured to capture and account for risk in "likely" scenarios, however the computer models used to predict these risks are not equipped to handle severe changes to markets which can happen literally overnight, in rare cases in history, as this book suggests will occur in 2015.

For a company to stop using derivatives and deploy greater amounts of capital to ensure it has the materials, commodities, interest rates, etc. required to operate its business, will be nearly impossible for most. The pressure to perform, in the near term, for shareholders is simply too great and deploying large amounts of capital in this manner will greatly reduce a company's leverage and theoretical profitability---in the near term.

But, this is exactly what should be done today. If companies wean themselves off of the derivatives gaming table, AS SOON AS POSSIBLE, and start migrating their assets away from banks playing the derivatives game, they will stand a very good chance of avoiding the trap being laid for them by the 4 Horsemen of the D'Apocalypse™ and their co-conspirators.

For those who laugh at this advice, many thousands of companies will fall, becoming unexpected prey of the 4 Horsemen, with perhaps only one of the 4 Horsemen even left standing at the depths of the great D'Apocalypse™. As was seen in the credit crisis, even and especially the largest banks are at risk of failure in a financially apocalyptic scenario.

Depositors' assets will vanish, literally overnight, as new banking regulations will call for the seizure of DEPOSITOR'S FUNDS to pay for banking failures, following exactly the same path taken by Cyprus. The FDIC will NOT be there for depositors because governments, already, KNOW the derivatives time bomb represents monstrous systemic risk! This is why they are already making regulatory changes, accordingly.

Bureaucrats and politicians are floating regulations through Congress and in Brussels which will cause depositors to lose their money and be forced to accept worthless stock in a failed bank, if it goes under. (If you are, or represent, a company, a sovereign state, or individual, make sure you read Chapter 9, "What To Do Now!").

The cabal which started it all, however, will KNOW what to do---they will FORECLOSE and ACQUIRE for peanuts (or own greater percentages of) the best firms and institutions who are *idiotically* participating at the gaming tables of the derivatives marketplace.

Institutions with hundred-year histories and trusted brands and billions of dollars of assets will become owned by the banking cabal and their elite owners. The taken-over companies long-term and underlying value will remain, but through the evil and despicable planning of the bankers and through the fraudulent termination of credit facilities, the seizure of cash, manipulation of pricing and the collapse of the derivatives market---even great companies shall fall.

BASEL III Tightening Worsens D'Apocalypse™--Bankers Only Reflate Once in Control

Basel, Switzerland, is home to the Bank for International Settlements, which serves central banks in their pursuit of monetary and financial stability, fosters international cooperation in those areas and acts as a bank for central banks. The Basel Accords are a set of recommendations for regulations in the banking industry.by the Basel Committee on Banking Supervision (BCBS). The BCBS maintains its permanent office at the Bank for International Settlements. (Source: as retrieved from BIS web site: http://www.bis.org/about/index.htm).

After the control over the global money supply is granted to the bankers during the middle, to end, of the next panic (which will be timed after the already approved, phased-in capital requirements of BASEL III are completed by January 1, 2018), the bankers will magically "reflate" the system and begin the recovery process. They will revise BASEL III—just as they had BASEL I and BASEL II---ultimately sending asset prices skyrocketing upward again. They will likely be valued in a new currency, or global digital currency and clearing system, they control. Their members will also own a considerably larger number of assets due to the crash of D'Apocalypse™.

But, as you might expect, BEFORE the D'Apocalypse™, Assflation™ is destined to reign and the markets will experience a blow-off like no other in history. More evidence of this piled up in early 2014 when the Basel Committee for Banking Supervision softened the rules on banks for reporting risk.

Wall Street Journal

"The Basel Committee for Banking Supervision, made up of banking regulators from around the world, said it had revised the definition of its leverage ratio in ways that will allow banks to report lower levels of overall risk. The leverage ratio measures capital held by a bank against its total assets, so the changes will lead to higher reported capital ratios. That will reduce the pressure on banks to either shed assets or raise more capital to meet the requirement.

The biggest beneficiaries of the changes appear likely to be banks most involved in securities and derivatives markets. Most important, the rules no longer require banks to count 100% of their off-balance-sheet assets. That not only includes most of <u>banks' derivatives exposures,</u> but also the guarantees and letters of credit that are essential to greasing the wheels of international trade." (Source: <u>The Wall Street Journal</u>, "Banks Get a Break on Leverage-Ratio Rules," by Geoffrey T. Smith, January 12, 2014, as retrieved from <u>http://online.wsj.com/news/articles/SB10001424052702303819704579316584090630274</u>, bold italics emphasis of author).

As you can see, the Basel Committee is important and they will loosen and tighten credit, and rules, in accordance with their grand plans, as outlined in this book. In this case, you can see the elephant's footprints in the butter, because the bankers, ***internationally***, are setting up their tee shot for a rip-roaring Assflation™ party! By loosening capital ratios, they allow the banks greater liquidity---and capital to push their favorite asset classes higher! They will make sure they dupe everyone to ensure they can unload their positions, and take full advantage of the cataclysm of doom which occurs via D'Apocalypse™, and the Doomsday Cycle.

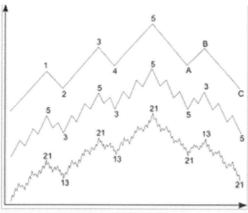

From R.N. Elliott's essay, "The Basis of the Wave Principle," October 1940.

Image as retrieved from Wikipedia:
http://en.wikipedia.org/wiki/Elliott_wave_principle).

The market "bottom" of the Doomsday Cycle should appear in the period 2018-2020, with a tremendous, initial shock wave happening in 2015 and 2016, with a multi-year, Elliott wave-like drop into an ultimate "low," thereafter. Elliott Wave Theory should work this time because there will not be market interference--- the bankers *want* it to crash because they can then effect a stunning land grab and seize control of the banking authority, worldwide (note: Most Elliott Wave technicians, including one of the most prominent, simply refuse to acknowledge the power of Assflation™ and market manipulation by the banks and the Federal Reserve. Most of them are in a constant state of bearishness which has destroyed their credibility on the Street. The major exception to this is Glenn Neely of Neowave, who is an outstanding technician. The author has no interest in Neowave, or Mr. Neely's business, FYI).

The implementation of BASEL III and the reversing of the recent loosening of rules regarding capital rations, shall see the banks using a more stringent set of capital and credit requirements on a scaled-in basis, the implementation and impact of which will cause a tremendous tightening of the money supply and tremendous shock to the entire, global economic system—further contributing to the pain of D'Apocalypse™ by design.

The worst of the effects of these new rules should be in place by the latter part of this date range (e.g., 2019-2020). Many companies will not be able to renew credit lines, or establish credit facilities, and will resort to massive asset sales to try and survive the attack from the wide-open jaws of the bankers.

The BASEL III requirements are scaled-in through January 1, 2018 and by then, the system will be well on its way to a devastating depression and collapse, exacerbated by distressed asset sales, which shall be far worse than experienced in the credit crisis of 2008-2011, or the Great Depression in the United States in the 1930s.

During the credit crisis, the bankers received nearly $30 Trillion to inflate certain asset sectors for their own benefit and through the monetization of debt, kept government spending alive via outright direct purchases of U.S. Treasury securities by the Federal Reserve and the banks. There will be no bailout this time for government---until the bankers achieve the control they want and have long desired.

The devastation and impact to <u>real</u> economies on earth (not just the stock and bond markets) will be felt through at least 2021 and possibly as late as 2025. 2021 may be the economic "bottom" of the dark malaise which drops over mankind, depending on the policy actions of the then President's administration. By this time, it will be pushing the newly empowered bankers to print money (see, in this section, "BASEL III— The Key to the Bottom), to stay in power.

Much will depend on if the bankers consider this particular President a friend, or a foe. A foe in power will mean the desperation and plight of nations will go on for years afterward, but this will not occur if books like those of the Federal Reserve Trilogy are successful in influencing the opinion of lawmakers and they induce radical change upon the banking system (e.g. the people in the U.S., Europe and Japan win during D'Apocalypse™ and they stand up, revolt, throw officials out of office and take over the control of money in their respective sovereign territories).

However, assuming the bankers and elite prevail, they will ensure the recovery calendar will provide enough time to legally foreclose and consolidate their latest round of acquisitions. Thousands of assets and target companies will be falling into their laps during their self-engineered demolition of the derivatives markets.

As the economy and people suffer, the bankers will use the BASEL III accord to provide themselves with camouflage and shelter from public scrutiny during this upcoming "Doomsday Cycle" of D'Apocalypse™ (e.g., "But, we were just following the conservative rules of BASEL III!"). Rest assured, once they have global control of the printing presses, the bankers and elite will magically "reflate" the system. They will then send asset prices skyrocketing upward, again, likely valued in a new currency, or system. Credit will be flowing and asset sales will be taking place, finding the bankers and elite exponentially wealthier. They will use

D'Apocalypse™ to become owners of even greater percentages of the prized assets on planet earth.

The derivatives bubble is their greatest work and is designed to take down all competitors and target-rich environments on earth. Most governments, companies and institutions use derivatives' securities to speculate and/or hedge their portfolios and national economic interests, and are vulnerable to attack. Perhaps the most devious part of their plan is using the Wall Street Wizards' overpowering "brilliance" and mesmerizing influence to assure the targets of something along these lines:

> **"The likelihood of a 7-standard deviation move**
> **is one chance in a billion years, so it is "safe"**
> **to sell this premium based on our risk analysis!"**

For the lay person: institutions WORLDWIDE, have hired a lot of book-smart, statisticians, and mathematicians, who ALL manage risk in the same manner, called VaR. They are brilliant, but at times have a very difficult time seeing the forest from the trees, like most "geniuses."

VaR—Value at Risk

The reader has read a little bit about Value at Risk, or VaR and has seen it is a key risk measurement tool at the big banks. It is an extremely important concept to grasp because VaR, as it is used by the banks and other large organizations, looks at the history of a financial portfolio, security or even a company, and develops a "bell curve." This curve tells a bank, government, firm, hedge fund, pension fund, or other manager of money if it can assume a certain risk, or not, given certain assumptions. It can supposedly tell the portfolio manager and/or institution the expected loss in a worst case scenario over a given time period, given the pricing history of a specific asset and given a specified degree of confidence.

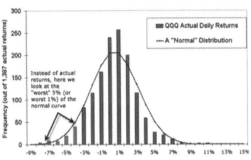

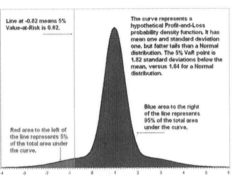

(Source: Top image "An Introduction to Value at Risk," retrieved from http://www.investopedia.com/articles/04/092904.asp, bottom image by AaCBrown, Wikipedia, retrieved from http://en.wikipedia.org/wiki/Value_at_risk).

For example, JP Morgan Chase, Goldman Sachs and Morgan Stanley calculate VaR using a 95% confidence interval, but if those firms used a 99% confidence interval, as does Bank of America and Citigroup, their VaR estimates would be meaningfully higher. (Source: OCC's Quarterly Report on Bank Trading and Derivatives Activities Third Quarter 2013, retrieved from http://www.occ.gov/topics/capital-markets/financial-markets/trading/derivatives/dq313.pdf, Page 10).

> **"We typically employ a one-day time horizon with a 95% confidence level."** (Source: Goldman Sachs 2012 Annual Report, page 89).

It should be emphatically stated, however, the "confidence levels" used by the banks (whether at 95% or 99%) amount to worthless propaganda. This is because the assumptions behind the models are foolhardy and most VaR models do not account for counter-party risk. Please read, later in this chapter, "Leverage is Astronomically Too High."

These kinds of valuation formulas do not typically provide for "out of the box" thinking and catastrophic risk management planning---man-made, or otherwise. When risk changes dramatically and rapidly, as in a nano-second in real-time, and events occur which are outside of a mere three-year historical analysis window, these formulas fall apart. This is also when you will see the statisticians and mathematicians run for cover and go back to being nerds. When D'Apocalypse™ arrives, you will see them frozen in terror, studying their screens, with the system blowing up all around them!

These particular "Wall Street Wizards" will be unable and incapable of taking any action to protect portfolios, institutions and countries from skyrocketing losses and catastrophic failure when the firestorm strikes.

The end result is the cabal of bankers and the elite families (and the thousands of shell companies they control) will wind up owning many, many of the counterparties---or their prized assets. These will include some of the most cherished assets of municipalities, states, federal governments, companies, pension funds, insurance companies and other institutions who use these kinds of formulae to determine their hedging strategies and calculate risk, all supposedly in adherence with BASEL III regulations.

This trap was purposely laid by the Federal Reserve and the central bankers. They pushed rates down and forced asset managers, worldwide, into a virtual stampede in the SELLING of risk premiums to enhance their yields. Furthermore, they based these sales upon idiotic assumptions of "book-smart" mathematicians and statisticians, who ignored the OBVIOUS catastrophic risk within the system---a system which is a derivatives market time bomb. It completely ignores the onset of a massive and impending change of events, easily foreseeable, which shall ultimately pulverize their risk assumptions and calculations.

By selling risk and generating income for themselves—sell-side market participants ("sell-side" in Wall Street parlance means Wall Street banks and firms who sell securities to investors) received additional income in a low-interest rate environment. It worked for a while, as they increased their yield. However, when actual risk (and devastating market performance due to this risk) exceeds the "expected" probability and "expected" number of standard deviations in a VaR formula, LOSSES can and will, occur. In this case they will become catastrophic and shall devastate institutions—large and small.

The towering and enormous derivatives system will be set on fire and destroyed, where just like an out-of-control California inferno it will destroy everything in its path in a blazing hell storm.

By mid-year 2013, institutions had placed bets on <u>below-investment grade</u> and <u>not even rated securities</u> totaling $9.121 TRILLION---the equivalent to nearly 60% *of the U.S. GDP!!*

Credit Default Swaps by Category and Maturity

Table 5

Credit default swaps, by rating category[1]

Notional amounts outstanding, in billions of US dollars

	Total			Investment grade (AAA-BBB)			Non-investment grade (BB and below)			Non-rated[2]		
	H1 2012	H2 2012	H1 2013	H1 2012	H2 2012	H1 2013	H1 2012	H2 2012	H1 2013	H1 2012	H2 2012	H1 2013
Total contracts	26,931	25,069	24,349	16,714	15,102	15,229	5,151	5,147	4,387	5,066	4,819	4,734
With reporting dealers	15,747	14,149	13,728	9,575	8,303	8,270	3,360	3,018	2,723	2,812	2,828	2,735
With other financial institutions[3]	10,997	10,720	10,429	7,042	6,693	6,822	1,759	2,098	1,625	2,195	1,929	1,972
Central counterparties[3]	5,209	4,891	5,548	3,720	3,464	4,013	686	848	715	802	578	821
Banks and security firms	2,919	2,963	2,236	1,759	1,747	1,364	613	758	450	548	459	402
Insurance firms	278	258	230	130	113	117	39	61	37	109	84	76
SPVs, SPCs and SPEs	458	587	377	198	289	174	44	52	44	217	246	155
Hedge funds	1,008	957	1,076	637	553	685	200	199	222	171	204	169
Other financial customers	1,125	1,063	986	599	527	479	178	179	157	348	357	350
With non-financial customers	187	200	193	96	106	127	31	32	38	59	63	27
Single-name credit default swaps	15,566	14,309	13,135	10,693	9,712	9,150	3,224	2,830	2,490	1,649	1,767	1,495
With reporting dealers	10,031	9,031	8,559	6,492	5,845	5,669	2,485	2,087	1,899	1,034	1,098	990
With other financial institutions[3]	5,441	5,170	4,498	4,138	3,806	3,421	726	732	580	577	632	498
Central counterparties[3]	2,352	2,078	2,047	2,080	1,728	1,735	178	135	141	95	195	172
Banks and security firms	1,840	1,778	1,363	1,241	1,223	959	320	337	223	279	218	181
Insurance firms	111	114	84	66	63	55	8	23	14	37	28	16
SPVs, SPCs and SPEs	131	225	98	68	158	60	28	36	21	35	31	17
Hedge funds	497	464	443	329	282	294	113	104	104	55	78	45
Other financial customers	509	511	463	354	352	319	79	77	78	76	82	66
With non-financial customers	114	108	78	63	59	60	13	11	11	38	37	7
Multi-name credit default swaps	11,364	10,760	11,214	6,021	5,390	6,078	1,926	2,317	1,897	3,417	3,052	3,239
With reporting dealers	5,736	5,118	5,169	3,084	2,457	2,601	875	931	825	1,778	1,730	1,744
With other financial institutions[3]	5,555	5,549	5,931	2,904	2,887	3,411	1,083	1,366	1,046	1,618	1,297	1,475
Central counterparties[3]	2,856	2,813	3,501	1,640	1,736	2,278	509	683	574	708	383	649
Banks and security firms	1,079	1,185	853	538	523	405	293	421	228	369	241	221
Insurance firms	166	144	146	64	50	63	31	36	23	72	56	60
SPVs, SPCs and SPEs	327	362	274	130	131	114	15	16	23	182	215	138
Hedge funds	511	493	633	271	271	391	87	95	118	116	126	123
Other financial customers	616	552	523	245	176	160	99	102	80	272	275	283
With non-financial customers	73	93	114	33	46	67	18	21	27	22	25	20

[1] See footnote 1 to Table 1. [2] Without rating or rating not known. [3] Both contracts post-novation are captured.

(Source: Bank For International Settlements, June 2013, "Statistical release OTC derivatives statistics at end-June 2013 Monetary and Economic Department," page 23 retrieved from http://www.bis.org/publ/otc_hy1311.pdf).

$22.7 TRILLION In Credit Default Swaps Comes Due For Settlement Within 5 Years!

Table 6

Credit default swaps, by remaining maturity[1]

Notional amounts outstanding, in billions of US dollars

	Total			One year or less			Over one year up to five years			Over five years		
	H1 2012	H2 2012	H1 2013	H1 2012	H2 2012	H1 2013	H1 2012	H2 2012	H1 2013	H1 2012	H2 2012	H1 2013
Total contracts	26,931	25,069	24,349	5,615	5,078	4,316	18,248	18,056	18,360	3,068	1,935	1,674
With reporting dealers	15,747	14,149	13,728	3,562	3,173	2,728	10,546	9,360	10,106	1,639	1,613	905
With other financial institutions	10,997	10,720	10,409	2,026	1,879	1,566	7,579	7,953	8,139	1,391	888	722
Central counterparties[2]	5,299	4,891	5,548	948	761	744	3,661	3,827	4,588	690	302	235
Banks and security firms	2,919	2,963	2,216	649	692	497	2,025	2,061	1,604	344	210	115
Insurance firms	278	258	230	38	33	27	161	171	162	78	54	41
SPVs, SPCs and SPEs	458	587	372	45	88	29	293	429	289	121	70	54
Hedge funds	1,008	957	1,076	174	155	155	657	686	800	177	116	121
Other financial customers	1,125	1,063	986	169	150	95	781	778	695	175	136	196
With non-financial customers	187	200	193	26	25	30	129	141	136	34	34	27
Single-name credit default swaps	15,566	14,309	13,135	3,508	3,519	3,156	10,432	9,725	8,817	1,628	1,065	1,160
With reporting dealers	10,011	9,021	8,559	2,384	2,312	2,114	6,669	6,106	5,749	958	613	695
With other financial institutions	5,441	5,170	4,490	1,120	1,188	1,036	3,683	3,546	3,622	669	437	443
Central counterparties[2]	2,352	2,078	2,047	464	470	486	1,665	1,468	1,438	223	139	113
Banks and security firms	1,940	1,778	1,363	468	487	391	1,207	1,177	890	165	114	80
Insurance firms	111	114	84	16	18	17	62	73	51	54	23	19
SPVs, SPCs and SPEs	131	225	98	11	43	17	78	148	64	45	33	17
Hedge funds	497	464	443	65	81	49	339	327	325	70	56	69
Other financial customers	509	511	453	85	88	69	339	351	253	89	71	143
With non-financial customers	114	108	78	15	19	6	81	73	46	16	16	25
Multi-name credit default swaps	11,364	10,760	11,214	2,106	1,559	1,157	7,816	8,330	9,543	1,442	870	513
With reporting dealers	5,736	5,128	5,169	1,178	861	604	3,877	3,856	4,356	680	401	209
With other financial institutions	5,555	5,549	5,931	917	692	532	3,896	4,407	5,117	742	451	282
Central counterparties[2]	2,856	2,813	3,501	484	291	248	1,995	2,358	3,190	376	163	163
Banks and security firms	1,079	1,185	853	181	205	106	818	884	714	80	96	35
Insurance firms	166	144	146	22	14	10	99	98	110	45	31	22
SPVs, SPCs and SPEs	327	362	274	37	44	13	228	281	225	71	37	16
Hedge funds	511	493	633	108	74	106	318	359	475	84	27	52
Other financial customers	616	552	523	84	62	26	446	427	442	85	64	53
With non-financial customers	73	93	114	11	6	22	43	68	70	19	18	22

[1] See footnote 1 to Table 1. [2] Both contracts post-novation are captured.

(Source: Ibid, page 24).

58

Table 7

Credit default swaps, by sector[1]

Notional amounts outstanding, in billions of US dollars

	Total[2]		Sovereigns		Financial firms		Non-financial firms		Securitised products		Multiple sectors	
	H2 2012	H1 2013	H2 2012	H1 2013	H2 2012	H1 2013	H2 2012	H1 2013	H2 2012	H1 2013	H2 2012	H1 2013
Total contracts	25,069	24,349	2,941	3,243	6,420	6,404	9,299	8,360	903	732	5,505	5,606
With reporting dealers	14,149	13,728	2,114	2,430	3,491	3,340	5,421	4,916	455	509	2,668	2,532
With other financial institutions[3]	10,720	10,429	807	791	2,888	3,041	3,819	3,401	437	210	2,768	2,984
Central counterparties[4]	4,891	5,548	121	133	1,402	1,629	1,935	2,002	5	7	1,428	1,777
Banks and security firms	2,963	2,216	414	393	715	565	1,095	736	295	90	445	431
Insurance firms	238	230	14	16	68	47	59	57	45	31	73	79
SPVs, SPCs and SPEs	587	372	29	22	99	80	181	79	17	15	260	176
Hedge funds	957	1,076	119	118	308	462	305	304	32	36	194	157
Other financial customers	1,063	986	111	110	297	258	245	222	43	30	367	363
With non-financial customers	200	193	20	22	41	24	59	43	11	13	69	91
Single-name credit default swaps	14,309	13,135	2,799	3,098	3,853	3,202	7,657	6,836	0	0	0	0
With reporting dealers	9,031	8,559	2,011	2,325	2,502	2,174	4,518	4,060	0	0	0	0
With other financial institutions[3]	5,170	4,498	768	752	1,312	1,006	3,090	2,740	0	0	0	0
Central counterparties[4]	2,078	2,047	120	128	380	316	1,578	1,603	0	0	0	0
Banks and security firms	1,778	1,363	401	374	472	350	905	639	0	0	0	0
Insurance firms	114	84	14	15	54	29	46	49	0	0	0	0
SPVs, SPCs and SPEs	225	98	8	10	60	31	158	58	0	0	0	0
Hedge funds	464	445	117	116	126	98	221	172	0	0	0	0
Other financial customers	511	463	109	109	220	182	183	172	0	0	0	0
With non-financial customers	108	78	20	21	39	21	49	36	0	0	0	0
Multi-name credit default swaps	10,760	11,214	143	145	2,567	3,203	1,642	1,524	903	732	5,505	5,606
With reporting dealers	5,118	5,169	104	105	989	1,165	902	856	455	509	2,668	2,532
With other financial institutions[3]	5,549	5,931	38	39	1,576	2,035	729	661	437	210	2,768	2,984
Central counterparties[4]	2,813	3,501	1	4	1,022	1,312	356	400	5	7	1,428	1,777
Banks and security firms	1,185	853	13	19	243	215	189	97	295	90	445	431
Insurance firms	144	146	0	1	13	18	13	17	45	31	73	79
SPVs, SPCs and SPEs	362	274	21	12	40	49	23	22	17	15	260	176
Hedge funds	493	633	1	1	181	364	84	75	32	36	194	157
Other financial customers	552	523	2	2	78	76	62	50	43	30	367	363
With non-financial customers	93	114	1	1	1	3	10	7	11	13	69	91

[1] See footnote 1 to Table 1. [2] Due to an incomplete breakdown reported by one country, the sum of components is less than the total. [3] Both contracts post-novation are captured.

(Source: Ibid, page 25).

Some Very Smart People Understand What is Happening

Paul Singer of Elliott Management and now famous because of his fight with the government of Argentina over its lack of payment on debt obligations owed to him, said the outlook for the global financial system was bleak and there would be no safe havens in today's markets. He indicated bonds across the developed world were not priced correctly and were trading at the "wrong price," due to artificial government purchases of these securities.

He also stated debt balances for world governments did not indicate the true state of affairs or conditions of those governments. Social Security, Medicare and pension promise obligations make the true debt figures total up to 500% of national GDP---in nearly every major Western country.

Furthermore, he believes entitlement programs should be considered "long-term debt," due to the inability of the politicians to modify, even slightly, the programs. *Finally, Mr. Singer stated it was impossible to measure the true risks taken on by the major financial institutions because of their large derivatives' positions. Each large institution has $150 Billion to $200 Billion in equity, supporting notional derivatives of $50 Trillion to $80 Trillion.* (Source: Financial Times, May 8, 2013, "Japan Bear Warns on Impending Debt Crisis," Dan McCrum and Arash Massoudi, as retrieved from http://www.cnbc.com/id/100722143, Author's emphasis italicized.).

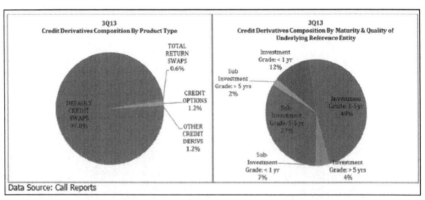

(Source: OCC's Quarterly Report on Bank Trading and Derivatives Activities 3rd Quarter 2013, page 11, retrieved from: http://www.occ.gov/topics/capital-markets/financial-markets/trading/derivatives/dq313.pdf).

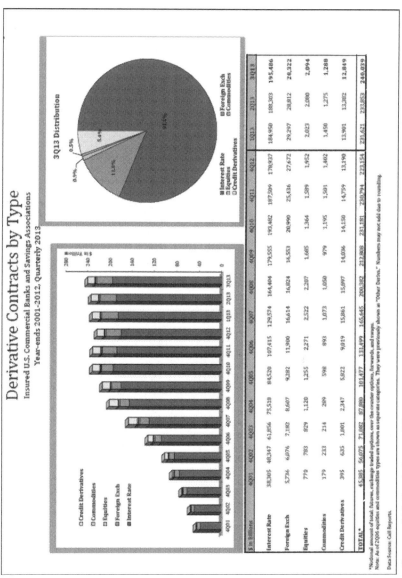

(Source: ibid, Graph 3, page 17).

4 Horsemen of the D'Apocalypse™ Control 93% of Derivatives Market

Even more frightening from an oligopolistic and liquidity perspective, JP Morgan Chase, Citigroup, Bank of America and Goldman Sachs **control and transact over 93%** OF ALL DERIVATIVES TRADING among the top 25 commercial banks in the United States. They also control over **40%** of the world's derivatives' transactions with their cohorts in the "G14," which consists of JP Morgan Chase, Bank of America-Merrill Lynch, Barclays Capital, BNP Paribas, Citigroup, Credit Suisse, Deutsche Bank, Goldman Sachs, HSBC, Morgan Stanley, RBS, Societe Generale, UBS and Wells Fargo Bank.

As discussed, the G14 controls over 80% of the world's $692 Trillion derivatives market.

> Anyone can understand the power of monopoly and oligopoly. We are regretfully at their mercy until real change is made to the system.

The Facts: Derivatives = Financial Weapons of Mass Destruction!
Let's now look at the facts which should convince you, unequivocally, Warren Buffett was indeed correct when he famously said:

"DERIVATIVES ARE FINANCIAL WEAPONS OF MASS DESTRUCTION!"

Derivatives are Financial Weapons of Mass Destruction
By Warren Buffett

"In my 2002 letter to shareholders I referred to derivatives as 'weapons of mass destruction.' Derivatives are really just a way to create a product with a very long fuse, for example, 100 years, as opposed to stocks which settle in 3 days. That kind of system allows claims to be built up. AIG called me in September and told me they were about to get downgraded which would have required higher posting requirements. Now this is an enterprise that has been built up over decades and was effectively destroyed in 48 hours by these products. With derivatives, you're exposed to counterparties and thus reliant on others. These claims built up over time to the tune of billions of dollars and when one falls, the whole system falls. Derivatives are not evil by themselves but rather everyone needs to be able to handle them. System wide, they're rat poison. Berkshire holds many derivatives but we always hold the money at Berkshire."
(Source: Investor Words, by Warren Buffett, as retrieved from http://www.investorwords.com/tips/389/derivatives-are-financial-weapons-of-mass-destruction.html#ixzz2bzBDYKBb).

Derivatives create tremendous trading income, commissions, bonuses and position income for banks, Wall Street and various participating institutions and individuals. This is only accomplished however, by over-leveraging an individual institution's, company's, or person's assets and balance sheet.

What has startled many is the sheer size of the positions within the derivatives market. As already discussed, it is impressive. It dwarfs the U.S. and world's GDP (U.S. GDP was $16 Trillion in 2013 and the world's was approximately $74 Trillion in 2013). The global derivatives market, notionally and conservatively is estimated at $692 Trillion, with the suspicion its actual size is far, far larger.

Many insiders in the business indicate the ***real size*** of this market is ***above $1.25 QUADRILLION DOLLARS***, double what the published figures indicate and may be as high as ***$1.5 QUADRILLION ---which would be the equivalent of 100 TIMES THE SIZE OF THE U.S. ECONOMY!***

G-U-L-P!!!

These financial time bombs have been the gravy train, of all gravy trains, for Wall Street. They keep many, many traders, partners and executives employed and well fed through enormous salaries and unbelievably egregious bonuses. As we discuss the problems underlying the derivatives market, please remember the mentioning of bonuses. They play a very powerful role in Wall Street's aggressive desire to trade derivatives and other exotic securities (see Chapter 3, Wall Street Profits & Compensation).

Why the Derivatives Time Bomb Will Go Off
WHEN this time bomb goes off, it will be caused by a number of factors, the most important of which is the improper use of leverage. It will cause ruination throughout the system.

For those confused by the hype and mystery surrounding "derivatives," if you take two minutes to read the following pages and highlighted tables, you will immediately become more educated on this subject than 99% of the rest of the population---and your education will help you protect your family. Don't worry---it will be "OK" to be in this 1% of the nation!

Also, please keep fresh in the back of your mind, the two categories of derivatives we explored earlier in this chapter (e.g., interest rate and CDS---Credit Default Swaps). The CDS market has nearly $10 Trillion in *below* investment grade bets and within five years, over $22.7 Trillion of CDS bets must be settled, in potentially, a dramatic interest rate environment!

Actual OCC Notional Derivatives Tables
D'Apocalypse™ Now! will demonstrate in the following pages A SIMPLE EXAMPLE ANYONE CAN UNDERSTAND which explains how dangerous the banks' leverage is in derivatives trading. We use the year-end 2012 annual financial statement data for the "4 Horsemen" of the D'Apocalypse™ and the year-end 2012 derivatives data from the Office of the Comptroller of the Currency in the example, providing clear, audited results for comparative purposes.

The 3rd Quarter 2013 derivatives figures, which follow the tables below, reveal no major changes in the lineup of culprits trading in this arena, or the absolutely dangerous leverage they are using to make a profit. Through 2014, no material changes in the major players have taken place.

The dangers of this leverage will become crystal clear, momentarily, as the reader will be taken into the world of derivatives, using a hypothetical family's capital. This book makes it easy to see the outrageousness of the banks actions, via a learning lesson which uses exactly the same ratios as the major banks, when they are trading derivatives. This lesson is presented in the tables, which follow.

What hopefully becomes obvious to every Congressman, Senator and citizen, is how the greedy actions of a small group of men and women place the entire nation at risk. Despite causing massive unemployment, spiraling inflation, out-of-control debt and deficits because of the secret bailouts and irresponsible government spending, the banks, the elite and their eager legions of employees have learned nothing---nor do they care.

They are the epitome of the old saying,

"Damn the torpedoes and full-speed ahead!"

Year-end 2012 Derivatives Data
From the Office of the Comptroller of the Currency (ONLY U.S.-Based Banks---DOES NOT INCLUDE International Transactions):

TABLE 3

DISTRIBUTION OF DERIVATIVE CONTRACTS
TOP 25 COMMERCIAL BANKS, SAVINGS ASSOCIATIONS AND TRUST COMPANIES IN DERIVATIVES
DECEMBER 31, 2012, $ MILLIONS

RANK	BANK NAME	STATE	TOTAL ASSETS	TOTAL DERIVATIVES	PERCENT EXCH TRADED CONTRACTS	PERCENT OTC CONTRACTS	PERCENT INT RATE CONTRACTS	PERCENT FOREIGN EXCH CONTRACTS	PERCENT OTHER CONTRACTS	PERCENT CREDIT DERIVATIVES
					(%)	(%)	(%)	(%)	(%)	(%)
1	JPMORGAN CHASE BANK NA	OH	$1,896,773	$69,003,973	3.5	96.5	75.8	12.6	3.0	8.9
2	CITIBANK NATIONAL ASSN	SD	1,313,401	55,402,433	2.8	97.2	81.1	12.3	1.0	5.6
3	BANK OF AMERICA NA	NC	1,474,077	42,479,208	3.3	96.7	80.4	11.5	0.8	7.2
4	GOLDMAN SACHS BANK USA	NY	118,536	41,197,310	4.0	96.0	93.8	5.1	0.1	1.1
5	HSBC BANK USA NATIONAL ASSN	VA	186,794	4,666,226	1.6	98.4	69.5	18.3	1.8	10.4
6	WELLS FARGO BANK NA	SD	1,266,125	3,670,050	3.9	96.1	68.4	5.5	4.5	1.6
7	MORGAN STANLEY BANK NA	UT	80,536	2,548,952	0.4	99.6	70.0	29.2	0.0	0.6
8	BANK OF NEW YORK MELLON	NY	282,443	1,189,685	1.8	98.2	70.0	29.2	0.8	0.6
9	STATE STREET BANK&TRUST CO	MA	218,655	934,598	0.2	99.8	0.6	95.8	3.6	0.0
10	PNC BANK NATIONAL ASSN	DE	295,026	354,776	24.7	73.3	95.7	3.1	0.2	1.0
11	SUNTRUST BANK	GA	169,077	270,623	14.6	85.4	82.3	1.8	14.3	1.7
12	NORTHERN TRUST CO	IL	97,139	216,355	0.0	100.0	4.2	95.8	0.0	0.0
13	U S BANK NATIONAL ASSN	OH	345,089	126,353	2.9	97.1	77.2	20.1	0.0	2.7
14	REGIONS BANK	AL	120,421	103,326	3.8	96.2	97.9	0.7	0.4	1.0
15	KEYBANK NATIONAL ASSN	OH	87,043	75,410	2.9	97.1	90.9	6.9	0.9	1.3
16	BRANCH BANKING&TRUST CO	NC	178,034	73,304	0.2	99.8	98.7	1.3	0.0	0.0
17	FIFTH THIRD BANK	OH	119,445	72,674	0.2	99.8	69.1	23.4	5.7	1.7
18	TD BANK NATIONAL ASSN	DE	203,986	70,569	0.0	100.0	81.4	17.5	0.0	1.1
19	UNION BANK NATIONAL ASSN	CA	96,323	59,575	11.2	88.8	77.6	6.8	15.5	0.1
20	RBS CITIZENS NATIONAL ASSN	RI	104,624	38,885	0.0	100.0	80.7	16.5	0.0	2.8
21	CAPITAL ONE NATIONAL ASSN	VA	230,961	36,260	0.1	99.9	98.2	0.1	0.0	1.7
22	BOKF NATIONAL ASSN	OK	27,934	33,696	4.1	95.9	88.4	1.1	10.5	0.0
23	FLAGSTAR BANK FSB	MI	14,069	29,120	40.5	59.5	99.9	0.0	0.1	0.0
24	HUNTINGTON NATIONAL BANK	OH	55,955	28,503	0.0	100.0	95.5	2.0	0.3	2.2
25	DEUTSCHE BANK TR CO AMERICAS	NY	56,397	23,410	0.0	100.0	51.4	36.3	0.0	12.3
	TOP 25 COMMERCIAL BANKS, SAs & TCs WITH DERIVATIVES		$9,059,062	$222,705,294	$7,471,082	$215,234,213	$178,552,783	$27,627,570	$3,337,269	$13,187,673
	OTHER COMMERCIAL BANKS, SAs & TCs WITH DERIVATIVES		3,590,615	448,277	10,212	438,064	383,928	44,856	16,881	2,880
	TOTAL FOR COMMERCIAL BANKS, SAs & TCs WITH DERIVATIVES		12,649,677	223,153,571	7,481,294	215,672,277	178,936,711	27,672,436	3,353,949	13,190,475
	TOP 25 COMMERCIAL BANKS, SAs & TCs % OF TOTAL COMMERCIAL BANKS, SAs & TCs WITH DERIVATIVES			(%) 99.8	3.3	99.5	80.0	12.4	1.5	5.9
	OTHER COMMERCIAL BANKS, SAs & TCs % OF TOTAL COMMERCIAL BANKS, SAs & TCs WITH DERIVATIVES			0.2	0.2	0.2	0.0	0.0	0.0	0.0
	TOTAL FOR COMMERCIAL BANKS, SAs & TCs % OF TOTAL COMMERCIAL BANKS, SAs & TCs WITH DERIVATIVES			100.0	3.4	96.6	80.2	12.4	1.5	5.9

(Source: OCC's Quarterly Report on Bank Trading and Derivatives Activities Fourth Quarter 2012, Table 3, retrieved from http://www.occ.gov/topics/capital-markets/financial-markets/trading/derivatives/dq412.pdf).

TABLE 8

NOTIONAL AMOUNTS OF DERIVATIVE CONTRACTS BY CONTRACT TYPE & MATURITY
TOP 4 COMMERCIAL BANKS, SAVINGS ASSOCIATIONS AND TRUST COMPANIES IN DERIVATIVES
DECEMBER 31, 2012, $ MILLIONS

RANK	BANK NAME	STATE	TOTAL ASSETS	TOTAL DERIVATIVES	INT RATE MATURITY < 1 YR	INT RATE MATURITY 1 - 5 YRS	INT RATE MATURITY > 5 YRS	INT RATE ALL MATURITIES	FOREIGN EXCH MATURITY < 1 YR	FOREIGN EXCH MATURITY 1 - 5 YRS	FOREIGN EXCH MATURITY > 5 YRS	FOREIGN EXCH ALL MATURITIES
1	JPMORGAN CHASE BANK NA	OH	$1,896,773	$69,003,973	$31,371,934	$7,760,123	$5,554,039	$44,802,786	$6,513,499	$648,364	$1,359,065	$18,360,086
2	CITIBANK NATIONAL ASSN	SD	1,313,401	55,402,433	25,264,853	7,072,235	4,627,638	36,964,726	5,021,160	371,293	137,516	5,523,999
3	BANK OF AMERICA NA	NC	1,474,077	42,479,286	5,961,264	4,382,353	2,691,356	13,035,973	2,410,363	735,777	122,441	1,468,581
4	GOLDMAN SACHS BANK USA	NY	118,536	41,197,310	18,518,099	8,679,898	6,061,661	34,079,658	572,064	721,293	679,991	1,983,349
	TOP 4 COMMERCIAL BANKS, SAS & TCs WITH DERIVATIVES		$4,802,787	$208,082,924	$81,116,150	$27,860,609	$19,848,694	$128,825,413	$14,517,116	$2,494,717	$2,359,065	$18,360,086
	OTHER COMMERCIAL BANKS, SAS & TCs WITH DERIVATIVES		7,946,890	15,070,647	1,955,459	2,647,818	1,599,886	6,203,165	3,880,294	393,709	83,836	4,297,839
	TOTAL AMOUNT FOR COMMERCIAL BANKS, SAS & TCs WITH DERIVATIVES		12,699,677	223,153,571	83,071,608	30,508,427	21,448,582	135,028,618	18,397,400	2,888,426	1,442,901	22,659,726

Note: Figures above exclude any contracts not subject to risk-based capital requirements, such as foreign exchange contracts with an original maturity of 14 days or less, futures contracts, written options, and basis swaps.
Therefore, the total notional amount of derivatives by maturity will not add to the total derivatives figure in this table.
Note: Numbers may not add due to rounding.
Data Source: Call Reports, schedule RC-R

(Source: ibid, Table 8, retrieved from http://www.occ.gov/topics/capital-markets/financial-markets/trading/derivatives/dq412.pdf).

66

2013 Derivatives Data

TABLE 3

DISTRIBUTION OF DERIVATIVE CONTRACTS
TOP 25 COMMERCIAL BANKS, SAVINGS ASSOCIATIONS AND TRUST COMPANIES IN DERIVATIVES
SEPTEMBER 30, 2013, $ MILLIONS

RANK	BANK NAME	STATE	TOTAL ASSETS	TOTAL DERIVATIVES	PERCENT EXCH TRADED CONTRACTS	PERCENT OTC CONTRACTS	PERCENT INT RATE CONTRACTS	PERCENT FOREIGN EXCH CONTRACTS	PERCENT OTHER CONTRACTS	PERCENT CREDIT DERIVATIVES
					(%)	(%)	(%)	(%)	(%)	(%)
1	JPMORGAN CHASE BANK NA	OH	$1,989,875	$71,810,058	3.6	96.4	77.5	11.6	2.6	8.3
2	CITIBANK NATIONAL ASSN	SD	1,344,751	62,963,116	2.6	97.4	81.6	12.2	1.2	5.1
3	GOLDMAN SACHS BANK USA	NY	111,117	47,467,154	4.0	96.0	94.7	4.6	0.1	0.7
4	BANK OF AMERICA NA	NC	1,438,859	41,286,713	4.7	95.3	80.6	11.5	0.9	7.0
5	HSBC BANK USA NATIONAL ASSN	VA	179,861	5,224,908	4.5	95.5	73.6	17.4	1.6	7.5
6	WELLS FARGO BANK NA	SD	1,328,010	4,332,672	4.5	95.5	89.6	5.1	4.2	1.1
7	MORGAN STANLEY BANK NA	UT	99,782	2,560,224	5.5	94.5	5.4	94.3	0.0	0.3
8	BANK OF NEW YORK MELLON	NY	291,475	1,196,907	2.6	97.4	67.3	31.0	1.7	0.0
9	STATE STREET BANK&TRUST CO	MA	212,689	1,121,877	0.5	99.5	0.9	96.6	2.5	0.0
10	PNC BANK NATIONAL ASSN	DE	298,486	381,329	27.7	72.3	95.2	3.3	0.3	1.2
11	NORTHERN TRUST CO	IL	95,631	243,907	0.0	100.0	3.8	96.2	0.0	0.0
12	SUNTRUST BANK	GA	167,525	238,202	14.3	85.7	77.8	2.2	18.2	1.8
13	TD BANK NATIONAL ASSN	DE	215,432	120,240	0.0	100.0	81.5	18.0	0.0	0.5
14	U S BANK NATIONAL ASSN	OH	356,590	104,411	3.2	96.8	71.5	24.5	0.1	3.9
15	REGIONS BANK	AL	116,068	81,364	2.7	97.3	97.0	1.3	0.5	1.2
16	BRANCH BANKING&TRUST CO	NC	175,616	66,783	0.1	99.9	99.5	0.5	0.0	0.0
17	KEYBANK NATIONAL ASSN	OH	88,093	65,874	8.0	92.0	89.9	7.1	1.6	1.5
18	FIFTH THIRD BANK	OH	123,338	63,207	0.9	99.1	61.6	28.5	7.5	2.5
19	UNION BANK NATIONAL ASSN	CA	104,956	61,693	10.0	90.0	76.7	7.3	16.0	0.0
20	CAPITAL ONE NATIONAL ASSN	VA	234,771	39,750	0.0	100.0	97.7	0.2	0.0	2.1
21	RBS CITIZENS NATIONAL ASSN	RI	98,283	39,429	0.0	100.0	78.3	18.9	0.0	2.8
22	BOKF NATIONAL ASSN	OK	26,912	32,765	4.3	95.7	87.5	1.0	11.5	0.0
23	HUNTINGTON NATIONAL BANK	OH	56,434	24,114	0.0	100.0	90.2	5.6	1.0	3.2
24	COMERICA BANK	TX	64,591	22,529	0.0	100.0	61.8	8.6	25.4	4.1
25	MANUFACTURERS&TRADERS TR CO	NY	83,616	20,092	0.0	100.0	96.1	3.9	0.0	0.0
	TOP 25 COMMERCIAL BANKS, SAs & TCs WITH DERIVATIVES		$9,302,762	$239,669,197	$8,904,186	$230,765,011	$195,164,725	$28,286,904	$3,370,890	$12,946,678
	OTHER COMMERCIAL BANKS, SAs & TCs WITH DERIVATIVES		3,592,622	369,417	16,445	353,271	321,596	35,135	10,716	1,970
	TOTAL FOR COMMERCIAL BANKS, SAs & TCs WITH DERIVATIVES		12,895,384	240,038,613	8,920,331	231,118,282	195,486,321	28,322,039	3,381,606	12,948,648
			(%)	(%)	(%)	(%)	(%)	(%)	(%)	(%)
	TOP 25 COMMERCIAL BANKS, SAs & TCs: % OF TOTAL COMMERCIAL BANKS, SAs & TCs WITH DERIVATIVES		99.8	99.8	1.7	98.1	81.3	11.8	1.4	5.4
	OTHER COMMERCIAL BANKS, SAs & TCs: % OF TOTAL COMMERCIAL BANKS, SAs & TCs WITH DERIVATIVES		0.2	0.1	0.0	0.1	0.1	0.0	0.0	0.0
	TOTAL FOR COMMERCIAL BANKS, SAs & TCs: % OF TOTAL COMMERCIAL BANKS, SAs & TCs WITH DERIVATIVES		100.0	100.0	3.7	96.3	81.4	11.8	1.4	5.4

(Source: OCC's Quarterly Report on Bank Trading and Derivatives Activities Third Quarter 2013, Table 3, retrieved from http://www.occ.gov/topics/capital-markets/financial-markets/trading/derivatives/dq313.pdf).

Leverage is Astronomically Too HIGH

The ratio between the banks' derivatives position values versus their Total Net Revenues, Net Income, Cash and Assets is staggeringly high---and their respective percentages vis-a-vis derivatives holdings, is staggeringly low. Most of these are *FAR, FAR BELOW 1%*, a recipe for disaster!! While God makes all things possible, it is difficult to imagine even the angels using this kind of leverage!!

Derivatives Positions Top 4 Banks
Expressed As Ratios Of Key Financial Statement Data

© 2013 Robert L. Kelly

Rank	Name	Total Net Revenues	Total Net Income	Total Cash & Segregated Cash	Total Assets	Total Derivatives Positions	Derivatives To Total Net Revenues Ratio	Derivatives To Total Net Income Ratio	Derivatives To Total Cash Ratio	Derivatives To Total Assets Ratio
1	JP Morgan Chase Bank NA	$ 97,031,000,000	$ 21,284,000,000	$ 53,723,000,000	$ 2,359,143,000,000	$ 69,003,973,000,000	711.15	3,242.06	1,284.41	29.25
2	Citigroup, Inc.	$ 70,171,000,000	$ 7,541,000,000	$ 36,463,000,000	$ 1,864,660,000,000	$ 55,402,433,000,000	789.53	7,346.83	1,519.83	29.71
3	Bank of America NA	$ 84,235,000,000	$ 4,188,000,000	$ 110,752,000,000	$ 2,209,974,000,000	$ 42,479,208,000,000	504.29	10,143.08	383.55	19.22
4	Goldman Sachs Bank USA	$ 34,163,000,000	$ 7,475,000,000	$ 122,340,000,000	$ 938,555,000,000	$ 41,197,310,000,000	1,205.90	5,511.35	336.74	43.89

Source: JP Morgan Chase 2012 Annual Report, page 62 & 190, Citigroup 2012 Annual Report, page 21 & 154, Goldman Sachs 2012 Annual Report, page 32 & 109.
Net Revenues Reported Net of Interest Expense.

Derivatives Positions Top 4 Banks
Expressed As Percentage Of Key Financial Statement Data

© 2013 Robert L. Kelly

Rank	Name	Total Net Revenues	Total Net Income	Total Cash & Segregated Cash	Total Assets	Total Derivatives Positions	% Total Net Revenues/ Derivatives	% Net Income/ Derivatives	% Total Cash/ Derivatives	% Total Assets/ Derivatives
1	JP Morgan Chase Bank NA	$ 97,031,000,000	$ 21,284,000,000	$ 53,723,000,000	$ 2,359,141,000,000	$ 69,003,973,000,000	0.141%	0.031%	0.078%	3.42%
2	Citigroup, Inc.	$ 70,171,000,000	$ 7,541,000,000	$ 36,463,000,000	$ 1,864,660,000,000	$ 55,402,433,000,000	0.127%	0.014%	0.066%	3.37%
3	Bank of America NA	$ 84,235,000,000	$ 4,188,000,000	$ 110,752,000,000	$ 2,209,974,000,000	$ 42,479,208,000,000	0.198%	0.010%	0.261%	5.20%
4	Goldman Sachs Bank USA	$ 34,163,000,000	$ 7,475,000,000	$ 122,340,000,000	$ 938,555,000,000	$ 41,197,310,000,000	0.083%	0.018%	0.297%	2.28%

Source: JP Morgan Chase 2012 Annual Report, page 62 & 190, Citigroup 2012 Annual Report, page 10 & 11 & 142, Bank of America 2012 Annual Report, page 21 & 154, Goldman Sachs 2012 Annual Report, page 32 & 109.
Net Revenues Reported Net of Interest Expense.

> In case you are having problems seeing the number of commas in the preceding "Total Derivatives Positions" column, we are talking about **TRILLIONS** of dollars here (e.g., JP Morgan had over <u>$69 TRILLION</u> in derivatives positions in 2012---By the end of the third quarter, 2013 it increased this amount to $71.8 Trillion)!

The range of leverage runs from a low of nearly 29 times (i.e., JP Morgan owns assets which collateralize only 3.4% of its derivatives positions) to a nose-bleed high of 10,143 times, based on the annual Net Income of Bank of America. This bank uses an incredulously low .010% (1/10,000!!!) of Net Income for every derivatives transaction made!

For purposes of clarity, this means for **EACH AND EVERY DOLLAR** of Net Income earned during the YEAR by Bank of America, the firm has leveraged exposure on derivatives positions worth a staggering $10,143 **PER DOLLAR OF NET INCOME** when the entire year's earnings are taken into account. *They are leveraging $42.5 Trillion in derivatives!*

Since income is fleeting and can go up and down dramatically, quarterly income becomes an important number because this is the income available immediately to deal with a potential crisis.

If one looks at Bank of America's *quarterly earnings* at year end 2012 (since we are looking at 2012 annual report data), this ratio rises to an *astronomically high 115,747.16* for every dollar of Net Income earned during the quarter (Bank of America had Net Income applicable to common shareholders of only $367 Million in the fourth quarter of 2012, leveraging over *$42.5 Trillion* in derivatives positions). Nothing much has changed in 2013, based upon the review of 3rd Quarter information as published by the banks, as they are still using ENORMOUS leverage and do not have the assets to back up their bets, in this writer's humble opinion. (Source: <u>Bank of America 2012 Annual Report</u>, page 136 and the OCC table reports on derivatives positions, discussed previously in this chapter in subsection, "Actual OCC Notional Derivatives Tables December 31, 2012").

NOW THIS IS INDEED IMPRESSIVE, IF NOT SPECTACULARLY OUTRAGEOUS, DANGEROUS AND MAD!

Bank of America is not to be singled out, either, because all the 4 Horsemen are using leverage in the most tragic and irresponsible manner possible. Please behold Goldman Sachs. They are leveraging themselves 336.74 TIMES against ALL cash at year end 2012! This actual percentage, per the tables above, is 0.297% (e.g., cash divided by derivatives)---far below 1%!! In fact, if you even include ALL ASSETS at Goldman Sachs, it only has slightly over 2% in assets to back up all its derivatives bets!

This means, across the board for every one of the 4 Horsemen, there is not enough cash, assets or revenues to even come close to paying off the liabilities which will be incurred as a result of even a slight disruption to these markets! It is the same situation at every one of the big banks because they are all, essentially, infinitely leveraged.

If you dig into the financial statement disclosures in their 10K filings and annual reports, you even discover these entities' VaR models base their assumptions on extremely SHORT historical time frames and do not account for counter-party risk in these models (see previous subsection, "Wall Street Wizards"). The banks claim they do "stress tests" to fill in the gaps, but these will not help them when D'Apocalypse™ arrives.

Congress should be holding all of these firms to account for their incredibly irresponsible and greedy business practices and astronomical leverage. These defy all law of reason and no regular customer could ever achieve this kind of reckless leverage. The 4 Horsemen have placed the entire country and world in jeopardy---all because of their own greed and ego.

Big Banks Put Taxpayers At Risk---Derivatives Liabilities FDIC Insured!

Each of the legal names used by the big banks in the OCC derivatives tables in this chapter is a federally chartered financial institution (as noted by "NA", National Association and "Bank USA") and is regulated by the Office of the Comptroller of the Currency and is insured by the FDIC!

JP Morgan Chase Bank NA, Citibank National Assn., Bank of America NA and Goldman Sachs Bank USA, the legal titles the OCC uses in its derivatives tables, are the entities where these sneaky firms have forced all of their derivatives trading and positioning to take place. Bank of America even transferred Merrill Lynch's derivatives exposure onto the back of the bank---forcing these liabilities onto the taxpayer in the event of a collapse!

This means when the derivatives market blows up, the Federal Deposit Insurance Corporation is on the hook to pay off depositors monies---put at risk because of the egregious risk taking of the big banks! It is absolutely surreal these satanically clever people have the chutzpah to pull this one off!

They gamble with OUR money, using nearly an infinite degree of leverage and when the world blows up in a massive derivatives meltdown, the U.S. taxpayer is on the hook for their losses!!

Where is the Congressional, Senatorial and Presidential outrage over these malevolent titans' actions, plans, strategies and tactics? It is nowhere to be found---all the banks wind up with, is a slap on the hands, in the form of a fine. No one goes to jail and no real reform takes place. Also, in case anyone is thinking, yes, but what about the $20 Billion, or so, JP Morgan Chase has been fined? Remember, they are the biggest gorilla on the block and had the benefit of the lion's share of the $30 Trillion Heist. $20 Billion is peanuts compared to what has been taken from America!

The "Smart Guys" Jeopardize Everybody

With this understanding, you have now "pierced the veil" and can see what the really "smart" guys on Wall Street have done to jeopardize everyone else around them---without caring one iota about the ramifications of their actions. These people only care if their paychecks bounce---or don't. Using improper leverage and excessive trading to enrich themselves is their only objective. One wrong move in any position could and ultimately WILL bring the whole house of cards crashing down around everyone.

When the counter-party failures and derivatives collapse happens, it is going to be one horrid, spectacular mess. It will ultimately result in a complete change of the monetary system, or will require such a mountain of money to be printed, your existing dollar will be relatively worthless.

This book expects an all-out revolution to occur, with tremendous ramifications for those people responsible for bringing this catastrophe to the regular citizens.

An Example of Derivatives Leverage a 3ʳᵈ Grader Can Understand

A simple example in the use of leverage will help you understand what this kind of leverage means—as well as the risks and rewards of using it. In this case, we will use the equivalent of the interest income generated on the bonds used in the following example to equal the premium received from entering this particular "derivatives" contract which you and your theoretical family decide to enter.

If we use the same "Derivatives to Total Net Income Ratio" Bank of America used in the 4th Quarter of 2012 (as discussed previously in subsection "Leverage is Astronomically Too HIGH"), it means if you had

$1 in earnings, you could go to Merrill Lynch and sell a put option. A put option, for those who don't know, is like a fire insurance policy. Its value goes UP if the house burns down. In this case, when you sell a put option at Merrill Lynch (i.e., you are acting like the insurance company and selling a policy), you give someone else **the right to sell you (and you must pay them)** $115,747 worth of bonds at a price of par, 100.00).

This **creates an obligation by you** to purchase the bonds at this price, all in exchange for a premium payment you collect up front of $3,472.41, equivalent to 3% interest on the underlying position.

This transaction was created all in exchange for only $1, allowing you to leverage your $1 in earnings with $115,747 worth of bond positions, which also create a potential liability for you---if the price of the bonds DROPS (i.e., the house burns down)!!!! Naturally, the $3,472.41 could dramatically increase your $1 in earnings---this is why you were tempted to use the leverage to begin with.

If the prices on the bonds don't change much (i.e., there was no change to the credit risk of the bond, market liquidity was still present and/or interest rates did not change), then Hip-Hip---HOORAY!!

Your family will be proud of you because you would have made a nice return on the derivatives contract for the bonds. You would have earned the entire $3,472.41, vastly increasing your $1 in earnings. Furthermore, you accomplished this by only putting up $1 in collateral to initiate the trade.

You are feeling quite smug at this point in time, strutting around like a peacock, with your chest pumped up like you were a teenager.

If, however, the price of the bonds fluctuates, and DROPS, because interest rates move UP, you could lose enormous sums of money, which will NOT BE COLLATERIZED BY THE MEAGER SUM OF $1 YOU PUT UP TO MAKE THE TRADE.

At the time of your "put" sale to the counterparty at Merrill Lynch, the counter party (now armed with insurance on bond price drops because of the put option purchased FROM you) ALSO buys bonds for $1000 per bond and owes $115,746* to Merrill Lynch. The counter party's purchase of a "put," buys THEM insurance IF the price of the bonds DROP, thus they are protected---as long as you pay the difference between $115,746, the counter party's purchase price of the bonds, and any lower fair market value of the bonds, realized during the holding period of the trade. You are the seller of the put and are "on the hook" for price drops. Within 6 months, if interest rates increase by only 1%, the price of the bonds DROPS to $828.50 per bond!!

*You can't buy a fraction of a bond, but for purposes of keeping the ratios identical to Bank of America in its use of derivatives, this example uses a fraction of a bond for exemplary purposes only.

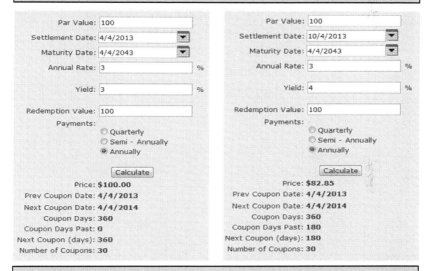

Interpretation:
A bond settling on 10/4/2013 with a par value of 100.00, a maturity date of 4/4/2043, a coupon rate of 3.00, and a market yield of 4.00 (after rates increase by 1% within 6 months of purchase) **will be priced at $82.85.** The difference between the settlement date and the maturity date is the length of time for which you may be holding the bond. The market yield is compared to the coupon's annual rate, and the larger the difference, the lower the bond's price will be. (Source: Investopedia & calculated from bond calculator at http://www.investopedia.com/calculator/bondprice.aspx).

In this example, leverage use turns against the seller of a put option (a form of derivative security) when rates go up by just 1% over a six-month period.

The preceding two bond analysis boxes indicate a price change in the bonds. This affects the put option you sold, due to the change in interest rates, and the drop in the fair market value of the bonds. Rates increased by only 1% in the six-

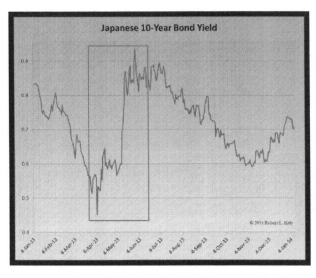

month period when you purchased the bonds, in this example (savvy readers will know Japan's interest rates on long-term bonds doubled, virtually overnight in the Spring of 2013, when its central bank announced massive "Quantitative Easing" plans to "help" the economy).

Of course, you are still "on the hook" for the bonds which were purchased at much higher prices of $115,746, because the put buyer purchased these bonds at the original purchase price at par value. ***The problem is---par value is now a lot higher than the fair market value of these securities***, which has dropped precipitously. You obligated yourself to provide price insurance to the purchaser, in exchange for receiving the premium payment of $3,472.41. Unfortunately, the bonds are now sitting in the insured's margin account at a major loss!

You had HOPED interest rates WOULD NOT increase during the time in which you were obligated to provide insurance, via the put option you sold. Unfortunately, it didn't work out the way you planned.

A short six months later, market interest rates went up ONLY 1%. This caused a loss on your "derivatives" holdings totaling $19,850.62!!! (the math is: $115,747-$95,896.99 = $19,850.62---with $95,896.99 equaling 82.85% of the "par" value of the bonds). Since you "sold" the derivatives contract in exchange for the premium of $3,472.41, this will offset against the $19,850.62 (we shall ignore, for purposes of this example, any time value remaining on the put option).

THE TOTAL LOSS IS: $16,378.21. IN A SHORT SIX-MONTH PERIOD (ASSUMING THE PUT IS EXERCISED), THIS LOSS WOULD HAVE WIPED OUT A FAMILY'S ENTIRE ASSET BASE IF IT WAS AN ABOVE AVERAGE AMERICAN FAMILY WITH EVEN $10,000 OF SAVINGS IN THE BANK!

REGARDLESS, THE LOSS IS MASSIVELY LARGER THAN YOUR INCOME FOR THE QUARTER. AS YOU KNOW WE PRETENDED YOUR INCOME WAS JUST $1, THE SAME RELATIVE AMOUNT AS BANK OF AMERICA'S NET INCOME IN THE 4TH QUARTER OF 2012, COMPARED TO THE DERIVATIVES CONTRACTS ON ITS BOOKS!

IN THIS SMALL PUT OPTION EXAMPLE, YOU CAN SEE HOW THIS KIND OF LEVERAGE SUBJECTS THE ENTIRE HOUSEHOLD TO ECONOMIC DANGER, AS THE DEBT YOU THEORETICALLY WOULD OWE WOULD BE IMPOSSIBLE TO REPAY, GIVEN YOUR INCOME!

IF YOU WANT TO USE BANK OF AMERICA'S ANNUAL INCOME TO DERIVATIVES RATIO, THIS NUMBER WAS 10,143.08:1! YOU DO THE MATH. WITH ONLY A SLIGHT BUMP UPWARDS IN RATES, TRILLIONS WILL BE LOST!

And, as they say, "Therein lies the rub…." (This saying is believed to have originated from Shakespeare's "Hamlet").

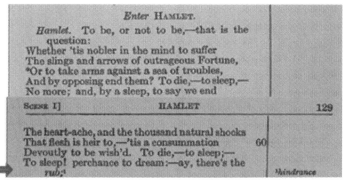

Enter HAMLET.

Hamlet. To be, or not to be,—that is the question:
Whether 'tis nobler in the mind to suffer
The slings and arrows of outrageous Fortune,
*Or to take arms against a sea of troubles,
And by opposing end them? To die,—to sleep,—
No more; and, by a sleep, to say we end

SCENE I]   HAMLET   129

The heart-ache, and the thousand natural shocks
That flesh is heir to,—'tis a consummation   60
Devoutly to be wish'd. To die,—to sleep;—
To sleep! perchance to dream:—ay, there's the
rub:¹   ¹*hindrance*

Source: "Hamlet, With Introductions and Questions For Review" by William Shakespeare, 1603, Act III, Scene I, pages 128 & 129, by F.A. Purcell, DD and L.M. Somers, M.A. Cathedral College, as adapted from Marshall and Woods Cambridge Edition, published by Scott Foresman & Company, Chicago and New York in 1916, retrieved from http://archive.org/details/hamletwithintrod00shak).

The Family Madness—Hell-Bent On "Investing" In Derivatives

Let us drill a little bit deeper here and imagine **YOU** are now an average family of four people who has obtained the permission of the President of the United States, the entire U.S. Congress and the Chairman of the SEC to enjoy certain trading advantages vis-a-vis everyone else in the neighborhood.

Let's further say Mom and Dad both work and they <u>each</u> bring home <u>$55,000 in income</u> for the year (their $110,000 in combined incomes will be leveraged in the following table under the "Revenue" column in accordance with the current leverage ratios used by the four largest derivatives players—the 4 Horsemen of the D'Apocalypse™). After all expenses are paid, they can save $2,000 in the family's checking account annually. Let's also say they have other cash savings in the bank of $10,000 and due to the housing market collapse, they have an underwater mortgage and they have no other real assets.

This means the theoretical family would be able to enter into transactions and control contracts which pays it premiums, interest or dividends and also, may create a profit or loss. Like any other kind of securities or investments, derivatives contracts CAN fluctuate in value—i.e., their prices may go up, or down, by the time of their contract's expiration date or termination.

The family also has permission from every firm on Wall Street, (e.g., Merrill Lynch, Citigroup, Wells Fargo, JP Morgan Chase, Goldman Sachs, etc.) to LEVERAGE OR MARGIN, the family's positions by MANY FACTORS---ORDERS OF MAGNITUDE above the normal allowances granted by the SEC for regular margin accounts. As most readers are aware, initial equity in margin accounts at any brokerage firm requires a minimum ratio of 2:1 in assets to debt when acquiring a leveraged equity position on an opening position for a marginable security.

The following table provides the aggregate derivative contract amounts which could be controlled by your little family. It assumes <u>identical leverage and ratios</u> being used by the 4 Horsemen of the D'Apocalypse™. Depending on which financial statement category you base your leverage on, the amount of leverage AND amount of derivatives' contracts you control, will vary.

Family Cash in Savings (i.e., called "Cash" in the following example): $10,000
Family Bank Account   (i.e., called "Assets" in the following example): $10,000
Family Annual Income (i.e., called "Revenues" in the following example): $110,000
Annual Family Savings (i.e. called "Income" in the following example): $2,000

Amount Of Derivatives Contracts Controlled By Family
With A 1% Profit On Derivatives Positions

© 2013 Robert L. Kelly

Using The Same Leverage Ratio As The "Big Four Banks," This Family Could Control

Family Leveraged Like	Derivatives To Cash	Profit/Loss	Derivatives To Assets	Profit/Loss	Derivatives To Net Revenues	Profit/Loss	Derivatives To Net Income	Profit/Loss
JP Morgan	$ 12,844,401	$ 128,444	$ 292,496	$ 2,925	$ 78,226,928	$ 782,269	$ 6,484,117	$ 64,841
Citigroup	$ 15,198,319	$ 151,983	$ 297,118	$ 2,971	$ 86,848,807	$ 868,488	$ 14,693,657	$ 146,937
Bank of America	$ 3,835,525	$ 38,355	$ 192,216	$ 1,922	$ 55,472,344	$ 554,723	$ 20,286,155	$ 202,862
Goldman Sachs	$ 3,367,444	$ 33,674	$ 438,944	$ 4,389	$ 132,649,478	$ 1,326,495	$ 11,022,692	$ 110,227

As you can see, based upon the industry ratios used to leverage "Cash," "Assets," "Revenues" and "Income," this table demonstrates how your "family" could leverage its relatively meager funds, of a few thousand dollars, into **OVER ONE HUNDRED MILLION DOLLARS** in derivatives securities' positions!

In ANY case you select, the theoretical dollar amount of contracts under your family's control is ENORMOUS, as measured relative to your cash, assets, income and savings! This amounts to family madness and insanity. IT WOULD NEVER BE PERMITTED UNDER U.S., European, Japanese or any other civilized country's LAW AND REGULATION.

However, the banks engage in this kind of leverage in derivatives securities, TODAY AND EVERYDAY, as a matter of regular business!!

The greater the leverage, the better it is for them (if it doesn't blow up!). They enjoy larger commissions, bonuses and revenues because they profit through manipulation and natural Street advantage. As a member of the Federal Reserve System, they have been allowed to build a new form of virtual oligarchy which controls the derivatives' market through sheer monopoly and oligopoly power.

As you can imagine, no household, or society, since God created mankind, would even THINK of doing, or effecting, such positioning given the use of such enormous and galactically huge leverage.

The RISKS of such an undertaking would put the ENTIRE FAMILY in danger of financial destruction---on a DAILY BASIS. With even the slightest little problem in the markets, price changes in the securities' positions could leave your theoretical family threadbare and on the streets without any food, heat, or water!

Let's take a look and see how some reasonable volatility would impact your family.

A postcard, dating from the 1910's, with the public domain "ME WORRY?" face which later inspired Mad Magazine's Alfred E. Neuman.

(Source: Wikipedia, as retrieved from http://en.wikipedia.org/wiki/File:Alfred_E._Neumann.jpg)

December 1956 Mad Magazine

Public Domain Image

WHAT???---ME WORRY?

In late 1959, *Mad Magazine* released a 45 rpm single entitled "What - Me Worry?" on ABC Paramount credited to Neuman and featured an unaccredited voice actor singing the song as Neuman.

WHAT COULD POSSIBLY GO WRONG???!!

The following tables present a quick summary of what happens if your family enters into a derivatives contract(s) which guarantees rates will NOT increase in the future. For purposes of this example, your family will have the privilege of using the same leverage as the 4 Horsemen.

From your perspective, the bet seemed like a good idea at the time you entered it. After all, the Chairman of the Federal Reserve stated rates will be "stable" until 2015 (Mr. Bernanke stated this when he began the QE programs and restated it many times thereafter) and the first Chairwoman, Ms. Janet Yellen, has echoed the same sentiment.

As a result, in exchange for the family's guarantee against a rise in rates, the family might earn a profit if it is correct in its bet (e.g. the family would keep the risk premium it was paid to guarantee rates would not increase). However, the family could also lose money if it bet incorrectly and rates do rise (or increase outside of certain boundaries), causing a loss.

The ratios used in the following tables are the exact same ratios utilized by the Big 4 Banks, using 2012 year-end information and the previously discussed OCC information on derivatives in this chapter. As discussed, the leverage the banks used in 2013 continued to be beyond outrageous. It is a leverage driven by greedy madness.

A theoretical variance in profitability (and/or loss) on the positions of 1% and 10% provides you with a good sense for the potential volatility of the position, given the leverage involved.

The following are the four different gambling scenarios.

Leveraged Derivatives Positions Showing a 1% Profit and a 1% Loss

Family Annual Income: $110,000   Annual Family Savings: $2,000   Family Bank Account: $10,000

Amount Of Derivatives Contracts Controlled By Family With A 1% Profit On Derivatives Positions

Using The Same Leverage Ratio As The "Big Four Banks," This Family Could Control

Family Leveraged Like	Derivatives To Cash	Profit/Loss	Derivatives To Assets	Profit/Loss	Derivatives To Net Revenues	Profit/Loss	Derivatives To Net Income	Profit/Loss
JP Morgan	$ 12,844,401	$ 128,444	$ 292,496	$ 2,925	$ 78,226,928	$ 782,269	$ 6,484,117	$ 64,841
Citigroup	$ 15,198,319	$ 151,983	$ 297,118	$ 2,971	$ 86,848,807	$ 868,488	$ 14,693,657	$ 146,937
Bank of America	$ 3,835,525	$ 38,355	$ 192,216	$ 1,922	$ 55,472,344	$ 554,723	$ 20,286,155	$ 202,862
Goldman Sachs	$ 3,367,444	$ 33,674	$ 438,944	$ 4,389	$ 132,649,478	$ 1,326,495	$ 11,022,692	$ 110,227

© 2013 Robert L. Kelly

Amount Of Derivatives Contracts Controlled By Family With A 1% Loss On Derivatives Positions

Using The Same Leverage Ratio As The "Big Four Banks," This Family Could Control

Family Leveraged Like	Derivatives To Cash	Profit/Loss	Derivatives To Assets	Profit/Loss	Derivatives To Net Revenues	Profit/Loss	Derivatives To Net Income	Profit/Loss
JP Morgan	$ 12,844,401	(128,444)	$ 292,496	(2,925)	$ 78,226,928	(782,269)	$ 6,484,117	(64,841)
Citigroup	$ 15,198,319	(151,983)	$ 297,118	(2,971)	$ 86,848,807	(868,488)	$ 14,693,657	(146,937)
Bank of America	$ 3,835,525	(38,355)	$ 192,216	(1,922)	$ 55,472,344	(554,723)	$ 20,286,155	(202,862)
Goldman Sachs	$ 3,367,444	(33,674)	$ 438,944	(4,389)	$ 132,649,478	(1,326,495)	$ 11,022,692	(110,227)

© 2013 Robert L. Kelly

Leveraged Derivatives Positions Showing a 10% Profit and a 10% Loss
Family Annual Income: $110,000   Annual Family Savings: $2,000   Family Bank Account: $10,000

Amount Of Derivatives Contracts Controlled By Family
With A 10% Profit On Derivatives Positions

© 2013 Robert L. Kelly

| Family Leveraged Like | Using The Same Leverage Ratio As The "Big Four Banks," This Family Could Control | | | | | | | |
	Derivatives To Cash	Profit/Loss	Derivatives To Assets	Profit/Loss	Derivatives To Net Revenues	Profit/Loss	Derivatives To Net Income	Profit/Loss
JP Morgan	$ 12,844,401	$ 1,284,440	$ 292,496	$ 29,250	$ 78,226,928	$ 7,822,693	$ 6,484,117	$ 648,412
Citigroup	$ 15,198,319	$ 1,519,832	$ 297,118	$ 29,712	$ 86,848,807	$ 8,684,881	$ 14,693,657	$ 1,469,366
Bank of America	$ 3,835,525	$ 383,553	$ 192,216	$ 19,222	$ 55,472,344	$ 5,547,234	$ 20,286,155	$ 2,028,615
Goldman Sachs	$ 3,367,444	$ 336,744	$ 438,944	$ 43,894	$ 132,649,478	$ 13,264,948	$ 11,022,692	$ 1,102,269

Amount Of Derivatives Contracts Controlled By Family
With A 10% Loss On Derivatives Positions

© 2013 Robert L. Kelly

| Family Leveraged Like | Using The Same Leverage Ratio As The "Big Four Banks," This Family Could Control | | | | | | | |
	Derivatives To Cash	Profit/Loss	Derivatives To Assets	Profit/Loss	Derivatives To Net Revenues	Profit/Loss	Derivatives To Net Income	Profit/Loss
JP Morgan	$ 12,844,401	$ (1,284,440)	$ 292,496	$ (29,250)	$ 78,226,928	$ (7,822,693)	$ 6,484,117	$ (648,412)
Citigroup	$ 15,198,319	$ (1,519,832)	$ 297,118	$ (29,712)	$ 86,848,807	$ (8,684,881)	$ 14,693,657	$ (1,469,366)
Bank of America	$ 3,835,525	$ (383,553)	$ 192,216	$ (19,222)	$ 55,472,344	$ (5,547,234)	$ 20,286,155	$ (2,028,615)
Goldman Sachs	$ 3,367,444	$ (336,744)	$ 438,944	$ (43,894)	$ 132,649,478	$ (13,264,948)	$ 11,022,692	$ (1,102,269)

Each line in this table shows how the exact same leverage ratio used by JP Morgan Chase, Citigroup, Bank of America and Goldman Sachs is applied to the family's respective cash, assets, revenues and income, as well as the amount of derivatives contracts your theoretical family could control (and the resulting profit, or loss, depending on market action).

Things are just great AND EXTREMELY PROFITABLE, as long as the market goes your family's way. You could make MILLIONS, depending on how your family deployed its leverage. You'd surely be clicking your heels and doing high fives if this were the case!

You can also see why stories of wild and crazy parties abound on Wall Street, particularly when a trader is correct about his, or her, bet's direction. A correct bet earns them earthly success too astounding for most of these people to NOT party like wild animals, erstwhle placing their spiritual lives in jeopardy.

Unfortunately, what becomes immediately apparent from the tables is with even a small 1% loss, your family's entire savings **FOR THE YEAR** are **WIPED OUT**! Depending on which leverage ratio you use and how aggressively your family bets, the entire family could become BANKRUPT, as its cash and assets could literally disappear overnight.

The strain of catastrophic losses caused by simple, normal market movements of supply and demand in the interest rate arena has wiped your family out and made it very poor. The family would have to liquidate anything and everything it owned to pay for its losses!

How could a legal and regulatory system permit this little family earning only $110,000 in an entire year, to lose up to over $13 MILLION, with even a modest 10% change in the portfolio value of the derivatives positions???!!!

Believe it, or not, this is EXACTLY the game the banks are playing...BUT THEY DO IT WITH YOUR MONEY!!

It is hard to believe we are not living in dreamland---with the dream about to become our worst nightmare. With this simple example, you have a better understanding than most other Americans and Europeans, of the ENORMOUS risks being taken by the large, commercial banks!

It is absolutely OUTRAGEOUS Congress, the EU and Japan aren't up in arms about this (as well as everything else written about in this book and The $30 Trillion Heist!).

Many Different Types of Derivatives

While this example uses interest rates, there are many, many types of derivatives for many kinds of securities and/or transactions. Some of them include foreign currency, like the Japanese Yen, some are commodity based, like Gold or Silver, some are related to Equities, Futures and Options, in addition to many, many others, including debt of just about any kind!

You have learned about the dangers inherent with leverage, which is the core problem associated with the derivatives markets. The other problem is obfuscation! Basically, the market is non-transparent and the control over the market is under the iron-grip grasp of only a handful of banks.

Sprawling, Unregulated, Uncontrolled Markets

The government's own watchdog, the GAO (Government Accounting Office), created a terrific table which attempts to summarize the risks in the securities marketplace. About the best they could do was merely *describe* some of the potential problems because the GAO has NO AUTHORITY to make changes.

You will find their descriptions are 100% in line with the warnings of risk and the reality of risk presence, as written and contained in this book.

Post-credit crisis, not much has changed, except for the infusion of nearly $30 Trillion in additionally heisted cash. This has made the system even more unstable and problematic. The coming crash will be spectacular in the pain and anguish it causes all of mankind.

Most derivatives transactions are effected "off-exchange" and "off-balance sheet," directly between the hedge funds, banks and others players in the arena. These transactions are executed over the phone and by computer, leaving the "real" market value to be determined by the management of the bank OR THE TRADER who initiated the transaction. Traders, banking executives and successful sales people on Wall Street hold significant influence over the compliance and financial oversight personnel in any of the banks on Wall Street.

GAO Chart Describing Risk in the Marketplace:

Developments in financial markets and products	Examples of how developments have challenged the regulatory system
Emergence of large, complex, globally active, interconnected financial conglomerates	Regulators sometimes lack sufficient authority, tools, or capabilities to oversee and mitigate risks.
	Identifying, preventing, mitigating, and resolving systemic crises has become more difficult.
Less-regulated entities have come to play increasingly critical roles in financial system	Nonbank lenders and a new private-label securitization market played significant roles in subprime mortgage crisis that led to broader market turmoil.
	Activities of hedge funds have posed systemic risks.
	Overreliance on credit ratings of mortgage-backed products contributed to the recent turmoil in financial markets.
	Financial institutions' use of off-balance sheet entities led to ineffective risk disclosure and exacerbated recent market instability.
New and complex products that pose challenges to financial stability and investor and consumer understanding of risks.	Complex structured finance products have made it difficult for institutions and their regulators to manage associated risks.
	Growth in complex and less-regulated over-the-counter derivatives markets have created systemic risks and revealed market infrastructure weaknesses.
	Investors have faced difficulty understanding complex investment products, either because they failed to seek out necessary information or were misled by improper sales practices.
	Consumers have faced difficulty understanding mortgages and credit cards with new and increasingly complicated features, due in part to limitations in consumer disclosures and financial literacy efforts.
	Accounting and auditing entities have faced challenges in trying to ensure that accounting and financial reporting requirements appropriately meet the needs of investors and other financial market participants.
Financial markets have become increasingly global in nature, and regulators have had to coordinate their efforts internationally.	Standard setters and regulators also face new challenges in dealing with global convergence of accounting and auditing standards.
	Fragmented U.S. regulatory structure has complicated some efforts to coordinate internationally with other regulators, such as negotiations on Basel II and certain insurance matters.

Sources: GAO (analysis); Art Explosion (images).

The Financial Accounting Standards Board published Statement 166, which eliminates the exemption from consolidation for certain SPEs (Special Purpose Entities). A second new standard, Statement 167, requires ongoing reassessments of whether consolidation is appropriate for assets held by certain off-balance sheet entities. These new standards will impact financial institution balance sheets beginning in 2010. (Source: GAO Report to Congressional Committees, July 27,20 09, "FINANCIAL MARKETS REGULATION, Financial Crisis Highlights Need to Improve Oversight of Leverage at Financial Institutions and across System" page 60, 61 & 62, as retrieved from http://www.gao.gov/new.items/d09739.pdf).

What has been approved by the Financial Accounting Standards Board is the banks can *assess THEMSELVES* to determine if certain off-balance sheet SPEs *need to be included* in their description of risk on the balance sheet.

Once again, the fox is put in charge of the hen house! This is why derivatives risk and positions are able to be smoke-screened out of financial reports! Their true liability is never reported upon.

It is simply impossible for any unregulated group engaging in highly complex transactions which DWARF the WORLD'S GDP to not fall apart. *The greed factor is far too great.* The system is too heavily slanted to reward profits and commissions earned from trading and selling securities. Every single employee in every single bank is employed in an environment focused on making money---and a lot of it. A reasonable trading and investing strategy, which does not use leverage, is at odds with the culture of greed and avarice which exists today, on Wall Street.

Quoting directly from the Bank of America (all of them use similar valuation techniques) this is what their auditors in the Notes to the Financial Statements had to say about derivatives:

"For non-exchange traded contracts, fair value is based on dealer quotes, pricing models, discounted cash flow methodologies or similar techniques for which the determination of fair value may **require significant management judgment or estimation.**"
(Source: Price Waterhouse Coopers, February 28, 2013, Bank of America 2012 Annual Report, page 159 (retrieved from http://investor.bankofamerica.com /phoenix.zhtml?c=71595&p=irol-reportsannual#fbid=ig2SqE5wRnM, author's emphasis, underlined and bold).

Just as the debacle in the mortgage-backed securities market unfolded after fraud was allowed to go unchecked for too many years (i.e., "Because this is how everybody does it…"), the entire derivatives' market for interest rates, foreign exchange, debt, credit, options, commodities, swaps, etc. will collapse in a planned orchestration. The banks will purposefully tighten the money supply, increase interest rates and then lower the boom on the value of thinly traded derivatives transactions and contracts.

The lust and urgency for the players involved to show profits will lead them down a road of heinous activity designed to steal trillions of additional dollars from the general public and unsuspecting companies.

Wall Street Compensation Is Skewed To Reward Large Risk

If this weren't enough, Wall Street and the banks have created performance-based incentives for their employees to maximize their profits—with little or no regard, for worrying about leverage and out-of-control trading. There is very little oversight, despite banking executives' self-righteous protestations otherwise and self-important testimonies provided to Congress by Wall Street's big-banking leaders.

Stolen 'Sachs' of $8B
Judge miffed over plea paralysis
By Mark Decambre, New York Post
April 3, 2013
"It's another black eye for Wall Street. A former Goldman Sachs trader, <u>hungry to boost his standing inside the firm and his bonus</u>, admitted yesterday he <u>secretly amassed an eye-popping $8.3 billion futures portfolio</u> — and then lied about it when supervisors came upon his scheme. Matthew Taylor, 34, eventually cost Goldman $118 million in losses as it unwound the sophisticated 2007 trade. "I accumulated this trading position and concealed it for the purpose of augmenting my reputation at Goldman and increasing my performance-based compensation," said Taylor, reading from prepared remarks as he pleaded guilty before Manhattan federal court Judge William Pauley."
(Source: New York Post, retrieved from http://www.nypost.com/p/news/business/stolen_sachs_of_ibJ5SIQCbyfhGu4szz9BZO).

You can see, above, where 34-year's young Mr. Taylor built an $8.3 BILLION position in futures (a form of a derivative bet), creating over $100 Million in losses. Many of you have also read about MANY other individuals on Wall Street who create BILLIONS of dollars in losses, virtually overnight for these firms. How is this possible?

Does it strike you as strange these people are only sussed out AFTER they LOSE money? There isn't even a whimper out of the Wall Street firms, OR the banks, when these people make millions and billions of dollars for the firm—WHEN THEY BET CORRECTLY.

Of course it IS strange, because the whole entire system is corrupt. Every one of these people, including the CEOs, the Board of Directors (who have stock options, salaries, etc.), management and every single employee receives extremely lucrative salaries during the year. THEY ALSO ALL receive stratospheric pay days at year end---tied nearly EXCLUSIVELY to YEAR-END "PERFORMANCE" BONUSES.

Those bonuses heavily rely on the derivatives market, which generates enormous commissions and profits for the banks and their employees because of the enormity of its size AND THE LEVERAGE traders are allowed to use. By now, you can probably understand the enormity of the problem---it is a problem driven by the greed of the banks and the greed of the employees. They do not truly care if the market blows up because they used too much leverage. As long as they "get theirs," these people do not care what happens to the Western financial world if the derivatives market blows up!

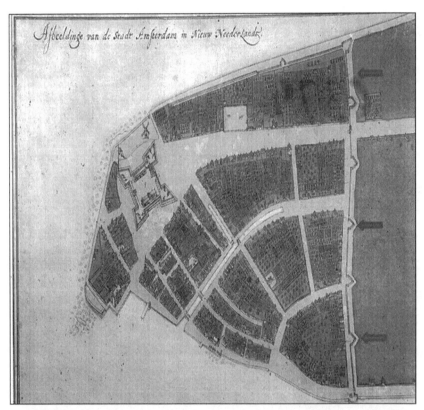

1660 Sketch of New York City---the "Wall" of Wall Street is shown on the far right, running vertically in the image. (Source: New York Public Library, Digital Gallery. Digital ID: 54682, Digital Record ID: 118555, as retrieved from http://digitalgallery.nypl.org/nypldigital/dgkeysearchdetail.cfm?strucID=118555&imageID=54682).

Plausible Deniability for Management When a "Rogue" Trader Blows Up

Because of the entire Street's core focus on making LOTS of money, you can see why there is no real management control over the Cowboys and Indians in the trading pits at the banks and Wall Street firms. The pomposity legendary among the "big" traders and "big" salesmen walking the floor of a Wall Street firm is *encouraged* by its acceptance among management and other personnel. It sends a signal to others who are successful in making big money for the firm:

"Yes, you too, can act like a horse's a__!"

The culture inbred on the Street is one of feigned, blissful ignorance by management, as long as the troops are making money. How they make money has become of secondary importance and has led to the growth of monstrous banks, filled with reckless and remorseless trading, sales and investment strategies. Together, they will accomplish one thing with certainty in the future: complete destruction of the financial system.

Derivatives trader: 'The trouble is, regulators are idiots'
The Guardian

"'It's a valid question: do we, as a society, want 25-year-old traders making £1m a year? If not, you need regulation, on a global scale. The trouble is, regulators are idiots. I am sorry to put it so bluntly but you can't expect it any other way. If an investment bank hires a graduate, two years later they will be making over £100,000. Meanwhile at the regulators you are getting £30,000. Why would a smart, aggressive, competitive 22-year-old decide to work for the Financial Services Authority?

You now have a generation who were told as graduates by their bank: we'll make you rich. *They weren't taught to think in terms of risk. Basically at banks it's quite simple: if you are generating £100m a year in profits, you can be the biggest arsehole and get away with it.*...I am also angry about the crisis. When I think of the CEO of some Wall Street bank that went bust, and he still has his $400m ... I mean, I owned shares in some of these banks, and they've gone to zero.

Bank CEOs are like salespeople. They are selling the dream to the outside world of how they are going to make the bank more profitable...The short-termism is endemic. In my career I have almost never seen anyone

---

trying to build something. There are just cycles of new guys coming in. They put forward a plan promising to make money in three or four years.

So the pressure is huge, and the easiest way is take more risk. It doesn't always have to be obvious, visible risks, sometimes it can be 'shadow' risks that are harder for outsiders to see.'"
(Source: The Guardian, by Joris Luyendijk, May 10, 2012, "Derivatives Trader: 'The Trouble Is Regulators are Idiots,'" retrieved from http://www.guardian.co.uk/commentisfree /joris-luyendijk-banking-blog/2012 /may/10/derivatives-trader-regulators-are-idiots. Author's emphasis italicized).

Management believes it has insulated themselves from any culpability, whatsoever, from the reckless acts of their trading and sales staffs. They would let the world believe they have done nothing wrong because they were, or are, doing business as usual---and in their particular business, it is "OK" and perfectly legal to be trading, overall, with global leverage equaling over 10 TIMES the world's GDP, with only 14 banks controlling over 80% of the transactions.

It is all justified, at least they believe, because they have "counter parties" to offset the risks. The reality is they engage in these fantastically and highly-leveraged transactions to put astronomical profits and compensation into their greedy pockets, while compromising the entire civilized world in the process.

There was a lot of hype and scrutiny surrounding these bandits and the income they brought home right after the credit crisis. Being as shrewd as they are, the bankers just took a lesson from sports stars and implemented compensation plans pushing income out to later years, even substituting stock for cash. The bankers didn't mind this at all, because they knew Assflation™ was just about to go into high gear—with a powerful rally coming their way in the equity markets.

The bankers took PUBLIC bailout TARP money as well as nearly $30 Trillion in secret bailout money from Ben Bernanke, courtesy of the U.S. taxpayer. Despite these funds coming directly from U.S. taxpayer-backed funds, these people had no conscience and insisted on being paid hundreds and hundreds of billions of dollars in salaries and bonuses.

You have to hand it to these tricky little devils—they really know how to get paid!! Even with current cash bonus numbers OUTRAGEOUSLY high, Wall Street and the banks further hide and obscure their piggish behavior by creating multi-year, cash, stock, loan (how about a lifetime loan which never has to be repaid?—note: author speculation), profit sharing, dividends, warrants and compensation schemes designed to hide the truth from investors, Congress and MAIN STREET.

Too Big To Jail

Perhaps the biggest factor which will cause the collapse in derivatives and create the Doomsday Cycle of D'Apocalypse™ is the fact the Federal Reserve, the bankers and the elite believe they are impervious to the regulatory system. Even the Attorney General of the United States testified before Congress the banks are just too big to prosecute! Attorney General, Eric Holder, stated:

"I am concerned that the size of some of these institutions becomes so large that it does become difficult to prosecute them…When we are hit with indications that if you do prosecute, if you do bring a criminal charge it will have a negative impact on the national economy, perhaps world economy, that is a function of the fact that some of these institutions have become too large. It has an inhibiting impact on our ability to bring resolutions that I think would be more appropriate. That is something that you all need to consider."

(Source: CSPAN, March 5, 2013, Eric

Holder, Attorney General of the United States, response to Senator Charles Grassley (R-Iowa) at time stop 2:19:25 retrieved from http://www.pbs.org/wgbh/pages/frontline/business-economy-financial-crisis/untouchables/holder-big-banks-clout-has-an-inhibiting-impact-on-prosecutions/).

Mr. Holder created the "Too Big To Jail" movement, whose attitude permeates Wall Street and serves to further empower the maniacs inside these institutions with an additional false sense of security and egos the size of the universe.

It brings to mind an old saying….

"Absolute power corrupts absolutely!"

John Emerich Edward Dalberg Acton (1834–1902), known simply as Lord Acton. (Source: Historical Essays and Studies, by John Emerich Edward Dalberg-Acton, edited by John Neville Figgis and Reginald Vere Laurence, London: Macmillan, 1907, as retrieved from http://oll.libertyfund.org/index.php?option=com_staticxt&staticfile=show.php%3Ftitle=2201&chapter=203934&layout=html&Itemid=27).

really don't know whether you exempt them because of their rank, or of their success and power, or of their date. . . . But if we might discuss this point until we found that we nearly agreed, and if we do agree thoroughly about the impropriety of Carlylese denunciations and Pharisaism in history, I cannot accept your canon that we are to judge Pope and King unlike other men, with a favoured presumption that they did no wrong. If there is any presumption, it is the other way, against holders of power, increasing as the power increases. Historic responsibility has to make up for the want of legal responsibility. Power tends to corrupt, and absolute power corrupts absolutely. Great men are almost always bad men, even when they exercise influence and not authority: still more when you superadd the tendency or the certainty of corruption by authority. . . . The inflexible integrity of the moral code is to me the secret of the authority, the dignity, the utility of history. If we may debase the currency for the sake of genius or success or reputation, we may debase it for the sake of a man's influence, of his religion, of his party, of the good cause which prospers by his credit and suffers by his disgrace. Then History ceases to be a science, an arbiter of controversy, a guide of the wanderer; . . . it serves where it ought to reign, and it serves the worst cause better than the purest. . . . Of course I know that you do sometimes censure great men severely; but the doctrine I am contesting appears in your preface. . . . I am sure you will take this long and contentious letter more as a testimony of hearty confidence and respect than of hostility, although as far as I grasp your method I do not agree with it. Mine seems to me plainer and safer, but it has never been enough to make me try to write a history, from mere want of knowledge. . . .

'I remain yours most sincerely,

'ACTON.'

To Lord Acton   'The College, Worcester: [April 9, 1887].

'My dear Lord Acton,—Your letter is an act of true friendliness, and I am very grateful to you for it—more grateful than I can say. It is a rare encouragement to me to have such a standard set up as you have put before me. Judged by it, I have nothing to say except to submit; *efficaci de manus scientia*. Before such an ideal I can only confess that I am shallow and frivolous, limited alike in my views and in my knowledge. You conceive of History as an architectonic for the writing of which a man needs the severest and largest of training; and it is impossible not to

"You ignore, you even deny, at least implicitly, the existence of the torture chamber and the stake. . . . The same thing is the case with Sixtus IV. and the Spanish Inquisition....In what sense is the Pope not responsible for the Constitution by which he established the new Tribunal? ....If there is any presumption, it is the other way, against holders of power, increasing as the power increases. Historic responsibility has to make up for the want of legal responsibility. <u>Power tends to corrupt, and absolute power corrupts absolutely. Great men are almost always bad men, even when they exercise influence and not authority:</u> still more when you superadd the tendency or the certainty of corruption by authority...." (Source: ibid, excerpt of letter to Bishop Mandell Creighton, April 5, 1887 from "The Right Honorable, The Lord Acton" Member of British Parlament 1865 – 1866, where Lord Acton discusses what happens to men in powerful positions—he was criticizing past Popes and the actions of the Church during the Spanish Inquisition and the wide use of torture chambers, as retrieved from http://oll.libertyfund.org/?option=com_staticxt&staticfile=show.php?title=2201&chapter=203934&layout=html&Itemid=27).

It will truly be interesting to see what happens to the bankers and elite when America, Japan and Western Europe break down and dive head first into the derivative's crisis---a crisis which will not be fixed by printing money.

The results will very likely witness people physically attacking the banks and anyone involved with the nefarious activities which brought the system down. Is it hard to imagine here in America? Just wait and see.

If people can't afford to eat (or there is no food available), or housing only really becomes affordable for the rich, or the unemployed get tired of living off of the bread crumbs from the food stamp program of the Obama Administration, the people will rise up.

No one in their right mind should want to be a banker, or a Wall Streeter, when this happens! Hungry and desperate people ALWAYS HAVE SOUGHT OUT those who are to blame for their plight and misery. This is just a simple lesson from history---and there is no army which can stand in the people's way---not even a Department of Homeland Security which has ordered over 2 BILLION BULLETS and a couple of thousand tanks to police the homeland.

As much as this book desires radical changes be made to the banking and Federal Reserve systems, one thing you can bet the bank on is there will be *no change* on Wall Street until there is a systemic failure.

After D'Apocalypse™, if the bankers and elite can control the politicians via the debt bargaining chips, the populations will have to suffer further. It will take the bankers and elite time to finish their cleanup of asset acquisitions (for pennies on the dollar) and it will take quite a while for the system to become reflated. Provided they negotiate as expected with governments, worldwide, they will have the grasp of the horns of global monetary policy and authority. This will allow them to quickly start the cycle all over again, becoming even wealthier at the expense of everyone else.

As much as this writer would prefer to have the bankers go out of business with D'Apocalypse™, via the outrage which shall surely bubble through all lands---this book expects the bankers to succeed. Even though their attack is viscous, deliberate and calculating, their strategy and tactics are enviable, insofar as they are designed to win and achieve their key objectives. When the derivatives' time bomb explodes, due to a deliberate tightening of credit conditions by the banks and elite, interest rates will be forced to rise. At this point, these carpet bagger bankers will again, tell all of us, they were just doing "business as usual," and did nothing wrong! They will undoubtedly blame the interest rate increases, on an "upturn" in the business cycle. The truth of the matter, however, is this willful and pre-planned tightening of credit will be a calculated and forceful bet the politicians will be incredibly frightened, when this occurs.

The politicians will be petrified because of the disastrous economic conditions, directly caused by the tightening of credit and resulting increases in interest rates. It will be then the bankers and elite strike. They will dangle the carrot of debt forgiveness, and easier credit conditions, in the faces of the politicians, in exchange for expanded monetary authority—ceded to the banking elite. In the hope the supply of money will be turned back on, and interest rates will subside, the politicians will cave.

When D'Apocalypse™ strikes, you will see a veritable Broadway show right on Wall Street, when you see the number of bankers pointing their fingers in every other direction, except at themselves, when the great firestorm approaches and the aftermath of D'Apocalypse™ ruins the land.

There is no country with the resources to bail out the pompous, egregious and outrageous greed infecting the banks of Wall Street and the people employed by it. It makes no difference if those banks are in New York, London, Tokyo, Hong Kong, Paris, Moscow, Frankfurt, or anywhere else.

Much has been said about how much money bankers and Wall Streeters take for their own pay, but what are we really talking about in salary, bonuses and compensation, really—

HOW MUCH ARE THEY GETTING PAID?

Chapter 3
Wall Street Profits & Compensation-
How Much Are They Getting Paid?

"Hot Money, Dirty Money!"

As the faces of our Founding Fathers look down in disgust, the bankers, Wall Street, Mr. Bernanke, Ms. Yellen and the Federal Reserve have taken the country for a ride. $30 Trillion secretly heisted without approval, or consent of Congress, has only served the owners of the Federal Reserve Bank of New York and its brethern Federal Reserve Banks around the country. It is simply unbelievable Congress sleeps while up to $30 Trillion was secretly taken, with a high probability much of the money was never returned!

Presidents Jackson, Wahshington, Grant, Lincoln and every other long-gone great President lies in their graves in shock at the size, boldness and sheer audacity of The $30 Trillion Heist and the spineless representatives in both houses of Congress unwilling to do anything about it. Not one administration, or government bureacrat, has tried to criminally prosecute any banker or elite benefactor of the heist, despite overwhelming evidence of fraud, abuse and gross violations of the law, damaging America forever.

The Federal Reserve Trilogy hopes to awaken a sleeping giant—the U.S. Congress---to go after every banker and elite owner hiding behind shell companies and family trusts and recover what has been plundered from all Americans. These modern-day Barbary Pirates have left us all with a legacy of debt, unemployment and spiraling cost-inflation hurting 80% of all Americans. The only people who benefited from Mr. Bernanke's actions are the elite---by using U.S. taxpayer-backed cash to cause Assflation™---ensuring the top 2% of all Americans were reimbursed for their losses during the credit crisis. One thing is certain, Mr. Bernanke will be welcomed with open arms on Wall Street---as is evidenced by his stunning pay for speeches---with one, alone, yielding him $250,000!

"Hot Money, Dirty Money," is dedicated to the modern-day pirates, in the following pages, enjoying their spoils. Artwork: By Robert L. Kelly. Original photo: credit Petr Kratochvil, as retrieved from http://www.publicdomainpictures.net/view-image.php?image=22050&picture=dollar-wallpaper).

The New York State Comptroller issued his annual report on compensation and Wall Street neared record levels, again, with the total rising to <u>more than $60 billion</u> (salary and bonus) in 2012. This was higher than any total except those in 2007 and 2008 — before the financial crisis fully took its toll on pay. 2013 appears to be a bit weaker, purportedly down 20% because of the impact wrist-slap fines are having on some of the banks' bottom lines. As of the printing of this book, 2013 information was not yet published.

The average pay package of securities industry employees in New York State was $362,950, up 16.6 percent over the last couple of years, but this is spread over approximately 175,000 workers.

Bonuses for the elite traders and their management reach the multi-million dollar levels. The highest paid (salary and bonus) CEO during 2012 in the securities industry (outside of hedge funds) was at Wells Fargo & Co. (WFC), where it awarded Chief Executive John Stumpf $22.9 million in salary and bonus for 2012, making him the highest-paid chief of a major U.S. commercial bank. Jamie Dimon, the CEO of the largest bank, JP Morgan Chase was paid $11.5 Million, down from $23.1 Million in 2011. This reduction was attributed to the major losses incurred by JP Morgan from the "London Whale," yet another rogue trader in derivatives which inflicted, seemingly overnight, billions of dollars of losses on JP Morgan Chase Bank.

4 Bailed Out Horsemen of the D'Apocalypse™--$12.7 MILLION PER EXECUTIVE!!

The summary tables, which follow later in this chapter, present the salaries and compensation for the twenty-six top commercial banks, according to SEC filings.

To reiterate, this author has nothing but praise for any executives who earn great sums of money honestly for shareholders, because ultimately, the shareholders have the power to rout them out if they are not doing a good job. Capitalism is a **good thing** because it rewards those who do great jobs! It is up to the individual to do good works with the blessing they have been given---or not. God leaves it up to everyone to make this choice---with obvious ramifications for those who remain selfish.

Setting this issue aside for a moment, the problem this book has with the bankers is they were and are secretly **subsidized** by the American taxpayer and have been since 1913. They are also likely involved in many wrong doings based upon the knowledge we have all gained because of the secret bailouts and continuing heists of money from the taxpayer-backed and U.S. Government-backed Federal Reserve.

It is simply outrageous these men and women can take home the kinds of compensation packages they have lined their pockets with—some of them have taken hundreds of millions of dollars, individually. This is also part of the big problem. The bankers, in conjunction with a sleeping, or in cahoots Congress, have apparently "legalized," in their own minds, what amounts to pure thievery.

They have issued to themselves absolutely enormous compensation plans---all subsidized by U.S. taxpayers, without Congressional, or taxpayer consent. Furthermore, they self-justify their egregious compensation plans through a thinly veiled "competitive" review of compensation at the other major banks. This stinks to high heaven because there are only 4 major banks which control the derivatives markets in the United States and they act as an oligopoly. It is no wonder why the following compensation tables are eerily similar to each other!

Some of these executives even have the audacity to tell the world they are doing "God's work!" This is an outrageous blasphemy in this writer's opinion. While the sweat of labor rolls off everyone else's brows with 32% unemployed (see Chapter 7, A Word on Unemployment), the amounts these people have taken when they collapsed the system during the credit crisis and ever since, are astounding and just plain wrong.

These are the SAME executives who were responsible for the credit crisis and mortgage bubble in the first place and when it blew up, Congress ONLY approved $700 Billion in TARP money. We find out, because of a partial audit by the GAO (General Accounting Office of the United States Government) they were ALSO the recipients of nearly $30 Trillion in heist money---SECRET BAILOUTS from taxpayer-backed Federal Reserve credits, cash, Treasury securities and other cash equivalents! The lack of outrage and action from Capitol Hill, the Justice Department and the Administration smacks of complicity.

The 4 Horsemen of the D'Apocalypse™, comprising the executive staffs of JP Morgan Chase, Citigroup, Bank of America and Goldman Sachs, with 15 individuals listed in SEC filings, paid their lead executives a total of $280,480,337—*a staggering average per person of approximately $12,749,106!* (The compensation was derived from available public sources for 2011 and 2012).

You will see the amounts per executive generally stay very consistent among the six largest commercial banks. These institutions paid compensation to individuals totaling nearly ½ **BILLION DOLLARS**---a total of $406,653,322, *an average of $12,322,827.94, per person.*

They appear to keep the salaries around the same levels to provide their oligarchy with "competitive" salary information which convolutedly they use to justify their own egregious salaries and bonuses, in and among their board rooms and supposedly independent "compensation committees."

In fact, if you look at the Top 25 Commercial Banks as ranked by derivatives, the AVERAGE compensation is $6,532,578 per executive.

REMEMBER, THESE ARE THE SAME GUYS WHO CAUSED THE CREDIT CRISIS IN THE FIRST PLACE AND WERE PUBLICLY AND THEN ADDITIONALLY, SECRETLY BAILED OUT, ALONG WITH THE ENTIRE INDUSTRY, TO THE TUNE OF TRILLIONS AND TRILLIONS OF DOLLARS, OF WHICH ONLY $700 BILLION WAS APPROVED BY CONGRESS VIA THE TARP FUND!!!

All of them should be in jail if it is found they were willing participants in a conspiracy which defrauded America and appears to have compromised entire generations of people.

This book's simple question to every Congressman, Senator and Administration official is:

"Are you going to let them get away with these egregious compensation plans when they were using secret bail-out money to prop up their failing companies? They clearly sent hundreds of billions of dollars out the back door to pay themselves, and their elite owners---outrageous amounts of money---WHAT ARE YOU GOING TO DO ABOUT IT?"

Most people would call this activity a clear-cut case of fraud, as they paid themselves outrageous salary and bonus packages (and also paid out billions of dollars in dividends to elite owners) on the back of taxpayer-backed dollars, secretly taken from the Treasury-backed Federal Reserve. These people have no shame because **they never disclosed any of it until well after the fact and kept secretly taking the money handed to them via taxpayer-backed funds, courtesy of the Fed.**

Legally, this is a most interesting point. This group of people has potentially defrauded the American public because of a lack of disclosure by the Federal Reserve and member banks, of the outrageous, secret bailouts, and greedy backdoor compensation schemes carried out by the banking elite. These schemes were created to enrich themselves, at the taxpayer's expense. The banks used the Fed-provided, U.S. taxpayer-backed heist money to secretly restore bankers' and elites' balance sheets, while also paying outrageous compensation to bank employees, with egregious dividend payments being paid to their owners. This was ONLY made possible by the SECRET heist of taxpayer-backed monies.

TOP 25 COMMERCIAL BANKS	
COMPENSATION FOR TOP 25 COMMERCIAL BANKING EXECUTIVES 2011 & 2012	
Information Derived From SEC Proxy Statements & Other Publications	
TOTAL COMPENSATION PAID TO EXECUTIVES IN TOP 25 BANKING COMPANIES*:	$849,235,188
AVERAGE PAY OF THE 135 LISTED EXECUTIVES IN TOP 25 BANKING COMPANIES:	$6,532,578
TOTAL PAYMENTS TO "BIG FOUR" EXECUTIVE MANAGEMENT:	$280,480,337
AVERAGE PAY OF 22 THE LISTED EXECUTIVES IN THE "BIG FOUR" OF DERIVATIVES TRADING:	$12,749,106

*Information not available for Union Bank and RBS Citizens. They were operating and obtaining bailouts from U.S. taxpayers, but are wholly owned subsidiaries of foreign corporations and not subject to reporting of salary information. Additionally, Deutsche Bank 2012 was unavailable.

Top Commercial Banks' Compensation to Lead Execs

A bank by bank breakdown of executive compensation follows, ranked in order of the size of the institution's derivatives positions. Please note not all executive compensation levels are published, or known.

The compensation figures have been collected from a variety of proxy statements and other public information and **may not be accurate**, however the author believes they are (or were at the time of collection). To investigate further, the reader should search **www.sec.gov**, **enter the company name** and use the **search** criteria **"Form DEF 14A."** Form DEF 14A is the proxy statement each firm files containing the compensation tables for its executives.

The exact amounts, frankly, don't matter. They are all astronomically high and any reasonable person can see what kinds of greed, avarice and conniving has taken place at the expense of the American taxpayer.

As the artwork, "Hot Money, Dirty Money!" explains, George Washington, Abraham Lincoln, Thomas Jefferson, John F. Kennedy, Theodore Roosevelt and many other great Presidents are rolling in their graves right now at the site of this outrageous abuse of the American public. The success the bankers and elite have had in manipulating our laws and legal system to nefariously attempt to justify their activities and actions defies imagination. The $30 Trillion Heist---Scene of the Crime? and The $30 Trillion Heist---Follow The Money! go into great detail exposing the results of these activities and efforts by the bankers and elite.

Twisting Laws---Elite Create a New Form of Despicable Oligarchy

When a set of laws is no longer for the people, by the people and of the people, but merely serves the interests of a small group of elite families and their caretakers, change must be made. The Declaration of Independence stated many, many violations the King and country of England had committed against the colonies. By twisting the legal system and instituting a corrupt Federal Reserve, the bankers and elite have effectively created a new form of despicable oligarchy—with them controlling the throne.

Our nation and citizens must fight to change this and recover what has been stolen from the people.

The following are the compensation summaries for the secretly bailed out banks. This should create outrage for every single person in America who is NOT on the take from the Federal Reserve System. This includes the poor, the middle class, <u>as well as the wealthy and the uber wealthy who made their money honestly</u>.

Nearly every single one of these executives should have suffered the pain of bankruptcy of their companies due to the systemic failure of the banking industry. They should have been swept away because of their poor management decisions. Furthermore, the people and companies who had their monies and assets on deposit, or account, at these institutions should have been protected by the government---but these institutions should have been allowed to fail.

New owners should have been allowed to take them over, wiping out the banks common and preferred stockholders, as well as the bond owners of these banks. This is called capitalism and falls under the principle of business and market risk!

Finally, nearly every one of the paid minions listed should be walking in shame---and not strutting like peacocks into Harry's on Wall Street, pretending to do "God's work." Thankfully, they do stick out like neon-striped zebras, "Jack Assbankers™," if you will!!

Compensation Tables Top 25 U.S. Banks
© 2013 Robert L. Kelly

JP Morgan Chase	SALARY & BONUS	NON-CASH (e.g. stock, warrants, etc.)	OTHER	SHOULD TAXPAYERS RECEIVE THIS MONEY?
James Dimon Chairman & CEO	$5,916,667	$17,000,000	$143,277	$23,059,944
James E. Staley CEO Investment Bank	$6,029,167	$11,125,400		$17,154,567
Mary Callahan Erdoes CEO Asset Management	$5,429,167	$9,925,400		$15,354,567
Ina R. Drew Chief Investment Officer	$5,429,167	$9,516,900		$14,946,067
Douglas L. Braunstein Chief Financial Officer	$3,620,833	$7,776,900		$11,397,733
Total Compensation To Top Management				$81,912,878

Citibank	SALARY & BONUS	NON-CASH (e.g. stock, warrants, etc.)	OTHER	DID THEY REALLY DESERVE IT?
Vikram Pandit Former CEO	$5,541,101	$3,998,589	$15,000	$9,554,690
Manuel Medina-Mora CEO, Global Banking, Latin America	$10,695,829	$2,852,650		$13,548,479
John Gerspach CFO	$6,896,375	$1,650,000	$15,000	$8,561,375
Michael Corbat CEO	$8,356,764	$2,250,000	$1,766,529	$12,373,293
Gene McQuade CEO, Citibank, N.A.	$7,584,159	$2,100,000	$15,000	$9,699,159
Don Callahan CTO	$8,517,414	$2,250,000	$15,000	$10,782,414
Total Compensation To Top Management				$64,519,410

Bank Of America	SALARY & BONUS	NON-CASH (e.g. stock, warrants, etc.)	OTHER	DID THEY REALLY DESERVE IT?
Brian T. Moynihan Chief Executive Officer	$950,000	$6,111,959	$420,524	$7,482,483
Thomas K. Montag Co-Chief Operating Officer	$3,700,000	$10,569,294	$29,310	$14,298,604
Charles H. Noski Vice Chairman	$2,210,000	$4,153,442	$58,752	$6,422,194
Bruce R. Thompson Chief Financial Officer	$5,200,000	$5,841,816	$37,420	$11,079,236
Gary G. Lynch Chief Legal, Compliance	$3,015,930	$4,238,865	$22,410	$7,277,205
David C. Darnell Co-Chief Operating Officer	$3,700,000	$4,491,114	$37,420	$8,228,534
Total Compensation To Top Management				$54,788,256

Goldman Sachs	SALARY & BONUS	NON-CASH (e.g. stock, warrants, etc.)	OTHER	DID THEY REALLY DESERVE IT?
David A. Viniar CFO	$4,850,000	$10,710,073	$243,325	$15,803,398
Lloyd C. Blankfein Chairman & CEO	$5,000,000	$10,710,073	$449,556	$16,159,629
Gary D. Cohn President & COO	$4,850,000	$10,710,073	$242,674	$15,802,747
John S. Weinberg Vice Chairman	$4,850,000	$10,710,073	$188,348	$15,748,421
J. Michael Evans Vice Chairman	$4,850,000	$10,710,073	$185,525	$15,745,598
Total Compensation To Top Management				$79,259,793

HSBC	SALARY & BONUS	NON-CASH (e.g. stock, warrants, etc.)	OTHER	DID THEY REALLY DESERVE IT?
Patrick J. Burke Chief Executive Officer	$1,513,885	$825,000	$103,220	$2,442,105
C. Mark Gunton Senior EVP, Chief Risk Officer	$969,694	$227,500	$540,587	$1,737,781
Michael A. Reeves EVP, Chief Financial Officer	$570,008	$66,000	$15,462	$651,470
Eli Sinyak Senior EVP & COO	$841,346	$753,228	$1,336,304	$2,930,878
Eric Larson Senior EVP, Chief Compliance Officer	$782,693	$510,000	$185,000	$1,477,693
Total Compensation To Top Management				$9,239,927

Wells Fargo	SALARY & BONUS	NON-CASH (e.g. stock, warrants, etc.)	OTHER	DID THEY REALLY DESERVE IT?
David A. Hoyt Sr. Exec. VP, Wholesale Banking	$3,900,000	$8,744,736	$15,000	$12,659,736
John G. Stumpf Chmn., Pres. & CEO	$6,800,000	$12,500,004	$15,000	$19,315,004
Carrie L. Tolstedt Sr. Exec. VP, Community Banking	$3,230,000	$5,500,008	$15,000	$8,745,008
David M. Carroll Sr. EVP, Wealth Management	$2,925,000	$5,500,008	$15,000	$8,440,008
Timothy J. Sloan Sr. Exec. VP & CFO	$3,261,686	$5,621,358	$15,000	$8,898,044
Avid Modjtabai Sr Exec. VP, Consumer Lending	$2,925,000	$5,500,008	$87,838	$8,512,846
Total Compensation To Top Management				$66,570,646

Morgan Stanley	SALARY & BONUS	NON-CASH (e.g. stock, warrants, etc.)	OTHER	DID THEY REALLY DESERVE IT?
Colm Kelleher EVP & Co-President of Institutional	$5,017,973	$7,775,267	$754,852	$13,548,092
James P. Gorman President & Chief Executive Officer	$3,516,011	$9,442,773	$9,800	$12,968,584
Gregory J. Fleming EVP & VP Asset & Wealth Mgmt	$4,150,018	$5,860,752	$0	$10,010,770
Ruth Porat EVP & Chief Financial Officer	$3,950,003	$7,167,076	$14,927	$11,132,006
Paul J. Taubman EVP, Co-President of Inst. Securities	$4,150,018	$7,779,753	$13,116	$11,942,887
Total Compensation To Top Management				$59,602,339

Bank of New York Mellon	SALARY & BONUS	NON-CASH (e.g. stock, warrants, etc.)	OTHER	DID THEY REALLY DESERVE IT?
Gerald L. Hassell Chrmn, President & CEO	$4,045,938	$8,640,014	$140,611	$12,826,563
Thomas P. Gibbons Vice Chairman & Chief Financial Officer	$2,618,169	$2,554,385	$112,579	$5,285,133
Brian G. Rogan Vice Chairman & Chief Risk Officer	$2,618,169	$2,554,385	$147,604	$5,320,158
Curtis Y. Arledge Vice Chair & CEO Investment Management	$6,802,735	$5,107,767	$163,111	$12,073,613
Karen B. Peetz President	$2,093,069	$2,591,993	$18,729	$4,703,791
Total Compensation To Top Management				$40,209,258

State Street Corp	SALARY & BONUS	NON-CASH (e.g. stock, warrants, etc.)	OTHER	DID THEY REALLY DESERVE IT?
Edward J. Resch	$2,288,000	$4,323,913	$252,345	$6,864,258
Chief Financial Officer				
Joseph L. Hooley	$3,608,000	$8,076,905	$310,600	$11,995,505
Chairman, President & CEO				
Joseph C. Antonellis	$2,260,000	$4,679,751	$2,315,211	$9,254,962
Vice Chairman				
James S. Phalen	$2,308,000	$5,197,456	$460,687	$7,966,143
Executive Vice President				
Scott F. Powers	$2,358,000	$4,332,332	$224,210	$6,914,542
Executive Vice President				
Total Compensation To Top Management				$42,995,410

PNC Bank	SALARY & BONUS	NON-CASH (e.g. stock, warrants, etc.)	OTHER	DID THEY REALLY DESERVE IT?
James E. Rohr	$1,200,000	$4,922,847	$135,475	$6,258,322
Chairman & CEO				
Joseph C. Guyaux	$1,605,400	$3,610,221	$21,438	$5,237,059
Chief Risk Officer				
William S. Demchak	$2,575,840	$4,416,686	$58,894	$7,051,420
President				
Richard J. Johnson	$1,503,650	$1,597,424	$40,638	$3,141,712
Chief Financial Officer				
E. William Parsley III	$1,179,315	$4,380,190	$12,762	$5,572,267
Treasurer & Chief Investment Officer				
Michael P. Lyons	$700,000	$5,982,880	$336,352	$7,019,232
Head of Corporate & Institutional Banking				
Total Compensation To Top Management				$34,280,012

Suntrust Bank	SALARY & BONUS	NON-CASH (e.g. stock, warrants, etc.)	OTHER	DID THEY REALLY DESERVE IT?
Mark A. Chancy	$1,352,400	$3,391,661	$70,479	$4,814,540
Corporate EVP & Wholesale Banking				
William H. Rogers Jr.	$2,798,100	$5,708,325	$99,473	$8,605,898
Chairman & Chief Executive Officer				
Thomas E. Freeman	$1,123,500	$2,778,871	$55,144	$3,957,515
Corporate EVP & Chief Risk Officer				
Aleem Gillani	$1,156,500	$2,778,871	$53,640	$3,989,011
Corporate Executive VP & CFO				
Anil Cheriyan	$802,500	$2,890,698	$7,500	$3,700,698
Corporate EVP & CIO				
Total Compensation To Top Management				$25,067,662

Northern Trust Company	SALARY & BONUS	NON-CASH (e.g. stock, warrants, etc.)	OTHER	DID THEY REALLY DESERVE IT?
William L. Morrison	$1,700,000	$2,091,960	$31,364	$3,823,324
President & Chief Operating Officer				
Frederick H. Waddell	$2,975,000	$4,183,909	$85,283	$7,244,192
Chairman & Chief Executive Officer				
Steven L. Fradkin	$1,400,000	$1,255,180	$25,799	$2,680,979
President-Corporate & Institutional				
Jana R. Schreuder	$1,425,000	$1,255,180	$29,733	$2,709,913
President-Personal Financial Services				
Michael G. O'Grady	$1,318,750	$1,255,180	$4,312	$2,578,242
ExVP & Chief Financial Officer				
Total Compensation To Top Management				$19,036,650

US Bancorp	SALARY & BONUS	NON-CASH (e.g. stock, warrants, etc.)	OTHER	DID THEY REALLY DESERVE IT?
Richard K. Davis Chairman, President & CEO	$4,144,392	$6,000,000	$17,572	$10,161,964
Andrew Cecere Vice Chairman & Chief Financial Officer	$1,984,189	$3,750,000	$30,185	$5,764,374
Pamela A. Joseph Vice Chairman, Payment Services	$1,659,682	$2,000,000	$16,619	$3,676,301
Richard C. Hartnack Vice Chair, Consumer & Small Business	$1,781,206	$1,800,000	$29,720	$3,610,926
Richard B. Payne Jr. Vice Chairman, Wholesale Banking	$1,183,769	$2,200,000	$29,720	$3,413,489
Total Compensation To Top Management				$26,627,054

Regions Bank	SALARY & BONUS	NON-CASH (e.g. stock, warrants, etc.)	OTHER	DID THEY REALLY DESERVE IT?
O.B. Grayson Hall Jr. President & Chief Executive Officer	$850,000	$3,605,000	$167,864	$4,622,864
John C. Carson Jr. Executive MD & CEO of Morgan Keegan	$1,500,000	$1,025,000	$4,325	$2,529,325
David J. Turner Jr. Senior EVP & Chief Financial Officer	$575,000	$876,600	$69,336	$1,520,936
Fournier J. Gale Senior EVP, General Counsel & Secretary	$916,667	$751,303	$29,693	$1,697,663
C. Matthew Lusco Senior EVP & Chief Risk Officer	$1,666,346	$525,620	$28,325	$2,220,291
Total Compensation To Top Management				$12,591,079

Keybank	SALARY & BONUS	NON-CASH (e.g. stock, warrants, etc.)	OTHER	DID THEY REALLY DESERVE IT?
Jeffrey B. Weeden Chief Financial Officer	$1,319,932	$2,624,370	$58,888	$4,003,190
Thomas C. Stevens Vice Chair & Chief Administrative Officer	$1,334,803	$1,244,100	$72,897	$2,651,800
Charles S. Hyle Chief Risk Officer	$1,386,812	$689,900	$55,823	$2,132,535
Henry L. Meyer Chairman of the Board & CEO	$1,389,683		$82,333	$1,472,016
Beth E. Mooney Chairman & CEO	$2,224,139	$2,608,671	$117,564	$4,950,374
Christopher M. Gorman President Key Corporate Bank	$1,921,891	$1,692,836	$37,697	$3,652,424
Total Compensation To Top Management				$18,862,339

BB&T	SALARY & BONUS	NON-CASH (e.g. stock, warrants, etc.)	OTHER	DID THEY REALLY DESERVE IT?
Kelly S. King Chairman & Chief Executive Officer	$5,811,964	$2,503,855	$238,935	$8,554,754
Christopher L. Henson Chief Operating Officer	$2,601,737	$1,021,770	$121,101	$3,744,608
Daryl N. Bible Senior EVP & Chief Financial Officer	$2,099,026	$777,769	$105,966	$2,982,761
Ricky K. Brown Sr EVP & President, Community Banking	$2,598,487	$1,021,770	$123,574	$3,743,831
Clarke R. Starnes III Sr EVP & Chief Risk Officer	$2,099,026	$777,769	$110,203	$2,986,998
Total Compensation To Top Management				$22,012,952

Fifth Third Bank	SALARY & BONUS	NON-CASH (e.g. stock, warrants, etc.)	OTHER	DID THEY REALLY DESERVE IT?
Kevin T. Kabat	$3,115,002	$5,596,412	$195,327	$8,906,741
Vice Chairman & Chief Executive Officer				
Robert A. Sullivan	$1,147,503	$1,358,752	$88,335	$2,594,590
Executive Vice President				
Greg D. Carmichael	$2,025,002	$2,692,293	$300,092	$5,017,387
President & Chief Operating Officer				
Paul L. Reynolds	$1,337,494	$1,402,395	$81,036	$2,820,925
EVP & Chief Risk Officer				
Daniel T. Poston	$1,287,490	$1,553,691	$223,642	$3,064,823
EVP & Chief Financial Officer				
Total Compensation To Top Management				$22,404,466

TD Bank	SALARY & BONUS	NON-CASH (e.g. stock, warrants, etc.)	OTHER	DID THEY REALLY DESERVE IT?
Ed Clark	$3,225,000	$7,525,047	$134,192	$10,884,239
Group President & CEO				
Colleen Johnston	$1,180,000	$1,770,068	$53,424	$3,003,492
Chief Financial Officer, Group Head				
Bob Dorrance	$3,100,000	$4,650,051	$8,017	$7,758,068
Chrmn CEO TD Securities, Head Bank Grp				
Bharat Masrani	$2,391,186	$3,512,542	$1,074,733	$6,978,461
CEO TD Bank, Group Head U.S. Banking				
Tim Hockey	$1,840,000	$2,760,063	($394,946)	$4,205,117
President & CEO TD Canada Trust, Group Head Canadian Banking				
Mike Pedersen	$1,840,000	$2,760,063	$196,095	$4,796,158
Group Head, Wealth Management				
Total Compensation To Top Management				$37,625,535

TD Ameritrade	SALARY & BONUS	NON-CASH (e.g. stock, warrants, etc.)	OTHER	DID THEY REALLY DESERVE IT?
William J. Gerber	$932,400	$601,555	$53,125	$1,587,080
EVP, Chief Financial Officer				
Fredric J. Tomczyk	$2,326,240	$4,164,626	$32,473	$6,523,339
President, Chief Executive Officer				
J. Thomas Bradley Jr.	$1,235,831	$1,041,469	$88,430	$2,365,730
Executive Vice President, Retail Distribution				
Marvin W. Adams	$1,658,400	$1,646,325	$113,797	$3,418,522
Executive Vice President, Chief Operating Officer				
Thomas A. Nally	$752,692	$525,784	$25,159	$1,303,635
EVP, TD Ameritrade Institutional				
Total Compensation To Top Management				$15,198,306

Union Bank	SALARY & BONUS	NON-CASH (e.g. stock, warrants, etc.)	OTHER	DID THEY REALLY DESERVE IT?

UnionBanCal Corporation, a wholly-owned subsidiary of The Bank of Tokyo-Mitsubishi UFJ, Ltd. (BTMU), is a financial holding company and bank holding company whose major subsidiary, Union Bank, N.A., is a commercial bank. BTMU is a wholly-owned subsidiary of Mitsubishi UFJ Financial Group, Inc.

IN UNION BANK'S FORM 10K ON FILE WITH THE SEC FOR 2012, **THEY REFUSED TO INCLUDE THEIR EXECUTIVE COMPENSATION NUMBERS, CLAIMING IT, AS A SUBSIDIARY, IS EXEMPT FROM SUCH REPORTING.**

THEIR ABILITY TO TAKE SUCH AN EXEMPTION FROM REPORTING, DEFIES THE IMAGINATION-- PARTICULARLY SINCE THEY TOOK BILLIONS FROM U.S. TAXPAYERS IN BAILOUT MONEY!

THIS IS THE PROVISION THEY CLAIM THEY ARE ENTITLED TO, IN ORDER TO PREVENT DISCLOSURE OF

ITEM 11. EXECUTIVE COMPENSATION

The information called for by this item has been omitted pursuant to General Instruction I(2) of Form 10-K.

---IF ANY READER KNOWS THEIR COMPENSATION LEVELS, PLEASE SEND ANY INFORMATION TO THE CONTACT AT THE FRONT OF THIS BOOK AND WE SHALL POST IT IN ANY UPDATES!!

HERE IS A LIST OF THEIR OFFICERS OPERATING IN AMERICA:

Officer				Deserve?
Masashi Oka				??????????
President & Chief Executive Officer				
John C. Erickson				??????????
Vice Chairman & Chief Risk Officer				
Mark W. Midkiff				??????????
Vice Chairman, Chief Retail Banking Officer				
Timothy H. Wennes				??????????
Vice Chairman & Chief Financial Officer				
John F. Woods				??????????
SEVP, Commercial Banking				
Robert C. Dawson				??????????
SEVP, Head of Community Banking				
Pierre P. Habis				??????????
SEVP, General Counsel				
Morris W. Hirsch				??????????
SEVP, Chief Information & Operations Officer				
Kazuo (Kaz) Koshi				??????????
SEVP, Deputy Chief Financial Officer/Chief Liaison Officer				
Erin Selleck				??????????
SEVP, Treasurer				
J. Michael Stedman				??????????
SEVP, Real Estate Industries				
Annemieke van der Werff				??????????
SEVP, Chief Human Resources Officer				
John M. Wied				??????????
SEVP, Independent Risk Monitoring Group				
Total Compensation To Top Management				?????????

RBS First Citizens	SALARY & BONUS	NON-CASH (e.g. stock, warrants, etc.)	OTHER	DID THEY REALLY DESERVE IT?
RBS First Citizens is a wholly owned subsidiary of the Royal Bank of Scotland and compensation not disclosed for U.S. Executives. The Royal Bank of Scotland received BILLIONS and BILLIONS of support from the U.S. Federal Reserve U.S. Government-- your taxpayer dollars saved RBS!! It is now owned by the U.K. Government, as it is yet another bank that would have failed.				
Royal Bank of Scotland (UK Bank Execs)				
Stephen Hester	$1,812,000		$634,200	$2,446,200
Group Chief Executive				
Bruce Van Saun	$1,132,500		$616,080	$1,748,580
Executive Director				
RBS First Citizens (US Bank Execs)				
Mr. Lawrence K. Fish				
Executive Chairman				
Mr. Brian S. Block				
Executive VP & Chief Financial Officer				
Mr. Robert M. Curley				
CEO Bank New York				
Ms. Richelle Vible				
CEO of Citizens of Bank Delaware				
Mr. Robert E. Smyth				
CEO of Citizens Bank of Massachusetts				
93 TOP EARNERS IN RISK-TAKING JOBS				$140,430,000
293 EMPLOYEES EARNING OVER $1 MILLION IN RISK-TAKING JOBS				$310,161,010
Total Compensation To Top Management				$4,194,780

The Telegraph   Rachel Cooper | Telegraph – Fri, Mar 8, 2013

"The Royal Bank of Scotland is to pay out $916.75 million in bonuses, according to the bank's Annual Results 2012. Royal Bank of Scotland (LSE: RBS.L - news) revealed on Thursday that 93 of its staff earned more than $1,510,000 in 2012, a year which the bank has previously described as "chastening." In its annual remuneration report, the state-backed lender said that total pay for its highest ranking staff - its eight most senior executives - was $31,700,000, down 16pc from 2011. The bank's 386 "code staff""

Capital One Financial	SALARY & BONUS	NON-CASH (e.g. stock, warrants, etc.)	OTHER	DID THEY REALLY DESERVE IT?
Richard D. Fairbank	$2,187,500	$20,325,060	$89,264	$22,601,824
Chairman, CEO & President, Director				
John G. Finneran Jr.	$907,760	$4,507,783	$198,199	$5,613,742
General Counsel & Corporate Secretary				
Gary L. Perlin	$1,267,452	$6,215,289	$240,571	$7,723,312
Chief Financial Officer				
Peter A. Schnall	$929,211	$4,318,226	$204,759	$5,452,196
Chief Risk Officer				
Ryan M. Schneider	$1,032,394	$4,826,774	$204,151	$6,063,319
President, Card				
Total Compensation To Top Management				$47,454,393

BOKF (Bank of Oklahoma)	SALARY & BONUS	NON-CASH (e.g. stock, warrants, etc.)	OTHER	DID THEY REALLY DESERVE IT?
Stanley A. Lybarger	$1,827,483	$1,469,939	$41,613	$3,339,035
President & Chief Executive Officer				
Steven G. Bradshaw	$848,839	$569,308	$41,862	$1,460,009
Senior Executive Vice President, BOKF				
Daniel H. Ellinor	$882,265	$575,731	$25,920	$1,483,916
Senior Executive Vice President, BOKF				
Steven E. Nell	$734,870	$280,048	$30,000	$1,044,918
Executive Vice President, CFO				
Norman P. Bagwell	$670,610	$386,159	$25,473	$1,082,242
Chief Executive Officer, Bank of Texas				
Total Compensation To Top Management				$8,410,120

Flagstar Bank	SALARY & BONUS	NON-CASH (e.g. stock, warrants, etc.)	OTHER	DID THEY REALLY DESERVE IT?
Paul D. Borja EVP& Chief Financial Officer	$749,999	$0	$0	$749,999
Matthew I. Roslin EVP & Former Chief Legal Officer	$774,999	$0	$0	$774,999
Joseph P. Campanelli Chairman,, President & CEO	$2,650,001	$0	$7,311	$2,657,312
Matthew A. Kerin Executive Vice-President & Managing Director	$774,999	$0	$23,083	$798,082
Salvatore J. Rinaldi Executive Vice-President & Chief of Staff	$849,999	$0	$34,784	$884,783
Steven J. Issa EVP & Managing Director	$685,578	$0	$9,750	$695,328
Total Compensation To Top Management				$6,560,503

Huntington National Bank	SALARY & BONUS	NON-CASH (e.g. stock, warrants, etc.)	OTHER	DID THEY REALLY DESERVE IT?
Mary W. Navarro Senior Executive Vice President	$1,210,000	$800,007	$32,906	$2,042,913
Donald R. Kimble CFO& Senior Executive Vice President	$1,550,000	$920,003	$35,112	$2,505,115
Stephen D. Steinour Chairman, President & CEO	$2,966,800	$3,500,041	$197,509	$6,664,350
James E. Dunlap Senior Executive Vice President	$1,125,000	$700,002	$43,280	$1,868,282
Helga S. Houston Chief Risk Officer & Senior EVP	$1,117,900	$499,998	$471,116	$2,089,014
Total Compensation To Top Management				$15,169,674

Deutsche Bank	SALARY & BONUS	NON-CASH (e.g. stock, warrants, etc.)	OTHER	DID THEY REALLY DESERVE IT?
(2011 Data-Some Executives May Have Departed)				
Anshuman Jain Co-Chairman-Mgmt Board				7,612,762
Jurgen Fitschen Co-Chairman-Mgmt Board				3,736,662
Stefan Krause CFO/Member-Mgmt Board				3,768,333
Henry Ritchotte COO/Member-Mgmt Board				N/A*
Stuart Lewis Chief Risk Ofcr/Member-Mgmt Board				N/A*
Stephan Leithner CEO:Europe/Member-Mgmt Board				N/A*
Angharad Fitzwilliams Head:Capital Introduction Asia-Pacific				N/A*
Marlin Naidoo Co-Head:Capital Introduction Americas				N/A*
Hermann-josef Lamberti Chief Operating Officer				3,768,333
Hugo Banziger Chief Risk Officer				3,768,333
Rainer Neske Member of Management Board				3,736,662
Josef Ackermann Chairman of the Management Board (stepped down in May 2012)				8,250,660
Total Compensation To Top Management				$34,641,746

*Information not available for Union Bank and RBS Citizens, as they are operating and obtaining bailouts from U.S. taxpayers, but are wholly owned subsidiaries of foreign corporations. Additionally, Deutsche Bank 2012 were unavailable.

General Compensation Data Wall Street

The Securities Industry in New York City

Thomas P. DiNapoli
New York State Comptroller

Kenneth B. Bleiwas
Deputy Comptroller

Report 7-2014   October 2013

Wall Street Cash Bonus Pool

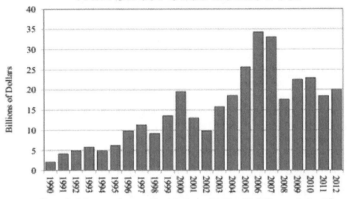

Note: Cash bonuses for securities jobs located in New York City; excludes deferred
components that have not yet been paid.
Sources: NYS Deparment of Labor; OSC analysis

"It's good work if you can get it," said Thomas P.
DiNapoli, the New York State Comptroller.

Securities Industry Wages in New York City

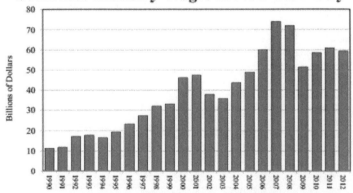

Note: 1990-1999 data are on the Standard Industrial Classification (SIC) basis;
2000-2012 data are on the North American Industrial Classification System (NAICS) basis.
Sources: NYS Department of Labor; OSC analysis

(Source: Thomas P. DiNapoli New York State Comptroller, Kenneth B.
Bleiwas Deputy Comptroller, "The Securities Industry in New York City,
October 2013, as retrieved from http://osc.state.ny.us/osdc/rpt7-2014.pdf).

110

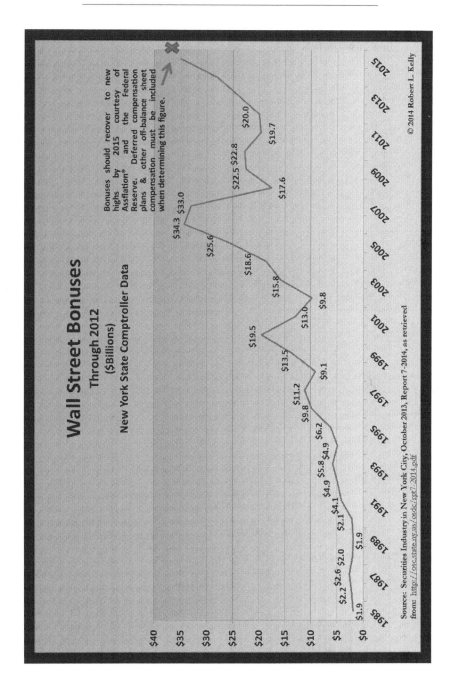

Wall Street Bonuses
Through 2012
($Billions)
New York State Comptroller Data

Bonuses should recover to new highs by 2015 courtesy of Assflation* and the Federal Reserve. Deferred compensation plans & other off-balance sheet compensation must be included when determining this figure.

Source: Securities Industry in New York City, October 2013, Report 7-2014, as retrieved from: http://osc.state.ny.us/osdc/rpt7-2014.pdf

© 2014 Robert L. Kelly

Business Insider, St. Louis Fed

The blue line (or top line if reading in black and white) represents the total number of employees in private industry in the U.S. (i.e., does not include government employees). The red line (i.e. middle line) represents the number of employees in the "financial services" industry, which includes Wall Street. The green line (i.e. bottom line) represents the number of employees in the securities industry (i.e., Wall Street).

Most of the cash from bonuses and salaries is spread around a few thousand people, distorting the "average" figures published in the press.

Median Work Pay In U.S. Only $40,092
A quick glance at the sampling of executive team salaries and bonuses at the big commercial banks shows they are paid greatly in excess of industry averages and paid enormously more than other Americans.

The top executives took, on average, $12,749,106/person vis-à-vis $362,950/person for the mere mortals who work on Wall Street!

Minimum wage in 2014 for New York is $8.00/hour, or $16,640 per year.

The median income in the U.S. was $40,092 (i.e., 771 x 52 = 40,092) according to the Bureau of Labor Statistics in July 2013.

 **BLS**
BUREAU OF LABOR STATISTICS
U.S. DEPARTMENT OF LABOR

NEWS RELEASE

For release 10:00 a.m. (EDT) Friday, November 1, 2013　　　　　USDL-13-2078

Technical information: (202) 691-6378 • cpsinfo@bls.gov • www.bls.gov/cps
Media contact:　　　　　(202) 691-5902 • PressOffice@bls.gov

USUAL WEEKLY EARNINGS OF WAGE AND SALARY WORKERS
THIRD QUARTER 2013

Median weekly earnings of the nation's 105.5 million full-time wage and salary workers were $771 in the third quarter of 2013 (not seasonally adjusted), the U.S. Bureau of Labor Statistics reported today. This was 1.7 percent higher than a year earlier, compared with a gain of 1.6 percent in the Consumer Price Index for All Urban Consumers (CPI-U) over the same period.

Data on usual weekly earnings are collected as part of the Current Population Survey, a nationwide sample survey of households in which respondents are asked, among other things, how much each wage and salary worker usually earns. (See the Technical Note.) Data shown in this release are not seasonally adjusted unless otherwise specified. Highlights from the third-quarter data are:

- **Seasonally adjusted median weekly earnings** were $777 in the third quarter of 2013, little changed from the previous quarter ($775). (See table 1.)

(Source: U.S. Government Bureau of Labor Statistics, as retrieved from http://www.bls.gov/news.release/pdf/wkyeng.pdf).

Table 1. Median usual weekly earnings of full-time wage and salary workers by sex, quarterly averages, seasonally adjusted

Year and quarter	Number of workers (in thousands)			Median weekly earnings					
				In current dollars			In constant (1982-84) dollars		
	Total	Men	Women	Total $	Men $	Women $	Total $	Men $	Women $
2004									
3rd Quarter	101,148	56,931	44,217	635	712	574	335	376	303
4th Quarter	101,658	57,288	44,369	646	720	577	337	376	302
2005									
1st Quarter	102,091	57,710	44,381	647	723	580	336	376	302
2nd Quarter	103,201	58,099	45,101	647	714	584	334	369	301
3rd Quarter	104,310	58,843	45,467	651	723	588	331	368	299
4th Quarter	104,605	58,967	45,638	658	730	585	332	368	296
2006									
1st Quarter	104,708	58,960	45,748	662	737	594	332	370	298
2nd Quarter	105,798	59,831	45,966	663	732	597	329	364	296
3rd Quarter	107,041	60,060	46,981	678	755	603	334	372	297
4th Quarter	106,847	60,140	46,707	681	748	607	337	370	300
2007									
1st Quarter	107,175	60,105	47,070	687	752	610	336	368	298
2nd Quarter	106,827	60,351	46,476	683	765	610	335	370	295
3rd Quarter	107,155	60,215	46,940	698	774	621	336	372	298
4th Quarter	108,178	60,508	47,670	700	774	615	332	368	292
2008									
1st Quarter	107,786	60,378	47,408	713	783	633	335	368	298
2nd Quarter	107,046	59,586	47,460	722	802	636	335	372	295
3rd Quarter	106,136	59,273	46,863	724	802	637	331	367	291
4th Quarter	105,617	58,511	47,106	727	806	647	340	377	302
2009									
1st Quarter	101,680	56,299	45,381	732	815	645	344	384	304
2nd Quarter	99,990	55,233	44,757	736	818	652	345	383	306
3rd Quarter	99,049	54,481	44,567	742	820	664	345	381	308
4th Quarter	98,569	54,412	44,156	747	823	666	344	379	307
2010									
1st Quarter	98,149	54,102	44,048	748	836	662	344	385	304
2nd Quarter	99,598	55,038	44,559	742	813	671	342	374	309
3rd Quarter	100,419	55,618	44,792	746	822	670	342	377	307
4th Quarter	99,960	55,469	44,491	750	826	676	342	376	308
2011									
1st Quarter	99,690	55,338	44,353	750	821	679	338	370	306
2nd Quarter	100,343	55,848	44,495	754	828	688	336	369	306
3rd Quarter	100,487	56,053	44,434	759	837	681	336	370	301
4th Quarter	101,316	56,643	44,674	761	838	686	335	369	302
2012									
1st Quarter	102,194	57,113	45,081	764	842	693	335	369	304
2nd Quarter	102,491	57,102	45,389	772	867	688	337	379	301
3rd Quarter	102,637	57,236	45,401	765	838	693	333	364	301
4th Quarter	103,681	57,701	45,980	772	868	690	334	376	298
2013									
1st Quarter	103,972	57,914	46,058	769	862	699	331	371	301
2nd Quarter	103,846	57,964	45,983	775	863	705	334	372	304
3rd Quarter	104,492	58,143	46,350	777	860	706	333	368	302

NOTE: Updated population controls are introduced annually with the release of January data.

(Source: Ibid, page 5).

Hedge Fund Heroes?

It is also no secret many of those in the hedge fund world have done extremely well, including massive payouts to executives during 2012 and rumors of a continuing avalanche of pay during 2013. They include:

- David Tepper of Appaloosa Management earned approximately $2.2 billion from big bets on Citigroup, Apple and U.S. Airways.
- Raymond Dalio made approximately $1.7 billion from the management fees and incentive fees Bridgewater Associates charges.
- Steven Cohen, whose firm SAC Capital Advisors has been under scrutiny from investigators and recently settled with the SEC with a fine of $1.8 Billion, earned approximately $1.4 billion.
- James Simons earned approximately $1.1 billion, partly on the large sum of money he has personally invested in Renaissance Technologies funds, a large hedge fund in New York.
- Kenneth Griffin, the head of Citadel, earned $900 million beating the market.

The biggest difference here, of course, is these funds and their leadership did not DIRECTLY receive bail out money from the Federal Reserve System (or at least this is not known from the available evidence). If this is the case, then these people are providing a valuable service to their clients and deserve to earn what their agreements state with their fund, given the contracts they have in place with the investors supporting them.

These are PRIVATE transactions and HAVE NOTHING TO DO WITH HOW THE BANKS AND WALL STREET FIRMS received heist money directly from the Federal Reserve, provided a given hedge fund did not use the Fed window to reimburse itself for bad bets made during the credit crisis.

Government has no right to get between investors and businesses if they are not bailing them out. This distorts the free market system which ultimately, if left alone, guarantees the most efficient allocation of capital possible. As bad as greed is, we all have a sinful nature and capitalism best harnesses it for optimal production, and use of resources, for the betterment of society at large. God leaves it up to each and every individual to make a decision to help, or not help, others, in accordance with our own drives, desires and impulses.

The Poor Widow's Offering:

⁴¹And Jesus sat over against the treasury, and beheld how the people cast money into the treasury: and many that were rich cast in much. ⁴²And there came a certain poor widow, and she threw in two mites, which make a farthing. ⁴³And he called unto him his disciples, and saith unto them, Verily I say unto you, That this poor widow hath cast more in, than all they which have cast into the treasury: ⁴⁴For all they did cast in of their abundance; but she of her want did cast in all that she had, even all her living. (Source: The Bible, Luke 21:1-4 King James Version, http://biblehub.com /kjv/luke/21.htm).

The Widow's Offering

⁴¹Jesus sat down opposite the place where the offerings were put and watched the crowd putting their money into the temple treasury. Many rich people threw in large amounts. ⁴²But a poor widow came and put in two very small copper coins, worth only a few cents. ⁴³Calling his disciples to him, Jesus said, "Truly I tell you, this poor widow has put more into the treasury than all the others. ⁴⁴They all gave out of their wealth; but she, out of her poverty, put in everything—all she had to live on." (Source: The Bible, Mark 12:41-44 New International Version, http://biblehub.com/niv/mark/12.htm)

It is up to the individuals involved with the capitalist system, or any economic system for that matter, to RESPOND to God and the Holy Spirit to help others. Ultimately, this is for the good of humanity. As a Christian, we are instructed to do good works not because it will get us into heaven (good works, alone, will not make this happen), but we perform good works because we are eternally *grateful* for being saved through the blood of, and our faith in, Jesus Christ. We WANT and DESIRE to do good works *because* we are thankful for His sacrifice on our behalf; we know God doesn't want any man, or woman, to boast his or her way, into heaven.

Of course, not everyone will follow a path to do good and help others---- this we all know. Nevertheless, God provides us with a freedom of choice---a one-way ticket to heaven, which we receive as a free gift, or a rejection of His gift and damnation for all eternity.

It's pretty simple and cut and dried. He didn't leave any wiggle room on this one!

The Sky Should be the Limit if No Bailout Used

In a free society, a capitalistic system supposedly guarantees the most efficient allocation of capital possible. Therefore, ***the sky should be the limit*** for hedge fund people. They should not be treated with the same scorn and disdain as those up to their eyeballs in the secret bail out, heist and conspiracy money issued to them by the Federal Reserve!

If the hedge funds have investors investing in their hedge fund and freely agreed to their compensation plans and structure, allowing the hedge fund manager to earn even $10 Billion, ---well, then BULLY FOR THEM AND CONGRATULATIONS!!

This is an HONEST example to the world, which shows what ingenuity and brains can do to help oneself and hopefully other people in a vibrant capitalist system!! Where the system fails, lately, is the fact greed has overcome nearly everyone and most people just take the money and hoard it, or spend wildly and shamelessly on extravagance and self-indulgence.

No one should want to be in those shoes on judgment day.

HOWEVER, MANY, MANY, MANY of these men and women DONATE significant sums of money to charity and make it their task to help others. These are saintly examples for all of us. Hopefully, every wealthy person will take lessons from some of the wealthiest people on earth who have made a pact to give their wealth away ***before*** they die. If they are a good steward of the money entrusted to them, they could help millions of people in the upcoming collapse of the D'Apocalypse™.

Of course, there is a <u>very important argument</u> the hedge funds and their managers should have been wiped out, too. ***They were all doing business with Wall Street.*** Rightfully, the credit crisis <u>should have shut down the whole system</u>---with their clearing house and banking partners going belly up, thereby making most of them bankrupt, also.

Any government bailout would have entailed some kind of a haircut, no doubt. The smartest of them even recognized this as a high probability and took steps to protect themselves, accordingly. Unfortunately for these truly brilliant people, the system screwed them because they would have been the ones to take over the banks!

As we know, the Federal Reserve nefariously bailed out the banks using unapproved and unauthorized U.S. taxpayer-backed money, preventing them from going bankrupt. This is an event virtually no one could have predicted and was a completely unfair use of U.S. taxpayer-backed monies. It may have also been illegal.

Most hedge fund managers assumed a business risk to deposit investor funds and securities into institutions and systems designed to systemically fail. This risk should have been an assessment of the management of the fund, but it wasn't. Some of the wisest managers, like Jim Rogers, did everything they could to prepare for the credit crisis and placed their capital in locations outside the U.S., away from the derivatives craps table.

Other managers also saw the collapse coming and did the right thing--- they diversified and went offshore to other financial markets because they saw the condition of the banks and firms in the West. As most know, one of the most famous money managers, Jim Rogers, who manages billions of dollars, left and went to Singapore. Readers may also know Mr. Rogers from his work as an author, where he has written many best sellers, including: Street Smarts, Hot Commodities, Adventure Capitalist, Investment Biker, A Gift to My Children and A Bull In China.

It is simply not fair to people, who planned in accordance with their reading of the tea leaves EXACTLY CORRECTLY, to have the Federal Reserve System secretly bail out the failed bankers and rest of the elite---at the expense of everyone else.

As discussed in this chapter in subsection, "Banks Should Have Failed— Protect Depositors with New Investors Ready to Jump In," the system would have recovered if the banks were allowed to fail, with people like Jim Rogers willingly becoming the next owners of the banks. The depositors' monies could have been wholly protected by the U.S. Government (or European, Japan, etc.).

This would have been a far better alternative than spending nearly $30 Trillion in taxpayer money to secretly bail out the Federal Reserve's shareholders and reimburse the wealthy for their stock and bond market losses. This did nothing to help the general economy, or people of America.

Hedge fund men and women are among the brightest people on earth--- hopefully, they are taking steps to evade the death trap awaiting them and their firms when the derivatives' time bomb goes off. If they are not, their funds (and THEIR OWN BILLIONS) may go up in smoke---particularly if they have their portfolios and capital sitting with the banks and any Wall

Street firm. When the fuse goes off and D'Apocalypse™ strikes, this time, the banks will steal THEIR money, too.

Congress Shouldn't Push Through Legislation Harmful to Hedge Funds, Unless....

To the extent ANY of these hedge funds exchanged worthless securities through their clearing-firm banks, or otherwise, in exchange for U.S. Treasury securities, cash, or U.S. taxpayer-backed cash-equivalent Fed credits (which can only be known by extensive audit of the Federal Reserve), these funds would appear to have also fraudulently participated in the Fed's scheme. IF this occurred, the related funds should be seized and returned to the U.S. Treasury.

The actions by the Fed and the willing participants are simply wrong. The entire affair of taking, on an undisclosed secret basis, nearly $30 Trillion, twice the size of the United States' GDP, was unauthorized conduct by the Federal Reserve and the Reserve Banks. All participants should be held accountable for their part in this heist from the U.S. taxpayer.

WITH THIS SINGLE EXCEPTION (i.e. if a hedge fund participated in the $30 Trillion heist) AND IN ANY EVENT, <u>Congress should NOT be pushing through legislation which prematurely taxes hedge fund positions.</u> Further tinkering with a free market which provides important liquidity for investors around the world is very, very bad business and will only serve to drive more capital offshore to other countries, where it is not within regulators reach, or authority.

New York Post
"The most feared man on Wall St.
Rep. Camp is a hedgie horror"
"He's become Wall Street's Public Enemy No. 1 — Dave Camp, a Republican Congressman from Michigan and chairman of the influential Ways and Means Committee....Camp is working on a huge tax-reform proposal that would eat into the Street's lucrative hedging operations. The draft covers a half-dozen changes in how hedging strategies are taxed, including imposing mark-to-market accounting for financial derivatives, changing the tax-basis calculations for these securities and preventing phantom income and deductions....The proposal calls for taxes to be paid much sooner and often at higher rates than in today's more favorable treatment." (Source: New York Post, by Gregory Bresiger, June 1, 2013, retrieved from http://www.nypost.com/p/news/business/the_most_feared_man_on_wall_st_YDG4q9InLiq4kwgIjmwJWM).

...Or, Hedge Fund Pirates?

As you have seen, the big bank executives and hedge fund managers are taking home paychecks totaling BILLIONS OF DOLLARS (some of them, individually this much!), despite the fact the entire system should have collapsed because of the Street's use of derivatives, leverage and fraud.

Thanks to the American taxpayer and the secretive actions of the Federal Reserve to take taxpayer-backed money and bail out the banks and elite, their system was allowed to continue. This allowed their leadership ranks, across the board in the hedge fund industry, to continue taking hundreds of billions of dollars in total compensation. If the Fed had not pulled off the $30 Trillion heist, this absurd amount of compensation, very likely, would NOT rightfully have been paid out.

This is because nearly the ENTIRE INDUSTRY would have been declared bankrupt, as a direct result of the credit crisis, due to the certain failure of the banks and major investment banking firms, had the free market been allowed to operate. Remember---the banks and investment banks would have merely been taken over by NEW owners. Those who invested and bet wrongly would be penalized, as they should be.

If Congress had been awake, the depositors would have been protected. Unfortunately, socialism for the rich was hard at work, destroying the very foundations of American capitalism.

No bankrupt industry on earth pays out compensation like the hedge fund industry has received since the commencement of the credit and mortgage crisis. It is only because the American taxpayer was secretly taken advantage of, were these people able to receive their billions of dollars in compensation.

The Fed will likely claim they didn't use "tax dollars" to secretly bailout the banks and elite.

Nothing could be further from the truth. Each and every dollar and Federal Reserve cash-equivalent, printed and heisted by the Federal Reserve, are backed by the full faith and credit of the U.S. Government!

Banks Should Have Failed—Protect Depositors with New Investors Ready to Jump In

What should have happened was the banking industry should have been allowed to fail, with only the strongest banks and hedge funds surviving, will ALL depositors protected. The "strongest" banks, by the way, were likely the small, responsible community banks sprinkled throughout the United States! The "strongest" hedge funds were those offshore and not playing in the derivatives game.

Those in power at the major institutions, and those vested in those holding power, should have been severely penalized—i.e., they should have lost their money! The elite didn't lose a penny, however, because the Federal Reserve bailed out both <u>member and non-member</u> institutions, as well as the elite behind the curtain.

If these organizations and family powers were allowed to go bankrupt and a "bank holiday" was declared, <u>new owners</u> would have stepped in QUICKLY.

There are many, many investors who would **love** to own a bank (e.g., the list of people with the capital and connections to take over the control of the banks is endless and could include such luminaries as Bill Gates, Warren Buffett, Jim Rogers, Mayor Michael Bloomberg, Larry Ellison, Mark Zuckerberg, Carlos Slim, Sergey Brin, Larry Page, etc.). This could have been easily accomplished by having the government step in and guarantee **NOT** the investors and bond holders of the banks and the people running them---but, instead, the government **should have guaranteed** the depositors' accounts!

As a result of blundering politicians and their sheer desire to stay in power, along with the abominable actions of the Federal Reserve, the banks, the executives, traders, sales people and wealthy elite owners of the banks were the benefactors of the biggest heist of all time.

They were able to continue their disastrous trading methodologies, leverage and risky bets in the set up for D'Apocalypse™ because they were able to escape ALL of their losses on their last round of bad, MULTI-TRILLION DOLLAR bets made during the mortgage and credit crisis.

"The Corruption, As Far As The Eye Can See, Is Everywhere!"
While this book comes down on the side of free enterprise, very strongly, there are some very serious questions being raised regarding corruption and the use of monies to avoid regulatory issues, and other problems. In what Professor Jeffrey Sachs, of Columbia University, believes may be a wholly criminal undertaking in the financial sector, the following is a summary (along with the author's interpretive thoughts and comments) of what Professor Sachs, an economist, had to say about compensation levels on Wall Street, at a <u>meeting attended by members of the Federal Reserve</u> in April of 2013:

> *"The corruption, as far as I can see, is everywhere....*
> *Massive illegality has been exposed in the system."*

—Professor Jeffrey Sachs, speaking to members of the Federal Reserve, April 2013.

Professor Sachs recounted in front of the camera, how he had just met with approximately 100 U.N. Ambassadors, discussing U.N. plans for the period 2015-2030. What was "palpable in the room," he said, was anger against the American financial system. The developing world feels like they are the victims. They believe the 2008 crisis contributed to instability and economic stress in other parts of the world, while the IMF and U.S. treats them as if nothing has happened and everything is normal. They know the U.S. failed badly in financial management and the implications for this have had an enormous impact around the world.

The entire experience of the last five years, Professor Sachs continued, brings into question the Fed's role as a regulator and the real lessons behind the financial crisis. The reality is there is massive illegality in the system. New settlements with banks and hedge funds are announced on nearly a daily basis, via SEC and other courtroom agreements pointing to a mountain of criminal and fraudulent behavior---which go way beyond a "bubble" and "mistakes." <u>The amount of the criminality is ENORMOUS.</u>

We have seen scandal upon scandal, including LIBOR, insider trading, Abacus (Jon Paulson's hedge fund) selling toxic mortgage assets in league with Goldman Sachs, etc. and a judge approving a settlement with SAC Capital for $600 Million---without SAC having to admit, or deny, any guilt, or liability!

The head of SAC, Steven A. Cohen, took home $1.4 Billion in personal compensation for his management of the company, while his top trader was arrested in handcuffs! This is the American financial system. It is an unregulated, lawless, environment.

<u>What we find in the evidence is many of these financial leaders are making massive political campaign contributions.</u> Mr. Cohen, for example, gave $217,000 in campaign contributions to the politicians, with the result being Mr. Cohen was given ample protection from the Senators and other legislators, insulating him from prosecution. The complete impunity of the system is massive.

The bottom line is, just like in 2008, today we find a continuing abuse of power and authority where massive, massive bonuses are paid out at the top of the pyramid, while massive fines are being paid out for unlawful behavior---with all of it supported and made possible by massive campaign contributions being paid to the politicians.

Author's Note and Research: The New York Times depicted a number of hedge fund managers and compensation they received, with half of the hedge funds failing to beat the market in 2012. Some of the highlights included:

- **David Tepper who received a $2.2 Billion paycheck, while donating $601,000 in campaign contributions;**
- **Ray Dalio received a $1.7 Billion paycheck;**
- **Steven Cohen received a $1.4 Billion paycheck;**
- **Daniel Loeb received "only" $380 Million and gave $551,000 in campaign contributions;**
- **Ken Griffin took $900 Million from Citadel and gave $2.7 Million in campaign contributions;**
- **While Leon Cooperman took home $560 Million.**

(Source: New York Times, "Hedge Fund Titans' Pay Stretching to 10 Figures," By Julie Creswell, April 15, 2013).

Jon Paulson's gold share bet lost $1.5 billion in 2012, with Professor Sachs doubting very strongly if Mr. Paulson was going to put $1.5 Billion back into the fund to cover the loss (the author concurs with Mr. Sachs presumption)! There is only upside for these people, no downside, as the fee structure is independent from performance.

(Author note: this is not entirely true because most hedge funds have a blended compensation structure where they are paid partially

for performance, usually 20% of the profits based on a "high-water" mark, and also a fixed fee as a percent of assets under management).

Mr. Sachs continued there is no justification for the incomes these people are taking, because there is no way their productivity is close to their income levels and it is disgusting they can also make large political contributions. Many of these funds are involved in lawsuits and settlements. By being domiciled in the Cayman Islands, they have no real accountability for much of anything. Furthermore, most of them create reinsurance companies in Bermuda and the Cayman Islands, allowing them to reinvest in their own firms--thus further avoiding taxes.

Where is the Fed in all of this? Basic regulatory practice is politically out of control and is out of legal bounds---there is no fairness and Wall Street is lawless. The regulatory system has broken down. The symptoms are massive government failure, with massive money payments taking over the regulatory bureaucracies and nearly the entire political arena.

We need to change the system to ensure the banks and hedge funds can't overly leverage themselves. Liquidity needs to be ensured and separated from the current speculative investing and betting taking place in the banking sector---Lehman Brothers was damaging because it infected the inter-bank loans, the money markets, with a lack of liquidity being the real loss.

The Glass-Steagall Act* once protected the banks and Wall Street from this kind of danger for a long time. However, the likes of Robert Rubin, Larry Summers, Bill Clinton, Phil Graham and others got rid of Glass-Steagall because their personal interests were tied to the outcome of Wall Street's desire to see the Act repealed.

*Author note: "The Gramm-Leach-Bliley Act, also known as the Financial Services Modernization Act of 1999 was enacted on November 12, 1999, during the Clinton administration, following extensive lobbying by investment banks and other financial services companies. The Act repealed the legal restrictions on combining banking and financial service firms found in the Glass-Steagall Act of 1933. This allowed commercial banks, investment banks, securities companies and insurance companies to merge with each other. The Glass-Steagall Act had prohibited any company from acting as both an investment bank and a commercial bank. Both were prohibited from owning insurance companies by the Bank Holding Company Act of 1956" (Source: sourcewatch.org http://www.sourcewatch.org/index.php?title=Gramm-Leach-Bliley_Act).

Particularly stunning, was in early 2009, many of these same people who were responsible for causing the credit crisis in the first place, were invited back into the White House to "fix" it.

The whole time, Larry Summers fought vigorously against limits on compensation, while the *Federal Reserve continued to print money and bail out the banks and the wealthy elite—with the Obama administration's firm blessing. All of these dastardly activities were accomplished, no doubt, to the chorus and the cacophony of loud laughter echoing down the halls of the Rothschilds, the Rockefellers, the Morgans, the Mellons, the Warburgs and every other bank board room around the world, who were members of the Federal Reserve System* (author's comments are italicized and bold from "Federal Reserve" onward in the above paragraph).

Toward the end of Professor Sachs talk, he asked the big question: "Can you separate the politicians from the crooks?"

Wrapping up his discussion he said there is an extremely deep crisis in values, as the regulations and legal structures need reform, while the Wall Street environment is pathological. These people are out to make billions of dollars and their attitude is nothing should stop them. They have no responsibilities to anyone---not for paying taxes, not to counterparties--- NO ONE. They have gamed the system and benefit from having a docile President, as well as a docile court and docile political system.

They have corrupted politics to the core and both political parties are up to their necks in this, as it has nothing to do with left wing, or right wing.

(Author note: Just as bankers and the elite historically paid off for media protection, it is even better documented, as to their support of BOTH political parties. This is critical for them to accomplish their objectives— the bankers and elite don't care who wins, as long as they can stay in their banking suites and earn money the old fashioned way---by TAKING IT!).

There is a sense of impunity from all of these people on Wall Street and not one person speaks in a moral language. (Source: Professor Jeffrey Sachs, 2013, of Columbia University in New York, video conference he held at a meeting attended by members of the Federal Reserve in April 2013, as (retrieved from http://www.youtube.com/watch?v=FLYQ_72CDWU).

Professor Sachs is doing everyone a great service by asking these excellent questions. He is largely correct.

The one point this book disagrees with is seemingly painting everyone who makes a fortune as "bad" (and should be taxed to death!). Professor Sachs, in this discussion, is particularly focused on the hedge fund managers, but these funds and managers did not directly receive public bailout money and may, or may not, have been exchanging worthless, toxic debt with the Fed for taxpayer-backed, good-as-gold U.S. Treasury securities, Fed credits, or cash.

His excellent point about collusion with Goldman Sachs and the shorting of toxic mortgage pools (e.g., Jon Paulson and Abacus) and other villainous activities of the funds should obviously not be allowed to occur.

A Contractual Right to Free Market Compensation is Intrinsic to the Constitution
For the record, if a CEO, or a hedge fund manager, makes a lot of money LEGALLY, WITHOUT TAKING TAXPAYER-BACKED, SECRET, HEISTED BAILOUT MONEY, there should be no problem with this.

Hedge fund investors are sophisticated, by definition, and if they entered into an agreement allowing for exorbitant compensation to be paid out to these managers, then the managers earned it in accordance with their contracts. Contracts are binding guarantees, in accordance with the U.S. Constitution. Contract rights go all the way back to the Magna Carta! They form one of the most basic, founding legal principles of our country. A contract is a contract and Congress cannot usurp a contract.

Our country is founded on a system which honors the letter of the law, as well as the contracts in hand. It is not a good decision to begin to try and manage, as socialists and communists do, the kinds of decisions individual investors make with respect to where they place their investments and the compensation arrangements they freely agree to with the smart and/or stupid people managing their monies! If the manager is "stupid," he, or she, will not last long and the capital will flow to someone else who is "smart" (supposedly), if the system is allowed to work.

In a normal world of "old school" America, this is how it is supposed to function in a capitalistic system. However, the problem today, is many of these Street people are operating in a manner where there appears to be overwhelming evidence of fraud, and a gross breach of fiduciary duty. Even more deeply troubling is how the regulatory and political systems are remaining silent as to their prosecution, holding NOT ONE OF THEM accountable criminally for any of their actions.

The banks, for example, not only secretly took U.S. taxpayer-backed money, but used their newly found TRILLIONS in capital to goose bond and stock markets into big, billowing bubbles, ready to pop (in the case of the bond market) and soon to pop (in the case of the equity market)! They are also making additional bets using OUTRAGEOUS leverage in their derivatives' positions.

Their financial recklessness combined with the aggressive behavior of fund managers who also have a "nothing to lose" and "everything to gain" attitude, has created a towering spire of HUNDREDS OF TRILLIONS OF DOLLARS in derivatives transactions and positions. This spire is destined to fall down and crash to earth---in a burning blazing ball of fire, with thousands of counter parties being torched along the way.

Cui Bono?

A financial system which has been allowed to build itself into this kind of an unregulated monster, capable of destroying entire nations, with one wrong bet, is simply beyond belief. The idiocy and/or duplicity, of every single administration, Congressman, Senator and regulator since 1987, are obviously apparent. The only question remains is, "Cui Bono?" Who benefits?

Upon reading this book, you will know the answer to this question. While the people profiled in these pages are sacking Rome with their billion-dollar paydays, the Kings and Queens directing them sit in stony silence behind their fortresses---ensuring the Federal Reserve and their working minions protect their interests. This is the key to understanding the great scheme and manipulation which has fallen on top of all us.

Derivatives are not the biggest revenue producer for these firms, but derivatives are the most profitable, or among the most profitable business sectors for Wall Street (when they work!). The firms are getting away with murder right now in the way they can legally deploy leverage.

Because derivatives produce such HUGE PROFITS from commissions, interest and premium payments, while also creating enormous profits from correct bets made on a given position, or transaction, the banks are vicious with determination to keep this market out of the purview of regulators.

The banks themselves control the market, in an oligopoly, and the game is rigged from the get go, with the odds stacked heavily in favor of the "house." All of the revenues and profits are created by using someone else's money, with little or no collateral required, of any kind.

As you know, the U.S. oligopoly is run by the 4 Horsemen of the D'Apocalypse™, JP Morgan Chase, Citigroup, Bank of America and Goldman Sachs, with over 90% control of all transactions in the United States and the number of people who control this market is VERY SMALL.

A regular board room will accommodate all key members of the Group of 14 Dealers (G14), which controls over 80% of the $692 Trillion "nominal" derivatives market. When they decide operation "D'Apocalypse™" is a "go", they will force another massive market change. Their members and followers will all know what to do.

The entire system is an unheard of set up for any other person, business, industry, or government in the history of mankind---and it is a system doomed for failure (at least for the counter parties!), as part of the grand design of the elite.

The Banks "Miraculous Profit Turnaround" is on the Tab of the U.S. Taxpayer!

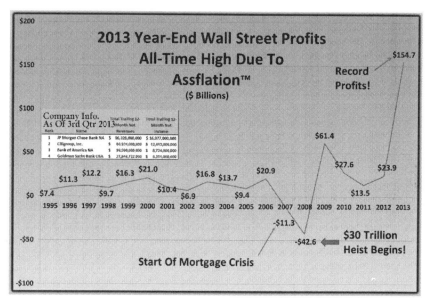

As you recall from the simple example in Chapter 2, "Derivatives---the Ticking Time Bomb!", if things go the right way, a theoretical family, earning a relatively modest (in comparison with Wall Street) $110,000 combined salary, with $10,000 in the bank, could make MILLIONS using derivatives by deploying the same leverage and playing by the same rules as Bank of America. Of course, it could also lose its shirt, which is precisely what happened to Wall Street in 2007-2009.

Don't let the profit figures fool you when the banks and Wall Street quickly "recovered" and made money during the "recovery" time period (per the sharp recovery spike, above). The banks were exchanging worthless and toxic mortgage paper, as well as other potentially worthless collateral, with Ben Bernanke and Janet Yellen at the Federal Reserve System, HAND OVER FIST! IN EXCHANGE, they received 100% cash back---in the form of taxpayer-backed Federal Reserve electronic account credits totaling trillions of dollars, along with U.S. T-Bills, U.S. Notes, U.S. Bonds and cash, courtesy of the U.S. taxpayer! As you know and surmise, the author calls these activities, collectively, "The $30 Trillion Heist."

THEY ALSO PAID THEMSELVES BILLIONS and BILLIONS OF DOLLARS IN DIVIDENDS, *siphoning the money directly from the*

Fed's payments, as backed by the American taxpayer (see The $30 Trillion Heist, Volume II, Follow The Money!, Chapter 1 "The $30 Trillion Heist---How the Scam Worked" and in this book, this chapter's subsection, "How Much did the 4 Horsemen of the D'Apocalypse™ Pay Out To Shareholders?").

What is clear from the history, is the banks took the nearly $30 Trillion surreptitiously given to them by the Fed and received up to a 3% risk-free return on it when the banks invested in risk-free, long-term U.S. Treasury Bonds. They used the rest to goose the equity and other fixed income markets and effectively drove rates to near zero, causing yet another unsustainable, massive bubble in these markets.

The bond market bubble will burst quite soon, as interest rates will skyrocket, ultimately leading to the destructive power of D'Apocalypse™ in, or around, the fall of 2015 and prior to the U.S. Presidential elections in 2016. Until this time, investors can count on the Fed to be pumping like crazy, as the Democrats and any other elected officials struggle to stay in power. Their only hope of not being voted out is to inflate the bubble in the hopes people with 401K plans also do not vote against them.

As readers of The $30 Trillion Heist know, outrageously, the U.S. taxpayer paid for a bailout of London's Financial Center and many, many other foreign banks around the world. This, along with the highly likely scenario Americans received worthless securities in exchange for the $30 Trillion the Fed gave away, is one of the key reasons why the Federal Reserve will not allow its books to be fully audited.

Even if you take Mr. Bernanke's word the backdoor bailouts were over $16 Trillion (but, you don't have to, because the General Accounting Office of the United States of America already published a report indicating over $26 Trillion was secretly used to bail out the banks!), this is MORE than the ENTIRE United States Gross Domestic Product. From this report and admission, it is easy to see what ONE YEAR'S profit would be for the banks!

REMEMBER, the banks, as permitted by Ben Bernanke and the Directors of the Federal Reserve, have been able to EXCHANGE their toxic and likely worthless mortgage-backed securities (AND OTHER DERIVATIVES WITH EXPLOSIVE RISK AND QUESTIONABLE VALUE) for taxpayer-back Federal Reserve electronic credits (and/or cash equivalents)—WHICH BEAR NO RISK. In other words, the banks have been able to offload their bad loans and risky, worthless securities positions AT FULL FACE VALUE in exchange for 100% CASH— COURTESY OF THE U.S. TAX PAYER---WITHOUT THE CONSENT OF CONGRESS.

This heist is the most brazen in the history of humankind.

The banks exchanged their toxic and likely worthless securities with the Fed and could turn around and invest the Fed's taxpayer-backed proceeds at a risk-free return of 3% in United States Government long-term bonds, or other maturities at slightly lower rates of return! It is literally like robbing Peter once, robbing him again and never paying Paul---they just keep the money for themselves!

When those rates were driven low enough, the banks and the elite switched to equities. The Fed's actions created Assflation™ in both of these preferred market sectors (e.g., bonds and stocks) of the elite, while continuing to drive their highly profitable, revived but completely dangerous, derivatives markets to new ground.

Now, with all the talking heads on TV asking themselves each morning why isn't the economy moving and why aren't the banks' lending money....what bank in their right mind would lend money to get the economy moving??

If you could exchange worthless securities (literally, Monopoly money which can't even buy a stick of gum outside of the game board) for risk-free, 3% U.S. Government-guaranteed Treasury paper, why would you ever lend money at risk to a single, solitary consumer? Each year, the $16 Trillion given to American banks, alone, could earn the banks $480 BILLION in risk-free interest income!! **$480 BILLION!!!**

As you have seen in this chapter, something "miraculous" happened to immediately restore the banks to profitability between 2008 and 2009. This book is betting the $30 Trillion heist had everything to do with it!

With this simple lesson, you know why the banks all became, all of a sudden, "healthy" in the middle of the raging storm of the mortgage and credit crisis. They simply heisted the money from you and every other citizen in the United States of America.

Jesus, in his only act of anger in The Bible, stormed the money changers and became righteously indignant with them, bowling over their tables in the process—Jesus called them a "den of thieves." Nothing much has changed since Jesus walked through the Temple in Jerusalem, except the amounts being stolen have increased exponentially.

Matthew 21:12:
And Jesus went into the temple of God, and cast out all them that sold and bought in the temple, and overthrew the tables of the moneychangers, and the seats of them that sold doves, And said unto them, It is written, My house shall be called the house of prayer; but ye have made it a den of thieves. (Source: The Bible, Matthew 21:12, King James Version).

Ultimately, society will track down the bankers and elite who took the money, along with all of their holding companies. When the economic firestorm of D'Apocalypse™ hits, the people will be woken from their slumber as extreme economic hardship sets in. If the bankers fail in their mission to establish global control of monetary policy via their use of their government-debt gambling chip, the people will stand a good chance of recovering the property stolen from them. This will require a group of righteous men and women, whose God-conscience and desire to seek justice overcomes their fear of retribution from the powers that be.

This could happen with a miracle in 2016 by the voters sweeping out of office every single politician who voted for and supports the Federal Reserve System, the banks and the elite---this is a vote which transcends political parties. By then, D'Apocalypse™ and its dramatic impact on every non-elite person's life should be quite apparent.

If millions of people in need of help unite, they stand a chance of changing the system and recovering the stolen goods, while expunging from the system the money-sucking leaches preying on all of our citizens.

Jesus called the money changers and the sellers of merchandise "thieves." I wonder what He would say about people receiving multi-million dollar paydays (see this chapter's previous subsection, "Top Commercial Banks' Compensation to Lead Executives") from nefariously received, taxpayer-backed monies, without prior disclosure, and what He thinks about just a few families siphoning off trillions of dollars in wealth, robbing the hard-working people of earth along the way?

If the Fed were fully audited and the actual securities the Fed has in its vaults and in the clearing firms around the world were physically seen and valued at their fair market values, people would THEN very likely learn a robbery of staggering proportions has indeed taken place, without any question at all, in anybody's mind! Fortunately, we have a clear, undisputable evidence trail which can allow Congress, the people and a future set of uncorrupted regulators pursue a path to prosecute these evil doers.

A Detective Story Unveiled

D'Apocalypse™ Now! and The $30 Trillion Heist, in both of its volumes, did not enjoy the advantage of a full audit of the Federal Reserve, but they have together, pieced together a detective's story, which is beyond fascinating. Each book in the trilogy goes to great lengths to document the evidence of the apparent fraud and thus evidence a robbery may have indeed been committed against the American people and the Republic.

What about operating PROFITS from the Federal Reserve? Is there any limitation on how profits are split up between the banks and/or the government? How do the member banks get the money to the **interested elite** (e.g., the largest, family-controlled, shareholders), who hide behind the shadows and corridors of power of these institutions?

How the Federal Reserve Makes Money

According to the Richmond Federal Reserve Bank, the Federal Reserve's income is derived primarily from the interest on U.S. Government securities which are also traded through open market operations. Other sources of income are the interest on foreign currency investments held by the System; fees received for services provided to depository institutions, such as check clearing, funds transfers, and automated clearinghouse operations, as well as interest on loans to depository institutions (the rate on which is the so-called discount rate). (Source, Federal Reserve Richmond, retrieved from http://www.richmondfed.org/faqs/frs/).

Of course, the Federal Reserve web site for Richmond does not make any mention of the Fed exchanging $30 Trillion of U.S. Cash-equivalent Fed credits, cash, or U.S. treasuries for worthless securities. This, it seems, is not supposed to be a way for the Fed and its member Reserve Banks to make money—at least according to the Richmond Federal Reserve. However, this is exactly what Mr. Bernanke and Ms. Yellen did and permitted, while running the Fed.

Most people would call this a robbery in plain sight.

How Much of the Federal Reserve Earnings Must be Returned to the Treasury?

According to the late Wright Patman of Texas, who was Chairman of the Committee on Banking and Currency for the House of Representatives:

"No law or regulation specifies how much of the Federal Reserve's earnings must be returned to the Treasury, but in practice the Federal Reserve spends all of the income it cares to spend, pays dividends to member banks on their "stock" and sets aside a large amount as "surplus." The remainder is then returned to the Treasury. It usually returns an amount several times the amount of its expenses." (Source: COMMITTEE ON BANKING AND CURRENCY, HOUSE OF REPRESENTATIVES, SUBCOMITTEE ON DOMESTIC FINANCE, 88th Congress, 2nd Session, SEPTEMBER 21, 1964, by Wright Patman, Chairman, CHAPTER IV, "WHY WAS THE FEDERAL RESERVE ACT PASSED?", point number 92, retrieved from http://www.baldwinlivingtrust.com/pdfs/AllAboutMoney.pdf).

With this knowledge as a backdrop, it is then interesting to listen to the Federal Reserve sing through the media (using them as its mouth piece), to brilliantly announce its "earnings" are sent back to the U.S. Treasury. There is no mention about any surplus returned to the Fed's balance sheet, nor is there any mention of any dividends paid to member banks; of course, there is absolutely no mention of the swapping of 100% good-as-gold U.S. Treasury securities and U.S. taxpayer-backed cash-equivalent Fed electronic credits for junk bonds and junk collateral from the banks!

When sensible people really understand the cloak of invisibility hanging over the Federal Reserve, shielding it from scrutiny, it will lead to incalculable suspicion, and will immediately put into question, the manner in which the Fed conducts its operations.

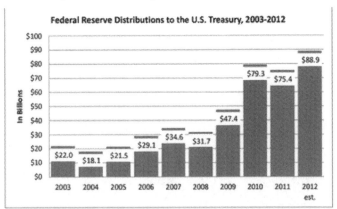

Source of 2003-2011 data: 2011 Annual Report of the Board of Governors of the Federal Reserve System
99th Annual Report 2012 of the Board of Governors of the Federal Reserve System, page 100, as retrieved from (http://www.federalreserve.gov/publications/annual-report/files/2012-annual-report.pdf).

The Fed isn't fully audited, and according to its very own specialized and suspect accounting rules (instituted by only its own pronouncement--- without oversight), **the Fed can value, on the Fed's own balance sheet, acquired junk bonds from the banks---even those which are worthless, AT THEIR FULL FACE VALUE.**

This capability appears to intentionally defraud the American public and mislead the people by showing a far higher valuation on a pool of securities than what is really the case. Because of the Fed's arcane and self-promulgated accounting rules, they can bury and hide worthless securities and worthless securities transactions in off-balance sheet vehicles and international accounts.   These are shielded from auditor eyeballs, Congress and the American people!

What will ultimately occur, long after Ben Bernanke retires, is there will be a HORRIFIC loss shoved back onto the U.S. Treasury and the taxpayers who will foot the bill. A full audit will reveal, with very high likelihood, the extensive use of "off balance sheet" vehicles designed to shield the Fed's surreptitious activities and tactics from the public's and Congress' prying eyes.

The actual 2012 distributions to the U.S. Treasury were only slightly more than $88 Billion. How do you like this number, when you know a $30 Trillion Heist was committed?

How Much did the 4 Horsemen of the D'Apocalypse™ Pay Out To Shareholders?
The bankers apparently believe they did such a great job during the credit crisis from 2007-2012, in dividends alone, **they paid their shareholders over $100 BILLION! Even during the worst of the collapse**, when the industry was getting and receiving secret and non-secret bailouts totaling nearly $30 TRILLION, the 4 Horsemen, along with most other banks, continued to pay TENS OF BILLIONS OF DOLLARS in dividends to their owners.

The following table shows how much those funds *would have meant* to the people of Los Angeles, Chicago, Columbus, Detroit, Baltimore, Atlanta and Miami if they were given to those cities, instead of to the banks and the elite.

By funneling the money to the elite and the banks, the Federal Reserve destined the cities and towns of America to lifetimes of poverty, welfare, rising prices and unrest---quite a legacy for the combined actions of Mr.

Greenspan and Mr. Bernanke and every single person, or entity, they conspired with, before, during and after the mortgage crisis and credit collapse.

Why Congress and the Administration are not up in arms about nearly $30 Trillion in secret, unapproved and unauthorized secret bailouts for the banks and their elite owners is a mystery. The people must take action with every single Congressman, Senator and Administration official to affect justice over these incredible and galactically diabolical actions by the Fed, the banks and the elite behind them.

Dividends & Beneficial Transactions To Shareholders							
The 4 Horsemen of the D'Apocalypse®							
From Consolidated Statement of Changes in Stockholders' Equity Statements							
				$ in Millions		© 2013 Robert L. Kelly	
	2007	2008	2009	2010	2011	2012	Total
JP Morgan Chase	DIVIDENDS PAID, BENEFICIAL TRANSACTIONS & NET INCOME						
Preferred		$ 674	$ 2,440	$ 642	$ 629	$ 647	$ 5,032
Common	$ 5,165	$ 5,633	$ 820	$ 835	$ 4,030	$ 4,729	$ 21,212
Net Income	$ 15,365	$ 5,605	$ 11,728	$ 17,370	$ 18,976	$ 21,284	$ 90,328
2007-2009 annual report 2009 page 148, 2010-2012 annual report 2012 page 191							
Citigroup							
Preferred	$ 45	$ 1,477	$ 3,202	$ 9	$ 26	$ 26	$ 4,785
Common	$ 10,733	$ 6,050	$ 36	$ (10)	$ 81	$ 120	$ 17,010
Pfd. & Com. Special Div.		$ 37	$ 4,610	$ 1	$ (1)	$ (1)	$ 4,646
Noncontrolling Interest	$ 226	$ 168	$ 17	$ 99	$ 67	$ 33	$ 610
Transactions & "Other"	$ 406	$ 3,650	$ 526	$ 520	$ 571	$ 183	$ 5,856
Net Income	$ 3,617	$ (27,684)	$ (1,606)	$ 10,602	$ 11,067	$ 7,541	$ 3,537
Common dividends in 2010 represent a reversal of dividends accrued on forfeitures by departing employees.							
2007-2009 annual report 2009 page 123, 2010-2012 annual report 2012 page 144							
Bank of America							
Preferred	$ 182	$ 1,272	$ 4,537	$ 1,357	$ 1,325	$ 1,472	$ 10,145
Common	$ 10,696	$ 10,256	$ 326	$ 405	$ 413	$ 437	$ 22,533
Net Income	$ 14,982	$ 4,008	$ 6,276	$ (2,238)	$ 1,446	$ 4,188	$ 28,662
2007-2009 annual report 2009 page 128, 2010-2012 annual report 2012 page 156							
Goldman Sachs							
Preferred	$ 192	$ 208	$ 1,124	$ 641	$ 2,002	$ 183	$ 4,350
Common	$ 639	$ 642	$ 588	$ 802	$ 769	$ 903	$ 4,343
Net Income	$ 11,599	$ 2,322	$ 13,385	$ 8,354	$ 4,442	$ 7,475	$ 47,577
2007-2009 annual report 2009 page 87, 2010-2012 annual report 2012 page 110							
Total Dividends Paid	2007-2012						$ 100,522
Total Net Income	2007-2012						$ 170,104

Equivalent Dividend Per Person:						
	Los Angeles	Chicago	Columbus	Detroit	Baltimore	Atlanta	Miami
City Population (U.S. Census--Chap. 2)	3,819,702	2,707,120	797,434	706,585	619,493	432,427	408,750
$ Per Person	$ 26,317	$ 37,132	$ 126,057	$ 142,265	$162,265	$ 232,460	$ 245,925
# True Unemployed (see Chap. 2--see calculation Chapter 13)	840,334	595,566	175,435	155,449	136,288	95,134	89,925
$ Per Person	$ 119,621	$ 168,784	$ 572,587	$ 646,656	$737,570	$1,056,636	$1,117,843

© 2014 Robert L. Kelly

(Source: The above table was produced from analyzing the annual reports for the "Big 4," JP Morgan Chase, Citigroup, Bank of America and Goldman Sachs for the years above. These can be Googled by the reader if interested, for example, a simple of search of "JP Morgan Chase Annual Report 2012" will bring you to this choice: http://investor.shareholder.com/jpmorganchase/annual.cfm).

These are the top institutional beneficiaries of the dividends on common stock, as obtained from public records:

Controlling Institutional Shareholders
4 Horsemen of the D'Apocalypse®
2013

© 2013 Robert L. Kelly

Bank	Vanguard	Franklin	Black Rock	Fidelity	T. Rowe	SPDR	BONYMellon	Goldman Sachs	JPM	Citigroup	Wells Fargo	Total
						Percentage Ownership of Bank						
JPM	9.7		2.35	2.57	2.87	5.32	1.28					25.28
Citibank	8.94	1.19	1.52	3.84		6.12	0.57					20.99
Bank of America	8.76		0.84	1.9	1.19	6.29		0.72	0.76	1.64		22.89
Goldman Sachs	7.67		0.83	0.38	0.68	5.56	0.58			3.21	0.79	18.91

> As you can see, less than 10 shareholders control a huge block of stock in each of the 4 Horsemen.

Knowing who the common and preferred shareholders are of the commercial banks is the key to understanding the money, dividend and ownership trail. This necessarily means finding out *who are the real owners of common stock—the people, families, or beneficiaries who disguise their ownership underneath the umbrella of thousands of obscurely named limited partnerships and shell companies.*

Regulatory change will be required to make this possible and will be critical in recovering the fraudulently taken monies from the American people.

Chapter 4
Public Scrutiny Required—Without it, Doom Awaits

Who are the Actual Owners of the Federal Reserve Banks' & Commercial Banks' Shares?

The need for a full-fledged audit as to the identity of the shareholders for all Federal Reserve Banks and their corresponding commercial member banks needs to be performed. <u>Despite the fact the Federal Reserve Banks are private corporations, these entities accepted public monies and have no right to privacy.</u> One of the requirements of this audit is full disclosure of the INDIVIDUALS who are the benefactors of all the issued and outstanding common and preferred shares. This means NO TRUSTS, SHELL COMPANIES, and OR OTHER MASKS HIDING IDENTITIES OF BENEFACTORS OF THE HEIST FROM AMERICA SHOULD BE ALLOWED!

Identification of the individual benefactors will allow proper public scrutiny to identify who participated, at the taxpayers' expense, in the $30 Trillion heist. The banks and shareholders behind the banks were the benefactors of taxpayer monies and should have no rights to privacy with respect to who owns what shares and who took how much money from the Federal Reserve. They must be fully identified.

This is the only way to know who actually controls, owns and benefits from the Open Market Operations, manipulation and control of the Federal Reserve System. It is critical to allow this public scrutiny of who, indeed, controls the Federal Reserve because of the astonishing and brazen heist and the taking of nearly $30 Trillion without any kind of oversight, whatsoever. The $30 Trillion is a hidden tax on the American people and is causing economic blight and the potential for outright collapse of government.

The ownership structure of the Federal Reserve is designed to confuse and obfuscate. It provides anything but a clear view as to who owns what, with opacity the operating byword of the system. Many authors have written a great deal about this subject, but the bottom line is the money has been taken away from the people it belonged to—and placed into the hands of the elite.

We must get it back.

Exchanging Worthless Securities for Public Monies Avoided Massive Losses for the Banks

Of course, thanks to the exchange of worthless debt securities and other equally questionable collateral, the bankers did not have to write trillions of dollars of losses off (see Chapter 3, "Wall Street Profits & Compensation-How Much are They Getting Paid?," subsection "The Banks 'Miraculous Profit Turnaround' is on the Tab of the U.S. Taxpayer"). If they were held responsible for their poor business decisions, like everyone else in America and around the world, the banks would have become totally bankrupt—with a takeover by other wealthy and successful companies and individuals (as discussed in "…Or, Hedge Fund Pirates?" in chapter 3).

Instead, these scoundrels were able to happily report profits and dividends in every year since the secret bailouts began (except Bank of America, which took a little longer to catch on to how the game was being played, apparently).

To place the dividend situation into perspective, if JP Morgan Chase, Citigroup, Bank of America and Goldman Sachs had donated the $100 Billion (in dividends they paid out to shareholders), as a thank you to the country for saving their skins, they could have helped MILLIONS of people.

If the money had been given DIRECTLY to some of the hardest hit locations in the United States, as a result of the banker-engineered mortgage fraud and credit crisis, EACH AND <u>EVERY CITIZEN OF Columbus, Detroit, Baltimore, Atlanta and Miami could have received a check for $33,906! This is ONLY dividends to the elite we are talking about. The $30 Trillion from the heist is ABOVE AND BEYOND A MERE $100 Billion!!!</u>

Helping even these aforementioned cities would have ensured NOBODY LIVED IN POVERTY IN THOSE TOWNS and it would have at least given those who got evicted and foreclosed upon by the banks, a fighting chance of saving their homes. It would have further kicked off an economic recovery which would have spread in those geographic locations.

$100 Billion in dividends is "big" money, no question about it and it could have helped millions. But, remember, $30 TRILLION DOLLARS was secretly taken by the Fed and paid directly to the banks and elite. This sum is an amount **300 times as large as the $100 Billion**!!! The amounts of money are beyond criminal. In the annals of history, if the author's questions are investigated and these people are prosecuted and found guilty, there will be no other crime bigger than this, except for D'Apocalypse™.

As discussed thoroughly in The $30 Trillion Dollar Heist, Americans still don't know who actually receives the TRILLIONS paid out by the Federal Reserve in dividends. This is because the shareholder and beneficial owner lists of the Federal Reserve Banks, are not publicly available in sufficient detail to establish what actual PEOPLE beneficially own the shares, and the benefits, of the Fed's largess.

It is important to put some prespective on the monies taken because we are talking about being able to save the ENTIRE COUNTRY of the United States, directly and IMMEDIATELY helping over 300,000,000 people---and no one would be out of work. If the money had been given directly to the people and economy, instead of to rich elitists and bankers, the economic malaise would have vanished, as quickly as it arrived. The only thing which would have happened, if this action were taken and the money given directly to American cities, was a lot of rich people would have lost their money----because of their poor business decisions.

The monies taken directly from the people in America, who need it the most, is simply staggering in its scale and in the skullduggery utilized in heisting it in favor of the rich. It simply makes one's stomach turn.

Here are the poverty "threshold" limits for 2012, according to the U.S. Census Bureau:

U.S. DEPARTMENT OF COMMERCE BUREAU OF THE CENSUS WASHINGTON, D.C. 20233 PRELIMINARY ESTIMATE OF WEIGHTED AVERAGE POVERTY THRESHOLDS FOR 2012	
Size of Family Unit	Estimated Threshold
1 person (unrelated individual)	$11,722
Under 65 years	11,945
65 years and over	11,011
2 people	$14,960
Householder under 65 years	15,452
Householder 65 years and over	13,891
3 people	$18,287
4 people	23,497
5 people	27,815
6 people	31,485
7 people	35,811
8 people	39,872
9 people or more	47,536

Source United States Census Bureau, retrieved from http://www.census.gov/hhes/www/poverty/data/threshld/

Any kind of recovery of the stolen riches would help the impoverished by directly injecting it into the local economies of the hardest-hit cities in America. Overall, we would experience an enormous recovery, instead of sector asset inflation in favor of the rich----which this author defines as Assflation™.

Hopefully, now you can better understand where the inspiration came from for coining this word.

Scrutiny of Record Shows Conflicts of Interest Abound
After reviewing and reading even just some of the exerpts in this book, *how* could the Fed, the banks and the elite accomplish the degree of manipulation and power it required to allow the SECRET transfer of nearly $30 TRILLION of U.S. taxpayer-backed dollars to the banks and the elite---without Congressional approval???

As is obvious by now, these transfers required autonomous control over monetary policy and the money supply----all made possible through the Federal Reserve. This is directly what allowed secret multi-trillion-dollar-pass-throughs to be given to the elite and their banks.

Is the Fed acting in the public's interest---or, as this book and trilogy suggests, the Fed is acting solely for the elite and the banks?

The public ownership records provide some clues, however, in an important congressional investigation, which built upon the late Chairman Wright Patman's exploration of the inner workings of the Federal Reserve, the 1976 Congress compiled an exhaustive report detailing the conflicts of interest at the Federal Reserve and Federal Reserve Banks. The Chairman of this Committee, Henry S. Reuss from Wisconsin, in his forward to the 120-page report stated:

"I transmit herewith a staff study of the corporate, banking and trade association relationships of the directors of the 12 Federal Reserve Banks.

This Committee has observed for many years the influence of private interests over the essentially public responsibllities of the Federal Reserve System.

As the study makes clear, it is difficult to imagine a more narrowly-based board of directors for a public agency than has been gathered together for the twelve banks of the Federal Reserve System.

Only two segments of American society – banking and big business-have any substantial representation on the boards, and often even these become merged through interlocking directorates.

The study raises a substantial question about the Federal Reserve's oft-repeated claim of "independence". One might ask, independent from what? Surely not banking or big business, if we are to judge from the massive inter-locks revealed by this analysis of the district boards.

The big business and banking dominance of the Federal Reserve System cited in this report can be traced, in part, to the original Federal Reserve Act, which gave member commercial banks the right to select two-thirds of the directors of each district bank But the Board of Governors in Washington must share the responsibility for this imbalance. They appoint the so-called "public" members of the boards of each district bank, appointments which have largely reflected the same narrow interests of the bank-elected members.

The parochial nature of the boards affects the public interest across a wide area, ranging from monetary policy to bank regulation These are the directors, for example, who initially select the presidents of the 12 district banks—officials who serve on the Federal Open Market Committee, determining the nation's money supply and the level of economic activity. The selection of these public officials, with such broad and essential policymaking powers, should not be in the hands of boards of directors selected and dominated by private banking and corporate interests.

* The nation would be better served by making the Federal Reserve System truly independent of big business and banking, freed of its built-in conflicts of interest, and more open in its activities for example.

* Voting membership, on the Federal Open Market Committee should be restricted to officers appointed by the President of the United States.

* The three Class A directors, who by law must be bankers, should be prohibited from participating in decisions bearing directly or indirectly on bank or holding company regulatory matters....

...Until we have basic reforms, the Federal Reserve System will be handicapped in carrying out its public responsibilities as an economic stabilization and bank regulatory agency. The System's mandate is too essential to the nation's welfare to leave so much of the machinery under the control of narrow private interests. Concentration of economic and financial power in the United States has gone too far. We should celebrate our Bicentennial by reversing the trend away from Thomas Jefferson."

Henry S. Reuss

HENRY S. REUSS, *Chairman,*
Banking, Currency and Housing Committee
Of the U.S. House of Representatives.

(Source: "Federal Reserve Directors: A Study of Corporate and Banking Influence, Staff Report for the Committee on Banking, Currency and Housing," House of Representatives, 94th Congress, Second Session, August 6, 1976, pages III & IV, as retrieved from http://adabyron.net/FederalReserveDirectors.pdf).

The report provides a treasure chest of information from nearly 40 years ago regarding the detailed makeup and inherent conflicts of interest of the members and directors of the Federal Reserve System, as well as their ownership and relationship interests with major companies and elite families around the world.

These conflicts carry forward to this very day (see Senator Bernie Sanders comments on conflicts in The $30 Trillion Heist---Follow The Money! Volume II, Chapter 2, "The Fed's Conflicts, Lack of Transparency & Control of The Business Cycle") and their ingrown presence RESULTED in the manipulation of Congress and the American people to the tune of nearly $30 Trillion over a two-and-a-half year period (and **God** only knows how many more trillions have been taken since 1913...).

Allowing a system of conflicts to exist simply inspires subterfuge in the ongoing operations of the Federal Reserve System.

Chairman Reuss' report focused on only the direct links of the Federal Reserve directors to the banking and corporate community and did not attempt to detail all of the massive conflicts which occur through secondary interlocks. Many of the directors of the Federal Reserve Banks are chief operating officers and chairmen of companies whose boards, in turn, have major links among other industrial and financial giants.

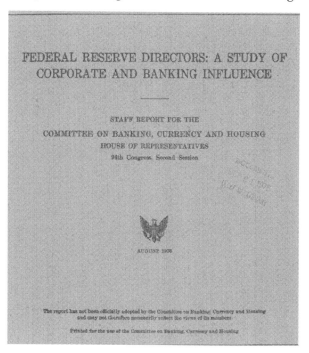

As the report shows and tells us:

"The tabular charts clearly show that substantial segments of corporate/banking power have a channel of communication and influence into the Federal Reserve Bank of New York—<u>easily the most important of the district banks</u>, with substantial roles in monetary policy and international operations of the entire Federal Reserve System. While these secondary links spread out through the twelve district banks like an international cobweb, this study does not determine the extent to which these links influence Federal Reserve directors. However, they are, at a minimum, additional evidence of the dominance of big corporations and big banking institutions in the backgrounds and the day-to-day lives of the great majority of Federal Reserve directors."
(Source: ibid, page 56, underline, author's emphasis).

Here are the conflicts, interrelationships and interests as Congress saw them. The Fed is entangled with rich owners who do not serve the American public's interests---these people only serve their own.

Chart 2-A

District Two

FEDERAL RESERVE BANK OF NEW YORK
Class A Directors

DAVID ROCKEFELLER	STUART MC CARTY	HARRY J. TAW
Chase Manhattan Corporation, Chairman , (Holding company for nine banks, including Chase Manhattan Bank, N.A.) $37.8 billion/assets, Holding Company Rank: 2	First-City National Bank of Binghamton, N.Y., President, $231 million. Rank: 395.	-First National Bank of Cortland, N. Y., President, $53.5 million. Rank: 1,782.
-Chase Manhattan Bank, N.A., New York, New York, Chairman, $33.8 billion. Rank: 3.	-Lincoln Firstbanks, Inc., Dir. And Vice-President (bank holding company which owns above bank). $2.6 billion/assets; Holding Company Rank: 28	-Cortland County Development Corporation, Vice-President.
-Chase Manhattan Bank, (Switzerland), Director.	-Crowley Foods, Inc., Director.	-Independent Bankers Assoc. New York State, Director., 1975-1976.
-Chase International Investment Corporation, Chairman, (wholly- owned foreign financing subsidiary of the Chase Manhattan Bank, N.A.)	-Systems Manufacturing Company, Director.	-New York State Bankers Assoc. Treasurer and Member Board of Directors.
-Chase Manhattan Bank Foundation, Chairman. -Rockefeller Brothers Fund, Trustee, Vice-Chairman and Member of Executive Committee, Chairman, nominating Committee. - Rockefeller Family Fund, Trustee, member of Executive Committee.	-Security Mutual Life Insurance Company, Director.	-New York State Bankers Assoc. Member at Large, Council of Administration. 1969.
	-New York State Bankers Association, Member, Government Relations Committee, September, 1974- .	-Comptroller of the Currency's Regional Advisory Commission, Member, 1970-1971.
-Rockefeller Center, Inc., Director& Member, Finance Comm.	-Comptroller of the Currency's Regional Advisory Commission for the 2nd National Bank Region. Member, 1968-1969.	

49
Tabular Chart A

David Rockefeller Chairman of
the Board Chase Manhattan Corp

Chase Manhattan Corp.
Officer & Director Interlocks

Private Investment Co. for America	Allied Chemical Corporation (2)	American Express Co. (2)	AT&T	United Sates Steel Corp.
Firestone Tire & Rubber Company	General Motors	Hewlett-Packard	Pacific North-western Bell Co.	
Orion Multinational	Rockefeller Family & Associates	FMC Corporation	BeachviLine Ltd.	Richardson Merrill Inc
ASARCO, Inc. (2)	Chrysler Corp. (2)	Utah Int'l Inc.	Bveleth Expansion Company	Metropolitan Life Insurance Co
Southern Peru copper Corp.	Int'l Basic Economy Corp.	Exxon Corporation	Fidelity Union Bancorporation	Private Investment Co
Industrial Miners Mexico S.A.	Selected Risk Investment	International Nickel/ Canada	Cypress Woods Corporation	May Department
Continental Co.	R. H. Macy & Co.	Equitable Life Assurance Soc.	International Minerals &	Norton-Simon Inc.
Honeywell, Inc.	Selected Risk Investment & Co.	Federated Capital Corporation	Burlington Industries	Sperry Rand Corporation
Northwest Airlines, Inc.	Omega Fund, Inc.	Federated Dept. Stores	Wachovia Corporation	Stone-Webster Inc.
Northwestern Bell Telephone Co.	Squibb Corporation	General Electric	Jefferson Pilot Corporation	San Salvador Development Company
Minnesota Mining & Mfg. Co	Olin Corporation	American Petroleum Institute	Private Investment Co. for America	Standard Oil of Indiana
	Mutual Benefit Life Ins. Co. of New Jersey (2)	Scott Paper Co.	R. J. Reynolds Industries, Inc	
		American Petroleum Institute		

50
Tabular Chart B

William S. Sneath President,
Union Carbide Corporation

Chase Manhattan Corp.
Officer & Director Interlocks

Private Investment Co. for America	Canadian Pacific Steamships, Ltd.	ASARCO	Morgan Guaranty Trust Company	J. C. Penney
Firestone Tire & Rubber Company	Pacific Logging Co.	American Title Insurance Co.	J. P. Morgan Company	Great American Reserve Insurance Co.
Orion Multinational Services Ltd.	Marathon Realty Co., Inc.	Chrysler Corporation	Depository Trust Company	
ASARCO, Inc. (2)	Soo Line Railroad Co.	Continental Corporation	Metropolitan Life Insurance Company	
Southern Peru copper Corp.	Great Lake Paper Company	Continental Insurance Company	Canadian Pacific Investments, Ltd.	
Industrial Miners Mexico S.A.	Trans-Canada Pipe Lines, Ltd	Security Reinsurance Corp., Ltd	Canadian Pacific Securities, Ltd.	
Continental Co.	Canadian Marconi Co.	Putnam Trust	Chase Manhattan Cortp. (Member, International Advisory Board)	
Honeywell, Inc.	Canadian Fund, Inc.	Toronto Dominion Bank & Trust	The Royal Bank of Canada	
Northwest Airlines, Inc.	Great American Reserve Insurance Company	National Reinsurance Corporation	Sun Life Assurance Company of Canada	
Northwestern Bell Telephone Co.	Manufacturers Hanover Trust Co. (Former Chief Exec. Officer)	Chemical Bank (Member, East Side Advisory Board)	Canadian Investment Fund	
	American Century Mortgage Investors			

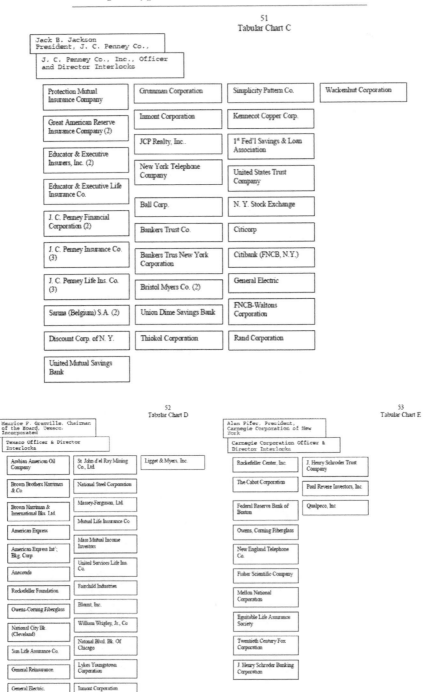

51 — Tabular Chart C

Jack B. Jackson
President, J. C. Penney Co.,

J. C. Penney Co., Inc., Officer and Director Interlocks

Protection Mutual Insurance Company	Grumman Corporation	Simplicity Pattern Co.	Wackenhut Corporation
Great American Reserve Insurance Company (2)	Inmont Corporation	Kennecot Copper Corp.	
Educator & Executive Insurers, Inc. (2)	JCP Realty, Inc..	1ˢᵗ Fed'l Savings & Loan Association	
Educator & Executive Life Insurance Co.	New York Telephone Company	United States Trust Company	
J. C. Penney Financial Corporation (2)	Ball Corp.	N. Y. Stock Exchange	
J. C. Penney Insurance Co. (3)	Bankers Trust Co.	Citicorp	
J. C. Penney Life Ins. Co. (3)	Bankers Trus New York Corporation	Citibank (FNCB, N.Y.)	
Sarma (Belgium) S.A. (2)	Bristol Myers Co. (2)	General Electric	
Discount Corp. of N. Y.	Union Dime Savings Bank	FNCB-Waltons Corporation	
United Mutual Savings Bank	Thiokol Corporation	Rand Corporation	

52 — Tabular Chart D

Maurice F. Granville, Chairman of the Board, Texaco, Incorporated

Texaco Officer & Director Interlocks

Arabian American Oil Company	St. John d'el Rey Mining Co., Ltd	Ligget & Myers, Inc.
Brown Brothers Harriman & Co	National Steel Corporation	
Brown Harriman & International Bks. Ltd.	Massey-Ferguson, Ltd.	
American Express	Mutual Life Insurance Co.	
American Express Int'l; Bkg. Corp	Mass Mutual Income Investors	
Anaconda	United Services Life Ins. Co.	
Rockefeller Foundation	Fairchild Industries	
Owens-Corning Fiberglass	Blount, Inc.	
National City Bk. (Cleveland)	William Wrigley, Jr., Co	
Sun Life Assurance Co.	National Blvd. Bk. Of Chicago	
General Reinsurance.	Lykes Youngstown Corporation	
General Electric.	Inmont Corporation	

53 — Tabular Chart E

Alan Pifer, President, Carnegie Corporation of New York

Carnegie Corporation Officer & Director Interlocks

Rockefeller Center, Inc.	J. Henry Schroder Trust Company
The Cabot Corporation	Paul Revere Investors, Inc.
Federal Reserve Bank of Boston	Qualpeco, Inc
Owens, Corning Fiberglass	
New England Telephone Co.	
Fisher Scientific Company	
Mellon National Corporation	
Equitable Life Assurance Society	
Twentieth Century Fox Corporation	
J. Henry Schroder Banking Corporation	

54
Tabular Chart F

Robert H. Knight, Partner,
Shearman & Sterling,
Attorneys, N.Y.C.

Law Firm represents:

The First National City
Corporation, N.Y.

The Bank of Nova Scotia
Trust Company of New York

The Canadian Bank of
Commerce Trust Co. (N.Y.)

The Fuji Bank and Trust
Company, N.Y.C.

55
Tabular Chart G

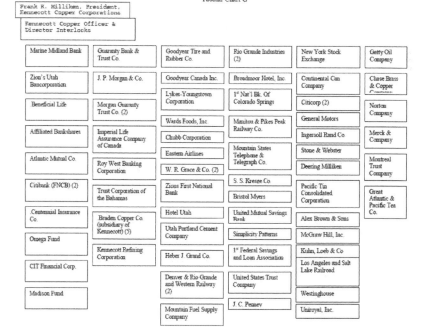

Frank R. Milliken, President,
Kennecott Copper Corporation

Kennecott Copper Officer &
Director Interlocks

Marine Midland Bank	Guaranty Bank & Trust Co.	Goodyear Tire and Rubber Co.	Rio Grande Industries (2)	New York Stock Exchange	Getty Oil Company
Zion's Utah Bancorporation	J. P. Morgan & Co.	Goodyear Canada Inc.	Broadmoor Hotel, Inc.	Continental Can Company	Chase Brass & Copper Company
Beneficial Life	Morgan Guaranty Trust Co. (2)	Lykes-Youngstown Corporation	1ˢᵗ Nat'l Bk. Of Colorado Springs	Citicorp (2)	Norton Company
Affiliated Bankshares	Imperial Life Assurance Company of Canada	Wards Foods, Inc.	Manitou & Pikes Peak Railway Co.	General Motors	Merck & Company
Atlantic Mutual Co.	Roy West Banking Corporation	Chubb Corporation	Mountain States Telephone & Telegraph Co.	Ingersoll Rand Co	Montreal Trust Company
Citibank (FNCB) (2)	Trust Corporation of the Bahamas	Eastern Airlines		Stone & Webster	
		W. R. Grace & Co. (2)		Deering Milliken	
Centennial Insurance Co.	Braden Copper Co. (subsidiary of Kennecott) (5)	Zions First National Bank	S. S. Kresge Co	Pacific Tin Consolidated Corporation	Great Atlantic & Pacific Tea Co.
		Hotel Utah	Bristol Myers		
Omega Fund	Kennecott Refining Corporation	Utah Portland Cement Company	United Mutual Savings Bank	Alex Brown & Sons	
CIT Financial Corp.		Heber J. Grand Co.	Simplicity Patterns	McGraw Hill, Inc.	
		Denver & Rio Grande and Western Railway (2)	1ˢᵗ Federal Savings and Loan Association	Kuhn, Loeb & Co	
Madison Fund			United States Trust Company	Los Angeles and Salt Lake Railroad	
		Mountain Fuel Supply Company	J. C. Penney	Westinghouse	
				Uniroyal, Inc.	

(Source for the preceeding charts, ibid, pages 9, 49-55)

"A 1975 study of the expense vouchers of Federal Reserve district banks revealed relatively heavy expenditures for entertainment, dinners and other functions, including joint meetings between the Federal Reserve district banks and the commercial bankers associations. The same expense reports contain a substantial number of outlays for dues and fees to various private organizations—at least some of which apparently fall within the 'public relations' area.[7] At the national level, some of the activities of the Federal Reserve directors are masked behind their corporate shields, and it is often difficult to distinguish the lobbying generated by the Federal Reserve banks from that of the corporate-banking lobby.

Throughout 1975, directors of Federal Reserve district banks <u>flooded the Congress with letters urging the defeat of the audit legislation.</u> For example, Malcolm T. Stamper told the Congress he was opposing the legislation 'in my capacity as president of the Boeing Company and as Chairman of the Seattle Federal Reserve' branch. Since that time Mr. Stamper has been promoted. He is now a class B director at the San Francisco Federal Reserve Bank.

Crown Zellerbach was another major corporation which lobbied against the audit bill. Its president—Charles Dahl—is another Class B director on the Federal Reserve Bank in San Francisco.

Similar letters opposing the audit bill came from Dresser Industries, an energy industry manufacturing conglomerate, whose chairman was a Class C director of the Federal Reserve District Bank of Dallas.

This was the pattern across the country, with the Federal Reserve calling on its corporate-banking directors to lead the lobbying campaign. In some cases, former directors were enlisted in the battle. At least one of these former directors—from the Federal Reserve branch in El Paso, TX— informed the Banking Committee of attempts by the president of the Federal Reserve Bank of Dallas to have him join the letter-writing campaign.

This type of lobbying activity is not limited to the audit proposals, but is available to the Federal Reserve on a wide range of banking, regulatory and legislative issues. In addition, these boards of prestigious businessmen serve as an on-going public relations front for the entire System...."

…While Corporate America has wide representation—through director interlocks—with all twelve banks in the Federal Reserve System, analysis of each district bank and cross-checking one district bank with the others reveals not only the narrow pool of talent but the "club" nature of the system.

This "club" approach leads the Federal Reserve to consistently dip into the same pools—the same companies, the same universities, the same bank holding companies—to fill directorships. This is particularly true in connection with those positions where the Board of Governors and/or the distinct banks have the right of appointment—the Class C directorships on the district boards and the various branch director positions:"

7 *"The Federal Reserve System: Accountability or Waste"*, Staff Report of the Subcommittee on Domestic Monetary Policy. Committee on Banking, Currency and Housing. U.S. House of Representatives. 94th Congress. 1st Session. July, 1975, 41 Pages.

(Source: "Federal Reserve Directors: A Study of Corporate and Banking Influence, Staff Report for the Committee on Banking, Currency and Housing," House of Representatives, 94th Congress, Second Session, August 1976, page 56-57, 62, Henry S. Reuss, Chairman, author's emphasis underlined, as retrieved from http://adabyron.net/FederalReserveDirectors.pdf).

The Federal Reserve System of the United States is hopelessly conflicted and needs to be dissolved. The Congress needs to take back the authority to control the United States' money supply and monetary policy. This is the only solution which will help save the country from a continuing explosion in the number of poor people and an overall reduction in the standard of living for the vast majority of Americans.

It is only logical these travesties would happen to the masses when an elite group is literally siphoning off trillions and trillions of dollars from taxpayer's pockets---forcing them to pay more taxes and live with higher inflation costs to pay for the greed, avarice and malevolent intentions of the Federal Reserve, the banks and the elite.

Rampant Greed and Theft Means Doom

Ultimately, these gross conflicts of interest and resulting rampant greed and apparent theft will prove to be the doom of the Western financial system. When it fails, the entire fractional banking system, based upon usury and control of monetary policy by a select handful of private citizens, will be thrown in our faces for ages to come.

We'll first hear about it from faithful Muslims (who forbid the paying of interest on any loans, or transactions) and many millions of Catholics will wonder why the Church changed its view on usury. The church knew of the admonition God gave the Israelites in Deuteronomy 15, where God prophesied the Israelites would lend to many nations. The founders of the Catholic Church saw this as a grave threat to the faith and didn't want to have the people enslaved by money lenders---whether they were Jewish, Catholic, Protestant, or otherwise. The reversal of the position of the Catholic Church undoubtedly contributed to the system of usury with outrageously high interest rates being used today, as practiced in modern-day banking activities on a regular basis. Anyone with a credit card statement knows this.

Today, these very same usurious bankers and bank employees are accepted and embraced by churches---in both the Catholic and Protestant faiths, while Muslims have developed clever ways to charge fees and payments in lieu of interest. As we see and realize, the greed of men has wandered into the pulpit and into religions, worldwide.

Usury, at the Heart of the Problem

The system which God admonishes against is a system which builds too much debt and leverage. He knows this can cause a man, a woman, or an entire society to become enslaved to a master---OTHER THAN GOD. Usury and debt are things everyone knows are bad. Together, they create social evil. They take time away from families and take time away from worshipping God. God wanted to set men and women FREE and created this earth to be our bread basket. With a little work, we could feed, clothe and house our families--inexpensively. He did not want His people to become debt slaves. Here are the words of wisdom from the Jews out of the book of Deuteronomy:

> ### The Year for Canceling Debts
>
> "¹At the end of every seven years you must cancel debts. ²This is how it is to be done: Every creditor shall cancel any loan they have made to a fellow Israelite. They shall not require payment from anyone among their own people, because the

Lord's time for canceling debts has been proclaimed. ³You may require payment from a foreigner, but you must cancel any debt your fellow Israelite owes you. ⁴However, there need be no poor people among you, for in the land the Lord your God is giving you to possess as your inheritance, he will richly bless you, ⁵if only you fully obey the Lord your God and are careful to follow all these commands I am giving you today. ⁶For the Lord your God will bless you as he has promised, and you will lend to many nations but will borrow from none. You will rule over many nations but none will rule over you.

⁷If anyone is poor among your fellow Israelites in any of the towns of the land the Lord your God is giving you, do not be hardhearted or tightfisted toward them. ⁸Rather, be openhanded and freely lend them whatever they need. ⁹Be careful not to harbor this wicked thought: "The seventh year, the year for canceling debts, is near," so that you do not show ill will toward the needy among your fellow Israelites and give them nothing. They may then appeal to the Lord against you, and you will be found guilty of sin. ¹⁰Give generously to them and do so without a grudging heart; then because of this the Lord your God will bless you in all your work and in everything you put your hand to. ¹¹There will always be poor people in the land. Therefore I command you to be openhanded toward your fellow Israelites who are poor and needy in your land." (Source: The Bible, Deuteronomy 15: 1-11 New International Version).

As a country, our usury laws were originally designed to protect consumers from the unscrupulous, high interest rates the banks charge today. These laws were largely gutted over the last thirty years through a constant corruption of the politicians who approved legislation changing the law in favor of the banks. Even the bankruptcy laws have been gutted to not allow relief when people get into trouble. Obviously, the spirit of Deuteronomy does not exist in America because, otherwise, the banks would be "forgiving the debt" after seven years---a Godly principle.

Instead, what has occurred is the banks and the elite PAID OFF our Congressmen and Senators to eliminate traditional usury laws and thereby allowed the banks to charge EXCRUCIATINGLY high interest rates. This really means most Americans and Europeans have already paid off their debts to the banking pirates under any kind of rational usury rate system, in place historically, prior to those old laws being swept away by corrupt politicians.

Allow Our Historic Interest Payments be Applied to Principal
This is an important fact which goes to the heart of reform. All people should have their historic interest payments credited toward a direct reduction in the principal they owe the banks---on ANY LOAN. If needed, people could pay the banks a 1% fee <u>over their cost at the Fed window</u> (which has hovered near 0% for five years and only a few percent going back to 2000, after the NASDAQ and stock market crash. This is also when the real estate bubble began, caused by Alan Greenspan's artificially low interest rates at the Fed window).

Just like Julius Caesar, *we need a law allowing all Americans to apply their past interest payments against the principal owed* (see Chapter 9, "What To Do Now," subsection, "Specific Plan for Countries Already Ruined by Bankers," under the topic of "Julius Caesar"). This will go a long way to aiding the 99% who have been abused and used by the banks and the elite.

This, along with another law forcing the banks to repatriate the homes stolen from millions of Americans, will help restore moral and civil order---which will be OUT OF CONTROL during D'Apocalypse™.

When the derivatives roof comes crashing down, it might just be the prelude to what this book believes will be the true Apocalypse, as promised from God above. As we know all too well, no war has ever been fought unless there was an underlying economic reason for it---even in the Middle East. Whenever you have less than 1% of the people controlling all the wealth, unrest is inevitable, even if they claim it is about "religion."

God works in mysterious ways. If one looks at the gigantic, derivative's time bomb, one can see where literally, overnight, He could send a wakeup call and remind mankind greed is NOT good and is not a preferred quality for entering heaven!

Derivatives...the Destroyer of all Destroyers
The morning the news hits and the derivatives market has blown up, <u>entire nations may be destroyed, financially speaking</u>. Plagues have come in all types and kinds throughout human history, but the derivatives plague will be the destroyer of all destroyers because it has the destructive power

to globally reach every single unprepared household on earth in the civilized world.

Unlike previous bubbles and "manias," whether it was the Tulip Bubble in Holland, the NASDAQ bubble in the United States, or whether it was the global real estate bubble, this time there will be no way to print enough money or lower interest rates enough, to cover the failed bets related to a derivatives collapse. The entire system's confidence will be destroyed and will lead to the collapse of many nations.

It is through such means God works to sort out the good from the bad. He also uses these opportunities to expose evil doers and ultimately, He removes them---reminding everyone who is in charge. This is the moment when public scrutiny will have a chance to make some real changes in how the bankers and elite are controlling everything.

With successful scrutiny and action, there is a slight chance we can save the system. Without change, the bankers will rule the day and use their debt hold over governments, worldwide, to expand their control over monetary policy and the money supply, as discussed.

> In the meantime, we are heading into an enormous storm. All the elements are there to kick start not only an economic Armageddon, but the Apocalypse predicted in the Book of Revelation, as any nation which cannot receive its capital from the West is going to be beyond angry. This is how major wars begin!

Do not, under any circumstances, listen to the hogwash on television from the talking heads when they pay reverence to the Fed. This writer recalls, vividly, at the height of the credit and mortgage crisis when the Fed was secretly buying and supporting the stock market, a famous talking head nearly shouting on TV: "We have the greatest Federal Reserve System in the WORLD!" (Note: this quote is from the author's memory and came from a prominent broadcaster of a major financial TV channel during the credit crisis when Assflation™ reflation of the markets took place through the now known nearly $30 Trillion in secret bailouts). The broadcasters, with a few very prominent exceptions, know not what they are talking about!

To be fair, there are also many highly intelligent people who don't believe there is any kind of conspiracy related to the Federal Reserve, the banks and the elite behind them. With respect to these people, this book agrees

COMPLETELY---there is NO conspiracy because what is being reported here in this book and The Federal Reserve Trilogy are FACTS!

The only possible wiggle room is there has NOT BEEN a FULL-BLOWN, UNRESTRICTED audit of the Federal Reserve using "mark-to-market" accounting and other generally accepted accounting principles every other firm in America must adhere to and utilize to report their financial statements (a must read in this area is in The $30 Trillion Heist, Volume II, Follow The Money! Chapter 11, "The Crystal Ball and the Acquisition of Giants" in its subsection, "The Continuing Sale of Toxic Securities to the Public—Even After They Were Caught!").

Each and every year of the Fed's existence needs to be audited, in each and every area of its operations, as well as its physical and virtual work spaces, each warehouse, every storage facility and every on- and off-balance sheet asset and asset vehicle it has created, used and/or otherwise disposed of.

Until this kind of independent and thorough audit is accomplished, we must assume the Fed has many, many secrets buried in off-balance vehicles with some very ugly surprises in store for the American consumer and the American Republic. All of this may get discovered after the towering inferno of the derivatives tower falls to the ground and the country is earnestly and finally, seeking answers.

This battle will be brought to the bankers' and elites' front door and the only question is will they have the political capital left to stay in power when the Doomsday Cycle begins!

The realization and real reason the banks, the elite and the members of the Federal Reserve could sit back and allow the gigantic and monstrous tower of derivatives to form, which permits the D'Apocalypse™ to even happen to begin with, was made clear in a sudden vision of authorship:

When these people were children, they MUST have been AVID readers of MAD MAGAZINE and students of Alfred E. Neumann, himself, because they think exactly the same way he thought, over 50 years ago!!

"What, Me Worry?"

Alfred E. Neuman
Mad Magazine
Public Domain Image.

How can a Federal Reserve System be trusted when they don't even show dividend distributions on their published income statements to the member banks, anymore? You have to find them buried in statistical data!

The answer is: *YOU CANNOT TRUST IT.*

(See Chapter 12 of The $30 Trillion Heist, Volume II, Follow The Money! and its subsection, "Honesty and Integrity of the Federal Reserve," "$1.6 BILLION 2012 DIVIDEND PAYMENT HIDDEN IN OBSCURE STATISTICS TABLE!").

If you have ears to hear, then listen. If you have eyes to see, then read---

DISASTER AWAITS....IF YOU ARE NOT PREPARED!

Chapter 5
No Risk Control—Say Goodbye to Your Assets on Deposit!

The existing language for banking and securities accounts in the U.S. and the European Union allows bankers to use "rehypothecation" in times of trouble to rob owners of ordinary bank and securities accounts. This can happen EVEN IF most of these unfortunate account holders made no "bets" in markets, whatsoever, and just wanted a "safe" depository for their capital. Customer agreements for new bank and/or securities accounts in most cases allow for rehypothecation, with these terms slipped into the contract, without the customer having a clue as to what can happen to their money if things go wrong. The banks know the regulators will do nothing to force a more open and clear-cut warning to account holders of the gigantic risk they are taking when they place their capital on deposit with one of these institutions.

Even the disclosures by the OCC for market risk on derivatives take only five short paragraphs. This is astonishing, given the fact the U.S. banks' derivatives positions are 15 times the size of the U.S. GDP.

"Banks control market risk in trading operations primarily by establishing limits against potential losses. Value-at-Risk (VaR) is a statistical measure that banks use to quantify the maximum expected loss, over a specified horizon and at a certain confidence level, in normal markets. It is important to emphasize that VaR is not the maximum potential loss; it provides a loss estimate at a specified confidence level...... Because of the unusually high market volatility and large write-downs in Collateralized Debt Obligations (CDOs) during the financial crisis, as well as poor market liquidity, a number of banks experienced back-test exceptions and therefore an increase in their capital multiplier.

Currently, however, none of the top 4 trading banks are required to hold additional capital for market risk based due to back-test exceptions."

(Source: OCC's Quarterly Report on Bank Trading and Derivatives Activities Third Quarter 2013, page 10, by Comptroller of the Currency, Administrator of National Banks, as retrieved from http://www.occ.gov/topics/capital-markets/financial-markets/trading/derivatives/dq313.pdf). Italics, bold author emphasis.

96% of Derivatives Traded in SECRET!

Any grade-schooler can see the OCC has completely IGNORED some of the greatest risks associated with derivatives. Most spectacularly, they do not address the primary issues of MASSIVE LEVERAGE, COUNTER-PARTY RISK AND TRANSPARENCY. OVER 96% OF DERIVATIVES TRADES ARE TRANSACTED IN **SECRET** (see Chapter 2, subsection, "Derivatives---$716 Trillion Unregulated Marketplace").

Most derivatives are not transacted on any exchange. If they were, market forces could create a natural guardian ensuring fair pricing and market corrections when values change. This would happen no matter if it meant prices were going up, or down. Even with the advent of Dodd-Frank legislation, where exchanges are supposed to be set up, there are many loopholes allowing the firms to avoid the transparency a truly free, exchange-traded market would provide.

It is clear Wall Street, the banks and the Federal Reserve System and nearly every single participant in this market, have learned NOTHING from the lessons they received from Long Term Capital Management (where a very small group of individuals nearly brought down Wall Street by using "back testing" and computer "models" to "prove" they were within acceptable confidence levels!—see Chapter 2, in this book, as well as The $30 Trillion Heist Volume II, Follow The Money!, in both its Chapter 6 "Assflation™ and VaR—it's Déjà vu, All Over Again!," and its Chapter 11 "The Crystal Ball and the Acquisition of Giants," subsection, "Bear Stearns"). They also have short memories when it comes to remembering traumatic market events and near-death experiences like the bubbles which burst in the NASDAQ and equity markets in 2000, as well as the credit and mortgage crisis, which started in 2007.

The greatest problem in the derivatives market lies in the spectacular leveraging which is used to generate irresistible profit figures across the industry. The sheer magnitude of the leveraging, globally **OVER 40 TIMES** the United States' entire Gross Domestic Product (U.S. GDP was $16 TRILLION in 2013), is the canary in the coal mine for the Western economies and our Western financial system.

When Will the Bubble Burst?

The only question is, when will this bubble burst?

This market will not blow up until the current administration is going into the fall <u>prior</u> to the next election cycle (e.g., **September/October/November 2015**)—this period will likely be marked by the beginnings of chaos, which will only grow worse through 2019.

This several-month period will witness an anxious administration attempt to brow beat the Fed into massive, additional rounds of quantitative easing prior to the Presidential election in 2016. If the Fed, the banks and elite are satisfied with the deal they strike with the Democratic Party's candidate for President, they shall hold the market up until the election in 2016. If not, they will tank the market and begin D'Apocalypse™ right then and there.

Either way, however and regardless, D'Apocalypse™ shall begin **no later than directly after the elections in November 2016.**

For the record, D'Apocalypse™ Now! expects the collapse to occur the year earlier, very likely in September of 2015, or October 2015. The market will lose confidence because of a myriad of factors and crash of its own weight. Interest rates should be soaring by then, causing severe economic turmoil and serious problems in the derivatives market.

Because of the sheer instability of the system and the towering structure of derivatives in place, everyone should be out of the markets by May 31, 2015.....and not a day later (see Chapter 9, "What To Do Now"!).

IF events change this thinking between now and then, which is certainly a possibility given the fact we are dealing with a large number of unknown variables, especially and including the decisions of the powers that be over the next year and a half, the author will publish an update.

The political and banking pressure from the member banks will be over-the-top on the Fed to keep printing money. If it becomes clear the next election cycle will see some major changes (at both the

CONGRESSIONAL and PRESIDENTIAL levels), the printing will stop and the markets will experience a major crush with severe consequences, as the outgoing party will do everything in its power to make things tough on the next administration---even if it is Hillary Clinton!

This will become crystal clear in the summer of 2015. The pollsters will be releasing findings of the presidential race and the market won't react until it "knows" which way the wind is blowing, as it gets closer to elections. However, the reality is the elections have nothing to do with much of anything, because the bankers are planning on this collapse to enable their consolidation of power over weakened governments, worldwide.

Perhaps the most interesting aspect of D'Apocalypse™ is IF people are HOLDING their own assets (e.g. stock certificates, bonds, precious metals, real-estate deeds, etc.), over time, their holdings will go UP in value. This is because the elite and bankers will likely win this round and ultimately inflate, enormously, the system with new capital (or new capital system which effectively devalues the old currencies). These actions, as discussed at length in The Federal Reserve Trilogy, will set off another planned escalation of the preferred assets of the elite and another massive round of Assflation™ in the process.

This asset-targeted inflation will once again be focused on the elite's assets of preference. In the run-up to D'Apocalypse™, and after a period of turmoil from the planned crush of markets and mayhem on the streets, these preferred assets include the following sectors: corporate (e.g., stocks and direct transactions with strong corporations), commercially viable real estate, agriculture of all types, precious metals, natural resources and high-end asset arenas.

These are primary areas of beneficial interest to the elite and will be a smart place to put your capital to work to protect yourself in the years ahead, using the timing suggestions in these pages. At the depths of the trough of D'Apocalypse™, you should be acquiring as many assets as you can---unloading at the top before the firestorm of D'Apocalypse™ reigns down on mankind---and finding a safe haven to protect your assets from risky banks prior to the cataclysm which is going to befall us.

By viewing the pieces on this chess board in this way, you can see how the components fit together, providing the bankers their next chance to cause yet another crisis and steal even more of the national treasuries from multiple governments and companies, around the world. While executing this plan, they will consolidate their grip and control over the global monetary system.

Many may read the foregoing and think, "Wouldn't they try and *prevent* the massive drop which would happen under such circumstances?" What these readers do not realize is the Federal Reserve System and member banks, in collaboration with other central banks around the world, **have purposely engineered this activity of swift contraction and then massive round of money printing and capital change to inflate the assets they fraudulently will obtain during the duress of D'Apocalypse™.**

Just like the mortgage crisis, it will be "Déjà vu, all over again," BUT EVEN BIGGER!

Warning to Foreign Governments
Any government with assets comingled at any of the world's central banks, or their associated members, are going to be in for a boat-load of problems in the coming years. Assets of all kinds will disappear into the pockets of the elite owners and the bonds they own will be repaid before anyone else---including a government.

Some governments understand what is happening. Venezuela and Germany, for example, know what they are doing, as they repatriated their gold reserves out of London and New York, back into their own vaults at home.

Germany Repatriating Gold From NY, Paris 'In Case Of A Currency Crisis'
"Germany's central bank announced Wednesday it will repatriate gold reserves held at the New York Fed and the Banque de France in order to have 'the ability to exchange gold for foreign currency [...] within a short space of time.'" (Source: Forbes Magazine, January 6, 2013, as retrieved from http://www.forbes.com/sites/afontevecchia/2013/01/16/germany-repatriating-gold-from-ny-paris-in-case-of-a-currency-crisis/).

Warning to Member Banks
Every single member of the cabal which originated the Federal Reserve and the Bank of England, along with their modern-day banking leaders and G14 members, are people who most would consider to be "brilliant." During D'Apocalypse™, some of these "brilliant" people will have become mesmerized by their own egos and belief systems and WILL be caught off

guard. This time, THEY WILL also be slaughtered in the financial markets by their own greed.

This is what caused the downfall of Bear Stearns, Lehman Brothers, AIG, etc. G14 members, be aware, the elite will eat their own kind!

Secret Bailouts Worked Last Time For Most Banks; Won't They Work During D'Apocalypse™?
The answer to this question and the reason why many member banks will be devoured is because a critical mass will be ignited in and throughout the derivatives system. Quite literally, D'Apocalypse™ will light a digital time bomb which destroys trillions of dollars of capital, overnight, making all those institutions which are unprepared, potential victims of the elites' master plan.

What does "critical mass," then, actually mean? The definition of a critical mass, in atomic-energy speak, certainly sheds some light on the use of this term. Both systems (i.e. atomic energy and derivatives) are highly complex and rely, critically, upon non-failure of the system:

Critical Mass
noun
1. *Term Used In Physics.*
2. The amount of a given fissionable material necessary to sustain a chain reaction at a constant rate.
(Source: Dictionary.com, as retrieved from http://dictionary.reference.com/browse /critical+mass?s=t).

Our scientists know how to create a critical mass using fission and have either destroyed things with this power, or have produced copious amounts of energy using it, all over the world. Obviously, the process can be used for good or evil, but no matter what, the process and reactions used to create the critical mass carry MASSIVE RISKS. We know what kinds of risks these are after the likes of Nagasaki, Hiroshima, Three-Mile Island, Chernobyl, Fukushima and God only knows how many reported and unreported radiation leaks and nuclear tests occurred during the last 75 years.

Now, from the Department of Energy we can see what, exactly, is "fissionable material:"

"Fissionable Material. A fissionable material is composed of nuclides for which fission with neutrons is possible. All fissile nuclides fall into this category. For fission to be possible, the change in binding energy plus the kinetic energy must equal or exceed the critical energy ($\Box$ BE + KE $\geq$ E$_{crit}$).

Uranium

235 fissions with thermal neutrons because the binding energy released by the absorption of a neutron is greater than the critical energy for fission; therefore uranium-235 is a fissile material. The binding energy released by uranium-238 absorbing a thermal neutron is less than the critical energy, so additional energy must be possessed by the neutron for fission to be possible. Consequently, uranium-238 is a fissionable material." (Source: *Atomic and Nuclear Physics DOE-HDBK-1019/1-93NUCLEAR FISSION*, page 51, U.S. Department of Energy, retrieved from http://www.hss.doe.gov/nuclearsafety/techstds/docs/handbook/h1019v1.pdf).

For fission to be possible, the change in binding energy plus the kinetic energy must equal or exceed the critical energy ($\Box$ BE + KE $\geq$ E$_{crit}$).

TABLE 4 Critical Energies Compared to Binding Energy of Last Neutron			
Target Nucleus	Critical Energy E$_{crit}$	Binding Energy of Last Neutron BE$_n$	BE$_n$ - E$_{crit}$
$^{232}_{90}$Th	7.5 MeV	5.4 MeV	-2.1 MeV
$^{238}_{92}$U	7.0 MeV	5.5 MeV	-1.5 MeV
$^{235}_{92}$U	6.5 MeV	6.8 MeV	+0.3 MeV
$^{233}_{92}$U	6.0 MeV	7.0 MeV	+1.0 MeV
$^{239}_{94}$Pu	5.0 MeV	6.6 MeV	+1.6 MeV

Since the laws of economically complex systems, like derivatives, ALSO rely on very logical, mathematical formulas for the system to operate in the first place, there is no argument these complex systems are subject to the laws of physics and math (i.e., with every action, there is a reaction!).

We all know what a functioning nuclear power plant is and everything works great, <u>under most circumstances</u>. There are even billion-dollar <u>safeguards</u> built-in to prevent meltdowns and reactor leaks. These plants even have REGULATORS inspecting the premises, night and day!

However, we also know these are extremely complex systems and when they are unstable and pushed too hard, they can and will create a catastrophic leak and in a worst-case scenario will melt down, potentially causing millions of deaths. **Inspectors, who are supposedly on duty, rarely know in advance a disaster is coming.**

Critical Mass Will Cause Chain Reaction in Derivatives' Marketplace

While the derivatives market is not a nuclear reactor, it is incredibly complex and prone, perhaps even more than a nuclear reactor, to human error. Derivatives also rely on technology to trade (e.g., massive computerized trading systems) and the most complex set of counter-party contracts on earth, each relying on the integrity of the other trading partner to fulfill his, or her, end of the bargain in a transaction. If events transpire which "overload" the system, or create a risk environment not foreseen by the computer models, massive failures WILL occur. This is because the events are outside of the modeling parameters the wizards of Wall Street created to trade, value and otherwise transact in the opaque, wild-west world of gambling on derivatives trading.

In the case of the coming derivatives debacle, it has been directly fed by the Federal Reserve through their over injection of energy (i.e., money, courtesy of the secret $30 Trillion heist and ongoing "QE" programs) into the system, ensuring the system is not in balance. We know this because injecting this amount of money, twice the size of the U.S. Gross Domestic Product is beyond question a destabilizing event, as time shall prove.

This **guarantees** a "critical mass" is reached where investors demand a much higher return for the risk they are taking to put capital to work. In the parlance of modern-day finance vs. nuclear energy, this is measured through interest rate movements---the cost of money, as well as the PRICE of assets (e.g., Assflation™).

With the Federal Reserve having primed the market's trading engine with the equivalent of 2 U.S. GDP's (e.g. $30 Trillion), interest rates and equity asset values will skyrocket into 2015. This, of course, is against a backdrop of enormous debt encumbrance by nearly all governments in the Western world. The governments will feel a tremendous "squeeze" because of the untenable interest payments they must make, along with the mushroom cloud of debt over their heads.

Ultimately, the markets WILL lose confidence in the ability of governments to PAY BACK the money they owe, and the capital will flee to safer ground, seeking better returns. This will create an out-of-control chain reaction which will bury the Western world's government spending plans---sending massive shockwaves through the system.

Like any good physics experiment, or math equation, the trading system will seek balance and a <u>return to an equality of relationships. It will also ensure the laws of nature are upheld.</u>

This will all happen while the "inspectors" of Wall Street (e.g. the regulators), the banks and the elite continue to sleep on the job and not do anything to prevent this disaster from happening!

The result of this catastrophe will be a complete economic collapse which the bankers will attempt to use as their opportunity to initiate another round of asset thefts (i.e., acquiring target companies for pennies on the dollar) and control of the monetary system. This should be relatively easy for them to pull off because governments will not be able to afford to finance their debts (i.e., interest rates will be high and the cost to cover the payments on debt and interest will prevent governments, states and municipalities from financing their debts). This means massive firings at the governmental level and enormous unemployment lines. People will be starving and will be beyond upset.

For the derivatives market, the largest portion of which transacts in and around interest rate movements, it means the artificially low interest rates implemented by the Federal Reserve, courtesy of Mr. Bernanke, Ms. Yellen and friends will rise, dramatically. This will create an explosion of losses across the derivatives, bond and equity markets (losses on bonds will be experienced first and then later for equities, as they are still being fueled by the Fed, the elite and the banks, along with capital pouring into the U.S. from international markets).

Derivatives will default when the Fed completely stops sending liquidity into the system and the banks shut down all lending and credit. This is done on purpose, as discussed. It also means the artificial practice of money injection and paying good money for bad money must also end, causing another tremendous change to and impact upon the system.

In a nuclear world, we have all witnessed the dramatic conclusions of systems out of whack. Whether they are from unexpected earthquakes, or intentional overload of energy to create uncontrolled reactions which result in massive explosions; the unexpected can and will happen when dealing with something tremendously powerful and incredibly complex and fragile.

The same dynamics apply to the massive, unregulated and out-of-control derivatives marketplace.

From a graphical perspective, the markets will experience this kind of general "big picture" wave pattern (see chapter 9 for more precise information):

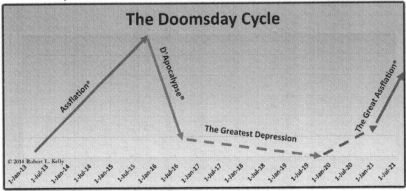

Please notice the above expected wave patterns have NOTHING to do with general economic employment, or the well-being of the nation. Assflation™ will occur in spite of HUGE unemployment for most people in the Western world. The above pattern merely looks at the actions of the elite to pump up assets aggressively, then cause a major collapse and crisis, which enables them to STEAL vulnerable assets during the collapse. Once their acquisition binge is complete, they will reflate the system and their preferred asset sectors, starting the cycle all over again! This is how they make money and take over treasured assets for pennies on the dollar.

Destructive Potential Power of Derivatives

How powerful is a $716 TRILLION UNREGULATED system holding and trading derivative securities OVER 40 TIMES the Gross Domestic Product of the United States and nearly 10 times the size of the world's GDP (e.g., approximately $71.8 Trillion in 2012, as reported by the CIA and about $74 Trillion as estimated by the IMF) WHEN THE SYSTEM ONLY HAS 2.5% IN ASSETS to use as collateral in backing up these transactions?

> **If the United States can project worldwide power and authority with an economy which is only 1/40th the size of the derivatives market, then the derivatives market, economically and powerfully, dwarfs the United States. We are talking about something demonically powerful here!**

And, remember---the numbers we are using ONLY include "notional" amounts (i.e., author's translation of bankers-speak definition of "notional" is: no one really knows how big it is!).

Many sources indicate the true size of the derivatives market may be as large as ONE QUADRILLION FIVE-HUNDRED TRILLION DOLLARS, WORLDWIDE!

G-U-L-P!!!

What is the scariest thing of all? No one really knows how big this market is. Every single OCC, U.S. Treasury, BIS, etc. document published ALWAYS refers to a "notional" amount of derivatives. The word, "notional" is pretty hilarious and probably took a room full of Ivy Leaguers to think it up, as far as its application to the derivatives market.

How most people were raised, when you have a "notion," you have a concept and most would just call it a "guess!"

Notion
[**noh**-sh*uh* n]
noun
1. a general understanding; vague or imperfect conception or idea of something:
a notion of how something should be done.
2. an opinion, view, or belief: *That's his notion, not mine.*
(Source: Dictionary.com, as retrieved from http://dictionary.reference.com/browse/notion?s=t).

As can be seen in the tables "Actual OCC Notional Derivatives Tables December 31, 2012," and from the 3rd Quarter of 2013 in this book's Chapter 2, "Derivatives---the Ticking Time Bomb!," the derivatives system is trading and betting in exactly the same manner which brought down Enron—remember them? Their leveraged trading and fraud destroyed an entire company and took down one of the most prestigious accounting firms on the planet (Arthur Andersen). Many of the executives involved went to jail. Over-leveraged trading ALWAYS fails, sooner or later.

If there is one lesson to take to heart in this book, this is the lesson. Over-leverage comes from the LOVE OF MONEY with the need to MAKE MORE MONEY in an unquieted zest to increase a person's lust for power, prestige and ego.

Unfortunately, we have failed to remember the warning our ancestors, for thousands of years, have told us driven from age-old warnings from <u>The Bible</u> about the love of money:

"The love of money is the root of all evil..."
(Source: <u>The Bible</u>, <u>1 Timothy 6:10</u>, King James Version).

Thomas Edison, one of the greatest inventors and pillars of American history, had a similar opinion of money, as can be seen from this excerpt from the New York Times on December 6, 1921.

" Gold is a relic of Julius Caesar and interest is an invention of Satan." Mr. Edison continued.. " Gold is intrinsically of less utility than most metals. The probable reason why it is retained as the basis of money is that it is easy to control. And it is the control of money that constitutes the money question. It is the control of money that is the root of all evil."

(Source: New York Times, December 6, 1921, "Ford Sees Wealth In Muscle Shoals...Edison Backs Him Up," as retrieved from http://query.nytimes.com/mem/ archive-free/pdf?res=9C04E0D7103EEE3ABC4E53DFB4 67838A639EDE).

WHEN the system of derivatives breaks down, which can literally happen overnight at any time during the next two years given its fragility and spectacular leverage, *the real reason for the breakdown will be the fact the "perfect" system created out of the love of money and the zest to maximize profits, will have reached a critical mass, causing an out-of-control, chain reaction, with explosive, global results.*

The weaknesses caused by the flagrant abuse of power, the pumping of money, astronomically high leverage and the accumulation of debt, worldwide, spells the death of the Western financial system as we know it. For the prepared, it will provide incredible opportunities to own assets and help other people during the crisis which will unfold before our very eyes.

Bankers Plan Controlled Demolition to Take Over Assets

The bankers' and the elite's master plan relies on their belief they can "control" any blow up which might occur in this market. In fact, just like the purposely implemented mortgage debacle they engineered, they will also cause the derivatives market to blow sky high!

D'Apocalypse™ will witness a banker-inflicted credit squeeze which tightens around the entire derivatives market, just like an Amazon Python wraps around its prey. It will create enormous pain and cause death to many corporations, with thousands of bankruptcies and takeovers—all available for pennies on the dollar.

> *"If the American people ever allow private banks to control the issue of their money, first by inflation and then by deflation, the banks and corporations that will grow up around them, will deprive the people of their property until their children will wake up homeless on the continent their fathers conquered."*
>
> **---Thomas Jefferson**
>
> Letter 1802 to Secretary of the Treasury, Albert Gallatin
>
> (Source: as retrieved from http://www.monticello.org/site/jefferson/private-banks-quotation)

The danger with their plan is JP Morgan Chase, Citigroup, Bank of America and Goldman Sachs (particularly) do not have the assets to back up their bets and neither does any government on earth. Many of the biggest banks in the G14 (see Chapter 2, "Derivatives---the Ticking Time Bomb!" subsection "4 Horsemen of the D'Apocalypse™ Control 93% of Derivatives Market") will very likely miscalculate their liability exposure and instead of being the hunter, they will become the "hunted," exactly like what happened to Bear Stearns and Lehman Brothers.

All it will take is one major counter-party transaction to go wrong and the entire structure will come down---leaving every single shareholder and account holder at risk of losing EVERYTHING THEY OWN. The bankers with the political clout (i.e., the ones who made the most payoffs), will likely be saved; however, there won't be enough money for everyone and government, if it even survives, will have to create a new currency, or currency system, in all probability. People will be robbed blind, and when they figure out the conversion rates into the new currency stole the majority of their wealth, they will be quite upset.

Citizens will become nasty mean!

You will no doubt remember these "really smart guys"--- the 4 Horsemen of the D'Apocalypse™, are trading in thousands:1 ratios on their derivatives bets, depending on which piece of collateral you want to use to measure by—e.g., cash, revenues, assets, or income.

Too Big to Fail Banks, Have Indeed Become the Too Big to Bail, Banks

Not even the United States Government will have the money to bail out this travesty. We will experience a stampede for market exits like no other before it in history because the system is cantilever leveraged---when you pull one key component out, or it fails, the entire house of cards will fall down. It is just too fragile and over-extended to survive.

The smart money is doing everything it can RIGHT NOW to protect itself. Please read Chapter 9, "What To Do Now." Those who read this book and forecast and prepare for these coming events will conquer them, or be far better prepared to deal with them than you are now.

Many of you will be in a position to help the 99%, as they will surely need it!

Ultimately, the people will seek justice—and the odds favor blood justice. Americans will realize most of the money in the system has already been hijacked offshore, or secretly tucked away by the wealthy. The common man will be left to starve and suffer. The only people left standing will be the preppers and the wealthy---those who have stored, or otherwise accumulated, assets they know have always kept their value over time.

This will work great for these 1%'rs, but what, pray tell, will happen to the common man in Detroit, Philadelphia, LA, New York, London, Paris and Tokyo, or nearly any place else in the world?

Chapter 6
Fractional Reserve Banking-Just the Tip of the Iceberg

Note: Reprinted from Volume I, The $30 Trillion Heist---Scene Of The Crime? Chapter 8, for those who have not read it.

Typically at the top of a credit bubble, or what the bankers like to call a "business cycle," is when banks PURPOSELY make credit easily available for nearly EVERYONE. When the time is right and the masses are in debt, the banks simply tighten the supply of credit, causing the bubble to burst, which forces the business cycle to go into a tail spin. With each "cycle" the bankers and wealthy elite know a certain percentage of the population will only be able to helplessly watch as the bank repossesses their property---stealing their hard-earned equity and assets away for pennies on the dollar.

"Steal" is harsh terminology, the author is aware of this; however, the "bubbles" and "cycles" are PURPOSELY created to take over coveted assets---AFTER other parties have invested significant amounts of capital in improving or creating the assets, during the upswing in the business cycle.

The bankers' ability to loosen and tighten the money supply can be accomplished in many ways, but among the simplest tools the bankers have to accomplish this goal is one they have used for centuries. It is the ability to use other people's money to make loans---and then simply not renew the loans, thereby tightening the supply of credit.

Bankers have made a lot of money through this practice in what is called in today's "Harvardized" terminology, "fractional reserve banking." This system allows bankers to receive your deposits, creating a liability for the bank. With each dollar you give them for safe keeping, they can lend out **at least** ten more dollars to other people---thereby creating credits in the borrowers' checking accounts and voila "money" (but not legal tender) out of thin air. These credits are available to the borrowers to spend with whoever will accept the draft of their checks, or if the bank will allow them, to withdraw funds. Fractional reserve banking is completely permissible under current law in the United States and Western Europe, as well as most Western countries.

The system is well known and older people will probably realize it is what caused the run on Jimmy Stewart's bank in the movie, "It's A Wonderful Life" in 1946, which recounted the hardships in America during the Great Depression in the 1930s. The fractional reserve system works for the bank IF all the depositors have <u>confidence</u> in the bank and the depositors don't all show up at once demanding their money.

Fractional reserve banking traditionally has created mega-wealth for the banks and the elite because when a person makes a deposit, the bankers can effectively earn not just 4%, 5%, 6% or 12% (or more) by loaning the depositor's money out, but they really earn at least 40%, 50%, 60% or 120% (or more), by simultaneously loaning the exact same deposit out to ten other people, thereby leveraging the loanable funds available to the bank by a factor of TEN! This is a great earnings stream on money which doesn't even belong to the banks!!!

Source: Still from "It's A Wonderful Life," 1946, filmed, produced and directed by Frank Capra. Jimmy Stewart and Donna Reed pictured-- public domain image. Rko Pictures .

This power of fractional reserve banking is why the elite fight so hard to protect their interests in it. It is also why it is dangerous to write about.

Think about it, if you were a bank and somebody GAVE you money for FREE and you could lend out TEN TIMES THE AMOUNT. This means you wouldn't earn 3%, 4%, 5%, 10% or even 30% (like most credit cards charge, today!). Instead, with the power of fractional reserve banking, you would earn 30%, 40%, 50%, 100% and even up to 300% on the "deposit" which wasn't even yours to begin with.

Is it no wonder why the banking elite want to keep control of the system and ensure they have absolute, effective control over the Federal Reserve?

Banks Create Money Out of Thin Air
There are some very interesting accounting studies performed on the banks and how they actually book the debits and credits on loans and deposit transactions. The obvious potential conclusion is the banks may actually be committing fraud when they lend people money, as they are not giving people legal tender in exchange for the borrower's legal obligation to repay a loan. By making loans, literally created from the banks' liabilities, the validity of the original loan agreement is certainly put

into question. This is an entirely different discussion and outside the purpose of this book; however, it is another interesting example of how the bankers have tried to legitimize what would be called fraudulent activity if anyone else were to try it.

The COMMITTEE ON BANKING AND CURRENCY, chaired by Wright Patman, agrees with the author and states:

Do private banks issue money today?
"Yes. Although banks no longer have the right to issue bank notes, they can create money in the form of bank deposits when they lend money to businesses, or buy securities. *The important thing to remember is that when banks lend money they don't necessarily take it from anyone else to lend. Thus they 'create' it.*" (Source: COMMITTEE ON BANKING AND CURRENCY, HOUSE OF REPRESENTATIVES, SUBCOMITTEE ON DOMESTIC FINANCE, 88th Congress, 2nd Session, SEPTEMBER 21, 1964, by Wright Patman, Chairman, Chapter II, What Is Money?, 33.). Author's emphasis underlined, as retrieved from http://www.baldwinlivingtrust.com/pdfs/AllAboutMoney.pdf).

Fractional reserve banking, by itself, allows bankers to manipulate the supply of money and creates enormous wealth transfers in favor of the bankers and generally and ultimately creates economic turmoil for the general public. *Why did we adopt this system?*

It is an important question and interesting to know how this system was ever invented, in the first place.

The Goldsmiths—Invented Fractional Reserve Banking
Fractional reserve banking dates back to the era of the "goldsmiths" in medieval Europe (in the 1600s) when goldsmiths stored gold and silver in their vaults in exchange for a formal receipt, which was signed and sealed by the goldsmith where the property was stored. These receipts became popular as a currency because they weighed less than the actual gold and silver sitting in the goldsmith's vaults. One day, the goldsmiths realized they could make new receipts, with NO gold or silver backing them up, thereby committing fraud. They lent this new currency to other interested parties in exchange for the party's gold interest payments back to the goldsmiths. Thus, the goldsmiths collected specie (gold interest payments) payments in exchange for the issuance of pieces of paper they created without anything backing them up, eerily reminiscent of our current monetary system and the bank's fractional reserve banking system.

These men had discovered customers would leave their gold and silver in the vaults untouched—leaving the goldsmiths with plenty of deposits to handle any demands for gold or silver. Ultimately, the word got out and people were quite upset, ending the goldsmith's role as trusted keepers of wealth for society, but not before the goldsmiths had walked off with most of all the money and property over an approximate 100-year period of time!

This was the birthplace of the modern-day fractional banking system. (Source: ibid, page 41).

As uncovered by George Selgin, Professor of Economics at the Terry College of Business at the University of Georgia and published on March 30, 2010, he wrote of the goldsmiths:

"Old-fashioned merchants complained bitterly that a class of men, who, thirty years before, had confined themselves to their proper functions, and had made a fair profit by embossing silver bowls and chargers, by setting jewels for fine ladies, and by selling pistols and dollars to gentlemen setting out to the Continent, had become the treasurers, and were fast becoming the masters, of the whole City. These usurers, it was said, played at hazard with what had been earned by the industry and hoarded by the thrift of other men. If the dice turned up well, the knave who kept the cash became an alderman: if they turned up ill, the dupe who furnished the cash became a bankrupt." (Source: The History of England, from the Accession of James the Second v. 4, London: Longman, Brown, Green, and Longmans page 514, as retrieved from http://www.english.gsu.edu/~mbrown/Texts/Misc/Macaulay_Hist_England_JamesII.pdf, page 1068).

Professor Selgin found this beautiful quote from a book by Thomas Babbington Macaulay, published in 1855, titled, The History of England, from the Accession of James the Second v. 4.

Usury—It Used to Be Bad

The practice of lending out currency and gaining interest on it is commonly known as "usury." Historically, usury was and still is outlawed by the Muslims, and was once outlawed by the Catholic Church. It is also forbidden in the Old Testament and Hebrew scriptures. The Jews even taught the word of God said any fellow Israelite you lent money to, if it is not repaid within seven years, should be forgiven because God wants his people to live in prosperity---not under the yoke and chain of debt (Source: The Bible, Deuteronomy 15, King James Version).

> We know, as Christians, Jesus is the Messiah and God made a provision for all men to be saved through faith in Christ. This means we should also forgive those who have debts, thus allowing those debtors to live a life of prosperity and not a life of slavery caused by debt. This is Godly instruction, taken directly from God's instructions to the Jewish people and applies in principle exactly the same way to Christians.

It is interesting the world turned its back on the teachings of these age-old religions, particularly on a subject as important as money. As more of the evidence of wrong-doing in these pages accumulates, you will inevitably "feel" a certain sense of foreboding, or day of reckoning approaching, because based upon God's principles the system in place is clearly against His will.

By Complicating Terminology, the Fed Keeps its Secrets Hidden from Joe Six Pack

If you read Mr. Samuel Leavitt's work (Our Money Wars, as discussed in The $30 Trillion Heist---Scene Of The Crime?, Chapter 7, with some excellent excerpts from his work in The $30 Trillion Heist---Follow The Money! Volume II, Chapter 17, "History Repeats Itself"), you will discover our present-day bankers have merely "Harvardized" the same banking terminology which was used in the 1700s and 1800s.

This is a transparent and vain attempt by them to sound intelligent and beyond reproach, when mere mortals might dare question their integrity and actions. You can see them complicate their speech and answers to direct questions whether they are testifying in front of Congress, whether they are speaking to reporters or whether they are just peering into a camera for benefit of a TV set.

Every chance they get bankers attempt to confuse anyone and everyone possible, using complicated words and structures in an attempt to hide their true activities and intentions. The elite have gone to great lengths to cover their tracks, even creating ingenious, innovative organizational names to hide their ownership interests and operational activities from the public's eye.

By using opaque names like the "Federal Reserve System," without using the word "bank" in the title of the original "Federal Reserve Act" and inventing words and terminology like "CDOs," "GMOs," "Futures," "Notional," "Quantitative Easing," "TARP," "SWAPS," "RESERVE," etc., while architecting a plan to have the Federal Reserve be run by the private sector, the bankers and the elite have tried to ensure their great deception has been kept secret from the American public.

Once again, please read these important comments and answers to questions from the work done by the COMMITTEE ON BANKING AND CURRENCY, HOUSE OF REPRESENTATIVES, SUBCOMITTEE ON DOMESTIC FINANCE, 88th Congress, 2nd Session, SEPTEMBER 21, 1964, by Wright Patman, Chairman, Chapter III, How is Money Created? Chapter 1, Preface, 10-15 (as retrieved from http://www.baldwinlivingtrust.com/pdfs/AllAboutMoney.pdf author's emphasis underlined):

10. Who really directs Federal Reserve operations?
Day-to-day operations in each of the 12 regional Federal Reserve banks are supervised by nine directors—six of them selected directly by privately owned commercial banks. <u>The most important monetary decisions for the system as a whole are made by the Open Market Committee, which is composed of 12 members.</u>

11. Do private bank interests influence Federal Reserve policy?
Yes. Of the 12 members of the Open Market Committee—the Committee which actually controls credit policy—5 are presidents of regional banks. These presidents are elected by the individual regional banks' nine-man board of directors with its preponderance of private commercial bank representatives. Further, all 12 of the regional bank presidents participate in the Open Market Committee's discussions, though only 5 can vote. The "discussion" Open Market Committee, then, has 19 members—12 regional bank presidents and the 7 members of the Federal Reserve Board.

12. Does it matter what amount of money is supplied the economy?
Yes, indeed. The money supply helps determine the general level of interest rates paid for the use of money, employment, prices, and economic growth. Many economists believe the money supply is the most important determinant of these variables.

13. Who determines the money supply?
The Federal Open Market Committee of the Federal Reserve System.

14. Why are interest charges important?
For many reasons. First, interest plays a large part in the cost of living. All business firms borrow to conduct their operations—some more than others. These include firms at every stage of production. So interest is a charge which is added on at each link of the production chain. This is a cost which must eventually be paid by the consumer. If it is not paid by consumers, output cannot be sustained. Thus, interest rates also are a determining factor of the level of business activity. Additionally, interest rates influence production because interest rates influence the amount business spends for investment in plant and equipment—the third largest amount of spending for the country's annual output. (Interest has this effect because a part of the country's annual investment is financed by borrowing.)

15. Do interest rate changes and tight money have other effects?
Yes. Consider what happens when the Government is restricting money and credit. Firms find loans difficult to obtain and investment tumbles. Small business is especially hard hit because the larger firms tend to have their credit needs catered to first. Further, when investment falls, firms which produce machinery or build factories find their orders slumping and lay off workers while cutting their own orders for goods. The economy pays for high interest in income not earned and in output not produced.

Federal Reserve Banks Are Not Owned By the Government
To keep their control of the Federal Reserve System, bankers have continued to mislead the general public and Congress ever since the Fed's founding in 1913. Many idiots, even today on CNBC, falsely believe the Federal Reserve is owned by the U.S. Government.

This author can still recall one of the most famous talking heads, a financial news reporter, proclaiming, "We have the greatest Central Bank in the whole world!" when the markets miraculously rose after the bank's self-engineered credit crisis hit.

The rise occurred, of course, because the fix was in and the $30 Trillion heist was on, as the Federal Reserve began secretly exchanging nearly $30 Trillion in U.S. taxpayer- and U.S. Government-backed electronic credits (and other cash-equivalents) for the worthless toxic securities on the books of the banks and elite.

It is remarkable how blind and utterly stupid some of the talking heads on TV are. Yes, even as a Christian, it is tough to sit and listen to sheer idiocy and not decry it.

"Quantitative Easing"—the Great Misnomer

There are many, many examples of the Federal Reserve's subterfuge, but one of this book's favorite mind-benders is the use of the phrase, "Quantitative Easing," or "QE3." Instead of plainly telling the public the Federal Reserve is using taxpayer-backed money via Fed credits (and/or U.S. cash and U.S. Treasury securities) to purchase worthless mortgage securities from the banks and government securities at auction because no one else will, the Fed attempts to disguise its true actions by creating the mesmerizing phrase, "Quantitative Easing." This terminology is designed to mislead the public and make it *seem like* the Federal Reserve is trying to help the economy!

In reality, the Fed is just giving the banks and rich people free money, as the securities they have been bringing to the Fed, in exchange for U.S. taxpayer-backed cash, are worthless, or worth only a fraction of their face value. With respect to its purchase of U.S. Government securities---this is purely inflationary and is a direct tax on the consuming public! As anyone on food stamps and anyone of the TRULY UNEMPLOYED (estimated at over 100,000,000 strong, now) understand, these bankers have done nothing to help the economy. They only realize they can't buy food for their families because costs keep rising and there are no jobs.

All the Federal Reserve and the bankers are doing is enriching the select by putting trillions of dollars into the pocketbooks of the banks—and the pocketbooks of their handlers---the elite owners of the Federal Reserve Banks.

Each word, every pronouncement and every incantation made by this den of vipers is carefully crafted to deceive and disguise their ongoing abuse of a typical American's natural good nature and trusting manner. Mr. Bernanke was a pro at using eloquent terms to diffuse and confuse, as he apparently learned well from the master of gibberish in banker-speak, his predecessor, Alan Greenspan.

This is the man who put the pieces in place to accomplish the grand heist by conditioning the public of the galactically stupid notion the Fed can't see a bubble forming and can't do anything about it…ergo, according to the Fed, artificially keeping rates low and exchanging good U.S. paper for toxic, bad paper has nothing to do with a bubble, or any other economic problem on the horizon! This, of course, is complete rubbish.

The utter nonsense which came out of this man's mouth, whether in front of Congress, the Queen of England or the general public is nothing short of stunning. It was even more stunning when uneducated Congressmen sat and became mesmerized by his arrogant gibberish, while he, in conspiracy with the Federal Reserve owners and members, set in motion the housing bubble and credit crisis.

As history reveals, it was Mr. Greenspan who initiated the major bailout of Wall Street during the Long Term Capital Management crisis and the NASDAQ collapse in 2000. This was accomplished by what Wall Street called the "Greenspan Put" and his easy money policies. He kept rates artificially too low and spent monies supporting markets---all in violation of the true spirit and workings of capitalism and the original intent of the Federal Reserve Act. Easy Al created the housing bubble through cheap interest rates and gushing flow of easy money in his effort to distort and artificially inflate the collapsing equity markets.

The Results of Mr. Greenspan's work was the raw destruction of millions of family's' wealth around the world, millions and millions of foreclosed homes and a very, very long unemployment line for the masses.

A couple of things which did increase, however, under the guidance of Mr. Greenspan and Mr. Bernanke were the number of people on food stamps. This has become a real gusher for their legacy, as the food stamp population has grown to approximately 50 million people in the United States and real unemployment numbers are above great depression levels (see Chapter 7 of this book, "A Word on Unemployment").

To Mr. Greenspan's wealthy, elitist partners (as well as Mr. Bernanke's) however, this matters not. These elite were all ultimately taken care of through the actions of the Federal Reserve and recovered 100% of their toxic paper losses and went on to create Assflation™, allowing them to make money in their targeted and preferred asset classes.

Are Bankers the gods of Death?

George Clooney in the movie, "Michael Clayton," says: "I am Shiva, the god of death!" Mr. Greenspan's actions certainly caused a credit crisis and mortgage bubble which inflicted pain upon tens of millions of people and there is no question, in this author's mind, the actions of the current members of the Federal Reserve System have served only the interests of the banks and their elite and directly heisted nearly $30 Trillion secretly from the American Republic.

Are this book's words too harsh for this group of elitists?

Are they gods of death (or trying to be?)? Nearly every single war in history has been caused by economics, with even most religious wars started and fomented because of the poverty of the masses. <u>Because bankers LEND money to governments (making wars possible to be fought even when tax receipts don't cover the war debt and payment for things like ammunition, tanks, planes and artillery!), bankers MAKE THE MOST MONEY when the government is at WAR.</u>

Through the bankers' restriction of credit and manipulation of the money supply, they also create depressions and economic hardship, forcing millions out of work. Ultimately if pushed long and hard enough, people become violent and revolt, or set themselves against other nations in an attempt to survive and thrive in an austere economic climate.

The Rothschild banking family in Europe and the U.K. learned this secret back in the days of Napoleon and nothing has changed since then. The bankers have no interest in a debt-free America, or debt-free world. The more debt we have, the greater the interest payments will become. Because of the banking elite's love for money, they think NOTHING of causing, creating or supporting conflicts between governments around the world. As discussed in Chapter 7, "Our Constitution---Just a Quick Word---You Won't Be Bored!," they have often financed both sides of a war, ensuring the loser is forced by the winner to make payments on the debt incurred fighting it. Of course, the winner must pay as well!

To add kindling to the raging fire of fractional reserve banking and the system of the Federal Reserve controlled by the wealthy elite, bankers discovered late in the 20th Century a whole new way to make money. Because people in love with money can never get enough of it, getting rich on the fractional reserve banking system wasn't enough for these greedy monsters. They have now ventured, on a nearly COMPLETELY UNREGULATED BASIS, into the infinitely leveraged world of derivatives and swaps---betting, trading, selling and buying derivatives securities positions totaling close to ten times the **world's Gross Domestic Product.**

> The derivative's system in place today, combined with the ongoing actions of the trading and selling regimes inside the banks, have placed the entire, civilized world at financial risk and has assured its doom. This is not an understatement. The evidence in these pages should overwhelmingly convince anyone of this fact.

The evidence should also, *especially,* scare the bankers and the ruling elite. Some of them might fear for their own salvations, because of the destruction set to befall so many, and even be saved---with the Holy Spirit convicting them, forcing their hearts to turn to God, instead of to self, and seek His forgiveness.

Perhaps some will even have the courage to give away their wealth and truly follow the path of righteousness, before the greatest destroyer arrives.

We can all be assured of one thing, however: in the end times, no matter what system the bankers and the elite have in place, if anything, the greatest destroyer WILL arrive and demolish whatever they have built under their current schemes, completely. The sheer wake and impact of destruction, wiping out trillions of dollars instantly will be God's way of destroying the modern-day temples these men and women have built as shrines to themselves. It will be awesome and frightening to behold the pure power and impact of the destruction---trillion, by trillion, by trillion! This author cannot imagine what the Day of Judgment will be like for those who are not saved.

Wholesale Destruction of the Banking System by the D'Apocalypse™

The major subject of this book is the D'Apocalypse™ (the DEBT AND DERIVATIVES APOCALYPSE), and includes a discussion about the wholesale destruction and compromise of the Western banking system, as a result of a pre-planned debacle brought about by the banks and the elite.

When D'Apocalypse™ arrives, and after they have caused enough pain, the bankers WILL bargain for global control over monetary policy and the money supply. Once this is accomplished, they will then reflate the system, in one form or another, to ensure future generations of elite families can continue to be served by the population of people around them.

The bankers will undoubtedly call in all their debt chips and threaten the politicians with continued economic doom if they are not bailed out on the backs of the taxpayer (once again), as they have many times before in history. This time, however, they will attempt to implement control on a centralized, world-wide basis, encouraging governments to consolidate the monetary system under one roof, for "better control, so this never happens again...."

It sounds incredible, but this is precisely what this book and trilogy expects they will attempt to do. To the outside world, it will appear their entire empire is collapsing around them, however, they will try to force a hard pivot and **make the world** bail them out---once again....this time not with a mere $30 Trillion, but **with an infinite supply of cash** supplied from their control over the world's printing presses!

The collapse should take place beginning in the mid-to-late part of 2015 (or, if the bankers cut the right deal with the next candidates for President, possibly right after the election in 2016, but this seems less likely) and the grasp for global monetary control to happen before 2020.

Their grab for power will only come after there is a lot of pain, suffering and hopelessness among the people---this is when the bankers and elite will strike. This could be any time after the market starts falling apart in 2015, but is more likely to be after a couple of years of economic agony, when 2017 begins.

Gold will be a great contrary indicator. The higher the price goes, the more out of control the system will be and the more likely the bankers will make their move for global monetary control.

Global Monetary Control—the End Game

The bankers believe this time, they will have such extensive leverage over politicians they can convince governments to deploy a newly created global, centralized banking system for the entire trading world. One of their tactics will be to feign magnanimity by offering to "forgive" some of the government debt (the bankers hold, or control, the debt of nations for nearly every major nation on earth) supposedly owed to them, in exchange for the elite's ability to run a new, global, centralized banking system.

This is the most likely scenario for how the banks and the wealthy elite will try to continue their scheme to defraud the people via the implementation of a global fractional reserve banking, monetary policy, money printing and a derivatives trading system they can ride rough shod over. They only care and want to ensure it is controlled by a handful of elite families and companies---this is the elite's dream and they are very close to making this dream a reality.

Their ultimate tactics may take a different form, but the damage which is going to be inflicted upon the wealth of nations and the common man, all over the world, will be TRAGIC when the derivatives collapse occurs.

God's Power Far Outweighs the Bankers

God's power far outweighs anything in the universe, as well as anything Wall Street, the bankers and the wealthy elite can throw at us and it is very likely, in their confidence and arrogance, they will underestimate what the response will be from the people, from God's people, all around the world.

As rioting and violence spreads from Greece, Brazil and Italy to the streets of America and the rest of Western Europe, with the youth unemployed, the middle class without jobs, crime skyrocketing and older people on fixed incomes finding the cost of bread and butter inflated beyond belief, the banks and the elite may have more on their hands than what they bargained for. This happened during the credit crisis and could easily happen again during D'Apocalypse™ . Most wealthy people keep their heads buried in the sand, sipping their Margaritas, driving their Ferraris and steering their yachts. It is interesting the wealthy are playing, while the U.S. Government is arming itself to the teeth, apparently preparing itself for a domestic revolution.

Just as happened at the height of the credit crisis, there will be exceptional, elite casualties due to their over confidence and oversized egos---the size of the universe. Of course, it is not likely to be one of the families who helped found the Federal Reserve (or their heirs).

The playbook for our economy is a playbook which came straight out of hell, with Satan's puppets calling the signals. God is stepping in soon to try and teach those who are in love with money a very big lesson, as knowingly, or unknowingly, they are helping to implement the devil's master plan.

The culmination of this plan is a system where every transaction is controlled and the beast emerges, where, indeed, if you don't have a number you won't be able to buy, or sell, anything from the elite's newly privatized, centralized bank with global banking power and authority.

There is no shortage of the love for money on Wall Street. If what The Bible says is true---"The love of money is the root of all evil..."---then Wall Street and the banks are purely evil and are destined for a confrontation with God Himself.

We should all make preparations to protect ourselves and our loved ones now, spiritually and otherwise—but especially if you work on Wall Street, or for one of the banks.

You need to ask yourself "What would God say if I was earning a living from one of these institutions?" It doesn't matter if you are a secretary, trader, salesman, executive or flunky bean counter—the monies they pay you with are dirty monies taken surreptitiously off the backs of the taxpayer.

Every single large bank should have been bankrupted during the credit crisis.

Chapter 7
A Word on Unemployment

(Reprinted from The $30 Trillion Heist---Follow The Money! Volume II, Chapter 15).

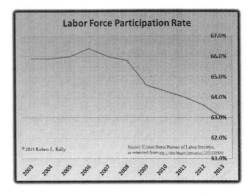

America has over 100 million people of working age who ARE NOT IN THE WORKFORCE. According to the U.S. Bureau of Labor Statistics, 10,271,000 Americans are officially unemployed and 91,521,000 working age Americans are "not in the labor force." Adding these together equals a **STAGGERING of 101,709,000** working age (ABOVE 16 years of age) Americans who do not have a job and who are really not in the work force!

The manipulated "Official" jobless rate fell to 7.6 percent from 7.7 percent and magically dropped to below 7% at the end of 2013 (Source: U.S. Labor Department July & November 2013). This is laughable when over 100 million are out of work! Statistical manipulation reminds many of how Germany in World War II, and Russia in the Cold War, fudged their numbers to pump out propaganda. Things seem to have come full circle.

How can any responsible human being in the U.S. Government publish such contrived nonsense, when the REAL unemployment rate is running at 31.8% of our total population, ACCORDING TO U.S. BUREAU AND LABOR STATISTICS! If we take the total number of working age people not really in the work force of 101,792,000 and DEDUCT 42,739,000*, for the estimated number of people OVER age 65 and also DEDUCT an estimated 13,002,000 full time students—the unemployment situation is beyond nasty. **This total equals 46,051,000 and is 31.8% of the entire civilian work force as of December 2013** (also called "PEOPLE WORKING" in the following table---Note: the table uses "NOT Seasonally Adjusted" figures and those numbers differ slightly from seasonally adjusted numbers from the U.S. Census Bureau).

(Source: U.S. Census Bureau: An estimated 40.268 million people over age 65 in 2010— author assumption expected growth rate of 2%; http://www.census.gov/compendia/statab/2012/tables/12s0007.pdf; U.S. Center for Education Statistics in the Statistical Abstract of the U.S.: 2011, Table 215, students attending American colleges and universities, est. in 2011 at 19.7 million). U.S. Department of Education: A record 21.6 million students in the fall of 2012, of which 13,002,000 are full-time).

True Employment Picture

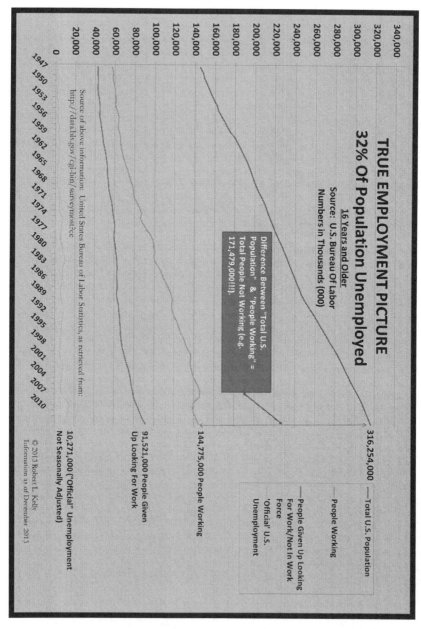

TRUE EMPLOYMENT PICTURE

32% Of Population Unemployed

16 Years and Older

Source: U.S. Bureau Of Labor

Numbers in Thousands (000)

Difference Between "Total U.S. Population" & "People Working" = Total People Not Working (e.g. 171,479,000!!!)

316,254,000 ——Total U.S. Population

——People Working

——People Given Up Looking For Work/Not In Work Force

——'Official' U.S. Unemployment

144,775,000 People Working

91,521,000 People Given Up Looking For Work

10,271,000 ("Official" Unemployment Not Seasonally Adjusted)

Source of above information: United States Bureau of Labor Statistics, as retrieved from: http://data.bls.gov/cgi-bin/surveymostcc

© 2013 Robert L. Kelly
Information as of December 2013

U.S. Bureau Of Labor Statistics Definitions

"Working-age population
According To the U.S. Bureau of Labor Statistics, working-age population in the United States is more specifically known as the civilian non-institutional working-age population:

- "Civilian" refers to persons who are not on active duty in the military;
- "Non-institutional" refers to persons who are not in institutions, such as prison inmates or those in a mental institution; and
- "Working-age" refers to persons 16 years of age and older.

Unemployment
In the United States, unemployment includes all persons who, during the reference week:

1. Had no employment,
2. Were available for work, except for temporary illness, and
3. Had actively sought work during the 4-week period ending with the reference week.

Employment
According to U.S. definitions, employment includes all persons who, during the reference week:

1. Worked at least 1 hour as paid employees, worked in their own business, profession, or on their own farm, or worked at least 15 hours as unpaid workers in a family-operated enterprise, and
2. All those who did not work but had jobs or businesses from which they were temporarily absent due to vacation, illness, bad weather, childcare problems, maternity or paternity leave, labor-management dispute, job training, or other family or personal reasons, regardless of whether they were paid for the time off or were seeking other jobs.

Each employed person is counted only once, even if he or she holds more than one job. For purposes of industry classification, multiple jobholders are counted in the job at which they worked the greatest number of hours during the reference week.

Who is not in the labor force?

All persons in the civilian non-institutional working-age population who are neither employed nor unemployed are considered not in the labor force. Many who do not participate in the labor force are going to school or are retired. Family responsibilities keep others out of the labor force. Still others have a physical or mental disability which prevents them from participating in labor force activities.

In the United States, persons not in the labor force who want and are available for a job and who have looked for work sometime in the past 12 months (or since the end of their last job if they held one within the past 12 months), but who are not currently looking, are designated as "marginally attached to the labor force." The marginally attached are divided into those not currently looking because they believe their search would be futile—so-called "discouraged workers"—and those not currently looking for other reasons such as family responsibilities, ill health, or lack of transportation.

For discouraged workers, the reasons for not currently looking for work are that the individual believes that:

- No work is available in his or her line of work or area;
- He or she could not find any work;
- He or she lacks necessary schooling, training, skills, or experience;
- Employers would think he or she is too young or too old; or
- He or she would encounter hiring discrimination.

BLS Definition of Civilian no-institutional population: Persons 16 years of age and older residing in the 50 states and the District of Columbia, who are not inmates of institutions (e.g., penal and mental facilities, homes for the aged), and who are not on **active duty in the Armed Forces.**" (Source: http://www.bls.gov/fls/flscomparelf/definitions.htm# working age population).

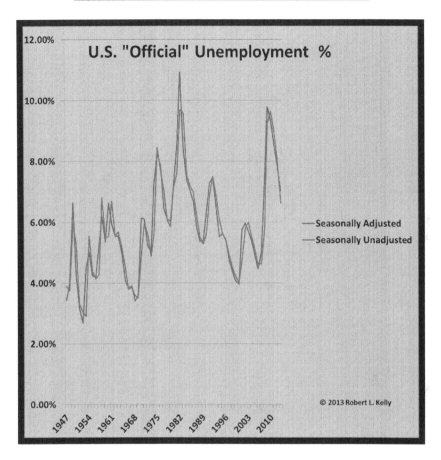

Most of us all know something just feels "funny" about the numbers which get published by the Federal Government---whether it is inflation (where they don't count food, energy, or housing—the key components of everyone's life!), employment (e.g., "7.6%? Anyone knows the real number is WAY higher than that!"), immigration (e.g., "Our borders are more secure now, than ever..." just as a poor Mexican woman hops the 18-foot international border fence near Nogales---right in front of the eyes of Senators John McCain, Chuck Schumer, Jeff Flake and Michael Bennet).

It seems just about any other piece of information coming out of the great government printing press in the sky is subject to a great big question mark.

Complementing the True Employment Picture chart seen previously, the following chart presents yet another look at the real picture. Using the government's own figures and after analyzing them to determine how many people are not really working, the following chart shows the actual number of people who are not working as a percentage of the Civilian Work Force.

There are many, many ways to "slice" data like this, but they all show a dramatic rise in unemployment since Alan Greenspan started "fixing" financial markets via the "Greenspan Put" when Long Term Capital Management blew up. As most recall, just a couple of years later, the NASDAQ bubble was bursting, creating the market chaos of 2000/2001.

This was when Mr. Greenspan first started his "Easy Money" policy of a free-wheeling Federal Reserve, unchained from key provisions of the Glass Steagall Act (courtesy of the Clinton Administration), while learning to capriciously violate the spirit and intent of the Federal Reserve Act through the massive infusion of money for the rich, along with other seeming violations, as covered in this book.

% of People NOT WORKING in Total Civilian Work Force

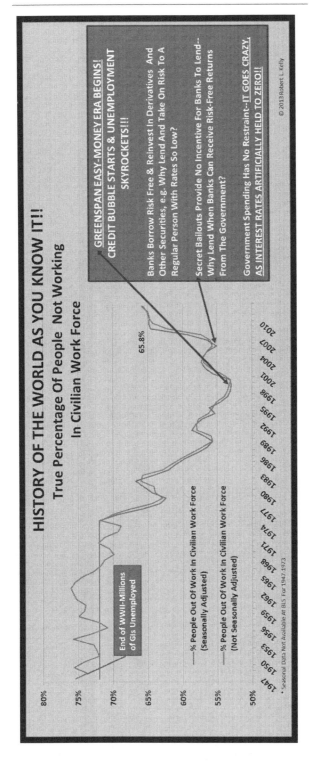

Chart updated through December 2013. (Source: ibid).

This is What the Government Wants You to Believe

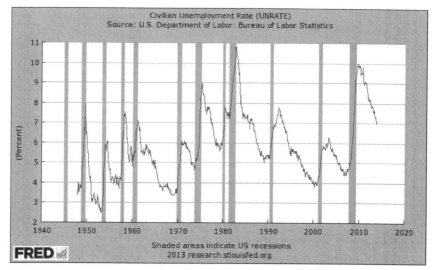

(Source: St. Louis Federal Reserve Bank, updated December 2013, as retrieved from http://research.stlouisfed.org/fred2/series/UNRATE/).

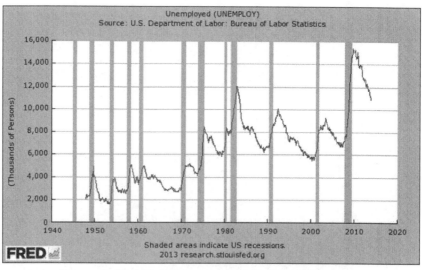

(Source: St. Louis Federal Reserve Bank, December 2013, as retrieved from http://research.stlouisfed.org/fred2/graph/?id=UNEMPLOY).

Which do you believe 31.8% "True" Unemployment, or 6 to 7 something % ?????

Chapter 8
The Coming Tightening...and Collapse

The Federal Reserve Banks and their controlling families are just following the path bankers throughout history have ALWAYS followed. WHEN AND ONLY WHEN bankers have been allowed to control the supply of money via a monopoly, they have always abused the system in many ways. The most common was for them to follow a two-step process of loosening and tightening of the money supply to achieve their objectives.

They FIRST make money *easy* to obtain via loans, credit lines, etc., which overheats the economy; then, SECOND, they suddenly take money *out of the system* by restricting borrowing and refusing to extend loans and/or credit lines. Banks continue to do just this today, but with an ally like the Federal Reserve who can globally increase, or decrease, what they call "M1," "M2" and "M3" (all measures of the supply of money), they can now manipulate economies on a macro AND micro-level.

With bankers in complete control of the money supply, interest rates and the supply of credit in the United States and Western Europe, they have a form of monopoly power over the world's economies. They have demonstrated their ability to orchestrate predatory raids on an entire industry (e.g., the "collapse" of the mortgage market), allowing the elite banks and the Federal Reserve to vastly increase their ownership of homes and real estate in America and around the world. While also showing their skills in seizing particular companies (e.g., Bear Stearns, Lehman Brothers, etc.), which is accomplished via the withdrawing of credit lines, imposting margin calls, forcing bankruptcy, etc.. This has happened to many companies around the world during the last five years.

Globally, we can expect their next step will be to increase interest rates and effect a *tightening* of the money supply, thereby causing a contraction which frightens politicians to the core. In the interim period, in the run up to the next Presidential election, expect all-out printing via QE programs and other actions by the Federal Reserve, as Mr. Bernanke did, and as his successor, Ms. Yellen, continues to do. The Fed will be under enormous political pressure from the incumbent administration to continue the fraud of Assflation™ and the Fed Chairwoman will do everything possible to not lose the game of musical chairs which will unfold before her very eyes.

Interest rates, because too much money (i.e., the energy needed to move markets) has been injected into the system, will shoot aggressively higher and will create an enormous additional burden for the U.S. economy, municipalities, states and the U.S. Government.

First, Increasing Interest Rates and Rising Stock Markets

Increasing interest rates will strengthen the dollar, causing U.S. exports to drop, further deteriorating a very weak domestic economic system. Between the $30 Trillion heist money, capital fleeing Japan and Europe, as well as new money being injected into the system by the Fed, an enormous rally in the equity markets will take place, particularly in the U.S. The double benefit of Assflation™ and international capital flowing into the U.S. market, attempting to flee a disaster in Japan and Europe, will find its way into "high-quality," highly liquid stocks and ETFs in the U.S.

Europe will be a major driver and factor here. The Euro will go bust (i.e., the Euro's exchange rate will drop precipitously vis-à-vis the U.S. Dollar) and the world will witness a tremendous short squeeze on the U.S. Dollar, causing it to strongly rise into the time when D'Apocalypse™ begins. This will create additional profits for international investors who converted early on into the U.S. currency and U.S. stock markets.

The excitement of the cacawing parrots (e.g. talking heads) on the financial television networks will be reflected in their cheer-leading Mr. Joe Six Pack back into the markets. This cacophony will be at a crescendo just in time for the 4 Horsemen of the D'Apocalypse™, their brethren bankers and elite, to unload inflated equity positions onto an unsuspecting public.

Naturally, once again, they will be selling just before the next great crisis, while their analysts push out bullish signals to investors! Insiders will be dumping like crazy at the top, just prior to the great firestorm of D'Apocalypse™ and the world, as we know it, will change forever.

For the record, while this author has an extremely low opinion of the talking heads, in general, some of them are outstanding---particularly those who have not been snow-balled by the Fed and the banks!

Stage is Set For the Banker-Engineered Global Collapse

The bankers and the now re-capitalized global banks, for their part, will finally now believe they are ready---courtesy of the U.S. taxpayer bailouts, the secret heist and the Fed-driven Assflation™ which will be roaring into 2015.

The stage will be set for the grand collapse which will catapult them into power and control of the global monetary system. Along the way, they will acquire many prized assets on planet earth which are encumbered with debt.

Loans Will Not Be Renewed

During D'Apocalypse™, no loans will be renewed. All those "iffy," below-investment grade bonds in the derivatives markets (as discussed in Chapter 2, "Derivatives---the Ticking Time Bomb!,") will go BELLY UP, with the banks seizing trillions of dollars of assets. The counter-party structure of the derivatives market will give way to a wasteland of bankruptcies by formerly large, overly-confident hedge funds, municipalities, states, governments, institutions and corporations. Too late, these once successful entities will finally learn their lesson in the dangers of using too much leverage.

Companies relying on debt for their normal business operations will go to their bank and attempt to renew their credit, or extend their loan. The bank will say----PAY UP! This will happen even if they have excellent credit ratings. Many of them will have BILLIONS of dollars in outstanding debt which needs to be refinanced, including normal lines of revolving credit. The banks, via a coordinated G14 and 4 Horsemen led premeditated attack, will go after asset-rich companies who utilize derivatives and debt in their operations.

> This kind of action is why men like Henry Ford and Thomas Edison despised the creation of the Federal Reserve System.

The abominable tactics of the banks and the Federal Reserve will engage their former, excellent customers (e.g., the Fortune and Global 1000 companies) in a frontal attack and the money trust will become infinitely stronger. The banks, elite and Federal Reserve will be fresh off of the $30 Trillion heist of the taxpayer's money and will have just sold their positions at the height of the biggest equity bubble of the major indices in history.

The banks who survive will see an extraordinary increase in power at the trough of the crushing depression. This will provide them the ability to likely take full control of global monetary policy, through their negotiations with sovereign states, all over the earth. The bankers will use their debt holdings against the sovereign states as bargaining chips and offer to reduce debt. Nothing comes for free and the bankers and elite will reduce the debt in exchange for control over the money supply and free rein of the system, with minimal political interference. This is the price the politicians must and will pay to turn the printing presses on again.

Many, many superior companies and organizations, employing tens of millions of people, will suffer dramatically during the major collapse from mid-to late 2015 onward. The cash flows these once fine companies had planned on using to pay off their operating expenses, as well as making the principal and interest payments on debt, will dry up---overnight, worldwide.

The banks and elite families, operating surreptitiously, will suddenly cut off the supply of credit, dramatically increase interest rates and make the terms of loans impossible. Their actions will wind up terrorizing companies, worldwide, with a calculated objective to foreclose upon and takeover, cherished targeted assets and companies.

These are tactics they honed their skills on during the mortgage crisis, allowing them to train an army of employees and attorneys in the now legalized art of stealing assets for pennies on the dollar because of the immoral laws on the books of nations, worldwide.

Thousands of Companies Will Be Taken Over
Some of the entities taken over will have been in operation over the course of two different centuries. Capital intensive industries, particularly manufacturing, energy, agricultural commodities, mining, precious metals, rare earth minerals and anything related to land which can produce cash flow (e.g., farms, real estate, office buildings, etc.), will be special targets for the predators of the D'Apocalypse™.

The Banks and Elite WANT Economic Collapse to Happen!
As the logic dictates, the banks and elite WANT an economic collapse to occur. This will allow them to call in loans which were designed to fail. Today, the banks are not generally lending to small businesses or John Q. Public. Currently, unless the security behind a loan is guaranteed by the government (i.e., they can resell the mortgage to FHA, FNMA, etc.), and can be repackaged and resold as a derivative security, or is backed by an absolute abundance of cash flow and assets, no loans are being made. In short, the banks are taking NO RISK on any transaction---except in their own trading and investment schemes. Here, they have the upper hand due to their complete domination of the derivatives and equity markets.

Bankers are very predictable. This behavior, where the bankers push credit out all over and then suddenly cut it off, has happened many times in history and is well documented. It also follows a logical path of behavior if one is driven, personally and corporately, by a profit motive.

If the profit motive happens to also be buttressed by the love of money and desire to continue building family dynasties, then these combined forces make the bankers' and elites' continued actions and outcomes inevitable. As long as the masses are kept in the dark about their long-term strategy and do not revolt in the process, they will remain in control.

Here is the master of banker-speak pronouncing for the entire world to hear, the Federal Reserve should now hit the brakes and STOP its "QE" programs. When this ultimately occurs, it will obviously tighten the money supply and when it happens for real in 2015, D'Apocalypse™ shall begin. Mr. Greenspan is beating on the war drums and sending the signal to TIGHTEN THE MONEY SUPPLY AND GET THE BANKERS AND ELITE READY---D'APOCALYPSE™ COMETH!

Greenspan: Fed Should Cut Back QE Now

"When you have very low, long-term 30-year yields, think about it in terms of price earnings ratio…we do have a problem here. This can move on us faster than we expect." When asked if the economy was strong enough to withstand a halt to the quantitative easy programs of the Fed, Greenspan replied, "We've got to do it even if we don't think it is strong enough." **Greenspan went on to say he believes we are underestimating the impact which high stock market prices can have in absorbing the impact of a rapid escalation in interest rates and a potentially large drop in the bond market.** (Source: CNBC video, June 7, 2013, retrieved from http://www.nbcnews.com/video/cnbc/52131722#52131722-author's emphasis bold).

JACK ASSBANKER™

Mr. Greenspan is a bit early because the tightening will not happen until at least 2015, as this book illustrates and teaches in detail, even if you hear the Fed insist it is reducing "QE" programs, etc. The Fed will not take its foot off of the gas pedal until then---even if they indicate otherwise.

Chairwoman Yellen WILL NOT like being the person who is seen in history as the one "holding the bag," when D'Apocalypse™ strikes. Once it is ordered and set in motion by the elite, she will stand out like Jack Assbanker™ the neon striped zebra!

When the music stops, the Fed will have nowhere to hide and nowhere to run---it will be exposed. For this reason, Ms. Janet Yellen will be viewed as completely expendable by the elite. Hopefully, with books like this one, people will realize there is much more to the story.

Don't worry too much about Ms. Yellen, however, because just like favored son Mr. Bernanke, she shall be rewarded for doing the bidding of her handlers--the elite owners of the Federal Reserve Regional Banks.

Additionally, anyone appointed to the Chair of the Fed knows how serious these people are behind the curtain and realizes the elite, the supreme elite, will DO ANYTHING to achieve their objectives. A person's life means nothing to them.

The stage is set. The bankers will cause the deflation with an orchestrated tightening of the money supply, after they have artificially goosed the stock market to higher highs. They shall, once again, prove they are only for the elite and their minion banks. They have no vision for the middle class, regular upper class and poor.

Their policies serve to merely blow huge bubbles which can only truly be exploited by the elite. As you can read yourself from the king of banker-speak, Mr. Greenspan, you see an "inner-circle" ex-Chairman of the Federal Reserve rooting solely for the elite via his support.

He is signaling to the elite world the bankers are going to halt the supply of money and credit on the Street. D'Apocalypse™ simply awaits the execution of their master plan when it is put in place.

1% Own 35% Of All Stock AND top 20% Own 92% Of All Stocks

The leaders in our government have been additionally bamboozled by the bankers because the bankers, a long time ago, got the politicians to pass laws permitting 401ks and IRAs. This allows everyone to supposedly own stocks.

This has caused the politicians to go along with the Federal Reserve and has empowered the Fed to continue, at all costs, to goose equity markets via Assflation™. This allows politicians to gather political support and money from the 20% of the country who own stocks. As you can see in the accompanying table, whose data was provided by G. William Domhoff from the University of California, 1% of the people own 35% of all stocks and 20% own 92% of the rest of the equity market!

This means any Assflation™ in equities (bonds are even more skewed to the wealthy) helps only the wealthiest 20% of the population! 80% of the people are simply cast aside and forced to fend for themselves.

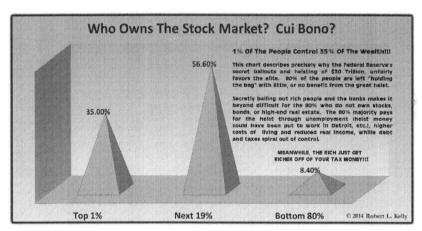

(Source: Wealth, Income, and Power, by G. William Domhoff, Table 6a: Concentration of stock ownership in the United States, 2001-2010, as retrieved from http://www2.ucsc.edu/whorulesamerica/power/wealth.html, chart created by author).

This is one of the key ways the Fed funnels money to the rich, using taxpayer-backed money from ALL AMERICANS to benefit a very small percentage of the population.

The rest of the 80% of the population are merely "bottom feeders," in the opinion of the elite. The reader can see from the distinguished Mr. Domhoff's work in the stock ownership graph above, 80% of the people RECEIVE NO BENEFIT, WHATSOEVER from the frantic antics of

Assflation™ creation by Mr. Ben Bernanke, Ms. Janet Yellen and the Federal Reserve!

It is just incredibly disturbing, given these facts, there is not one Congressman, Senator or President getting serious about the problem of the Federal Reserve. It is a cancer which must be cut out of our nation's system.

As any reader realizes after reading The $30 Trillion Heist, or D'Apocalypse™ Now!, things are decidedly WORSE for the 80% during the last decade. The Fed's and the politicians' supporting actions just build enormous bubbles—benefiting only themselves and their handlers. As we all know, bubbles ultimately crash and cause much greater harm to the general public and economy than would have otherwise occurred if free markets were allowed to rule. Bubbles also INCREASE the cost of living without reciprocation in the increase of WAGES. This is why standards of living are dropping for the masses!

The masses are left to clean up the mess. They will suffer from either massive inflation due to the Fed's printing of money, or an outright tax collection on EVERYONE, to pay for the elite's and banks' sins.

It is a system which will doom the country if it is not resolved to the benefit of the masses. This is why we need reform NOW and the country needs to recover the assets taken from it by the banks and the elite--- wherever they are in the world.

As is clear from all of the above, 80% of the people own precious little in the stock market and they certainly will not be stuffing safety deposit boxes with government bonds! Skewing markets via $30 Trillion heists and QE programs, for what amounts to a give-away to the top 1% of the population, with the next 19% going along with the party, is rapaciously wrong.

There is no question of the damage caused by the banker's indiscriminate lending and printing of money during Allan Greenspan's, Ben Bernanke's and Janet Yellen's credit and stock market bubbles. When these people blew their enormous, unsustainable equity and debt bubbles, they did and will do what all bubbles do---they pop!

This is always accomplished by the cessation of credit, lending and subsequent *tightening* of the money supply in a deliberate planned action to acquire assets for pennies on the dollars by the bankers and elite. They always try to blame their tightening of the money supply and credit squeeze on the fear of potential inflation and economic "recovery." It is incredibly convoluted because the Fed and the banks CAUSE inflation and today, there is no "recovery," only Assflation™ in the markets! All the jibber jabber about "recovery" is merely a smoke screen!

Over the last several years, particularly, their tactics have forced tens of millions of Americans to lose their homes and businesses and forced 50 Million people onto food stamps, with real unemployment rates significantly higher than in the Great Depression, at 32% (see Chapter 7, "A Word on Unemployment"). This is only 2014. The reader will be shocked at what will be seen in the unemployment figures in 2017, just three short years from now.

Another "**G-U-L-P**," please!

After living through and apparently surviving the pain of the credit crisis, at least some people, the top 20% by wealth, are breathing a breath of fresh air. Some of these "20%" are readers of this book and may disagree with the author's prognostications and wonder if the worst is behind us, after all, they are doing better than ever!

Most of them will subconsciously block out the evidence for D'Apocalypse™, as Americans particularly, are taught to always be optimistic (including, believe it, or not, this author!).

Sometimes in life, however, you must be realistic and objective. If you are, there is no way, in light of the facts and evidence, anyone can ignore the Doomsday Cycle approaching all of us. Its sentinel signal is burning brightly on the horizon, for all to see who care to look. The great firestorm of D'Apocalypse™ approaches, lighting up the dark sky ahead of us. It will engulf everyone who is unprepared and in its path of destruction.

Banks Reloaded With Cash, Balance Sheets Recovered...Time For Next Collapse!
The exchange over the last five years of worthless mortgage and worthless derivative securities by the banks and elite for **100% CASH** in the form of taxpayer-backed, U.S. Federal Reserve credits and cash-equivalents has done NOTHING but put money into the pockets of the bankers, their trading partners, rich people and wealthy foreigners.

With ALL Americans on the hook for 100% of the *interest and principal payments on trillions and trillions of dollars of U.S. Treasury securities given to the banks and elite,* we must ask ourselves, once again:

"Cui Bono?"...."Who Benefits?"

This is one of the most important questions to be answered in understanding who is operating in cahoots with the Federal Reserve—and what their next planned moves are. You will be much better equipped to protect your family and assets, whether you are rich or poor, if you can see and understand who will benefit the most from D'Apocalypse™ and what they plan to do.

We know it makes sense for the banks to crash the market. This will enable them to purchase assets inexpensively, prior to inflating them again, but is there something bigger happening here?

Because the numbers are staggeringly huge relating to the $30 Trillion heist and the trillions of dollars of debt involved, a reasonable person must ask:

"IS THERE SOMETHING BIG HAPPENING—BIGGER THAN BUYING COMPANIES AND ASSETS CHEAPLY---IN A CAREFULLY AND METICULOUSLY CRAFTED MASTER PLAN?????"

666 Empowers Control Over Global Monetary Transactions?
When the towering, burning tower of derivatives collapses and the markets are paralyzed with fear, it will *empower* the bankers to seize control of monetary policy and the supply of money, worldwide. This will be possible because governments will be in a panic and all debt will be called in by the 4 Horsemen of the D'Apocalypse™---JP Morgan Chase, Citigroup, Bank of America and Goldman Sachs in America and the G14, worldwide.

In the age of technology, an empowered monetary authority in support of governments' tax collection efforts will guarantee the repayment of debt and interest payments from governments *and* consumers, worldwide.

Because of a collapsing economic environment and the extreme hardship experienced by nearly all people during D'Apocalypse™, these conditions will necessitate from governments' perspective, a system which can track *all* transactions.

This would vastly improve tax collection and would also record and file away flow of funds information into a database. This database would allow governments and the empowered monetary authority to track wealth. This would be a spend-crazy politician's dream because they could then create a brand new "wealth tax" to tap, which would support their need to stay in power.

In this way, it would be easy for government authorities to track down wealth and tax it, while simultaneously ensuring *every single dollar transaction* is also taxed!

In exchange for this capability and their control of this tracking system, the bankers and elite are assured they will be guaranteed payment on their principal and interest, while maintaining supreme control over monetary policy and the money supply. Not a bad trade for giving up some debt to the governments of the world!

When the deal is struck between the banking cabal, the ruling elite and governments, worldwide, the "new" global banking authority will ensure there is little, or no, government interference in the operations of this global beast. The bankers and elite will have virtually free reign at this point in time.

The NSA already tracks every single online conversation and phone call and there are no technology impediments for the bankers and the elite to create this system. They will be able to track the flow of funds and transactions of all kinds and types. All they have to do is connect the dots on everyone's bank statements, cash transactions and security holdings.

The very last thing the bankers will do before they seize control of monetary policy is create another, even more powerful and dramatic panic. This will force every government to its knees. Politicians will pray to the elite and banking authority for relief. With the control of the debts of governments and begging politicians, worldwide, the Federal Reserve, the bankers and the elite will be in a unique and globally powerful position.

With such an entity and small group of people wielding and holding such incredible power, it is easy to remember the warnings from childhood <u>Bible</u> lessons and our studies, in later life.

The following passage describes certain events, as written in the Book of Revelation....THE BOOK OF THE APOCALYPSE.

The author will be the first to say it is very difficult to understand all aspects of <u>The Bible's</u> poetic imagery, but the parallels and the battle lines which are forming in and around money, are indeed striking and alarming:

Revelation 13

The Beast out of the Sea

1The dragon ᵃstood on the shore of the sea. And I saw a beast coming out of the **sea. It had ten horns and seven heads, with ten crowns on its horns, and on each head a blasphemous name. 2The beast I saw resembled a leopard, but had feet like those of a bear and a mouth like that of a lion. The dragon gave the beast his power and his throne and great authority. 3One of the heads of the beast seemed to have had a fatal wound, but the fatal wound had been healed. The whole world was filled with wonder and followed the beast. 4People worshiped** the dragon because he had given authority to the beast, and they also worshiped the beast and asked, "Who is like the beast? Who can wage war against it?"

5The beast was given a mouth to utter proud words and blasphemies and to exercise its authority for forty-two months. 6It opened its mouth to blaspheme God, and to slander his name and his dwelling place and those who live in heaven. 7It was given power to wage war against God's holy people and to conquer them. And it was given authority over every tribe, people, language and nation. 8All inhabitants of the earth will worship the beast—all whose names have not been written in the Lamb's book of life, the Lamb who was slain from the creation of the world.

9Whoever has ears, let them hear. 10"If anyone is to go into captivity, into captivity they will go.

If anyone is to be killed with the sword, with the sword they will be killed."

This calls for patient endurance and faithfulness on the part of God's people.

The Beast out of the Earth

11Then I saw a second beast, coming out of the earth. It had two horns like a lamb, but it spoke like a dragon. 12It exercised all the authority of the first beast on its behalf, and made the earth and its inhabitants worship the first beast, whose fatal wound had been healed. 13And it performed great signs, even causing fire to come down from heaven to the earth in full view of the people.14Because of the signs it was given power to perform on behalf of the first beast, it deceived the inhabitants of the earth. It ordered them to set up an image in honor of the beast who was wounded by the sword and yet lived. 15The second beast was given power to give breath to the image of the first beast, so that the image could speak and cause all who refused to worship the image to be killed. 16It also forced all people, great and small, rich and poor, free and slave, to receive a mark on their right hands or on their foreheads, 17so that they could not buy or sell unless they had the mark, which is the name of the beast or the number of its name.

18This calls for wisdom. Let the person who has insight calculate the number of the beast, for it is the number of a man. That number is 666.
(Source: The Bible, New International Version, Revelation 13, retrieved from http://biblehub.com/niv/revelation/13.htm, author's emphasis underlined).

The Bible's poetic imagery is quite powerful. God has ***already*** revealed to us what will happen in the end times and because most of us are mere mortals, it is extremely difficult to understand all the details of God's plan. What is very clear, however, is He wants us to use introspection and turn to Him for salvation. Christians know this through His son Jesus Christ. As we learn from the above passage, those whose names have been "written in the Lamb's book of life, the Lamb who was slain from the creation of the world," shall not worship the beast.

It is a Christian's solemn duty and obligation to
NEVER worship the beast. It is the most important
reason the Federal Reserve Trilogy is written.

In Revelation 13, He is clearly warning us of a coming evil and terrible beast, operating against God and His holy people on earth. It is quite clear this "beast" will have the power of controlling every single transaction on the planet.

Perhaps the bankers and the elite naively build a system which can track every transaction and it is simply taken over by the second beast, per Revelation 13--*or perhaps something more sinister is unfolding.*

In this day and age, given what we know---either way---it means one thing and one thing only: a global, centralized monetary authority with the power to report and process transactions, as well as the ability to dictate what will be used as a medium of exchange. Ultimately, The Bible says there will be a required mark on a person's body to buy, or sell, anything. As we all know, fingerprint swiping is already here, so the ability to digitally read a "mark," is a straight forward process, because the systems are already in place to implement this prophecy.

Digitally speaking, the monetary authority would also have the power to *prevent* anyone from making a transaction via the simple strokes of a keyboard, or refusal to honor a fingerprint, once it is digitally processed.

Unless a person is cleared and approved for processing, this futuristic monetary authority can shut off all access to checking accounts, savings accounts, brokerage accounts and safety deposit boxes. Cash, as we know it today, will not be used as much because the world will shift to a digital currency. Digital markings on cards, or the ability to convert unique human body marks into digital code, or the "mark," itself, will be the pathway to a person's wealth. When you sell a stock, a bond, or any other thing, your electronic account will be credited, as already occurs today, but on an institution-by-institution basis. The future will see global control by these monsters in a completely integrated database.

Forcing this kind of system upon society has to be taken in steps---but as you know, we are well on our way, as any bank today can seize any account in seconds if it desires to do so, or is otherwise ordered. To go the distance will require some enormous changes and shocks to the system.

These shocks have to be enough where an authority figure can dictate changes for the "good" of everyone, ensuring for example, "to recover, everyone must pay their fair share." The only way to do this is to get rid of cash as a primary medium of exchange. A logical first step would be to empower an international banking cabal, granting them authority over the world's monetary system, policy control, as well as its electronic and physical currency forms.

This is the real end-game for the bankers and the cabal of the elite. They will stop at nothing to complete their mission of achieving a complete dictatorship over the world's money supply, in league with governments. This will allow them and their future elite family members to continue stripping the world's wealth for their own accounts. With an expanded and global monetary authority as their new base camp, the elite will sit on top of the collection of interest, principal payments and transactional fees, while monopolizing all financial markets.

This guarantees their ongoing profitability, family lineage, as well as complete control over the derivatives, credit markets and business cycle. As you are beginning to understand and as Thomas Jefferson, our great President stated,

"And I sincerely believe, with you, that banking establishments are more dangerous than standing armies; and that the principle of spending money to be paid by posterity, under the name of funding, is but swindling futurity on a large scale. I salute you with constant friendship and respect."
---THOMAS JEFFERSON

(Source: The Works of Thomas Jefferson in Twelve Volumes. Federal Edition. Collected and Edited by Paul Leicester Ford. Thomas Jefferson to John Taylor, Monticello, May 28, 1816 and retrieved from http://memory.loc.gov/cgi-bin/query/r?ammem/mtj:@field (DOCID+@lit(tj110172))).

Unfortunately, the bankers and elite will likely succeed in causing suffering for hundreds of millions of additional people through their preconceived, self-engineered and devastating depression. The credit contraction and targeted deflation of assets and companies will witness the bankers' and elites' predatory pillaging and theft of trillions of additional assets for pennies on the dollar. It will also witness their bid to gain control of the world's monetary systems.

Out of the abyss of this deflationary morass, economic depravity and suffering, the banker's *will* seize control.

Prices will then, and only then, be allowed to rise across all asset classes. *The bankers' newly acquired assets and companies will then skyrocket in value,* with the world experiencing yet another, great "loosening" of credit. Credit shall be made available to one and all, with this loosening occurring *only after* D'Apocalypse™ and the Greatest

Depression, runs its course. While the bankers believe they are the clever ones, there is only one reason the bankers will achieve their temporal goal of global monetary control:

Because God already planned this as a precondition to His return!

The author is very happy he is not on the side of the bankers or the elite, as we all know who ultimately wins this war—and it sure isn't them...

Chapter 9
What To Do Now

If You Are A Government

While we await heavenly intervention, we must be prudent and proactive in our preparations. It is our absolute duty to God and every human being on earth to trumpet the warning call to empower people to protect themselves from the destruction which <u>will</u> occur during D'Apocalypse™.

Given freedom of choice by God above, certain men and women built the derivatives tower which becomes THE financial weapon of mass destruction. Mankind's love for money, and zest for power, ultimately will cause a calamity, which will ruin hundreds of millions of people's lives. It will not be God's fault. The fault will lie clearly with those responsible for building the derivatives doomsday tower of D'Apocalypse™, which is clearly designed to swindle trillions of dollars in assets away from their rightful owners, for pennies on the dollar.

For those in a position of governmental power and authority who can perceive the evil of what is about to befall us, we must ride and trumpet our horns to warn those who will listen. In this way, we can help others and potentially save and improve lives---possibly millions of them. This section of "What To Do Now," is written for governments, with potential application for serious hedge funds (who may have the freedom to move in the direction the author is suggesting). It provides detailed, serious and concrete suggestions to help your country and people.

During the last one hundred years, until quite recently, the United States has dominated world commerce. There can be no uncertainty or question, of this fact. It allowed the nation to become wealthy and great---with the wealth spread out amongst the people. It resulted in the largest and wealthiest "middle class" on earth. The principle reasons behind this rise to power were because of the U.S. tradition of free enterprise and a once non-obtrusive government. This instilled freedom in the people and allowed individuals and corporations to profit from innovations in technology, medicine, energy, agriculture, mining and industry, among many other sectors and businesses. This powered the country's fortunes and it was nearly all financed by the banks.

Both "guns and butter" were also possible in this unique era of American history because a balance was struck (e.g., balanced budgets, responsible spending and responsible bankers). There were also many additional "moral" checks on those working in government and in the financial system. People did not, generally, try and game the system for their own greedy desires. Sadly, this is not the case anymore.

The banks, historically, only leveraged their profits by using fractional reserve banking (which is bad enough), but through the advent of derivatives, the bankers have created a transactional environment riddled with non-regulation and what appears to be outright fraud. This has allowed the banks to effectively collateralize and hold hostage the entirety of the United States and world.

The actions of the bankers, the elite and the Federal Reserve (and its cast of supporting central banks around the world) are simply inexcusable.

Your nation is urged to take action NOW to protect itself from the coming collapse. Brilliant hedge fund managers may also be interested in these ideas. Hedge funds could easily team up with a country, large or small, and assist it in achieving the goals, ideas and opportunities presented herein.

In case any government wonders if this book is all just hype and thinks, "D'Apocalypse™ can't be possible….The system the United States has is strong and powerful---look at what the bankers and elite have helped finance and build!"

Well, it will be of interest to know, despite the historic track record and success of the United States, according to the CIA Factbook for 2012, <u>the United States was dead LAST in its current account balance, among ALL NATIONS.</u> The United States has a <u>STAGGERINGLY NEGATIVE $487,200,000,000 DEFICIT</u>—ranking 193rd---behind every nation on earth in the CIA survey of 193 nations.

| 193 | **United States** | $ -487,200,000,000 | 2012 est. |

(Source: CIA Fact Book, as retrieved from https://www.cia.gov/library/publications/the-world-factbook/rankorder/2187rank.html).

This deficit amounts to approximately $690,000 per person in Detroit and about $11,000 for every person on food stamps in America! It is very clear the other trading nations do not want American products, which is just another eerie sign something is not working too well in the American economy.

It also proves with 100% certainty the bankers, the elite and the politicians have absolutely failed in their supposed efforts to "help" the country. You know from reading this book, or The $30 Trillion Heist, however, they have succeeded tremendously in lining their own pockets with taxpayer monies.

Unique Opportunity to Wrest Control of the Western Grip on Finance

Because of sheer overwhelming avarice, the United States and its Western allies have exposed themselves to an overwhelming debt load, coupled with a toweringly high-risk situation in the derivatives markets. As a result, which happens very *infrequently* in history, there is a unique opportunity for a number of countries around the world to wrest financial control *away* from the U.S. and its Western allies.

This author loves his country; however, the politicians have buried it in a sea of regulation and an ocean of unfunded obligations and liabilities, while the bankers have robbed it blind. There is just no question they will drag the entire system down and it is extremely doubtful anything will change their reckless behavior, except God Himself. The politicians, bankers and the elite will *only* seek to save themselves and their highly paid positions (and pensions and golden parachutes) at all times and at *all costs*. The die is cast on this front.

More importantly, this Christian writer has a solemn duty to *all* mankind to speak the truth and hopes these words help as many as possible--- Christians and non-Christians, alike. We are all God's people.

The fact is, the bankers and elite have overreached and placed the entire system at risk. As history teaches us, someone will step in to fill the gap— someone always does. If you are in a position of power and authority to step in and implement the recommendations espoused herein, there will be a great opportunity for a nation (or group of nations) to wrest control away from the powers that be.

The situation is grave for the West and the opportunity is rare. This allows for the possibility a collection of wealthy individuals, or hedge funds, operating under the approval of government (somewhere), can follow the suggestions in this chapter and help nations which need help. They will also make a decent profit in the process.

The elite, the bankers and the politicians are extremely vulnerable and they either don't realize it, or they are trying to game the system as long as it lasts. They hope to survive on the other side. As you know, this book expects them to take control, or exercise far greater control over monetary policy, at the end of the day.

D'Apocalypse™ Now! suggests taking a page from the play book of the Federal Reserve's ancestors who long ago wrote the plan for America's central bank. This author believes a unique set of INDEPENDENT International Reserve Banks would provide remarkable capabilities for even the smallest country, or group of countries.

For any super powers reading this, you are potentially in the cat bird's seat and will have the opportunity to rain havoc on the Western banks. By following the suggestions in this chapter, you can give them a taste of their own medicine in the very near future. You must seize the moment when it arrives!

As a result of decades-long manipulation and outright greed, there are several emerging and important opportunities for the reader to understand. Even though this subsection of the chapter is written for "governments," depending on who you represent—e.g., self, family, trust, corporation, pension fund, state, OR government---you can take advantage of this situation, by taking action NOW and collaborating with other like-minded people.

If you do take action, it will likely make you, and those you care about, and those to whom you have a fiduciary responsibility to protect, very wealthy and very rich—all earned in an honest, God-fearing way. If this good fortune happens to you, you will likely remember to help others, as you won't forget where the advice came from and the fact God alone showed you the path forward, as this author has no desire for wealth, or accolades.

The changes coming to the markets don't happen very often and when they have been seen to be orders of magnitude (an order of magnitude from a technical perspective is a factor of 10...) above what historically has been "ordinary" market action, only the prepared will be able to take advantage of them.

Everyone else will be PETRIFIED and likely DESTROYED.

No recommendations are provided here for any specific government(s), even though there are examples highlighting interesting alliances which might occur.

Finally, the author is happy to provide assistance and counsel to any governments or other parties, who seek help in establishing these forward-thinking, concrete solutions and ideas. The author's email address is dapocalypsenow@gmail.com, attention: Mr. Robert L. Kelly.

Governments, Large and Small, Have a Huge Chance to Change the Game
There are only a few governments not wholly compromised by the Western bankers. Large countries have very powerful military forces at their disposal and can protect their citizens, be independent and maintain successful, sophisticated financial markets and monetary policy systems. Other governments are struggling and do not, necessarily, have the same military or financial capabilities other great nations enjoy.

The best news is --- IT DOES NOT MATTER!

For any large, great country, you have the opportunity to dominate the West, however, if you are a small country, your world is about to change, forever. You are going to learn by exercising a little creative diplomacy with your regional trading partners and practicing strong ethics, you can become the next Switzerland!

Many smaller governments have made extraordinary strides in implementing strong financial banking systems and depositories for the benefit of their countries, while receiving capital from depositors from all over the world. If you look at Panama, Uruguay, Singapore and Labuan in Malaysia, for example, as well as many of the successful "offshore" banking centers including the Cayman Islands, Macau, the Marshall Islands, etc. they have all been *extremely* successful in attracting capital. These territories do not have frightening armies to protect themselves, either! They rely on the United Nations, their own modest military and police (by superpower standards) and common law to ensure security and justice over their banking systems (with the exception of Macau, which is tightly bonded with China).

Be forewarned, however, some of these centers will be in big trouble during D'Apocalypse™, especially those whose economies and banking centers are dollar based.

Beware of OECD

Historically, many of these countries and offshore banking centers have been successful, but nearly every one of them has allowed itself to be involved with the OECD (Organisation for Economic Cooperation and Development), which brandishes policy on behalf of Western governments and Western banks under the guise of "economic cooperation and development."

In reality, OECD (and other Western financial organizations) is a tax collector for bloated Western government spending. This organization actually *hinders* and prevents most emerging countries from attracting significant amounts of capital.

The reader should know, most Western countries' will reject this opinion, as many leaders and bureaucrats are bought off, at the highest levels. This assures control of an emerging country's financial system by the OECD and the Western banks. Under the auspices of fighting "terrorism" and "money laundering," the OECD and the Western governments have been able to control the flow of capital causing it to wind up, primarily, in New York and London.

Quoting directly from the OECD's web site:

"20/07/13 - The OECD today presented to G20 finance ministers plans for a two-pronged attack on tax avoidance and evasion from both companies and individuals." (Source: http://www.oecd.org/newsroom/oecd-calls-on-g20-finance-ministers-to-support-next-steps-in-clampdown-on-tax-avoidance.htm).

To make a bold change for your country and region and prevent the wrath of D'Apocalypse™ from falling on your people, leaders will have to make strategic and bold choices with decided, steadfast and determined precision—and SPEED. This will necessitate creating a hub which does not violate any laws, but allows your region or country to ATTRACT capital with complete PRIVACY.

The suggestions which follow are an easy way for an existing government, which may not even be a leader in the international banking community, to develop a POTENTIALLY VERY STRONG FINANCIAL DEPOSITORY SYSTEM. This system can potentially generate billions of dollars in profits which can be used to help develop a country's, or region's, resources and economies, thereby increasing employment and the well-being of citizens across the land.

By harnessing capital for the good of the people (and NOT a small number of elite families), countries deploying this plan will make an enormous leap forward in their goals to defeat poverty and advance the standard of living for all peoples in their nations. You will also accomplish this with the best system on earth, a capitalistically-driven system. It shows no favors to the wealthy and elite, but allows them to invest their capital and earn an honest return on their monies, in exchange for interesting ownership participation in a new, International Reserve Bank, as further described, later in this section of the book.

> For a country which is already successful, or is already mighty, but perhaps at odds with the U.S. and Western Europe (but not their respective citizens!) over their haughty, unwieldy and irresponsible use of leverage and debt, you have a particularly **huge chance** to upset the global balance of financial power in the 21st Century.

Assured Doom-- D'Apocalypse™ COMING!

Unfortunately, the United States has changed dramatically and taken away countless rights of citizens during the last several decades. This, in combination with a staggering debt and derivatives burden resembling a tower built out of playing cards, has sealed the fate of not only the government, but also the people. Perhaps a miracle will happen to stop the devastation and ruin which will befall this great land, but it is too late at this point in time, in the opinion of this humble author.

After thoroughly looking at scripture, studying God's word, reading hundreds of books, thousands and thousands of articles, absorbing the nearly three-hundred year nefarious history of the Federal Reserve System and its predecessors---the evidence is clear and overwhelming.

The author is *NOT* Paul Revere riding and warning "THE BRITISH ARE COMING, THE BRITISH ARE COMING!," the author *IS*, however, *writing and warning* you:

"D'APOCALYPSE™ IS COMING!!
D'APOCALYPSE™ IS COMING!!"

The evidence points to no other resolution than a complete system meltdown, which will have global ramifications.

The only way to save the West's system is if the politicians and the banks do a full-scale reboot. They need to return the homes stolen by the banks from the citizens and cancel significant amounts of debt. This should be accomplished through the application of past interest payments on principal, while reducing taxes and spending dramatically (i.e., run a SURPLUS, while reducing the tax burden, debt burden, fee burden and regulatory burden foisted on Americans *and* Europeans during the last forty years).

ADDITIONALLY, the politicians MUST BREAK UP THE BANKS and aggressively seek the return from the elite and the banks of ALL fraudulently-heisted capital, assets and property taken from the people. The elite cannot be allowed to hide behind the walls of the banking empires and their thousands of shell corporations, which mask their true ownership.

**Piercing the corporate veil of their fraud
is crucial to extracting justice for the people!**

Unless they do all of the preceding, the system is doomed in its current form. The damages will be seen in additional, rapidly rising unemployment (yes, even higher than the 32% number calculated in Chapter 7, "A Word on Unemployment"), increasing interest rates, astronomically skyrocketing deficits, mountains of debt, huge inflationary increases in the costs of the staples of life and soaring asset prices defying reason. These will all, predictably, cause a devastating crash resulting in a complete system shut down.

Governments Vicious On Taxes—Your Government Should NOT Be
The governments on both sides of the Atlantic in the Northern Hemisphere, particularly, are focused aggressively on raising taxes and making it exceptionally difficult for capital to freely move offshore or even within the respective nations. One of their biggest mistakes is not doing and implementing the REVERSE policy.

Legislators should be LOOSENING the laws and allowing capital to more FREELY and PRIVATELY be moved around. It is utter nonsense to be making laws disguised under the auspices of protection from "terrorism" and "money laundering," when the government is really only after tax money to pay for its bulging budgets and spending binges.

This enormous tax crackdown by the politicians will only get worse, as long as they are in power. It will cause the system to fail more rapidly, as well. Their actions cause a massive slowdown in the velocity of money because capital flees to where it will not be prosecuted and will not be overly taxed.

This will be the Democrats and Republicans downfall in 2016.

They have both created a massive, deflationary shock wave to the economies which penalizes capital. As interest rates rise to a crescendo in 2015 and their policies continue to drive capital underground, they will create a witch's brew of economic evil which become the prime catalysts of D'Apocalypse™...and the bankers stand by to light the match!

Governments should always keep the <u>traditional</u> Swiss model in mind. <u>Strict secrecy</u> for investors will require a <u>guarantee by the state</u>, particularly for smaller nations. This guarantee from the state must cover all capital deposited, as well as guarantee very low taxes onshore and <u>no taxation offshore</u> on investment capital brought into the country via the International Reserve Banks (see subsection, "The Big Spenders Are the Problem---Not the Solution!," in this chapter).

This book does NOT advocate illegal tax avoidance, but is merely pointing out the utter stupidity of politicians. They always wreck everything via overregulation. For all you Americans out there---MAKE SURE YOU PAY YOUR TAXES, if you are able to, because it is a Biblical principle---

"Then saith He unto them, Render therefore unto Caesar the things which are Caesar's; and unto God the things that are God's." (Source: <u>The Bible</u>, King James Version, <u>Matthew 22:21</u>).

For those of you who can't pay your taxes due to tough times, just try and keep your chin up and know God has far, far better things planned for you and your life---whether it is in this life, or the next one. It is His promise and it is a promise this writer knows to be a fact.

Protect Your Government from the Mistakes of the West

Irresponsible government spending, highly paid civil servants (with enormous and unsustainable pension, benefits and entitlement plans), bloated budgets (with their resulting pressure on politicians to raise taxes, impose fees and increase regulations), profligate actions by the Federal Reserve System and galactically stupid, short-sighted actions of the banking system in the derivatives markets, are directly responsible for an America, Europe and Japan on the rocks.

The results of these collective actions have created a virtual dictatorship over money which is well on the way to destroying the system. The end result shall be *very few people* will want their capital in America. But, like every other major bubble in history, *first* there must be an unprecedented and spectacular Assflation™ blow-off which assures the world America is the only place to be.

Your country should be preparing, ***now***, to take advantage of smart capital seeking immediate safe harbor for its monies. When the crash occurs, "smart money" will lose enormous fortunes if it is not prepared; and if you are not ready to receive it, you will not benefit.

U.S. and European politicians, particularly, have made too many rules. They have also put their noses into too many areas which should be left alone to assure those governments remain attractive destinations for capital. This is why these two political regions have grown historically, but are quickly collapsing due to the extremely unwise and poor decision-making of the politicians. Their complicity and permission to allow the bankers to run rough-shod over the citizens in both the United States and Western Europe, by layering hidden taxes on the people and effecting grand heists against all citizens, have sealed their fate.

Together, they are responsible for rising taxes, continued wasteful and shameless spending, while creating the greatest unemployment since the Great Depression. This has become the cancer called **"Amerika" and the forthcoming tragedy we call D'Apocalypse™**.

Ultimately, the politicians, IF THEY ARE EVEN STILL IN POWER, will have a decision to make. Do they inflate away the debt and impoverish hundreds of millions of people because of a tremendous rise in the cost of housing, food, clothing, energy, etc., or will they unveil a new currency, as discussed at length in this book. A new currency, overnight, can steal the wealth of the nation and its investors. Printing money destroys the lives of nearly everyone! As you can see, the politicians are in between a rock and a hard place!

Either way, wealth will VANISH overnight, if investors are caught unprepared.

Your government should be prepared to do THE OPPOSITE of what the West has done. You simply need to enact STRICT privacy laws assuring anonymity for investors. You also need to create an interesting and easy system for wealth to be attracted to your country and/or region. If you have the courage to pass a constitutional amendment, or government decree, stating your government will not borrow any more money and will pay down its debts (if you have any) and operate ONLY a balanced budget,---***capital will be wildly attracted to your country.***

Specific Plan for Countries Already Ruined by Bankers

In the situation of a country which has already been ruined by the bankers (this INCLUDES THE UNITED STATES!), the ONLY solution is to pass a law which does as Caesar did (see Julius Caesar story, which follows). Your new law should allow citizen and corporation relief against the banks! Past interest payments for all people should apply **retroactively** to their debt, with the added caveat the people who may have been thrown out of their homes by the bankers, should receive a cash refund equaling the interest payments they made to the lender during the time they owned the home.

These reimbursements should be made, entirely, by the banks and the elite. The elite are the principal owners and beneficiaries of the banks who received secretly heisted bailout monies. This means they also participated in the banks' widespread fraud, which caused the global credit crisis and subsequent heist from the U.S. taxpayer.

If they don't have the money, then the people should be permitted to foreclose, collectively, on the banks and the elite's assets. No one should be able to hide behind the veil of a corporation, since all of the bankers' and elites' actions were based on fraud when they received the secret bailouts from the Federal Reserve. As the GAO audit revealed, they fiendishly deceived all of us and concealed the heist and defrauded, massively, consumers during the real estate bubble and its bust.

Implementing this kind of bold action would immediately help the global populations and economy of every country, but would provide huge relief to the citizens of the United States, Ireland, Greece, France, Spain, Italy, Brazil, the entirety of an indebted Eastern Europe and any other countries buried in debt related to the mortgage and credit crisis. These actions would immediately lighten the debt load and ignite the economies of nations instituting these reforms.

Also, please notice this does not take one thin dime from any honest wealthy person. It only goes after those who instituted the global fraud against the masses.

Next, pass the privacy laws and protections required to attract capital in the form of an International Reserve Bank. For countries which need to boost investor confidence, create a joint resolution between the military and political leadership of the host and/or regional country, as further described in this section of the book.

Given the grand scale of the elites' agenda, decisive, bold action must be taken to help millions of peoples' lives by instituting real economic and systemic reform in your country. These steps will increase investment and capital, while creating JOB growth through EMPLOYMENT, via the creative magnetism of a safe harbor for capital.

This is the best way to reduce poverty and produce real job growth for the young, the old and those in between.

Julius Caesar

When Caesar was rising to power in 59 BC when he was first elected to consul in the first Triumvirate, the Triumvirate included himself, Pompey (the foremost military commander to whom Caesar reported and to whom Caesar's daughter was married, also in 59 BC) and Crassus (a wealthy financier). As most are taught in their history lessons, the Roman Senate at the time was well known for its extreme corruption and jealousy, making it difficult for any one person to become a supreme emperor.

"Die Ermordung Cäsars"
Caesar surrounded in the Senate, being murdered. By Karl von Piloty (1826–1886), painted in 1865. The painting is located in the Lower Saxony State Museum (Source: Wikipedia, as retrieved from http://en.wikipedia.org/wiki/Julius_caesar).

During the next ten years or so, Caesar consolidated his power through a series of brilliant military and administrative actions which ultimately made him Rome's supreme dictator, effectively neutralizing the Senate. Militarily, his actions included the invasion of and conquering of Gaul (modern-day France) and Great Britain, WITHOUT the consent of the Senate, and ultimately destroyed Pompey's army in Spain.

By law, the armies of Rome were supposed to remain above the Rubicon River in Northern Italy, which divided Italy from Gaul. The Roman Senate had created this artificial barrier to ensure they had the run of the country, without military interference. When Caesar crossed the Rubicon on January 10, 49 BC, it is said he spoke the famous words:

"Alea iacta est, translated as "The die is cast."

Throughout this period, Rome was having a Civil War with many economic problems. Caesar had to pay his legions and the Senate was taxing the "citizens" to death---forcing many of Rome's citizens to flee the high taxation rate. This led to Caesar passing laws limiting HOW LONG a person could stay away from Rome (3 years) and he made other edicts which encouraged scientists and teachers of the liberal arts to live in Rome by FREEING them of taxes imposed by the city. This attracted the most brilliant minds of the day to live in Rome and encouraged others to live there, also, causing the tax base to rise. He took other actions, causing Rome to give public land away to 20,000 freemen, provided they had three children, or more, and to his soldiers. Caesar knew tax receipts increase if land was cultivated and population growth was increasing.

He also knew his soldiers would fight for him if they were rewarded for loyalty. Julius Caesar also *reduced* the number of people receiving corn at the expense of the public (i.e., welfare) from 320,000 to 150,000 people and he invoked taxes on the importation of foreign goods.

In one of his bravest decisions, which helped most people throughout the land, dramatically improved the economy and perhaps in itself, ended the civil war, Caesar issued a decree regarding the repayment of debt on property. Because of the civil war and high taxes, the economy was in rough shape and property prices had dropped precipitously, causing mortgages to be "under water." The lenders wanted to foreclose and the borrowers wanted to be let off the hook. Because of Caesar's appeal to the people, most thought Caesar would decree the

JULIUS CÆSAR. 29

XLII. Eighty thousand citizens having been distributed into foreign colonies,[1] he enacted, in order to stop the drain on the population, that no freeman of the city above twenty, and under forty, years of age, who was not in the military service, should absent himself from Italy for more than three years at a time ; that no senator's son should go abroad, unless in the retinue of some high officer ; and as to those whose pursuit was tending flocks and herds, that no less than a third of the number of their shepherds free-born should be youths. He likewise made all those who practised physic in Rome, and all teachers of the liberal arts, free of the city, in order to fix them in it, and induce others to settle there. With respect to debts, he disappointed the expectation which was generally entertained, that they would be totally cancelled ; and ordered that the debtors should satisfy their creditors, according to the valuation of their estates, at the rate at which they were purchased before the commencement of the civil war ; deducting from the debt what had been paid for interest either in money or by bonds ; by virtue of which provision about a fourth part of the debt was lost. He dissolved all the guilds, except such as were of ancient foundation. Crimes were punished with greater severity ; and the rich being more easily induced to commit them because they were only liable to banishment, without the forfeiture of their property, he stripped murderers, as Cicero observes, of their whole estates, and other offenders of one half.

XLIII. He was extremely assiduous and strict in the administration of justice. He expelled from the senate such members as were convicted of bribery ; and he dissolved the marriage of a man of prætorian rank, who had married a lady two days after her divorce from a former husband, although there was no suspicion that they had been guilty of any illicit connection. He imposed duties on the importation of foreign goods. The use of litters for travelling, purple robes, and jewels, he permitted only to persons of a certain age and station, and on particular days. He enforced a rigid execution of the sumptuary laws ; placing officers about the markets, to seize upon all meats exposed to sale contrary to the rules, and bring them to him ; sometimes sending his lictors and soldiers to

[1] Principally Carthage and Corinth.

Excerpt from <u>The Lives of the Twelve Caesars</u> see source information at end of this section.

debt would be forgiven and borrowers would not have to repay the lenders. Caesar did not suggest this.

Instead, Caesar had the properties assessed at their respective values prior to the civil war--when the values were much higher--and allowed all interest payments to be deducted from those revised values, whether the borrower paid it back in money, *or in a personal bond. This was a personal obligation of the borrower, without the need for a banks' approval!* This allowed people who had no money to STAY IN THEIR HOMES and refinance in a manageable manner! This action reduced the debt by approximately 1/4th.

What a difference it would have made if any politician worth his or her salt, stood up against the bankers and declared---"All homeowners can write their own bond at the Federal Reserve Borrowing rate (it has been at nearly zero percent for the banks all throughout the crisis) and self-finance not only their home, but also enjoy an immediate credit against their owed principal with the deduction of all historically made interest payments!"

Collectively, Caesar's actions helped him end the civil war, enthroned him to power and set Rome off in the right direction, which led to the establishment of the Roman Empire, formed Europe and allowed Rome to rule for centuries. The history books tell us of the jealousy and fear Senators had of Caesar disbanding the Senate. As we know, Caesar was murdered. It would be interesting to know if the murderers, Gaius Cassius Longinus and Marcus Junius Brutus, were also lenders who had to forgive ¼ of the debts owed to them!

(Source: The Lives of the Twelve Caesars, by C. Suetonius Tranquillus, as translated by Alexander Thompson and revised and corrected by T. Forester, Esq. A.M., pages 14, 15, 18, 19, 24, 25, 28, 29, published by George Bell & Sons, Covent Garden, London 1890, as retrieved from http://files.libertyfund.org/files/1888/1235_Bk.pdf and http://www.ultimatebiblereferencelibrary.com/The_Twelve_Caesars_of_the_1st_Century_-_Suetonius.pdf).
Author comment: this work, "The Lives of the Twelve Caesars," as of 1500 A.D. (after the printing press was invented), no less than 18 editions were printed, with the world's scholars artfully and carefully translating each and every word. This work is held in very high regard by scholars, worldwide, with respect to Caesar and his lasting legacy.

Follow the Yellow Brick Road

The reason why the most successful financial centers have THRIVED during the last 100-200 years is for only one reason: they convinced millions of wealthy people and governments to follow the yellow brick road—right to the entrance of their financial castle (or island!). The financial centers have succeeded because they knew the key to collecting investor gold and investor capital was to pass strict laws and provide those investors with great confidence regarding the security of their money. Without this unquestionable security in place, they knew there would be no yellow brick road leading to their castle, as the gold and capital would be taken elsewhere on a different golden road the investor knew would be secure *and* protected.

STEP ONE is to realize what INVESTORS BELIEVE makes countries and offshore locations viable, attractive international depositories for their investment: security of capital. This realization is critical and must be unambiguously translated into the laws, land, military and police of any country desiring to implement the recommendations this book presents. The critical realization is:

SECURITY OF CAPITAL = PRIVACY & ORDER.

PRIVACY & ORDER = THE ABILITY TO SLEEP AT NIGHT.

THE ABILITY TO SLEEP AT NIGHT = BILLIONS OF DEPOSITS BEING SENT TO YOUR INTERNATIONAL RESERVE BANK.

If you are thinking about liberty for your people and a flourishing society, you may also need to make reforms. You may need to create strict laws ensuring the mistakes the West has made, shall NOT be repeated by your country, or regional treaty group (as further explained in this chapter).
You can see, or should see, the West's political and monetary decisions have threatened some of the most critical principles for attracting capital:

Security and Privacy.

The only way to make sure your country, as a whole, benefits from the attraction of capital is to *guarantee* investor capital is not attacked. You *also need to make sure* a few people don't steal the inside track to wealth---to the enormous disadvantage of everyone else. Unfortunately, this is what has been the case in the United States and Western Europe, with the

Federal Reserve System and its cohort central banks. As time will prove, it will be one of the leading, prima facie causes of D'Apocalypse™.

Additionally, if your country lacks control over its politicians' and bankers' ability to borrow, lend, spend and/or manipulate the money supply, this will result in a significant, additional tax burden on the people. This is wildly evident in the United States and Europe through everything we have all witnessed in the last thirty years---secret bailouts, inflation and the manipulation of the economic and political system. All of these activities have led to a massive debasement of the dollar and have set up the systemic collapse which lies just dead ahead of all of us.

Unless there is real, legal and political reform, any actions taken via the recommendations in this book will be negated and REVERSE the economic progress you will have worked hard to implement for your people.

Western Governments Forgot the #1 Rule
Governments in the West, across the board, have forgotten the #1 rule, which also ensures they can continue to attract capital.

In the West, there is <u>NO SECURITY</u> for capital anymore because of the trillions of dollars of debt and derivatives outstanding which dwarf the world's GDP! Security is also in peril as a result of a quagmire of regulations and legal quicksand, which are all designed to steal investors' money when the system fails.

Most people don't choose to recognize the facts regarding this serious matter, which is human nature. No one likes to change and often, when change occurs, people act like a deer caught in head lights. They refuse to move until it is too late. It was true with the millions of people who perished in WWII and it has been true thousands of other times in history. In WWII, we all know the signs were all there, but only the most decisive and courageous made preparations to depart, often leaving nearly everything behind in order to save themselves and their families. The smartest nations, during and after WWII, made it EASY for the most talented people to immigrate to their shores. Those nations became leaders in the aftermath of that great conflict.

Your country should do the same TODAY, in anticipation of the collapse. You should build up incredible incentives to attract, permanently, smartmoney capital and brilliant people, for the betterment of your entire nation. Just like Caesar did!

Noah was warned to build an ark in preparation for a great flood no one on earth believed would arrive. You know what happened next (e.g., the story of Noah is told in The Bible, Genesis 6:9 and referenced in Hebrews 11:7---Noah is commended and his family is ultimately rewarded for his radical faith which called for unusual actions on his part, saving his family). Whether you are Jewish, Christian, Muslim, Hindu, or just about any other religion on earth, as is also retold in countless cultures all around the world, the story of a great flood is ever present in Holy Scriptures, of many religions. This book, in a way, is an economic version of the story of Noah---at least in terms of building a financial ark!

While this book does not expect a flood of water to occur, it does expect a sea change to strike at the heart of the Western financial system and Western economic markets—with global impact for all to feel.

Western politicians have spent themselves into the grave and are driving capital away in their zeal to capture every last tax dollar from their subjects. They are also attacking entities operating inside and outside their borders with vengeance. This causes capital to not only flee, but also to become petrified and FREEZE. As a result, the capital stops doing nearly ANYTHING, except being invested in liquid market sectors which cause Assflation™. The end result is no real economic development or growth.

What is the U.S. Congress' solution to this obvious problem? These rocket scientists thought long and hard about the problem and their solution is to invoke legislation **taxing international corporations** for just moving funds from one country to another. These people are brain dead and really need to be pushed out of office!

Their ongoing disastrous and idiotic decision-making will make a great script for a movie on the downfall of America, someday. Immediately, however, this should be of great concern to companies based in the U.S.

Companies based there should be considering moving their operations and headquarters immediately offshore to a destination guaranteeing their protection and guaranteeing their capital. This is only a logical decision to make since the politicians are very focused on the monies people and corporations have deposited overseas. You must act with swiftness because the legislature will ultimately prevent companies from moving anything offshore, or it will be severely restricted and/or taxed.

For governments reading this and considering a major change to their monetary and economic security policies based on the recommendations in this book, you can see the opportunities are tremendous for attracting capital to a country which will not punish the best of the best!

Unfortunately for American and European companies, the severe strain of an out-of-control, decaying governmental system is about to bear its teeth against everything which made the United States and Europe great. Japan is in a very similar situation and faces many of the exact same issues of the West.

Nimble governments and nimble readers will benefit handsomely from the West's mistakes---if the suggestions outlined herein are followed.

Until 1913—No Income Tax in the USA
As most readers know, America didn't even have an income tax until 1913, *also* the year in which the Federal Reserve was created.

The income tax was passed to guarantee the payment of interest and principal on bonds the U.S. would sell through the Fed to the bankers and founders of the Federal Reserve System!

This flew in the face of the U.S. Constitution which stated and states categorically, no direct taxation should ever be placed on the citizens of our country. A hungry Congress and ravenous bankers weaseled their way around this law by making income taxes variable, based upon people's income! This was a dagger in the heart of the intent of the Constitution, but the courts have held taxes are legal in the U.S. and it is the law of the land which must be respected.

As part of the recommendations discussed for governments, your government should provide tax PROTECTION for investors.

As stated ad nauseum, when governments start seizing capital through the increasing of fees, endless taxes, tariffs and outrageous regulations which currently beset most Western nations, capital simply goes elsewhere---particularly when the system is about ready to collapse.

This is why some of the smartest money in America and Europe has *already* moved its wealth offshore. Take a look at the fine print of the balance sheets of some of the United States' greatest corporations, hedge funds and investors---they have trillions of dollars stashed overseas, which is their absolute and legal right, at least for today. The same holds true for companies based in Europe.

As you will read in the section "If You Are a Corporation Seeking to Survive the Derivatives Debacle" in this chapter, a handful of American companies already have over $262 Billion parked offshore. These companies should be key investor targets for your government and should be apprised of your plans to institute a world-class, secure and private financial depository system, named the "International Reserve Bank(s)." Following the conservative principles outlined in D'Apocalypse™ Now! --- The Doomsday Cycle will be magic to the ears of *every* treasurer and CEO of *every* cash-rich company.

To protect your government's investment and successful, long-term outcome of the depository system, it is essential your government controls spending through the passage of legislation, which requires a balanced budget. The U.S. Congress and many Presidential administrations in the United States have found it convenient to spend their way to reelection. Their spending was aimed at propping up financial markets, creating unfunded social spending programs, or approving plain old, "pork barrel" political bills. But regardless, the money has flowed, courtesy of the Federal Reserve.

It has also flowed in Europe with equal zest and is now at a point where the sovereign debt crisis throughout the U.S. and Europe, as well as Japan, is INESCAPABLE and is the root cause of an economic tsunami and destruction which will be devastating.

Big Spenders Are the Problem---Not the Solution!

The destructive power of D'Apocalypse™ and the impending economic collapse it implies is a situation which is known and reverberates down the halls of Congress on the Potomac, in Parliament on the River Thames and in Brussels, the throne of the EU. You can read about it every day in the newspapers and listen to it on television. Budgets are a disaster, economies are a train wreck and governments close (at least in the U.S.).

Everyone is at least aware of "derivatives," but no one makes any real attempt to tackle the core problem of leverage and debt hanging over

EVERYONE'S head. In short, politicians do NOTHING about ANYTHING. The only solution the politicians have is to INCREASE TAXES AND INCREASE SPENDING, WHILE DRIVING THE BUDGET HIGHER. The politicians are the problem---they are not the solution.

Not only do these political wags overpay themselves, but they have also buried our economies and peoples. The social welfare, benefit and pension plans they have passed, to make sure they are reelected and well-paid, have demolished the system.

Capital truly wants to flee both the U.S. and Europe, but the U.S. and Europe and their foils of the BIS, G8, OECD and other alphabet soup organizations, have attempted to scare every person and country on earth. This is a vain and hopeless attempt for them to remain in control.

They realize once the dam starts leaking and capital begins to flee, it will turn into a flood-raging torrent of ex-patriots moving their monies and wealth offshore. As a result, the U.S. passed "FACTA" and a laundry list of other regulations, which has caused a great deal of trepidation for investors to do anything drastic. Countries, even including the once sphinxlike Switzerland, have been threatened with asset seizures if they don't turn over depositors' and businesses' confidential information.

> This is old news now; however, the point is, among ALL THE NATIONS, there is an ENORMOUS OPPORTUNITY to become the NEXT SWITZERLAND. You can become the next city on the hill with a golden spotlight of freedom and privacy shining on and from it! A place where SECURITY OF CAPITAL IS THE #1 RULE!

Switzerland used to be unassailable. They were strong and never bended on confidentiality. Not any longer.

Do you know the real reason why they bent?

Switzerland No Longer Unassailable Because of Debt

It isn't the fact, alone, they had been threatened with asset seizures if they didn't disclose who had monies in Zurich, Geneva, etc. The primary reason the Swiss bent on their long-established rules pertaining to secrecy is because of one thing and one thing only: THEIR DEBT!

The tables in this chapter describe a series of recommendations, including establishment of new "International Reserve Banks" (consisting of highly advanced bank vaults and depositories), which will invite capital into secure locations, prior to the meltdown of D'Apocalypse™ which is certain to afflict the west.

Within the tables, you will see Switzerland's debt listed at the bottom of each theoretical alliance. Look at the size of the DEBT of Switzerland compared to its GDP. Switzerland will survive D'Apocalypse™, there is no doubt about it; however, DEBT is the real problem of all the developed Western nations. The idiots in charge of their governments have generally indebted the countries deeply and have spent their grandchildren's inheritance into oblivion.

Your country has a chance, with a new system of magnetic capitalism, to take advantage of the egregious mistakes made by modern Western leaders. If you do, you will create happiness and prosperity for your fellow countrymen.

Trillions of Dollars Just Waiting to Flee

Trillions of dollars of capital are just waiting to FLEE. This book provides your country with a solution which will make you an economic magnet and powerhouse, with an opportunity to save the world, or at least portions of it, financially speaking.

Every person of means knows the velocity of money has SLOWED dramatically and companies are NOT SPENDING capital because of their knowledge of the huge debt problem, the fragility of the financial system and the politicians banging the drum for increased taxation and regulation. If some creative and forward-thinking countries got behind these recommendations and implemented them, populations of people could be truly helped, with those responsible for their implementation making a very good profit, to boot.

The politicians in power among the leading Western nations suffer from the same disease---they have no discipline in spending and do not have term limits. As a result, they place their selfish need for reelection in front of the long-term prosperity of their respective nations. This is not true democracy, because a democracy should be free from the ability of politicians to pass laws and regulations which greatly stack the odds in favor of their reelection---allowing those in power to remain in power.

What has really happened to America, particularly, is it has become an oligarchy, where elected officials can control enough capital to fraudulently manipulate elections, while ensuring their constituents receive special benefits and ear marks for projects in their jurisdictions. This assures elected officials are placed in a favorable light, while greatly improving the odds of their reelection. The whole process is like Las Vegas stacking the deck in the house's favor. Needless to say, the bankers and the Federal Reserve completely and wholeheartedly support those in power who do not go against their interests!

The American system has inbred corruption throughout and now even the Supreme Court has ruled there are no limits as to the amount of money a corporation can spend to support a political candidate. Something is very wrong when the judicial and legislative branches of government virtually assures companies can spend billions of dollars, if they desire, to back a candidate, or group of candidates, for political office. Your government should have strict term limits on politicians. This will ensure more honesty by the elected officials and a commitment to work on the peoples' issues---and not the politicians' own agenda.

If a country, or several countries, was able to create a reasonable and secure way for corporations, pension funds and wealthy individuals to move capital to someplace safe, these investors and entities would make a move. As discussed, right now, Western investors are like the deer caught in headlights...they look up and know something isn't quite right, and believe the big light shining in their eyes is the light at the end of the tunnel, but unfortunately, it is a freight train bearing down right on top of them, full steam ahead!

Capital thrives best in a free, faith-based society. Having responsibility to God above ensures a characteristic of trust, in and throughout society, vital to capital's success. This has been the overriding reason, historically, for the United States' success because the country has believed in God (e.g., the motto on the front of U.S. currency, "In God We Trust"). If there is truly a spiritual awakening in a country and the law of the land reflects a newly found spiritual direction, ***capital will embrace it.*** Capital flocks to countries respectful and loving of God, as history has taught and shown us this many times before.

Unfortunately for the United States, while the currency still bears the words, "In God We Trust," it is not clear God even exists in the eyes, ears and hearts of the majority of Congress these days. As anyone can see,

233

U.S. laws have been dramatically changed during the last fifty years. Collectively, they make a mockery of God's laws and lessons, as they are revealed to us in The Bible. His wisdom has been there for all to see, hear and acknowledge. Because His wisdom has been outright rejected on many, many levels, this writer shudders to think what lies ahead when it comes to retribution time for the United States and many of her Western allies, who have followed similar disobedient paths.

Governments Should Wipe Out Repression and Endorse Faith

As this book is a warning about the coming derivatives collapse of D'Apocalypse™ and what to do about it, its intention is not to brow beat anyone on religion. Investment THRIVES because of the freedom people have enjoyed to privately own property, while also enjoying their right to privacy---which *includes* the freedom to worship God above, with their lives defended and protected by the government. Inherent in this framework has ALWAYS been a belief in God, above.

When the United States was founded and for nearly two hundred years thereafter, the vast majority of people in the country believed in the resurrection of Jesus Christ. The country practiced this faith throughout its history and it was only until about fifty years ago, or so, the country started turning away from Christianity. Today, we can see America embracing everything from Gnosticism, to Satanism, to Atheism, and a whole host of other religions---while making our laws more favorable for the elite few. Most who objectively look at the changes must conclude Christianity has been under nothing but an all-out, brutal attack, from all sides.

Additionally, with the revelation the U.S. is spying on its citizens, most know and realize it is the fascists, historically, who controlled and spied on their own people. All of us can remember the horror stories which came out of the repressive era of Communism, when it controlled Eastern Europe and Russia. This group of nations did not thrive when they had "anti-privacy" rules in place and they all, ultimately, crashed—and their economies burned.

Later, when the light of freedom was allowed to shine down on their citizens, they flourished. One can look at the remarkable growth rates of Russia, Eastern Europe and China during the last thirty years and immediately realize the bell of freedom has rung. Even though communism still prevails in China, the Chinese government has been wise and very shrewd in its deployment of freedom in its system. As a result, it has ignited amazing growth rates and created vast improvements throughout the country to the benefit of an entire population of people.

Now the pendulum is swinging the other way for America and the West. Where communist societies used to be much more restrictive, they have opened dramatically and have allowed CAPITAL TO FLOW, thus creating greater prosperity for their people!

THE ABSOLUTE REVERSE HAS BEEN TRUE FOR AMERICA AND WESTERN EUROPE. With capital controls, ever-increasing taxation, sky-high unemployment and a system catering only to the rich, the Western system is buckling under the strain. You can just feel it.

Importantly, make the attraction of capital into your country (or via alliances with other nations in your region, if necessary) easy to understand, secure and safe. Create a binding resolution between the military, ruling party and congress, if necessary, to commemorate and legalize your great step forward. If you do this, capital will leap into your vaults!

The system needs to be air tight with respect to the PROTECTION of privacy. This will ensure the FREEDOM Of MOVEMENT of capital and *its* privacy, once under your protection. In this way, your nation's people will benefit and prosper (you will see how in a moment).

Corporate wealth and individual wealth will desire to move to your protection and will do it in a big hurry.

Establishing International Reserve Banks for Your Country

Because of the impending collapse of the Western markets, your country requires a DIFFERENT banking system than what is currently deployed in the United States, Western Europe, Japan and throughout the G14. For purposes of attracting capital from a system extremely close to collapsing, you MUST guarantee and/or show new depositors:

1) The government stands behind their deposits---and the bond holders and the stock holders of any bank in this secure system will be the ones who will be punished for any bank failure, however unlikely one may be. There will be no repeat Cyprus performances.

a. Their assets shall ALWAYS BE GUARANTEED BY THE GOVERNMENT, REGARDLESS OF AMOUNT. There shall be strict controls and laws which dictate to the bankers in these banks they can only lend, or hypothecate in any way, <u>a maximum of 20% of the deposits</u> during the **first five years** of an International Reserve Bank's (also referred to as "IRB") life.

b. Audits shall be performed by auditors from OUTSIDE the country, who are designated as part of the "Vault Treaty" (as explained herein) and IRB franchise agreement. Audits are to be performed annually--- in and throughout all parts of the IRB. This will include assaying bullion holdings--assuring the integrity of any bullion on hand in bank vaults. This will protect the depositors and owners of those assets and assure them no one has hijacked their bullion holdings via laser-etched tungsten counterfeits.

c. They can invest a maximum of 6% of their *deposited capital* in the International Reserve Bank's preferred stock. The IRB shall pay a dividend to them of 3%, cumulatively, based upon their invested capital. If the bank fails to make at least an annual dividend payment during any three-year period, the government and the preferred shareholders shall have the right to foreclose on the bank and its existing owners. These owners shall have no legal recourse because an unappealable, default judgment, in favor of the government and the preferred shareholders, would be rendered as a condition of the original IRB agreement in the event of such a default.

IF the IRB is ever foreclosed upon and new owners take over, the preferred shareholders shall also be granted an opportunity to invest in common stock of the IRB at a per share cost pari passu with the new common stock owners, up to the maximum of their original preferred stock investment in the foreclosed upon IRB. The preferred shareholders shall also enjoy the continuing right to invest up to 6% of their deposits and assets in the new IRB preferred stock.

Any invested capital into the IRB shall be split between the government and the owners of the designated International Reserve Bank, with 20% being paid to the government, as part of the franchise and protection fee, to be split with the country's military, and 80% being paid into the operating capital of the International Reserve Bank. These monies shall be available for lending and investment on behalf of the bank's shareholders.

20% of all dividends paid out on common stock shall be set aside and paid to the banks' employees in an employee bonus pool. This pool shall be split evenly among the employees, ensuring a massive incentive for all to work together for the common good (i.e., common dividends declared shall be paid out 80% to the common shareholders and 20% to the employees). In the event of lazy employees not deserving of such largess, they may be fired by the management of the IRB, however, they should be entitled to their pari passu share of dividends for the time they worked during the year of their firing. This will prevent predatory firing practices by greedy management. It will also keep overhead costs low because all bank employees will be extremely efficient and productive.

Each bank shall have a seven-person board. The board of directors shall consist of two members from the preferred shareholders, two members from the common shareholders, two members from the employees and one member from government. Except for the government and employees (whose seats are appointed by those groups, however, in the case of the employees, their representatives shall be elected via a secret vote of all employees), the board of directors shall be elected by a majority vote of the shareholders of each class of stock being represented.

d. The government shall hold an international auction to run the IRB. The government shall keep these monies, to be split with the military. The winning entity shall also pay the government a franchise fee of ¼ of 1% (i.e., .25%) on every dollar (euro, yen, etc.) deposited and every asset on hand, each year. The ¼ of 1% shall be calculated based on the customers deposits and assets, as measured quarterly, with one-fourth of the .25% payable (i.e., .0625%) at the end of each calendar quarter, based on the quarter's ending deposits and assets on hand.

The government shall be able to audit, physically, any IRB at any time with at least a 5-day notice, if it deems necessary. The expense of the audit shall be borne by the government. This will avoid any shenanigans going on with accounting rules---making this process very simple. The government can count the beans and get paid its franchise tax on a timely and accurate basis.

The winning bidders for the IRB franchise shall place 20% of their entire equity and ownership interests in a trust for the benefit of the poor of the host country. The equity and ownership interests, and any money or profits derived from them, shall help build the infrastructure, education, food and shelter for the underprivileged people in that nation. These improvements shall be funded out of any dividends or income generated for shareholders by the IRB, of which the trust now has an interest. Additionally, if the owners sell their common stock ownership, then 20% of those sales shall be paid to the trust immediately upon the close of the transaction and funds are received. Please see the following analysis to show you what is possible with even modest assumptions on returns, reserves, etc.

International Reserve Bank
Pro Forma Projection

	Year 1	Year 2	Year 3	Year 4	Year 5	Year 6
Gross Deposits	$1,063,829,787	$2,127,659,574	$4,255,319,149	$8,510,638,298	$14,468,085,106	$21,702,127,660
Net Customer Deposits (6% Of New Deposits Invested In Preferred Stock)	$1,000,000,000	$2,060,000,000	$4,123,600,000	$8,247,416,000	$14,094,844,960	$21,245,690,698
New Depositor Investment In Preferred Stock (3% Cumulative Dividend)	$63,829,787	$67,659,574	$131,719,149	$263,222,298	$373,240,146	$456,436,962
Cumulative Preferred Stock Investment By Depositors	$63,829,787	$131,489,362	$263,208,511	$526,430,809	$899,670,955	$1,356,107,917
Additional Common Stock Investment into IRB (80% to IRB, 20% to Gov't)	$62,500,000					
Net Capital Available To IRB From Common Stock Investors	$50,000,000					
Fee to Government From Common Stock Investors	$12,500,000					
Depositor Investments -Preferred Stock (3% Dividend, @ 6% Of Deposits)	$63,829,787	$131,489,362	$263,208,511	$526,430,809	$899,670,955	$1,356,107,917
Fee To Government On New Depositors' Preferred Stock Investments	$12,765,957	$13,531,915	$26,343,830	$52,644,460	$74,648,029	$91,287,392
Net Capital Available To IRB From Depositors' Investments	$51,063,830	$105,191,489	$210,566,809	$421,144,647	$719,736,764	$1,084,886,333
Previous Year's Retained Earnings		$723,404	$1,047,234	$1,596,064	$2,687,479	$4,333,762
Total IRB Assets & Capital Available—Loanable Funds @ 20% of Deposits	$301,063,830	$567,914,894	$1,086,334,043	$2,122,223,911	$3,591,393,235	$13,886,634,514
Total IRB Assets & Capital Available—Loanable Funds @ 60% of Deposits						
Estimated IRB Revenues @ 4% of Available Capital	$12,042,553	$22,716,596	$43,453,362	$84,888,956	$143,655,729	$555,465,381
Estimated Operating Expenses @ 50%	$6,021,277	$11,358,298	$21,726,681	$42,444,478	$71,827,865	$277,732,690
Profit Before Franchise Fee & Preferred Dividends	$6,021,277	$11,358,298	$21,726,681	$42,444,478	$71,827,865	$277,732,690
Annual Government Franchise Fee (1/4 of 1% on Deposits)	$2,659,574	$5,319,149	$10,638,298	$21,276,596	$36,170,213	$54,255,319
Dividends Preferred Stockholders (3%, Hold Cumulative Rights)	$1,914,894	$3,944,681	$7,896,255	$15,792,924	$26,990,129	$40,683,238
Profit Before Common Stock Dividends & Employee Bonus Pool	$1,446,809	$2,094,468	$3,192,128	$5,374,958	$8,667,523	$182,794,134
Dividend Bonus Employees (20% Share of Common Stock Dividends)	$144,681	$209,447	$319,213	$537,496	$866,752	$18,279,413
Dividend Bonus Owners Of Common Stock	$578,723	$837,787	$1,276,851	$2,149,983	$3,467,009	$73,117,653
Total Dividends Common Stock	$723,404	$1,047,234	$1,596,064	$2,687,479	$4,333,762	$91,397,067
Retained Earnings (50% Of Profit Before Common Dividend & Bonus Pool)	$723,404	$1,047,234	$1,596,064	$2,687,479	$4,333,762	$91,397,067
Positive Cash Flow (Adds Dividend Payments Back In)	$3,361,702	$6,039,149	$11,088,383	$21,167,882	$35,657,652	$223,477,371
TOTAL FEES PER YEAR PAID TO GOVERNMENT	$27,925,532	$18,851,064	$36,982,128	$73,921,055	$110,818,242	$145,542,712

Growth Assumption: Deposits double in years 1-4, increase 70% & 50% years 5-6, respectively.

e. For any government in a regional alliance, 80% of the governmental franchise fees collected from an "in-country" International Reserve Bank shall be paid to the hosting country and 20% shall be placed in a pooled fund which shall be split evenly among the rest of the other members of the Regional Vault Treaty. This will allow poorer, or less populated countries, to benefit from larger, or more successful ones. This will encourage everyone to "pull together" for the common good and will increase economic development between nations and produce greater trade, which will promote peace---all very good things for people.

Year 1	
Net Customer Deposits	$ 1,000,000,000
Investable Capital From Depositors	$ 63,829,787
IRB Loanable Funds @ 20%	$ 301,063,830
Estimated IRB Revenues @ 4%	$ 12,042,553
Estimated Operating Expenses @ 50%	$ 6,021,277
Profit Before Franchise Fee & Dividends	$ 6,021,277
Government Franchise Fees	$ 2,659,574
Dividends Common Stockholders	$ 578,723
Dividend Bonus Pool Employees	$ 144,681
Retained Earnings	$ 723,404
Invested IRB Capital By Depositors	$ 63,829,787
Government Fee On New Preferred Stock	$ 12,765,957
Government Fee On New Common Stock	$ 12,500,000
Total Government Payout Year One	**$ 27,925,532**

Year 6	
Net Customer Deposits	$ 21,245,690,698
Investable Capital From Depositors	$ 1,356,107,917
IRB Loanable Funds @ 60%	$ 13,886,634,514
Estimated IRB Revenues @ 4%	$ 555,465,381
Estimated Operating Expenses @ 50%	$ 277,732,690
Profit Before Franchise Fee & Dividends	$ 277,732,690
Government Franchise Fees	$ 54,255,319
Dividends Common Stockholders	$ 73,117,653
Dividend Bonus Pool Employees	$ 18,279,413
Retained Earnings	$ 91,397,067
Invested IRB Capital By Depositors	$ 1,356,107,917
Government Fee On New Preferred Stock	$ 91,287,392
Total Government Payout Year Six	$ **145,542,712**

2) A MASSIVE REDUCTION in the ability of an IRB bank to LEND money and capital has been put in place. This involves outlawing the use of the "fractionalized banking system," as it is practiced in the West, which is at the heart of the problem in this system. Western bankers routinely can legally lend out up to at least 10 times what they have on hand in depositor cash. This effectively increases the money supply and causes inflation, while allowing the bank to charge interest on loans for money the bank does not own---simply an outrageous advantage for the owners of those banks. For the next several years, as the world deals with D'Apocalypse™, IRBs should be on the 80/20 rule, where 80% of their capital should be retained and accessible to depositors---with the strictest penalty to the bank, its executives and owners, if it exceeds the lending limit. Allow 20% of deposits (i.e., total deposits and audited, liquid assets) to be loaned out. There shall be no restrictions on loans made with the IRB's own capital, except for abiding by IRB loan policy, as established by the Board of Directors. Restricting, dramatically, the percentage of loanable funds for all IRBs will not lend itself to great growth at the moment, *but it will ensure your country and the IRB has the capital it needs to survive* and become a dominant player after the West goes through the biggest bust in history.

a. Part of the package an IRB can offer depositors shall include a passport and citizenship, for life in the host country, to anyone making a commitment to deposit a minimum of $250,000 ($100,000 for smaller countries) for at least five years, and make the 6% investment in the IRB. *Companies making large deposits shall have the advantage of extending this citizenship package to their employees,* as an added incentive to bring billions of dollars in capital to your country and the IRB.

b.   After the first five years of operation, allow the bank to lend, AT MOST, 60% of deposits (i.e., total deposits and audited, liquid assets) on hand.   There are no restrictions on loans made with capital invested in the IRB, except for abiding by IRB loan policy, as established by the Board of Directors.

The amount of money the IRB can lend out MUST be set in stone and can NEVER be modified by subsequent generations---this is the key to attracting capital to a safe haven which will have long-lasting, generational appeal, as sophisticated capital owners will come to admire the strict limits you have placed on fractional reserve banking. The limits on available and lendable funds need to be set by regulation in national law. If an IRB violates the lending limit, any investor can sue the IRB in an international court for treble damages and the government shall fine the IRB $10,000,000 per violation, if the lending limit is exceeded.

3)   A signed agreement between the leadership of your government and the military of your country has been signed (and/or your allies who are parties to a Regional Vault Treaty), providing for the international protection of any monies on deposit at the IRB in your country. This protection applies regardless of a person's citizenship, or source of funds, and regardless of whether, or not, there is war, or peace.

4)   Secret bank accounts shall be maintained which restore the privacy requirements of millions of corporations and investors. Pass strict laws which require any person caught revealing state and/or IRB secrets, to be imprisoned for up to twenty years.

a.   Ignore the various internationally bank-controlled organizations currently attempting to dictate whether your country is "grey" (e.g. the OECD assigns colors to countries who do not comply with its edicts), or any other "color," in an effort to intimidate you.   What is important is for your country to attract as much capital as possible prior to the collapse of D'Apocalypse™. *Most of the major international organizations (e.g., G8, IMF, OECD, etc.) are*

designed to do nothing more than restrict capital from flowing freely INTO your own country. Cooperating with them merely provides a country with loans from the IMF, IBS, or other Western bank-controlled institution, with your country prostituting its sovereignty to these Western, banker-controlled institutions.

5) You will advertise this capability in every major city on earth. This should be a very "big deal" with a marketing campaign designed to do nothing less than attract capital from those who have controlled it for far too long. You must also be prepared for the tremendous political pressure the powers that be will place on you and your country. It will be worth it.

6) Tax relief shall be provided for all who make deposits in your country and there shall be NO taxes and NO fees, of any kind, guaranteed by the Vault Treaty and IRB franchise agreement on any deposits, or assets, made into the IRB account. Additionally, there shall be no taxes, penalties, or deductions for withdrawing, or investing capital (of any amount); with the exception of the provision relating to the depositor's right to purchase capital stock in the International Reserve Bank, and/or any separate agreement the depositor has reached with the IRB (and/or government), with respect to a passport, as well as other investment opportunities the depositor voluntarily agrees with.

7) Your government shall demand all bullion be returned to your country ASAP. Just as Venezuela, Germany and other countries have insisted on the return of their bullion assets---your country should to. When it is returned and before accepting it, ensure each and every bar is TESTED for counterfeits. The ability to use lasers to perfectly etch over the top of a veneer of gold, hiding a brick of tungsten underneath, is a well-known capability and in use, worldwide. Be particularly careful of any gold received out of any central bank. There are, saying this politely, "delivery issues." Each IRB shall have at least one assayer, with modern assaying equipment, along with a world-class bullion storage capability.

8) In parallel with the formation of the International Reserve Bank(s), the national legislature of your country MUST pass a law making it a crime for any politician to accept a bribe, consulting contract, advisory fee or campaign contribution from any International Reserve Bank, or any of its employees, officials, board members, consultants, advisors, depositors, shareholders, debt holders, any other party affiliated in any

way with the International Reserve Bank, or any of the affiliated parties mentioned herein. The punishment should be severe (e.g., a minimum 20-year sentence for each person involved).

The objective is to instill investor confidence to attract capital. Laws must be tough and punishment severe in order to convince large investors, foundations, pension funds and corporations your government (and its allied IRB counterparts in other countries) is very serious about creating an historic "Swiss-like" character for the International Reserve Bank and its hosting nation(s).

Switzerland has recently caved and changed its laws, leaving this opportunity wide open for other governments who have a vision to create a safe-haven for capital. By implementing this vision, you will only serve to make your country FAR WEALTHIER and in turn, help feed a lot of hungry people through the creation of many, many jobs in your land.

9) Regional alliances shall share their profits among the nations involved with their respective IRBs and Regional Vault Treaty in a similar fashion as the professional U.S. sports leagues share their profits among themselves. Essentially, nations shall award franchises for multiple locations for the International Reserve Banks. These entities should earn a handsome profit. They first pay their franchise tax to the government of ¼ of 1% on all deposits and assets on hand and any other fees due because of investment (i.e., the government receives 20% of all invested capital). 80% of these collective fees are retained by the "host" country of the particular IRB, with 20% of the fees being split evenly between the other signatory nations of the Regional Vault Treaty. As discussed, this book highly recommends splitting these monies with the military of your respective countries.

This book realizes this advice flies in the face of what the G8 is suggesting because the G8's interests (particularly the Western members) are in hunting down every tax dollar it can because of the West's overspending. The G8 has no interest in teaching emerging nations the secrets to their historic success in attracting capital through the establishment of a forward-thinking, independent, International Reserve Bank.

The opportunity is here to create a region on earth where capital will FREELY FLOW TO---without fear of it being lost. Old-fashioned secrecy and privacy with respect to capital is a corner stone, historically, for all freedom-loving people, worldwide. The first region on earth to create a system like this will FLOURISH in this environment and insulate itself from towering debt and soon-to-collapse derivatives markets, worldwide. *YOUR COUNTRY WILL BECOME A SAFE HAVEN FOR SERIOUS CAPITAL.*

The one place which has come closest to implementing this vision and has gained tremendous respectability, is Singapore, however, they have signed tax treaties making them subject, ultimately, to the beck and call of the Western financial system.

The G8

The G8 is made up of heads of government from Canada, France, Germany, Italy, Japan, the United Kingdom the United States and until the uprising in the Ukraine, the Russian Federation. They were supposedly "kicked out" of the G8 as a punishment for invading the Ukraine. The European Union is also represented at

Russian Federation Coat of Arms
(Source: Wikipedia, as retrieved from http://en.wikipedia.org/wiki/Russ

Vladimir Putin
Russian President
(Source: Wikipedia, as retrieved from http://en.wikipedia.org/wiki /Vladimir_Putin).

meetings by both the President of the European Commission and the leader of the country which has European Union Presidency. Special mention needs to be made of Russia, as this country is beyond a super power.

Russia has a President who professes to be a Christian and has an opportunity to create a banking system which could attract trillions of dollars in capital from the West. Some might even say Russia is freer than America today, given U.S. propensity to over-regulate, over-legislate and over-tax just about everything. If Russia ever decided to make a marked departure from the Western bankers and implement the suggestions herein, it would very quickly and radically annihilate the West's financial system. Western politicians just do not get it. Capital is tired of being terrorized. It wants a free home.

China has a unique opportunity, as well. It has brilliantly attracted Western capital to help it completely transform its country. The pace of growth is a tribute to the strategic intelligence of its leadership. China is playing the long-term game and has made huge and significant investments in its

Flag of People's Republic of China

infrastructure, defense and industrial capabilities, while tying up rare and precious resources around the world. China has ensured it is in an excellent negotiating position for decades to come. Out of respect to the 1.3 billion people who live there and the thousands of leaders who are responsible for their transition to a freer economy, China is a country with the industry and might to make a huge impact against the current powers leading the West's financial system. It also has to solve its own debt bubble; however, it is far better off than the leveraged pinnacle of doom which towers over the Western financial system.

From a completely intellectual perspective, it will be interesting to see how this plays out. The West, loaded with debt and a towering financial system with massive derivatives exposure due to excess greed, versus two emerging and transformative markets which in many ways are freer than America!

Is this Athens and Sparta reenacted? Only time will tell.

Any way it is sliced and diced, both Russia and China are outstanding lessons in allowing capitalism and free enterprise to work. Though both modern-day China and Russia have a foundation built from communism, both have chosen free market policies---with relatively modest government intervention. This is one of the key reasons both economies are on a tear, despite the inevitable bubbles and busts which come with such rapid growth. Compare their growth with the West, where over-regulation and debt, caused by desperate politicians attempting to inflate economies based on unwise economic principles, have been the policy. Except for the upper class, the Western economies are in a real shambles and both the politicians' and bankers' actions have reached a tipping point. This tipping point is called D'Apocalypse™.

Many millions of people are going to be very, very upset with the West's politicians and bankers in the coming years, and it is highly likely massive changes in government will take place. As we see and hear the frustration in Brazil, Greece, Italy, Spain, etc., this action will be mimicked all around the globe---targeted at corrupt governments and the people who are supposedly running those governments whose only real agenda has been to stay in power.

There is a sense of change in the air on the world stage, particularly watching the body language of the world's leaders. Perhaps Russia will do its own thing and not hold itself at the mercy of the bankers and become a true, trusted leader of strength in the financial markets. Perhaps China will allow Hong Kong, or Macau, to adopt new, more private banking rules in order to attract capital from Switzerland, London, New York and Singapore.

The 21st century will be interesting—this is for sure.

G8 Ignores the Developing World, the G20 is Banker-Controlled

All G8 members originate from the developed, industrialized world. Unbelievably, it excludes China, India, South America, the entire Middle East, Thailand, Malaysia, Indonesia, Australia and many, many other countries! It also fails to represent any countries in Africa or Central America.

The G8 has ignored the issues concerning the developing world and with the exception of Russia, has spent itself into oblivion. Government employees, and elected officials, have enriched and entrenched themselves---particularly in the United States and Western Europe. The G8's policies and priorities fail to represent the majority of the developing world and every other great nation on earth.

The G20 doesn't help anything, either, because it is a forum for the international finance ministers and central bankers---the very ones who facilitated the $30 Trillion Heist and the inevitability of D'Apocalypse™!

The G20 Members.

Australia	India	Argentina	France	China
Canada	Russia	Brazil	Germany	Indonesia
Saudi Arabia	South Africa	Mexico	Italy	Japan
United States	Turkey	EU	United Kingdom	South Korea

The G20 is a group of finance ministers and central bank governors from 20 major economies. (Source: Wikipedia, as retrieved from http://en.wikipedia.org/wiki/G-20_major_economies).

The first nation, or group of nations in the developing world, particularly, which can create a Regional Vault Treaty and International Reserve Bank(s) will attract capital and will find itself being one of the key leaders of the world's future in the 21st Century. The West's governments are hopelessly corrupted by money, power and the need to maintain their power via the accumulation of debt. This will not last long.

The creation of International Reserve Banks can be done by any country itself, or could be led by another major nation, with invitations going out to "affiliated" countries, worldwide, via a Vault Treaty.

The two most obvious candidates for such a leadership position are China and Russia; however, the Middle Eastern countries are extremely well capitalized and could also be a very interesting leader in this regard. While they operate under Sharia law, their "investment" in an International Reserve Banking system, which helps developing nations, would significantly benefit them and geographically further diversify their assets. This would also ensure their integration into an emerging, new and revolutionary banking system.

Creation of capital is the key to helping the future of people. The profits from its accretion flow into the local economies where the IRBs are located. Ultimately, provided there is enough time, the tables will turn and the country, or region(s), who create International Reserve Banks will become DEBT FREE.

They will ultimately use their capital and power to reacquire treasures stolen long ago by the greedy Western bankers and established elite in the West.

Does this sound outrageous and impossible?

Please review the calculations on debt to GDP and see how badly the U.S. looks when unfunded entitlements are counted:

©2013 Robert L. Kelly

Selected Government Debt To GDP
Ranked By External Debt To GDP

GDP Rank	Country Name	GDP 2012	Public	Public Debt	External Debt	External	U.S. Debt + Unfunded	Total US
98	Macau	$47,190,000,000				0.0%		
31	Nigeria	$455,500,000,000	18.8	$85,634,000,000	$10,100,000,000	2.2%		
101	Paraguay	$41,550,000,000	14.7	$6,107,850,000	$2,245,000,000	5.4%		
3	China	$12,610,000,000,000	31.7	$3,997,370,000,000	$770,800,000,000	6.1%		
162	Suriname	$6,874,000,000	7.3	$504,300,000	$504,300,000	7.3%		
93	Bolivia	$56,140,000,000	32.7	$18,357,780,000	$4,200,000,000	7.5%		
4	India	$4,761,000,000,000	51.9	$2,470,959,000,000	$376,300,000,000	7.9%		
96	Uganda	$51,270,000,000	26.8	$13,740,360,000	$4,126,000,000	8.0%		
142	Malawi	$14,500,000,000	47.1	6829500000	$1,214,000,000	8.4%		
73	Ethiopia	$105,000,000,000	44.4	$46,620,000,000	$9,956,000,000	9.5%		
61	Ecuador	$155,800,000,000	23.3	$36,301,400,000	$15,480,000,000	9.9%		
76	Oman	$91,540,000,000	3.6	$3,295,440,000	$9,768,000,000	10.7%		
77	Myanmar	$90,930,000,000	8.1	$7,370,000,000	$11,000,000,000	12.1%		
84	Kenya	$77,140,000,000	50	$38,570,000,000	$9,526,000,000	12.3%		
106	Honduras	$38,420,000,000	34.5	$13,254,900,000	$4,884,000,000	12.7%		
42	Vietnam	$325,900,000,000	48.2	$157,083,800,000	$41,850,000,000	12.8%		
79	Ghana	$83,740,000,000	47.4	$39,692,760,000	$11,230,000,000	13.4%		
20	Saudi Arabia	$921,700,000,000	12.9	$118,899,300,000	$127,400,000,000	13.8%		
85	Tanzania	$75,070,000,000	34.4	$25,824,080,000	$11,180,000,000	14.9%		
29	Colombia	$511,100,000,000	40.2	$205,462,200,000	$78,640,000,000	15.4%		
34	Venezuela	$408,500,000,000	49	$200,165,000,000	$63,740,000,000	15.6%		
40	Peru	$332,000,000,000	18.3	$60,756,000,000	$52,590,000,000	15.8%		
68	Cuba	$121,000,000,000	35.1	4247100000	$22,160,000,000	18.3%		
62	Kuwait	$153,400,000,000	7.1	$10,891,400,000	$28,210,000,000	18.4%		
8	Brazil	$2,394,000,000,000	54.9	$1,314,306,000,000	$440,600,000,000	18.4%		
23	Argentina	$755,300,000,000	41.6	$314,204,800,000	$141,100,000,000	18.7%		
117	Nicaragua	$27,100,000,000	52.7	$14,281,700,000	$5,228,000,000	19.3%		
30	Malaysia	$506,700,000,000	53.5	$271,084,500,000	$98,650,000,000	19.5%		
60	Morocco	$174,000,000,000	71.7	$124,758,000,000	$33,980,000,000	19.5%		
164	Guyana	$6,256,000,000	66.1	$4,135,216,000	$1,234,000,000	19.7%		
12	Mexico	$1,788,000,000,000	35.4	$632,952,000,000	$352,900,000,000	19.7%		
25	Thailand	$662,600,000,000	43.3	$286,905,800,000	$133,700,000,000	20.2%		

	Country Name	GDP 2012		Public Debt	External Debt		U.S. Debt + Unfunded	Total
81	Guatemala	$79,970,000,000	29.9	$23,911,030,000	$16,170,000,000	20.2%		
16	Indonesia	$1,237,000,000,000	24.8	$306,776,000,000	$251,200,000,000	20.3%		
124	Zambia	$24,360,000,000	31.2	$7,600,320,000	$5,445,000,000	22.4%		
26	South Africa	$592,000,000,000	43.3	$256,336,000,000	$137,500,000,000	23.2%		
90	Costa Rica	$59,790,000,000	47.4	$28,340,460,000	$14,470,000,000	24.2%		
92	Panama	$58,020,000,000	41	$23,788,200,000	$14,200,000,000	24.5%		
138	Namibia	$17,030,000,000	28.2	$4,802,460,000	$4,204,000,000	24.7%		
7	Russia	$2,555,000,000,000	12.2	$311,710,000,000	$631,800,000,000	24.7%		
99	El Salvador	$47,090,000,000	57.4	$27,029,660,000	$12,840,000,000	27.3%		
17	Turkey	$1,142,000,000,000	40.4	$461,368,000,000	$336,900,000,000	29.5%		
43	Chile	$325,800,000,000	10.1	$32,905,800,000	$117,800,000,000	36.2%		
94	Uruguay	$54,670,000,000	57.2	$31,271,240,000	$21,070,000,000	38.5%		
135	Congo, Republic of the	$19,410,000,000	18.3	$194,100,000	$7,644,000,000	39.4%		
39	Ukraine	$340,700,000,000	38.8	$132,191,600,000	$135,000,000,000	39.6%		
182	Belize	$3,048,000,000	90.8	$2,767,584,000	$1,457,000,000	47.8%		
50	United Arab Emirates	$275,800,000,000	40.4	$111,423,200,000	$158,900,000,000	57.6%		
5	Japan	$4,704,000,000,000	214.3	$10,080,672,000,000	$3,024,000,000,000	64.3%		
64	New Zealand	$134,200,000,000	41.8	$56,095,600,000	$90,230,000,000	67.2%		
59	Qatar	$191,000,000,000	32.5	$62,075,000,000	$137,000,000,000	71.7%		
110	Bahrain	$33,630,000,000	56.2	$18,900,060,000	$25,270,000,000	75.1%		
14	Canada	$1,513,000,000,000	84.1	$1,272,433,000,000	$1,326,000,000,000	87.6%		
1	European Union	$15,970,000,000,000	85.3	$13,622,410,000,000	$15,500,000,000,000	97.1%		
2	United States	$15,940,000,000,000	73.6	$11,731,840,000,000	$15,930,000,000,000	99.9%	$182,580,000,000,000	1145%
57	Hungary	$198,800,000,000	78.6	$156,256,800,000	$202,000,000,000	101.6%		
11	Italy	$1,863,000,000,000	126.1	$2,349,243,000,000	$2,493,000,000,000	133.8%		
19	Australia	$986,700,000,000	26.9	$265,422,300,000	$1,403,000,000,000	142.2%		
15	Spain	$1,434,000,000,000	85.3	$1,223,202,000,000	$2,311,000,000,000	161.2%		
6	Germany	$3,250,000,000,000	81.7	$2,655,250,000,000	$5,719,000,000,000	176.0%		
47	Greece	$281,400,000,000	161.3	$453,898,200,000	$576,600,000,000	204.9%		
38	Austria	$364,900,000,000	74.6	$272,215,400,000	$808,100,000,000	221.5%		
10	France	$2,291,000,000,000	89.9	$2,059,609,000,000	$5,165,000,000,000	225.4%		
46	Norway	$281,700,000,000	30.3	$85,355,100,000	$659,100,000,000	234.0%		
35	Sweden	$399,400,000,000	38.6	$154,168,400,000	$1,034,000,000,000	258.9%		
36	Hong Kong	$375,500,000,000	30	$112,650,000,000	$1,047,000,000,000	278.8%		
56	Finland	$200,700,000,000	53.5	$107,374,500,000	$599,300,000,000	298.6%		
41	Singapore	$331,900,000,000	111.4	$369,736,600,000	$1,174,000,000,000	353.7%		
37	Switzerland	$369,400,000,000	52.4	$193,565,600,000	$1,563,000,000,000	423.1%		
9	United Kingdom	$2,375,000,000,000	88.7	$2,106,625,000,000	$10,090,000,000,000	424.8%		
147	Iceland	$13,040,000,000	118.9	$15,504,560,000	$100,200,000,000	768.4%		
58	Ireland	$195,400,000,000	118	$230,572,000,000	$2,163,000,000,000	1107.0%		

The Certainty of Marketing Success of the IRB

All investors should be excited to have their capital placed in a safe location (from a debt to GDP perspective), if they know:

1) They will not be robbed by the government, or the IRB employees.
2) The armed forces of the host nation and its allied nations will vow to protect and defend the investors' capital, as if they were citizens of the country, with all the rights this entails.
3) Corruption has been stamped out, and to the extent it still exists, the government shall guarantee AGAINST IT. If corruption occurs, under the new law, the offending parties should be sent to prison for a very long time. In certain countries where corruption is endemic and is the "normal," even more severe punishments shall be needed to restore order and accountability of the system guarding the depositors' capital.
4) They have complete 24/7 access to their capital.
5) They have a digital path to their funds, which requires other stringent security methods.
6) They can count on complete secrecy.
7) They can receive permanent citizenship.

Regional Partnerships Take on a Whole New Meaning With a Vault Treaty in Place

Governments will undoubtedly think through the possibilities for creating an International Reserve Bank via a Vault Treaty. Here are some interesting combinations which could attract capital, easily, from North America and Europe:

The Central & South American Alliance

As you can see from the countries listed, as follows, these GDPs DWARF the GDP of Switzerland. With reform and some tough new laws on the books, along with a strong military alliance among the countries agreeing to the Vault Treaty, a very powerful tool will be in place to attract capital which will transform the entire continent.

A Latin American Bank Vault—a Supreme IRB Strategy

Selected Government Debt To GDP
Latin American Bank Vault

GDP Rank	Country Name	GDP 2012	% of US	Public	Public Debt	External Debt	External Debt as %
23	Argentina	$755,300,000,000	4.7%	41.6%	$314,204,800,000	$141,100,000,000	18.7%
182	Belize	$3,048,000,000	0.0%	90.8%	$2,767,584,000	$1,457,000,000	47.8%
93	Bolivia	$56,140,000,000	0.4%	32.7%	$18,357,780,000	$4,200,000,000	7.5%
8	Brazil	$2,394,000,000,000	15.0%	54.9%	$1,314,306,000,000	$440,600,000,000	18.4%
43	Chile	$325,800,000,000	2.0%	10.1%	$32,905,800,000	$117,800,000,000	36.2%
29	Colombia	$511,100,000,000	3.2%	40.2%	$205,462,200,000	$78,640,000,000	15.4%
90	Costa Rica	$59,790,000,000	0.4%	47.4%	$28,340,460,000	$14,470,000,000	24.2%
68	Cuba	$121,000,000,000	0.8%	35.1%	$42,471,000,000	$22,160,000,000	18.3%
61	Ecuador	$155,800,000,000	1.0%	23.3%	$36,301,400,000	$15,480,000,000	9.9%
99	El Salvador	$47,090,000,000	0.3%	57.4%	$27,029,660,000	$12,840,000,000	27.3%
81	Guatemala	$79,970,000,000	0.5%	29.9%	$23,911,030,000	$16,170,000,000	20.2%
164	Guyana	$6,256,000,000	0.0%	66.1%	$4,135,216,000	$1,234,000,000	19.7%
106	Honduras	$38,420,000,000	0.2%	34.5%	$13,254,900,000	$4,884,000,000	12.7%
12	Mexico	$1,788,000,000,000	11.2%	35.4%	$632,952,000,000	$352,900,000,000	19.7%
117	Nicaragua	$27,100,000,000	0.2%	52.7%	$14,281,700,000	$5,228,000,000	19.3%
92	Panama	$58,020,000,000	0.4%	41.0%	$23,788,200,000	$14,200,000,000	24.5%
101	Paraguay	$41,550,000,000	0.3%	14.7%	$6,107,850,000	$2,245,000,000	5.4%
40	Peru	$332,000,000,000	2.1%	18.3%	$60,756,000,000	$52,590,000,000	15.8%
162	Suriname	$6,874,000,000	0.0%	7.3%	$504,300,000	$504,300,000	7.3%
94	Uruguay	$54,670,000,000	0.3%	57.2%	$31,271,240,000	$21,070,000,000	38.5%
34	Venezuela	$408,500,000,000	2.6%	49.0%	$200,165,000,000	$63,740,000,000	15.6%
Total		$7,270,428,000,000	45.6%	41.7%	$3,033,274,120,000	$1,383,512,300,000	19.0%
37	Switzerland	$369,400,000,000	2.3%	52.4%	$193,565,600,000	$1,563,000,000,000	423.1%

A Central American IRB Alliance

Creating a broad alliance with all of these countries could be a bit difficult, given the politics of the region and the many natural differences which occur between nations. However, when you look at nearly ANY combination of countries in Central and South America, their combined GDPs are far larger, and their collective debts are far smaller as a percent of GDP, than Switzerland! With some creative and aggressive diplomacy, even some of the very small countries, completely overlooked by the G8, have a shot at attracting capital on par with Switzerland. These countries would certainly be a lot safer, from an aggregate debt perspective!

Selected Government Debt To GDP
Central American Bank Vault

GDP Rank	Country Name	GDP 2012	As a % of US GDP	Public Debt as % GDP	Public Debt	External Debt	External Debt as % GDP
182	Belize	$3,048,000,000	0.0%	90.8%	$2,767,584,000	$1,457,000,000	47.8%
90	Costa Rica	$59,790,000,000	0.4%	47.4%	$28,340,460,000	$14,470,000,000	24.2%
61	Ecuador	$155,800,000,000	1.0%	23.3%	$36,301,400,000	$15,480,000,000	9.9%
99	El Salvador	$47,090,000,000	0.3%	57.4%	$27,029,660,000	$12,840,000,000	27.3%
81	Guatemala	$79,970,000,000	0.5%	29.9%	$23,911,030,000	$16,170,000,000	20.2%
164	Guyana	$6,256,000,000	0.0%	66.1%	$4,135,216,000	$1,234,000,000	19.7%
106	Honduras	$38,420,000,000	0.2%	34.5%	$13,254,900,000	$4,884,000,000	12.7%
12	Mexico	$1,788,000,000,000	11.2%	35.4%	$632,952,000,000	$352,900,000,000	19.7%
117	Nicaragua	$27,100,000,000	0.2%	52.7%	$14,281,700,000	$5,228,000,000	19.3%
92	Panama	$58,020,000,000	0.4%	41.0%	$23,788,200,000	$14,200,000,000	24.5%
162	Suriname	$6,874,000,000	0.0%	7.3%	$504,300,000	$504,300,000	7.3%
94	Uruguay	$54,670,000,000	0.3%	57.2%	$31,271,240,000	$21,070,000,000	38.5%
Total		**$2,325,038,000,000**	**14.6%**	**36.1%**	**$838,537,690,000**	**$460,437,300,000**	**19.8%**
37	Switzerland	$369,400,000,000	2.3%	52.4%	$193,565,600,000	$1,563,000,000,000	423.1%

The Mercosur IRB Alliance

The "Norte Del Sur" IRB Alliance

Selected Government Debt To GDP — Mercosur Bank Vault

GDP Rank	Country Name	GDP 2012	As a % of US GDP	Public Debt as % GDP	Public Debt	External Debt	External Debt as % GDP
23	Argentina	$755,300,000,000	4.7%	41.6%	$314,204,800,000	$141,100,000,000	18.7%
93	Bolivia	$56,140,000,000	0.4%	32.7%	$18,357,780,000	$4,200,000,000	7.5%
8	Brazil	$2,394,000,000,000	15.0%	54.9%	$1,314,306,000,000	$440,600,000,000	18.4%
101	Paraguay	$41,550,000,000	0.3%	14.7%	$6,107,850,000	$2,245,000,000	5.4%
94	Uruguay	$54,670,000,000	0.3%	57.2%	$31,271,240,000	$21,070,000,000	38.5%
34	Venezuela	$408,500,000,000	2.6%	49.0%	$200,165,000,000	$63,740,000,000	15.6%
Total		**$3,710,160,000,000**	**23.3%**	**50.8%**	**$1,884,412,670,000**	**$672,955,000,000**	**18.1%**
37	Switzerland	$369,400,000,000	2.3%	52.4%	$193,565,600,000	$1,563,000,000,000	423.1%

©2013 Robert L. Kelly

Norte Del Sur American Bank Vault

GDP Rank	Country Name	GDP 2012	As a % of US GDP	Public Debt as % GDP	Public Debt	External Debt	External Debt as % GDP
29	Colombia	$511,100,000,000	3.2%	40.2%	$205,462,200,000	$78,640,000,000	15.4%
61	Ecuador	$155,800,000,000	1.0%	23.3%	$36,301,400,000	$15,480,000,000	9.9%
164	Guyana	$6,256,000,000	0.0%	66.1%	$4,135,216,000	$1,234,000,000	19.7%
92	Panama	$58,020,000,000	0.4%	41.0%	$23,788,200,000	$14,200,000,000	24.5%
101	Paraguay	$41,550,000,000	0.3%	14.7%	$6,107,850,000	$2,245,000,000	5.4%
162	Suriname	$6,874,000,000	0.0%	7.3%	$504,300,000	$504,300,000	7.3%
Total		**$779,600,000,000**	**4.9%**	**35.4%**	**$276,299,166,000**	**$112,303,300,000**	**14.4%**
37	Switzerland	$369,400,000,000	2.3%	52.4%	$193,565,600,000	$1,563,000,000,000	423.1%

©2013 Robert L. Kelly

Those who change their laws first and either go it alone with a national IRB, or establish a Regional Vault Treaty, in complete alliance with the involved countries' respective militaries, will win the prize to be first out of the box to create a brand new safe haven for investors.

The beautiful part of this strategy is---who could denounce *any* government for trying to help the poor people of its country, or surrounding region? The answer is: no one.

With enough countries involved, the world cannot turn its back on you. There is certain strength in numbers!

Let's look at Africa, for a moment.

The African Alliance

Yes, even Africa has a great chance at forming such a banking system. The challenges here are more difficult, as certain areas are prone to extreme violence and corruption runs rampant; however, the biggest reason for the unrest is the extreme poverty. IF certain governments got together and the militaries united to establish the IRB, and share the profits with government, it could be a home run. Their combined GDPs also DWARF Switzerland's!

Selected Government Debt To GDP
African Alliance

©2013 Robert I. Kelly

GDP Rank	Country Name	GDP 2012	As % of US GDP	Public Debt as % GDP	Public Debt	External Debt	External Debt as % GDP
31	Nigeria	$455,500,000,000	2.9%	18.8%	$85,634,000,000	$10,100,000,000	2.2%
96	Uganda	$51,270,000,000	0.3%	26.8%	$13,740,360,000	$4,126,000,000	8.0%
142	Malawi	$14,500,000,000	0.1%	47.1%	$6,829,500,000	$1,214,000,000	8.4%
73	Ethiopia	$105,000,000,000	0.7%	44.4%	$46,620,000,000	$9,956,000,000	9.5%
84	Kenya	$77,140,000,000	0.5%	50.0%	$38,570,000,000	$9,526,000,000	12.3%
79	Ghana	$83,740,000,000	0.5%	47.4%	$39,692,760,000	$11,230,000,000	13.4%
85	Tanzania	$75,070,000,000	0.5%	34.4%	$25,824,080,000	$11,180,000,000	14.9%
60	Morocco	$174,000,000,000	1.1%	71.7%	$124,758,000,000	$33,980,000,000	19.5%
124	Zambia	$24,360,000,000	0.2%	31.2%	$7,600,320,000	$5,445,000,000	22.4%
26	South Africa	$592,000,000,000	3.7%	43.3%	$256,336,000,000	$137,500,000,000	23.2%
138	Namibia	$17,030,000,000	0.1%	28.2%	$4,802,460,000	$4,204,000,000	24.7%
135	Congo, Republic of the	$19,410,000,000	0.1%	1.0%	$194,100,000	$7,644,000,000	39.4%
114	Congo, Democratic Republic of the	$28,030,000,000	0.2%	36.6%	$10,258,980,000	$7,644,000,000	27.3%
Total		$1,717,050,000,000	10.8%	38.5%	$660,860,560,000	$253,749,000,000	14.8%
37	**Switzerland**	**$369,400,000,000**	**2.3%**	**52.4%**	**$193,565,600,000**	**$1,563,000,000,000**	**423.1%**

Looking once more at our friends in South America, we find even small governments could make a tremendous difference to their local economies by simply becoming a solid place to store and protect capital.

Selected Government Debt To GDP
Guyana, Suriname & Paraguay

GDP Rank	Country Name	GDP 2012	As a % of US GDP	Public Debt as % GDP	Public Debt	External Debt	External Debt as % GDP
164	Guyana	$6,256,000,000	0.0%	66.1%	$4,135,216,000	$1,234,000,000	19.7%
101	Paraguay	$41,550,000,000	0.3%	14.7%	$6,107,850,000	$2,245,000,000	5.4%
162	Suriname	$6,874,000,000	0.0%	7.3%	$504,300,000	$504,300,000	7.3%
Total		**$54,680,000,000**	**0.3%**	**19.7%**	**$10,747,366,000**	**$3,983,300,000**	**7.3%**
37	Switzerland	$369,400,000,000	2.3%	52.4%	$193,565,600,000	$1,563,000,000,000	423.1%

Here are three countries, all amazing places and the world basically ignores them. If they were to band together, even though they are much smaller in GDP than Switzerland, their collective debt is FAR LESS, as a percent of GDP. This makes them a much more fiscally safe place to store capital.

If they formed an alliance, they could totally transform their economies through the transference of capital, with the profits shared by the respective governments and military for the betterment of their people.

258

These countries are growing, but they are primarily at the mercy of the larger economies around them, as well as the bankers pulling their purse strings. Paraguay has tremendous resources, as does Guyana and Suriname. They are slowly being developed, however, the question once again is, "Cui Bono?"

Did those countries retain control, or are other people buying up large swaths of property for development---robbing, perhaps, future generations of citizens the good earth they were endowed with. By now, readers of this book know the answer to this question.

Asia and the Middle East have the largest and perhaps greatest opportunity to spring this plan into action. They are the least mired down by Western bankers. Granted, some of these countries did incur debt, but they have many resources at their disposal to remain independent and not be crushed by the inevitable Western collapse. Also, if they decide on a different monetary policy and capital investment strategy than their Western counterparts, they can defend themselves—either militarily, or economically speaking.

But, make no mistake; due to the far overreach by the Western banking establishment, those countries which can prepare a pathway protecting capital will enjoy the benefit of enormous inflows of assets, currency and capital, allowing them to become a 21st Century version of a new-Switzerland.

The Asian IRB Alliance
Hong Kong and Singapore have exceptional opportunities to exploit the debt explosion in the West and the massive derivatives bubble built by the Western banks.

These territories are unique because they could make minor revisions to their laws which could have an enormous impact on capital flows into their already well-established and trusted banking centers. It is only a matter of time before they do. The international competition to attract capital will heat up terrifically during the next several years. These two (and perhaps Macau, as well) provincial cities and territories are obvious candidates to implement IRB-type facilities especially suited for Western interests. Singapore has already built, perhaps, the world's most secure storage facility, which maintains strict privacy. These territories are extremely sophisticated and have established the long-term trust and respect of investors, worldwide.

Asian leaders, particularly China, have obviously thought through the benefit of establishing several "special" territories which attract capital and yet still allow China to protect its population from the overreach of the Western banking establishment. It also has largely protected China from the loose mores of the Western system of government. A little further tweaking of laws, guaranteeing privacy, security and accessibility to capital, will ensure they become THE global superpower everyone believes they will become. Frankly, Russia has the same, identical, opportunity IF they break from the G8, formally, or go about their business of state without informing the G8 of its IRB plans.

As China, Russia and a myriad number of other countries attempt to build IRBs, or a version of one, the world will witness an economic war for the *attraction of capital*. Historically, this has been a "no-brainer" in favor of the West because of security and the protection and safety of the system. This assumption and presumption has now changed because of the politicians' actions, as backed by the Federal Reserve, other central banks and the elite owners of the banks.

A crazy time is arriving because the West is already losing this emerging economic war, despite its attempts to use all of its resources to maintain control. These manipulations have included controlling the ratings agencies, issuing massive amounts of debt, the printing of money, controlling interest rates and the issuance of regulations which make it difficult to move capital overseas.

Western politicians are plainly incompetent. Capital *always* finds a way to flee when it is under attack and their politicians' actions, all designed to simply enhance reelection chances, simply cause irreparable harm to the entire system.

During the middle of the Edward Snowden debacle, Moody's issued this press release on June 24, 2013 against Hong Kong banks—there will be many more attacks on competitive banks outside the West in the coming years. The bankers and politicians will be PETRIFIED of capital flight:

Rating Action: Moody's takes rating actions on nine Hong Kong banks

Global Credit Research - 24 Jun 2013

"Hong Kong, June 24, 2013 -- Moody's Investors Service has changed the outlooks for the bank financial strength ratings (BFSRs)/Baseline Credit Assessments (BCAs) of eight Hong Kong banks to negative from stable, and one bank's BFSR outlook to stable from positive. In addition, Moody's has lowered Wing Lung Bank's BFSR by one notch, and affirmed all other ratings of the nine banks. Moody's has affirmed the deposit ratings of all the nine banks involved in this rating action. However, it has changed the outlooks on the deposit ratings for five of the nine banks concerned to negative from stable, while those for the other four banks are unchanged at stable….The rating actions follow Moody's decision to revise the outlook for Hong Kong's banking system to negative from stable. The change in the banking system outlook reflects the agency's concerns regarding persistent negative real interest rates and potential property bubbles in Hong Kong, as well as Hong Kong banks' growing exposures to Mainland China. These factors could result in adverse operating conditions for Hong Kong banks over the outlook horizon." (Source: Moody's press release, June 24, 2013, as retrieved from http://www.moodys.com/research/Moodys-takes-rating-actions-on-nine-Hong-Kong-banks--PR_275029).

All is fair in love and war!

The Emerging Asian Country Alliance

If the governments, in just about any combination of the emerging Asian nations, got together and formed a strategic, financial alliance focused on attracting capital for investment in their collective states, it would send shivers up the spine of the Western banking establishment. In the following table, only one country is significantly below Switzerland's GDP and this country, Myanmar, has tremendous assets which are just waiting to be developed. These countries, and many around them, have been totally ignored by the West and thrive at the hands of extremely industrious societies. The following is a politically and religiously challenging alliance, but in a global economic war for capital, sometimes the phrase, "politics makes strange bed fellows" is apropos.

Selected Government Debt To GDP Asian Alliance

GDP Rank	Country Name	GDP 2012	As % of US Public Debt — GDP	As % of US Public Debt — as % GDP	Public Debt	External Debt	External Debt as % GDP
42	Vietnam	$325,900,000,000	2.0%	48.2%	$157,083,800,000	$41,850,000,000	12.8%
16	Indonesia	$1,237,000,000,000	7.8%	24.8%	$306,776,000,000	$251,200,000,000	20.3%
77	Myanmar	$90,930,000,000	0.6%	8.1%	$7,370,000,000	$11,000,000,000	12.1%
25	Thailand	$662,600,000,000	4.2%	43.3%	$286,905,800,000	$133,700,000,000	20.2%
30	Malaysia	$506,700,000,000	3.2%	53.5%	$271,084,500,000	$98,650,000,000	19.5%
Total		$2,823,130,000,000	17.7%	36.5%	$1,029,220,100,000	$536,400,000,000	19.0%
37	Switzerland	$369,400,000,000	2.3%	52.4%	$193,565,600,000	$1,563,000,000,000	423.1%

In an emerging Asian Country scenario, a combination of Muslim and non-Muslim nations would be created with the knowledge Sharia law does not permit the use of interest payments, or charges, in the manner proscribed and practiced by non-Muslim bankers. However, many Muslim nations have established special zones for commerce with commercial partners (e.g., Malaysia's Labuan Territory, Bahrain, etc.), where non-Muslim banking practices are allowed.

If such an IRB alliance occurred between groups of countries in Southeast Asia, the combined GDPs, along with the STATURE of the governments involved, would cause an International Reserve Bank to grow very rapidly---attracting billions of dollars which would benefit the alliance and populations in the region.

Asia, the Middle East, Africa and Latin America—each of them has a tremendous opportunity to act.

International Reserve Bank Establishment Requirements Summary
The greatest issue in establishing an IRB will be convincing capital the integrity of the IRB system is beyond strong and is impeccable. This will require agreements, in many cases, ensuring the protection of capital by the military and police, in combination with government, in those regions. To summarize, establishing a successful IRB should include:

1) Building state-of-the-art vaults and storage facilities, which become a top, national priority to protect. They should be built in a manner similar to those in Switzerland and the newly constructed vault in Singapore (Freeport), where Deutsche Bank is storing $9 Billion in gold. The newly established IRB would allow:

a) Any depositor to access the facility 24/7, without any requirement to alert officials of their arriving to inspect, access, add to, or depart with, their savings, assets, capital, or holdings, unless certain deposits are pledged against a passport, or investments the depositor has made which ties up his, or her, capital for a certain period of time.

b) Digital, secure access to depositor capital. This system shall use multiple levels of security, including bio, personal and encrypted communications with no backdoor.

2) A passport and citizenship, for life, to anyone making a commitment to the country to deposit capital in a minimum amount of $100,000 for at least three years in smaller, developing nations and $250,000 in

larger ones. Corporations making large deposits shall have the further benefit of extending the citizenship offer to its employees, without charge. Each government can establish the required deposit amounts to enact this corporate right of citizenship. *A very smart government would call up the treasurer of one of the big U.S. companies with billions stashed offshore and establish a partnership with one, or many of them.*

The citizenship rights for individual depositors and companies will only be allowed during the first three years of the IRBs life, while the hosting nations and its IRB allies establish the system. The incentive of providing economic citizenship is a patriotic one to and for a host nation and its politicians. The politicians who make this happen are merely taking reasonable steps to protect their country from the coming collapse. Creating attractive incentives for capital to migrate to its shores, as soon as possible, is a brilliant way to quickly launch the IRB(s). Your country's objective in establishing capital and creating the IRB is far more strategic than simply gathering "economic citizens," as some small countries permit, today.

Your goal should be to become a player on the world financial stage, and thereby help your people. Providing a citizenship incentive at the initial stages of an IRB is a powerful carrot to dangle in front of investors. If the program works well, your government can always extend the three-year initial period when economic citizenships are offered.

3) The ability for depositors to invest 6% of their deposited capital in the International Reserve Bank's preferred stock. The International Reserve Bank will pay a dividend to them of 3%, cumulatively. If the bank fails to make at least an annual dividend payment during any three-year period, the government and the preferred shareholders shall foreclose on the bank and the existing common stock owners. These common stock owners shall have no legal recourse and shall suffer an immediate default judgment with immediate possession of the IRB by the government and preferred stockholders. This will be possible because the foreclosed upon owners shall be required to agree to the default judgment when they assume ownership and control of the IRB facility, if there is a foreclosure event. While the penalty for failure to pay a preferred dividend appears to be draconian, this will provide a mighty incentive for depositors to invest capital and make them one of the IRBs greatest marketing agents, as

they have an ownership interest in the bank. To protect common stockholders from unscrupulous and potentially Machiavellian tactics of withholding preferred dividends in order to create a phony foreclosure, the IRB must pay annual dividends to preferred shareholders, first, out of profits before any monies are paid to anyone else (e.g. employee bonus pool, common stock dividends, etc.).

4) Preferred shareholder rights, where if a foreclosure does take place, the preferred shareholders shall attain the right to acquire *common stock* in any new IRB which is organized, up to their existing actual investment in preferred stock of the foreclosed upon IRB. Said investment in common stock shall be on a price pari passu with new ownership. The preferred shareholders shall also enjoy the continuing right to invest up to 6% of their deposits and assets in the new IRB into its preferred stock. This keeps any depositor's equity loss who invested in a foreclosed IRB at a maximum of 6% of his, or her, deposits, while also allowing the investor to participate in *both* the common and the preferred stock in any new IRB which emerges. A "high-water" mark should be used to ensure any depositor's investment of 6% into IRB preferred stock is based upon their original deposit balance and any *new* deposits must cause the account balance to *exceed* the original, or "high-water" mark balance, before a depositor is permitted to acquire additional preferred stock. Sophisticated investors will want to participate in the emergence of a next-generation reserve bank and they will understand the risks associated with it. As you can read, any plan to create an IRB must also entail the possibility of failure and plan to protect the depositors.

5) A split of capital invested in the IRB between the government and the owners of the IRB in the following proportions: 20% to the government and 80% to the International Reserve Bank.

a) Allow an international auction to be held to run the International Reserve Bank. The winning entity shall pay the government a franchise fee of ¼ of 1% on every dollar of capital deposited, each year. This will avoid any shenanigans going on with accounting rules---make it very simple and enable the government to count the beans and get paid, with the ability to audit on short notice.

6) A government (and allied governments) guarantee of deposits. Investors want a government which stands behind the deposits, where

the bond holders and the shareholders of the bank are punished for any bank failure---not the depositors. Depositors' assets are ALWAYS GUARANTEED BY THE GOVERNMENT WITH STRICT CONTROLS ON THE BANKERS WHICH LIMITS THEIR LENDING AND/OR HYPOTHECATION CAPABILITY.

a) The severest punishment should be doled out to any banker who violates the lending-limit rules.

b) Audits need to be performed by auditors from OUTSIDE the country, which are expressly designated as an integral part of the Vault Treaty and IRB franchise agreement.

7) Creating a MASSIVE REDUCTION in the ability of an IRB bank to LEND money and capital. This involves outlawing the use of the traditional "fractional reserve banking system" commonly used today in the West, where bankers routinely lend out up to 10 times what they have on hand in depositor cash. This book suggests for the next several years the banks should be on the 80/20 rule. 80% of its deposits and assets on hand are retained and accessible---with the strictest penalty to the bank if it exceeds this lending limit. This would allow 20% of deposits (i.e., liquid deposits) and the IRB's capital to be lent out in the first five years of IRB life. This will not create great growth at the moment, but will ensure your country and IRB has the capital required to survive and thrive, while potentially becoming a dominant player after the West goes through the turmoil of D'Apocalypse™.

a) After the first five years of operation, allow the IRB bank to lend, AT MOST, 60% of liquid deposits and capital on hand. These lending standards MUST be set in stone and can NEVER be modified by subsequent generations---this is the key to attracting capital to a safe haven with long-lasting, generational appeal.

b) For any established, Western governments who institute this newer, stricter lending rule across all banks, you have to manage your economy to control deflation and a deep recession which will occur as a result of the transition to a more stable banking system. This may mean putting money into the hands of the people, directly, by forgiving debt and other means to allow the system to recover. This will be particularly important if your economy is deeply in debt and in trouble. You cannot permit a self-imposed belt-tightening and contraction of the effective money supply to stranglehold your people. Transition to the more conservative IRB system will also attract international capital and help offset a decrease in the velocity of and supply of money in the local economy.

8) A signed agreement between the leadership of your government and the military of your country (and/or your allies in the Vault Treaty), providing for the international protection of any monies, assets or capital on deposit in your country, regardless of a person's citizenship and regardless of whether, or not, there is war, or peace. The military will share with the government in the fees and royalties from the IRB.

9) Secret bank accounts are to be maintained, restoring the privacy requirements for millions of corporations and investors. Pass strict laws which will immediately indict any person caught revealing secrets of the IRB with a severe punishment of jail time, of up to twenty years. No single employee, or director of an IRB, shall have access to all depositor information, with strong internal controls established to prevent unauthorized access of sensitive information and accounts.

10) Advertising the IRB and its special capabilities to every major city on earth. This should be a very large marketing campaign designed to do nothing less than attract capital from those who have controlled it for far too long.

11) Provide tax relief for those who make deposits in your country. There shall be NO taxes and NO fees, of any kind, guaranteed by the Vault Treaty, IRB and/or host government, unless depositors engage in a separate agreement to do so (e.g. and incur fees on investments, services, etc. which they freely engage in).

12) All IRBs are exempt from any and all taxes.

International Reserve Bank
Pro Forma Projection

© 2013 Robert L. Kelly

	Previous Year's Retained Earnings	Year 1	Year 2	Year 3	Year 4	Year 5	Year 6
Gross Deposits		$1,063,829,787	$2,127,659,574	$4,255,319,149	$8,510,638,298	$14,468,085,106	$21,702,127,660
Net Customer Deposits (6% Of New Deposits Invested in Preferred Stock)		$1,000,000,000	$2,060,000,000	$4,123,600,000	$8,247,416,000	$14,094,844,960	$21,245,690,698
New Depositor Investment In Preferred Stock (3% Cumulative Dividend)		$63,829,787	$67,659,574	$131,719,149	$263,222,298	$373,240,146	$456,436,962
Cumulative Preferred Stock Investment By Depositors		$63,829,787	$131,489,362	$263,208,511	$526,430,809	$899,670,955	$1,356,107,917
Additional Common Stock Investment Into IRB (80% to IRB, 20% to Gov't)		$62,500,000					
Net Capital Available to IRB From Common Stock Investors		$50,000,000					
Fee to Government From Common Stock Investors		$12,500,000					
Total IRB Assets & Capital Available--Loanable Funds @ 20% of Deposits		$301,063,830	$567,914,894	$1,086,334,043	$2,122,223,911	$3,591,393,235	$13,886,634,514
Total IRB Assets & Capital Available--Loanable Funds @ 60% of Deposits							
Depositor Investments - Preferred Stock (3% Dividend, @ 6% Of Deposits)		$63,829,787	$131,489,362	$263,208,511	$526,430,809	$899,670,955	$1,356,107,917
Fee To Government On New Depositors' Preferred Stock Investments		$12,765,957	$13,531,915	$26,343,830	$52,644,460	$74,648,029	$91,287,392
Net Capital Available To IRB From Depositors' Investments		$51,063,830	$105,191,489	$210,566,809	$421,144,647	$719,736,764	$1,084,886,333
Previous Year's Retained Earnings			$723,404	$1,047,234	$1,596,064	$2,687,479	$4,333,762
Estimated IRB Revenues @ 4% of Available Capital		$12,042,553	$22,716,596	$43,433,362	$84,888,956	$143,655,729	$555,465,381
Estimated Operating Expenses @ 50%		$6,021,277	$11,358,298	$21,726,681	$42,444,478	$71,827,865	$277,732,690
Profit Before Franchise Fee & Preferred Dividends		$6,021,277	$11,358,298	$21,716,681	$42,444,478	$71,827,865	$277,732,690
Annual Government Franchise Fee (1/4 of 1% on Deposits)		$2,659,574	$5,319,149	$10,638,298	$21,276,596	$36,170,213	$54,255,319
Dividends Preferred Stockholders (3%, Hold Cumulative Rights)		$1,914,894	$3,944,681	$7,896,255	$15,792,924	$26,990,129	$40,683,238
Profit Before Common Stock Dividends & Employee Bonus Pool		$1,446,809	$2,094,468	$3,192,128	$5,374,958	$8,667,523	$182,794,134
Dividend Bonus Employees (20% Share of Common Stock Dividends)		$144,681	$209,447	$319,213	$537,496	$866,752	$18,279,413
Dividend Bonus Owners Of Common Stock		$578,723	$837,787	$1,276,851	$2,149,983	$3,467,009	$73,117,653
Total Dividends Common Stock		$723,404	$1,047,234	$1,596,064	$2,687,479	$4,333,762	$91,397,067
Retained Earnings (50% Of Profit Before Common Dividend & Bonus Pool)		$723,404	$1,047,234	$1,596,064	$2,687,479	$4,333,762	$91,397,067
Positive Cash Flow (Adds Dividend Payments Back In)		$3,361,702	$6,039,149	$11,088,383	$21,167,882	$35,657,652	$223,477,371
TOTAL FEES PER YEAR PAID TO GOVERNMENT		$27,925,532	$19,851,064	$36,982,128	$73,921,055	$110,818,242	$145,542,712
Growth Assumption: Deposits double in years 1-4, increase 70% & 50% years 5-6, respectively.							

Once again, this is what an IRB's performance might look like, starting with $50 Million and obtaining in year one a deposit base of $1 Billion, which is a "net" number and assumes depositors will take advantage of the preferred stock investment opportunity in the IRB.

Even with a conservative assumption of 4% revenue generation <u>on available and loanable funds and capital</u>, this IRB in a six-year period could possibly generate hundreds of billions of dollars in revenue for the GOVERNMENT(s) hosting and sponsoring the International Reserve Bank. As you can see, it is a serious opportunity any head-of-state should consider for his, or her, people.

The pro forma, above, restricts the capital pool to only 20% of available deposits for the first five years and is "ramped up" to meet the 60% loan level limit, in Year 6. As a result, earnings increase dramatically.

If You Are a Bank Competitor to the 4 Horsemen of the D'Apocalypse™

If you are a bank competitor to the 4 Horsemen of the D'Apocalypse™, or the G14, you should be disengaging from any and all counter-party derivatives transactions on and off your books. You do not want to have any reliance, or entanglements, with other parties who might possibly go bankrupt when the derivatives tower collapses.

Furthermore, you should not worry about maximizing bank profits for the next four to five years. What you should be focused on is the PRESERVATION of assets and the attraction of capital into your own storage facilities and banking network. This means you should radically INCREASE the amount of physical reserves on hand (i.e., don't rely on digital assets from, with, or to a clearing bank). This will, undoubtedly, add expense and reduce lending volume and profitability, however, the opportunity to *gain* depositors the first moment the next round of trouble sets in will more than offset the conservative action you take, today.

Furthermore, you should collaborate with a number of "like-minded" thinking banks in your region and set about the task of sharing resources with savings and loans, community banks and credit unions in the U.S. and small, well-run banks in other international regions. Create an agreement in which ALL OF YOU GUARANTEE depositors you will keep over 50% of their deposits on hand or physically within the regional banking system, you create.

You will all be able to advertise this ability and still maintain your relationships throughout the wire system and Federal Reserve. When the balloon goes up, your organizations will be in an enviable position to potentially take over hundreds of billions, if not trillions of dollars in assets, as many of the big banks will fail and shall be forced to break up. Your bank could be the one acquiring assets for pennies on the dollar!

Believe it, or not, perhaps the best banks are the small, responsibly run banks scattered throughout every township of America---provided they do not have their depositor's monies tied up with larger banks "upstream" and have not overly indebted themselves. The same is true in countries where the G14 operates. The smaller banks have to be well run, as they are primarily run by responsible families and businessmen---not wild-eyed traders and executives eyeballing million-dollar paydays.

If You Are a Corporation Seeking to Survive the Derivatives Debacle

Thousands of corporations use derivatives to free up capital and increase, or "lock-in," profits. It all looks great when the counter party is not in default. The trouble for a corporation is there is not only the default risk associated with the counter party, but there is also the DEFAULT risk of the bank, ALONG WITH THE FACT THE BANK COMPLETELY CONTROLS THE TRANSACTION AND THE TRADE. It can heavily influence TERMS, PRICING AND CONDITIONS OF THE DERIVATIVES TRANSACTION. The banks' abilities and powers, combined with the history-making, standard deviation changes which shall be brought about because of D'Apocalypse™, spells deep and woeful misfortune for thousands of companies.

When D'Apocalypse™ occurs it means there will be very little real liquidity in the derivatives markets. Since only a few big players dominate the trading (JP Morgan Chase, Citigroup, Bank of America and Goldman Sachs control over 93% of the market among the top 25 commercial banks in America and only 14 banks control over 80% of transactions, worldwide), when trouble arrives, the banks will throttle the trades, increase margin requirements and completely stack the odds in their favor. As we also have learned from this book, over 96% of the derivatives market is unregulated and their related transactions do not trade on an exchange.

This is a recipe for disaster if you are a company trading in the derivatives marketplace.

Even with the new legislation passed in the Dodd-Frank bill on July 21, 2010 (the same date on which the Federal Reserve ended their partial audit....what a coincidence...), there are many, many loopholes allowing the banks to avoid the light of scrutiny from a clearing exchange, as well as other regulators in this market.

Corporations, like their small-bank counterparts, should "tighten their belts" and use their capital to control their transactions, instead of using derivatives and leverage to bet on rate and price change, or product and commodity availability.

One of the biggest risks most CEOs, CFOs and Treasurers have not considered is a "what if" scenario where the BANK, always eager to foreclose on tempting, desirable assets, INCREASES its demand for MARGIN money based on the *bank's* conclusions about "risk." Banks can concoct all kinds of phony reasons to accomplish this. They could even point to economic conditions and demand a company comes up with, IMMEDIATELY, millions of dollars in additional collateral in order for it to control its derivatives trade/hedge. This is what caused AIG, Enron, LTCM and Jefferson County, as well as countless other entities to blow up.

In AIG's case, which was well publicized, a credit trigger was initiated against it in 2008, creating a credit default swap ("CDS") margin call to be made. This caused a bailout totaling $185 billion, the direct assistance of the United States Government and an untold huge number of secret, backdoor bailouts. AIG was lucky it was in bed with Goldman Sachs, because Goldman was in a disastrously risky situation. Ultimately, it was directly bailed out of its trades with AIG by the United States Government and Federal Reserve System.

As you probably know from the press, or from reading The $30 Trillion Heist, "Hank" Paulson, then Secretary of Treasury for the United States of America, was Goldman's ex-CEO. It was under his watch at Goldman which laid the ground work for the credit crisis to begin! One shudders to think of the conflicts of interest he had when he supported the bailing out of AIG. Who knows how many millions of shares in Goldman he owned and what kinds of assets he had tucked away in Goldman pension plans and Goldman golden parachutes. AIG was not a bank and not legally authorized under the Federal Reserve Act to be bailed out by the Federal Reserve.

As further discussed in Chapter 2, "Derivatives---the Ticking Time Bomb!," there are several key risks to using derivatives, including price risk of the underlying asset, product risk, the counter-party risk, the bank risk, the credit risk, as well as serious liquidity concerns in this marketplace. A credit rating downgrade, for example, could cause a requirement to obtain cash when cash is THE most difficult to secure.

Because derivatives are leveraged transaction vehicles and are traded up to many times the underlying collateral's value, a company may fail to obtain the funds which are demanded of it to meet a margin call. This forces other triggers to take place, which forces further margin requirements! In this way, a company is left open to the predators which shall surely follow. The first one to come knocking at the door will be the bank where you initiated the derivatives transaction!

In all likelihood, this bank will also be the place your company keeps its securities, checking and payroll accounts. The danger is plain to see. Those assets can be seized, immediately, potentially cutting off all credit for you and your company's operations!

The Cyprus Phone Call

There are many other risks in the derivative's market. Like it or not, and whether or not your company does any derivatives business, IF YOU ARE BANKING AT A BANK trading in, or otherwise transacting in derivatives, or is engaged in significant counter-party transactions with banks and other parties who trade in derivatives, then there is a very high likelihood you will receive the "Cyprus Phone Call."

If you have this kind of exposure, then the odds are extremely high one day in the not too distant future, your company will learn your bank is going "on holiday." Instead of your deposited funds and capital, you will receive non-liquid common stock in a "new" bank (because the old one has been closed!) and you MAY be left with 10%, 20%, or 30% of your assets once held at the bank. It is also a very real possibility your company receives NOTHING, as any monies on deposit shall be sucked out by insiders before the collapse is known on the Street.

Cyprus depositors lost 47% of their money. How much do you think your company will lose when the firestorm of D'Apocalypse™ arrives and burns down a tower of derivatives which stands 10 times taller than the world's Gross Domestic Product?

It is times like these where the wise build an ark.

The bottom line is there is real and tangible risk which is not priced into the marketplace and could cause many companies to become bankrupt, literally overnight. The major banks will put the squeeze on ANY company unprepared for the onslaught coming our way. Just as they cut off credit to Lehman Brothers, Bear Stearns, etc., they can and will do it again, except this time it shall not only be real estate, banks and investment banks which are acquired.

The bankers and the elite would just *love* to increase their ownership in and get their hands on a number of large corporations. They are especially interested in those laden with rich assets in the petroleum, agricultural, real estate, mining, and other commodity sectors, as well as several debt-dependent and leveraged industrial and commercial concerns.

Recently, JC Penney received this EXACT message from CIT, the largest commercial lender to the apparel industry. JC Penney is one of the largest retailers in the world and owns a tremendous amount of real estate.

Pinching Penney
Retailer's shares tumble after credit clampdown
"CIT — the largest commercial lender in the U.S. apparel industry — has abruptly stopped financing deliveries from smaller manufacturers to Penney stores, The Post has learned...Shares of the Plano, Tex., retailer plunged more than 10 percent, to $14.60, in the final 40 minutes of trading after CIT's move was first reported on nypost.com...insiders speculated that CIT grew skittish after getting a peek at Penney's financials..." (Source: New York Post, by James Covert, 8/1/2013, "Pinching Penney" as retrieved from http://nypost.com/2013/08/01/pinching-penney/).

The Banks Could Go Broke Overnight
Often, banks engaged in the trading of derivatives are selling risk. This creates a strong revenue and profitability stream for them, when conditions are "normal." It is highly likely their "sale" of risk is done by a bunch of really smart math wizards who have assumed there is NO LOGICAL WAY events will occur outside of "X" number of standard deviations (see Chapter 2, subsection, "When the Bubble Bursts" and "VaR—Value at Risk"). This assumption, of course, is a major problem given the towering height of derivatives and debt plaguing and threatening the global economy. Something can and will break....so be prepared!

You can bet the bank on the fact these wizards will be wrong, causing devastating losses to hit the banks---forcing even many of the largest ones to fail OVERNIGHT!

As discussed at length in this book already, politics and the banks' ability to utilize their debt leverage against governments, along with their battle cry of "too big to fail," will likely come into play to determine if any of the 4 Horsemen of the D'Apocalypse™ and G14 make it through the collapse.

For the CEO, one final word: no government is big enough to bail out these banks, or bail out an asset class in the derivatives market going virally wrong. What WILL very likely occur is the 4 Horsemen will get whittled down to 1 Horseman, or even just 2. The G14 could be cut in half. Just as they all turned on Bear Stearns and Lehman, you can believe greed mongering will force them down a path where they will attempt to eat one, or more, of the other big horses.

While this is transpiring, the markets will be in chaos and banks will be shut down. The banks and the elite will use their leverage over governments, along with their $30 Trillion in heist money, plus profits from Assflation™, to attempt to gain control of monetary policy and the money supply, on a worldwide basis, as discussed at length in Chapter 2 in subsection, "BASEL III Tightening Worsens D'Apocalypse™--Bankers Only Reflate Once in Control."

The EU is already adopting new regulations crippling the ability of depositors to access their cash. Large and small depositors will be targeted and their money will be stolen.

Companies should get the majority of their money OUT NOW---out of ALL "major" banks in the Western world (i.e., per recommendations which follow, diversify your cash, place it in private, secure and respected storage and only keep the bare minimum you need in commercial banks)!!

Do not associate with any banks doing business with correspondent banks in the derivatives market. Read the section, preceding this one, "If You Are a Bank Competitor to the 4 Horsemen of the D'Apocalypse™" and build up a relationship with a high-quality community bank (or regional bank outside of the U.S.). If you have a great deal of cash, make the investment of time and effort to cultivate many, many of them to spread out your risk. If you are seeking to truly help all of your employees and shareholders---have the CEO and CFO make the phone call to the country of your choice to establish, jointly, a new International Reserve Bank.

New EU rule savers need to fear credit under 100,000 euros
German Economic News, August 7, 2013

"In the case of bankruptcy of a bank, customers will experience massive problems when they believe their bank balance is guaranteed by official deposit insurance. The current EU proposal provides that customers can withdraw a maximum of only 100 to 200 euros, daily, in case of a collapse. This state may last for up to three weeks. Anyone planning major purchases should think ahead of time, if you are planning to use your money...Largely unnoticed by the public, the EU is pushing forward concrete steps it will take in the event of a banking collapse....In fact, this development means those savers with deposits of 100,000 euros, or more, blindly relying on the commitment of Angela Merkel and Wolfgang Schäuble, are sure to have to beg for their money...According to the EU proposal, <u>savers will now have to wait for weeks until they can be sure if they will ever see their money.</u>" (Source: Deutsche Wirtschafts Nachrichten, August 7, 2013, as retrieved from http://deutsche-wirtschafts-nachrichten.de/2013/08/07/neue-eu-regel-sparer-muessen-um-guthaben-unter-100-000-euro-bangen/).

Diversify Your Cash & Securities Holdings
As a corporation, you should be invested in your businesses producing strong cash flows which are likely to survive a major downtrend in the economy. The "downtrend" coming up will be an outright collapse. To the extent you can sell any divisions, or assets which are highly cyclical, NOW IS THE TIME TO DO IT, prior to June of 2015.

With respect to cash and securities, do not keep any significant amount of money at the large banks, or investment banks. Diversify your holdings into stronger banks. The best bet in the U.S. is to go to a well-managed bank outside of the control of the 4 Horsemen of the D'Apocalypse™, or G14, which is high in the Weiss Ratings (http://weissratings.com/banking-industry-research/). Weiss makes a serious effort to quantify risk and is not as prone to the conflicts of interest other ratings agencies seem to have. Internationally, there are many ratings agencies, but be careful and cross check between multiple, independent ratings (e.g. http://www.defaultrisk.com/rating_agencies.htm). Many of the agencies are directly paid off by the banks. Caution is the by word and smaller is usually BETTER, with respect to the kind of banking relationship you may want to consider.

In America, to the extent possible, follow in the footsteps of some of America's largest corporations, where reported recently, they have parked over $262 billion offshore---out of the clutches of Uncle Sam. The Sacramento Bee reported:

"Chevron, California's largest corporation, is holding $26.5 billion, the report says, and others from the state on the list, by size of the firm, include Hewlett-Packard, $33.4 billion; McKesson, $3.8 billion; Apple, $82.7 billion; Wells-Fargo, $1.3 billion; Intel, $17.5 billion; Safeway, $1.3 billion; Cisco Systems,$41.3 billion; Walt Disney, $566 million; Sysco, $910 million; Google, $33.3 billion; Ingram Micro, $2.1 billion; and Oracle, $20.9 billion." (Source: The Sacramento Bee, July 31, 2013, "Big California corporations parking $262 billion offshore," as retrieved from http://blogs.sacbee.com/capitolalertlatest/2013/07/big-california-corporations-parking-262-billion-offshore.html#storylink=cpy).

<u>U.S. companies should make asset transfers to separate offshore corporations which are then spun off to shareholders</u>. If your transfers overseas are merely to a "subsidiary," the U.S. Congress will take your money. NO money will be safe offshore if it is controlled by an entity which is owned by your U.S. company, directly.

The politicians are desperate to get reelected and will do anything they can to bring down harsh and severe laws against anyone and everyone who has assets offshore. European companies should do the exact same thing---no one will be safe from the greed of the politicians to steal capital. For the largest companies, or a combination of middle-sized companies, now is the time to contact a government and discuss the opportunity to establish your own International Reserve Bank. This is how you can control your own destiny when the storm hits.

As you can see, strategic diversification does not just mean geographical, it means political and corporate diversification, as well.

Do Not Keep More Than $99,000 (€99,000 euros) in Any U.S.A, or EU Bank

This means, specifically, you should not keep any more than **$99,000 dollars** in any single U.S. bank or **99,000 € euros** in any European Bank and no more than **99,000£ pounds** in any English bank. Even then, be prepared to lose at least 50% of those monies!! The governments are being told by the elite the banks DEPOSITORS should pay for a failed bank---not the stock or bond holders!! This seems unbelievable, but it is true. One of the best ways to protect the security of your cash, is to park your cash in a private storage vault which is HIGHLY regarded. This book mentions a couple of options; however, you can use Google and find your own without too much of a problem.

The author cannot be more serious in this matter. To the extent you need and have cash, protect it. Also bear in mind under any new currency scheme or inflation scenario, your cash will greatly diminish in value---a new currency and/or inflation is just another way of robbing you of what is yours. The best scenario is to do what Warren Buffett has done---own businesses whose products will maintain their relative value in any revised currency scheme, or inflation scenario. The section in the book urging you to sell any divisions or companies, before 2015, relates to businesses which are cyclical and could suffer during D'Apocalypse™.

Also, read the section on gold in this chapter, titled, "Buy Bullion" (also keep it stored privately).

You shouldn't own any securities which are kept at U.S. or EU investment banks for the next several years. The smaller firms typically all clear through the larger ones and the larger ones are all involved with derivatives. As we all saw in 2011, Man Financial collapsed overnight and it was headed by Jon Corzine, another ex-CEO of Goldman Sachs and ex-Governor of New Jersey! Over a billion dollars of supposedly segregated customer funds went missing and to this day, customers still don't have all their money back. No one was put in jail and the whole matter is just another example of the corruption between government and Wall Street. Mr. Corzine has not been prosecuted.

To the extent your company can diversify some of its cash into bullion, do this at the right time, but make sure you are receiving bullion from a reputable dealer and it is not stored in a bank deposit box. Anything in a bank deposit box can be seized, overnight, in the event of a financial crisis. Freeport, in Singapore, would be an excellent place to search out and inquire about the acquisition and storage of bullion there. ALSO, the "Buy Bullion" section in this chapter provides excellent insight as to WHEN to "buy" and WHEN to "sell" gold. The best "bullion" to purchase is gold coins from a reputable dealer---bags of them, if you have this kind of capital.

Switzerland also has excellent PRIVATE storage facilities which have long-standing and time-honored reputations for honesty. They can store cash in the form of just about any currency and they can buy and sell bullion, as well as just about any other security you can think of. See the subsections, "If You Are a Pension Fund" and "Buy Bullion" for further discussion on gold, silver and other precious metals.

As discussed at length, however, in this chapter, Switzerland has succumbed to the debt monsters and has caved on privacy.

Caveat Emptor is the advice provided for any services purchased there!

Finally, Canada, Australia and many countries in the Western financial markets boast secure, private, non-bank storage. A simple "Google" search, targeting your preferred location, will focus your search and provide you with better security, ultimately, than the banks.

If You Are a Pension Fund

Read and follow the recommendations for corporations. On a day-to-day basis, a pension fund and its money managers dutifully deal with the banks and brokerage firms, while faithfully investing in assets they hope will ensure their retirees the benefits they have been promised. When the collapse occurs, the value of government obligations (e.g., their bonds and notes) of all kinds will get crushed---either because of skyrocketing interest rates, or outright collapse and bankruptcy of government, or both. Long-term corporate bonds will get smashed because of the spike, across the board, in all interest rates. Investors shall demand a greater return on their money, particularly once the veil of deceit on the real risk of the derivatives market is uncovered. Furthermore, most funds have rules regarding what kinds of securities they may invest in and unfortunately, they have been led down a garden path which virtually guarantees their inability to meet their pension fund obligations.

Many of them realize they are "underfunded" and cannot meet those obligations, as the pension fund crisis is well documented. Unfortunately, what they don't expect is a complete shutdown of the system, where their clearing firms and banks literally shut down and the pension funds and retirees cannot access their capital and retirement income.

As discussed, D'Apocalypse™ is coming which entails a complete collapse of the financial system---this means the major banks and major brokerage firms will go under and just like Man Financial, there will be bankers who abscond with customer assets. Billions and billions will be lost with no warning.

Imagine the frightened and scared bankers who will be writing checks they can't cover and will do just what Jon Corzine ordered and permitted---the writing of checks using supposedly client-segregated funds for the business of MF Global!! People lost hundreds of millions of dollars due to the actions of Man Financial and its executives. The regulators have done nothing about it.

Do you seriously think the regulators and politicians will do anything at all when the system fails? They will be completely panic stricken and will have nowhere to run. The problem they will have is the sheer size of the coming collapse.

The Fed, using its traditional methods, will not be able to (and until global control of monetary policy is achieved, it will not want to) rebuild because this was their last great bubble---the final, bullish, blow-off run before D'Apocalypse™.

This created and is going to create for the equity markets (bonds have already seen their historic run and are soon to be pummeled by rising rates), the biggest Assflation™ of all time in this asset class—particularly for high-quality, highly liquid stocks. Like many unsustainable bubbles preceding them, both the stock and bond markets will fall with such a mighty crash, anyone unprepared will get wiped out, literally overnight.

To survive, pension funds must absolutely assume what happened with Mr. Corzine **will** happen again, but on a much broader scale than what occurred with Man Financial, *or* during and through the mortgage crisis. YOU MUST CHANGE how and where you are investing and increase the quality of the assets you choose to purchase for your portfolio. You should be desperately trying to make portfolio changes, while liquidity in the market is available because it could dry up in an instant.

If a fund does not adhere to this advice, it too shall fall victim to the bankers' thievery. All funds should be out of the equity and governmental debt markets before June of 2015.

Deal Direct With Corporations & Storage Facilities

This book suggests a dramatic change of strategy for a pension fund. You should <u>not</u> be invested in unsecured commercial paper and shouldn't allow one dollar to be invested in the repo, or government bond markets.

You should be in short-term, high-quality CORPORATE bonds where your fund <u>holds</u> the certificate and receives the payments directly from the company you are dealing with. You may have to negotiate, in private transactions, these investments directly with multiple companies. There are many blue chip companies, sporting very strong cash flows and/or assets, seeking capital. These should be the preferred investment vehicles for the foreseeable future, PROVIDED THOSE ENTITIES DO NOT USE DERIVATIVES.

Focus on the ones which will continue to sell their products, goods, or commodities in good times and bad. While everything will be affected in a collapse scenario, the world will more than likely survive this economic catastrophe. Fortunes will be made by those who thought outside of the box and planned accordingly. Some of these fortunes will be vast, accruing to those who are prepared.

To the extent your fund's rules permit, establish your own supply of bullion and have it stored in a secure area which is not inside a bank. Bullion will drop further in price (read subsection, "Buy Bullion" in this chapter), as there is a serious deflation coming and rising rates are coming. However, bullion will have its day in the sun and will ultimately soar. Timing of your bullion purchases is important.

Short-Term Non-Government Assets
If a fund makes a shift to corporate assets and corporate bonds---away from government bond investments—it will at least allow the pension fund to deal with a party and make an investment in an entity which is responsible for its balance sheet.

Good companies which have ongoing successful operations with strong cash flow will survive any kind of currency change. Their products will simply be sold at new prices under any new currency scheme which might be devised after D'Apocalypse™ arrives. This will provide for the protection of investments in those corporations because the underlying products, or assets, produced by those companies, will maintain their relative value in any new monetary system. "Currency destruction" will not impair their ability to stay alive as corporations, provided they don't have too much debt. Be very, very wary of any companies with dangerous debt-to-equity levels, or rely on lines-of-credit which will not get renewed. The bankers are literally planning to create a massive liquidity squeeze which will facilitate the foreclosure and seizure of vulnerable corporations and assets. Do not get caught in their trap.

Keeping investments SHORT TERM (less than 1 year) will ensure you can maneuver through the coming twists and turns of the markets with far better results than being locked into a 30-year bond bearing a yield of 3%, which is supposedly protected by an interest rate swap which will go belly up because your counterparty went bankrupt. This kind of transactional thinking, prevalent in today's derivatives markets, will leave thousands of unprepared funds, corporations and accounts breathless, as devastating losses will be taken on medium-term and long-term bond positions because interest rates spike to 5%, 10,%, 15%, or even 20%. This is a deadly serious threat to any bond portfolio.

Do not take this warning lightly.

Yes, for now, you will leave short term gains on the table; however, you are prioritizing the securing of your assets (immediately!) in order to take advantage of the coming crash. You want to have assets intact when interest rates skyrocket and governments and central banks unveil a new currency paradigm---foisting it upon one and all without any warning. Your firm, fund, or company will benefit because it will have made an investment in a corporation, or other non-governmental concern, whose survival is virtually assured because its underlying business will maintain its relative value in any kind of currency destruction, or change, which befalls us.

AGAIN, JUST MAKE SURE THE COMPANY YOU TRANSACT WITH DOES NOT INVOLVE ITSELF IN DERIVATIVES!

When the middle-to-end of the collapse is complete, you will be able to use your capital to acquire assets for a fraction of the price they are today. This timeframe could easily be pushed into the 2019-2020 period.

Finally, you should participate whole-heartedly in the equity rally into 2015 (see "Buy the Dow").

No Securities in Street Name, $99,000 per Account

Finally, this point is obvious, but EVERYONE (people, pension funds, insurance companies, corporations, individuals, etc.) should make sure they do not have more than $99,000 in any single banking or securities account. If you have accounts set up in different LEGAL names (e.g., different legal ownership, as in multiple corporate, trusts, your own account, your company's account or wife/husband joint account), then you may have multiple accounts with any bank, or firm, in accordance with each legal name. No account should ever hold over $99,000 or 99,000 € euros if you are in Europe. Brits shouldn't have any more than 99,000 £ in any account, or bank.

DO NOT PLACE ANY MONEY IN ANY BANK DOING BUSINESS IN THE DERIVATIVES MARKET PLACE!!

Also, do not under any circumstances allow your securities to be held in street name, if at all possible. Many brokers and investment banks will pitch you with, "We have insurance to $1 Million, $5 Million, etc.,"or greater amounts with private insurance. Do not believe a word of their promise of "insurance." There will be no insurance company capable of guaranteeing the collapse of this system. The federal government is our best hope (thus the $250,000 FDIC insurance guarantee), but this lifeline is highly suspect—and can be dramatically reduced at ANY TIME, which is why the author suggests only maintaining $99,000 in any account (or 99,000 €, or 99,000 £)!! The best bet is to make sure your assets are in a bank or institution with a very high WEISS rating (or strong international rating), as can be investigated easily at www.weissratings.com, or via Google, internationally.

If you are big enough and have the assets, you should start your own bank and **require it** to maintain the 80/20 rule espoused in this book for the International Reserve Banks, as discussed earlier in this chapter.

Understandably, in most cases, this will cause an enormous change in how a large fund, or company, is currently doing business. Many will say this is impractical advice and add: "How can you possibly suggest such a thing...we manage BILLIONS!"

The simple answer is if you want to keep your assets intact, YOU MUST FIND A WAY! It is not only possible, but practical.

If You Are a Trust Fund

If you are an heir and have had your Granddad's and great-Granddad's money being taken care of by any of the big banks, or perhaps you are even a shareholder of one of the 4 Horsemen of the D'Apocalypse™, or G14, you should assess your risk from a perspective of inevitable change.

The risks are monumentally high for those who have their fortunes in the banks, where the derivatives tower is soaring high over their heads. Particularly if you are an owner, or perhaps even an heir to one of the founders of the Federal Reserve System, the people running "your" bank *are employees* and you have allowed them to construct a remuneration system which rewards, almost exclusively, *short-term profits. This has led to a system of ridiculous and outrageous compensation plans architected around schemes rewarding high risk.*

You should immediately diversify your asset holdings away from these entities. While there is a good chance the bankers and the elite will be successful and actually take control of the global monetary system, there is also a very good chance there will be unexpected casualties along the way---including members of the current elite. This includes the possibility of losing your entire fortune and the awareness one, or more of the "Big 4," fails during the D'Apocalypse™ (and/or several of the G14).

You should be following the advice provided for pension funds, corporations and everyone else in this section. Caution is the by word.

If You Are an Individual

First of all, pray. Get on your knees and pray somehow God spares all of us from the collapse this book is predicting. While this author felt compelled to write this exhaustive warning and admonition, he doesn't wish it upon anyone. <u>To the extent possible, follow the advice provided previously to corporations and pension funds---even if it is on a small scale.</u>

Individuals come in all different shapes and sizes---both physically, as well as financially, but the advice to everyone is to make sure you have enough to eat and drink tucked away for you and your family. Don't tell **anyone** you have a store of supplies in your house, or in any other locations.

This is not prepping---this is really just good common sense. There are enough variables in play to cause a supply disruption from any one of a number of sources. These include financial Armageddon, which this book predicts, but also from other events including NBC (Nuclear, Biological and Chemical) attacks or even solar events which could take place and affect broad sections of your country---paralyzing and destroying supply chains everywhere.

As we all saw the violence which immediately occurred in Louisiana when there was no food, or water, for a few short days, there will be violence once again when D'Apocalypse™ arrives. People in Europe are seeing and reading about riots in Spain and other southern European countries.

Each and every person in America has a right to bear arms and it is your personal choice if you do, in accordance with the laws where you live. In a financially apocalyptic scenario, you want to stay off the streets because millions of people will be very hungry and very, very angry.

A Bank Collapse Can and Will Happen to a Bank Near You!

Finally, a collapse can and will happen to a bank near you!! Do not, for all classes of individuals (Wealthy, Middle Class, Poor and Unemployed), fall asleep at the wheel and assume the government will bail every bank out, again. The system is broken and there isn't enough money to fix it. If you print the money to "fix it," those monies will be worthless in TODAY'S dollars!!

Eventually, prices of EVERYTHING will skyrocket after the crash and after the bankers and elite steal assets at bargain prices, while gaining control of monetary policy, worldwide.

It is sickening to even write about it and see the writing on the wall, but it will happen---the bankers and the elite have all the control. They, if nothing else, have demonstrated time and time again in history how very greedy they are.

Keep enough cash at home to last at least a month and if you can, have enough for several months, because ATM machines will probably not work (or will be severely limited as to the amount of cash you can take from YOUR account). By the way, in a real melt down—it probably won't matter if you have spread your money around different banks in the U.S. because the government will know by your social security number and EIN (employer identification number) where ALL OF YOUR ACCOUNTS ARE!! <u>This is another very good reason to investigate highly regarded, private storage facilities in foreign countries.</u>

The best course of action is to geographically and physically diversify your checking, savings, securities and commodities holdings. Safety deposit boxes are not good options because you can be shut out of them at any time—and the contents of your safe seized without warning.

If you are wealthy, or have liquid assets, you should be worried about confiscation of your monies (e.g., cash, securities and safety deposit boxes) in a bank, or securities, account. Any banking failure in the future will very likely be resolved, at least partially, by stealing depositors' monies and assets---even if the depositors had nothing to do with the banks foray into the derivatives casino, counter-party transactions and other poor investment decisions made by the bank's executives, salesmen and traders. Diversify your monies into THINGS which actually create cash flow and security. Consider purchasing commercial property filled with good tenants if you are wealthy and make sure you own some bullion coins.

The new banking rules for the EU will very likely be put in place in the U.S. (or, alternatively, the banks will just seize and re-hypothecate your holdings without permission, just as occurred with MF Global).

Please note in the subsection of this chapter, "If You Are a Corporation," the finalized EU rules, as reported in August 2013, do not even include protection for "small" depositors! The following article is from June 2013:

"European Union finance ministers approved a plan Thursday for dealing with future bank bailouts, forcing bondholders and shareholders to take the hit for bank rescues ahead of taxpayers. The new framework requires

bondholders, shareholders and large depositors with over 100,000 euros to be first to suffer losses when banks fail....Shielding small depositors from losses is a top priority in Europe, especially after the public outrage over initial plans to bailout Cypriot banks using money from both large and small depositors. In the event of a future banking crisis, European finance ministers agreed there would be bank 'bail-ins' instead of 'bailouts' where investors would be forced to rescue struggling financial institutions."
(Source: "Europe bank rescue plan would hit investors," By Alanna Petroff @AlannaPetroff, June 27, 2013, CNNMoney, as retrieved from http://money.cnn.com/2013/06/27/news/world/eu-bank-rescue/).

For the Poor and Unemployed

For the poor and unemployed, get even more motivated and attempt to supplement any assistance you are receiving by doing odd jobs of any legal type you can find. You can exchange work for food and shelter in many cases. Try and stay clean, as this is also a key to obtaining work. Go to your local church, or synagogue, and volunteer your services---you will meet new people who may learn they can count on a good worker and hire you on the spot. God has a way of helping those who help themselves---especially if you believe in Him!

The burden of weakness through poverty and lack of work, is enormous, and this book expresses the sincerest hope there will be a spiritual awakening around the world to help those many billions who are living in poverty---and particularly those living at, or below, threshold poverty levels. There is room to help many---let us hope the people who have the means read this book and act, or find other enlightenment to help the poor and needy, as they shall truly find themselves in desperate conditions. The best way to help the poor is create good work for them and as we all know, help, without condition, starving people in any way you can.

For the Middle Class

For the middle class, the advice is to keep going to work and reduce your debts as best you can. If you have money in 401ks and IRAs, then be prepared for the equity ride of a lifetime in the Dow Jones and larger cap stocks. Large amounts of capital from the U.S. and overseas shall come to the mistaken conclusion the only "safe haven" and place to be are U.S. equities (e.g., large cap stocks). Abandon this market long before the 2016 election, NO LATER THAN late May 2015, even though there will be, very likely, big gains remaining to be had, which will likely include a "blow off" move to the upside.

When you do abandon it, place your 401K and IRA money into SHORT-TERM, HIGH-QUALITY (e.g., big oil, large pharma, large food and other cash-rich, low-debt, high cash-flow companies) corporate notes and bills.

> *The biggest question you will need to ask yourself is if you think the government will seize your 401k and/or IRA plans (or any other pension plan established by the government)?*

<u>This author believes the need to stay in power shall be so great for the politicians they will do exactly this.</u> If, after reading and learning from this book and <u>The $30 Trillion Heist</u>, as well as other writings on the subject, you come to the conclusion there is a strong likelihood the politicians will seize your investments, then take the penalty on an early withdrawal and protect your funds---per the recommendations in this book. By the way, "seizure" can come in multiple flavors. You might find yourself forced to purchase government bonds because all international purchases STOP and no one else wants them! This will leave your retirement plans scotched.

Additionally, each month, set some money aside to purchase at least extra canned goods and water. We are not talking about prepping; there are many others who focus on the best ways to acquire long-term food storage (e.g., freeze-dried is about the best). We are talking about surviving a several-year long depression where work may not be continuously available and you have to watch every penny to make sure you and your family can survive. Canned goods are typically the least expensive, long-term food available and have a decent shelf life.

Also, if you make an investment in food, know you have done, on a small scale, what much wealthier people have done. You are buying commodities which will not only hold their relative value, but will increase in value rapidly, in a systemic collapse. This book does not address the myriad of health issues concerning GMO, plastic coatings on cans, etc., but if you have to eat and have a slim budget, at least you can acquire some food with a decent shelf life.

For the Wealthy
For the wealthy, the advice is simple: follow the suggestions laid out for corporations, pension funds and trust funds. BUT, if this book is correct and you are thanking God you took precautions, then HELP others when the balloon goes up and HELP them GENEROUSLY. Millions of

people will need food, shelter and clothing. If you take the simple, practical and conservative steps recommended in this book, you will be in a position to not only have prospered during the collapse, but you will become a saint to thousands of others and shall be honoring God in the process—IF you help them.

Buy Bullion

Bullion is a hedge against <u>confidence erosion and </u>instability. Confidence, at its core, is about government, currency and price stability. With Europe in enormous trouble—because of debt, Japan on the brink of total collapse, because of debt, the United States on the verge of collapse, because of debt, China at risk of a bubble implosion, because of debt, and with derivatives transactions towering over every nation on earth, the Western world is teetering on the brink of something spectacularly devastating!!

This has never happened before in known human history. When this collapse occurs, or the world begins to see governments are failing and the system is spinning completely out-of-control, everyone will flee in panic to bullion. You may not be able to obtain it when this day arrives.

When to Buy Bullion

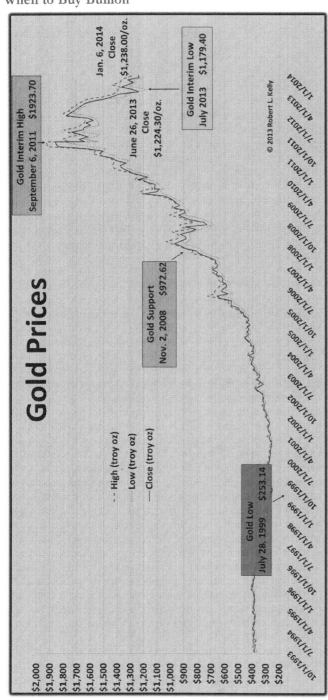

Out of prudence, everyone reading this book should <u>ultimately</u> own at least 30% of their holdings in gold. If you are an aggressive investor, WHEN gold drops, as interest rates continue to increase into 2015, load up the boat---particularly at the targeted price levels provided for you in the second gold chart in this section. Your investment in gold should be scaled in between $1,196.67 and $682.92---this is the range of the author's possible areas of support for gold. It does not mean gold will go to $682.92! If you are willing to sit on "paper" losses, then by all means find a reputable dealer, make sure you aren't purchasing counterfeit bullion, pull the trigger and load up early. It is very likely, however, gold will drop below the first level of support at $1,196.67 and the author believes as rates ratchet up and the dollar rallies, gold will drop even more. The best bullion to own is gold coins.

Don't be surprised, given the EXTREME levels of debt which need to be repaid, if gold heads all the way down to the **lower** end of the range. **Make sure** you own some "good gold" (non-counterfeit) at today's prices. The market is putting gold on sale, with more sales to come.

For speculators and people who want to take more risk, immediately invest 10% in gold, with the full knowledge gold's price, even in the $1,200 range (at its prices on June 26, 2013 at $1,224.30/oz., October 16, 2013 at 1281/oz. and January 6 at $1,238/oz.), will more than likely *drop further* to between $682.92 (the 1.00 Fibonacci retracement level) and $1,156.86 (the .618 Fibonacci retracement from the high and low of gold's big rally from $682.91 to its high above $1,900/oz.).

You will <u>VERY</u> likely experience a paper loss on the position, but anything and everything can happen in this marketplace. There are gigantic amounts of leverage involved, and any major problem could make the derivatives tower collapse. It will be too late to acquire gold, after the collapse occurs, at reasonable prices. Right now there is no panic in the air with regard to gold and you have a better chance of acquiring "good" gold from a reputable dealer---WHICH ASSAYS ITS BULLION.

Many people and organizations will be in the counterfeit gold business when prices for bullion soar.

Ultimately, gold's rise will come about because of a massive sea change in the erosion of confidence in Western governments---because of the debt and irresponsible actions of our collective politicians and bankers.

You may have a difficult time finding "good gold" when the balloon goes up, the music stops and everyone is scrambling for their chairs. Don't get caught without some gold on hand when D'Apocalypse™ strikes.

Remember, IF gold drops through one of the Fibonacci Retracement support levels listed in the following chart, *it will very likely* probe down to the next one. By using the retracement levels, and clearly marked downward trend channel, you can scale your purchases more aggressively as you experience price behavior in real time (the further it drops, the more aggressive you become, depending on your tolerance for risk).

For those readers who don't know what a Fibonacci number is, in mathematics, these are the numbers in the following integer sequence, where the previous two numbers, when added together, equal the next number: 1\1\2\3\5\8\13\21\34\55\89\144\...

When these numbers are divided by each other, "Fibonacci Ratios" are derived which frequently wind up being very useful in technical analysis for stocks, bonds, bullion, etc. For example, quoting from Wikipedia "the key Fibonacci ratio of 0.618 is derived by dividing any number in the sequence by the number that immediately follows it. For example: 8/13 is approximately 0.6154, and 55/89 is approximately 0.6180." (Source: Wikipedia, as retrieved from http://en.wikipedia.org/wiki/Fibonacci_retracement).

You want to make sure you have good gold before the conflagration of D'Apocalypse™ firestorms over ALL of us.

When gold reverses and heads up, breaking back up through the downward sloping "upper" trend line, you want to be fully invested.

If you didn't load up on bullion at sale prices, make absolutely sure you are fully invested when gold breaks back above 1923.70, the high made in September 2011. That is---if you can find a reliable supply of gold coins.

Right now, at the beginning of 2014, gold appears to be setting up for further downside action.

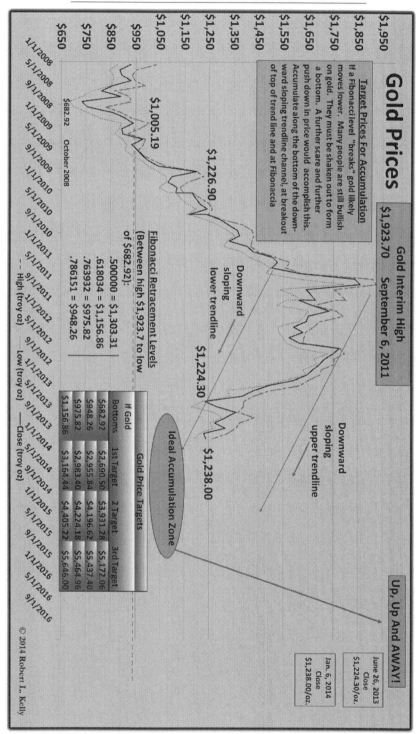

Gold Prices

Gold Interim High
$1,923.70   September 6, 2011

June 26, 2013
Close
$1,224.30/oz.

Jan. 6, 2014
Close
$1,238.00/oz.

Up, Up And AWAY!

Target Prices For Accumulation
If a Fibonacci level "breaks" gold likely moves lower. Many people are still bullish on gold. They must be shaken out to form a bottom. A further scare and further push down in price would accomplish this. Accumulate along the bottom of the downward sloping trendline channel, at breakout of top of trend line and at Fibonaccia

$682.92   October 2008

$1,005.19

$1,226.90

Downward
sloping
lower trendline

$1,224.30

Downward
sloping
upper trendline

$1,238.00

Ideal Accumulation Zone

Fibonacci Retracement Levels
(Between high $1,923.7 to low of $682.92):

.500000 = $1,303.31
.618034 = $1,156.86
.763932 = $975.82
.786151 = $948.26

If Gold	Gold Price Targets		
Bottoms	1st Target	2 Target	3rd Target
$682.92	$2,690.50	$3,931.28	$5,172.06
$948.26	$2,955.84	$4,196.62	$5,437.40
$975.82	$2,983.40	$4,224.18	$5,464.96
$1,156.86	$3,164.44	$4,405.22	$5,646.00

© 2014 Robert. L. Kelly

The well-defined trend channel (as the author has identified in the preceding chart) will also help you to time your purchases---accumulate gold along the lower boundaries of the channel. When gold breaks through the UPPER line on the trend channel, gold will be getting ready to break out to the upside for the next great push to very likely, over $3,000 per ounce. Don't be afraid to purchase more gold if you miss out on the "low" and it starts to break out. Gold will have a huge and enormous run, eventually, as real gold will skyrocket if you have it in your possession—or it is kept in a safe, reliable location.

Remember, gold is just a trade setting up---it is not the solution for the world. A return to a "gold standard" would be horrendous (see following subsection, "No Gold Standard"). Even this writer cannot predict precisely when the collapse in derivatives will occur and the Fed completely loses its grip on interest rates, but it is going to happen soon. The advice is to buy at least some "good" bullion NOW, as it is available.

Only Purchase Gold from a Reliable Dealer—Counterfeits Prevail!
Extremely volatile markets can be expected in the interim. The most important reason to purchase bullion today in the United States, particularly, is all parties have the ability to FREELY transfer currency, both inside the country AND OUTSIDE the country! You also have the ability to obtain and own gold, without intervention. Do not listen to the gold bugs who say there isn't any gold out there and the markets are being manipulated. There is plenty of gold out there.

People cannot eat gold and it is not productive! Just make sure you have 100% assayed gold, however, and purchase it from a reputable dealer---even paying them their typically higher fee. The phony, gold-plated, tungsten-wrapped bars and coins will rob you of your investment if you don't purchase bullion from a dealer who assays its bullion holdings when it receives and stores them. Be extremely cautious on this matter.

One final comment on gold's price action: the gold bugs point to how thousands of regular citizens were lining up in mid-2013 to purchase gold in India and other locations in Asia, particularly, at prices which were at significant premiums to the market's spot price. Since India has imposed significant penalties and has made it very difficult to acquire gold, people are smuggling it in---on nearly every single flight! <u>This is usually a great CONTRARY indicator the actual price of gold will drop FURTHER!</u>

These smugglers won't be feeling quite so flush:
Stash of gold bars worth £700,000 found in airplane toilet
"Jet Airways plane had been flying on international routes before landing at Kolkata * Cleaners discovered 240 gold bars hidden in a toilet compartment * Last month officials found £1.2million worth of gold on plane in Bangladesh (Source: The Daily Mail, By Richard Sears, 20 November 2013, as retrieved from http://www.dailymail.co.uk/news/article-2510606/Stash-gold-bars-worth-700k-Indian-airplane-toilet.html#ixzz2qKN2USNe).

Most people in the general population don't have a good sense for financial markets and act out of greed and fear---usually exactly *opposite* of what is required to earn a profit in the markets. For those people who are purchasing gold today, they will be ultimately rewarded, with a bit of patience, because the global monetary system is in a sad state of affairs. Perhaps the simple people lining up in India and Asia are wiser than this book gives them credit for...the bottom line is, gold will ultimately spike---very, very high.

How High is High? When Do You Get Out??
The price of gold, depending on the world's state of mind and the condition of the Western banking and governmental systems, could be as valuable as some of the stories you have heard. In times of tremendous panic and crisis, people have exchanged an ounce of gold for a building, or some acreage of land. It will depend on how panicked everyone is and on top of the panic, if the central banks print too much money and inflation kicks into very high gear---not because of the quantity of money directly, but because the psychology of the people will be to spend their paper dollars as quickly as possible on real items because prices keep escalating.

By the way, as long as the United States of America has an Army, Navy, Air Force and Marines which can hold their own in the world, there will NOT be a hyperinflation, as was seen in the Weimar Republic in Germany after World War I.

Our society will ultimately go through turmoil, deflation and serious inflation, but at the end of the day, IF THOSE PRINTED DOLLARS ARE BACKED BY THE GOOD FAITH AND CREDIT OF THE UNITED STATES GOVERNMENT and are also GOOD TO PAY TAXES, there will be no hyperinflation, at least insofar as experienced by the German republic after World War I. Moreover, right now, a DEFLATION is occurring of massive proportions due to the debt and the squeeze being placed on taxpayers, as the politicians attempt to pay for their outrageous spending habits and bloated budgets.

In a theoretical scenario, however, let's assume the Fed prints even more outrageous sums of money, further ruining the future of our grandchildren. Additionally, let's say there will be a major panic BECAUSE OF A CRISIS IN GOVERNMENT, SOCIETY AT LARGE, A BREAK OUT OF WAR, OR A COMPLETE MELT DOWN IN CURRENCY.

Gold Price Targets			
If Gold Bottoms	1st Target	2 Target	3rd Target
$682.92	$2,690.50	$3,931.28	$5,172.06
$948.26	$2,955.84	$4,196.62	$5,437.40
$975.82	$2,983.40	$4,224.18	$5,464.96
$1,156.86	$3,164.44	$4,405.22	$5,646.00

In any of these scenarios, it is not at all unlikely for gold to rise to $5,646.00 (Fibonacci 3.618), $4,405.22 (Fibonacci 2.618), or $3,164.44 (Fibonacci 1.618), assuming gold bottoms in the current cycle at $1,156.86.

The chart, above, provides you with potential EXIT points for a reader's gold bullion holdings (at various Fibonacci levels). Depending on the severity of the crisis, the higher the yellow metal will soar.

The rise will be fast and furious when it happens----***remember when it does, gold is just a trade.*** The bankers and the elite have a furious control over governments, due to all the debt governments' have accumulated. This means as gold spikes, it could (and likely will) quickly reverse back DOWN with the advent of a newly announced monetary system. Do not get psychologically attached to your gold.

By all means, be prepared to ***exit*** when it spikes into a ***panic high***. It can just as easily drop and the panic premium collapses, if confidence returns to government. The major panic high will be in the middle to the end of D'Apocalypse™ when confidence is about to return to government---right about the time the elite and the bankers announce their deal with government!

Watch the price targets, above, and don't get greedy. If you are blessed with massive profits during the D'Apocalypse™, take them and help others who will need your help. Acquire assets which can produce income in future years. At the depths of the collapse, there will be bargains to be had. Target and watch carefully for a spike high in gold---it can happen at any time after D'Apocalypse™ begins, but is likely to be in the 2017-2019 timeframe.

Don't Get Too Cute With Timing On Gold!
Before gold bottoms, interest rates will have to increase because of the market's demand for a greater return because of the high risks and fragile financial condition of governments worldwide, debt in all parts of society, and an ocean of money being flooded into the system. This spike in interest rates will apply further downward pressure on gold. The key point here is DON'T GET TOO CUTE WITH TIMING!

It is important you find pure bullion from a source which assays its bullion shipments (both bricks and coins)—and find a source which will stand behind its product. This is not likely a source on the Internet, but a physical location where you can meet the actual people who are responsible for their own bullion acquisitions and who have long track records. Stack's Rare Coins in New York City comes to mind. If you are unfamiliar with a reliable dealer, you can check the Professional Coin Grading Service web site at http://www.pcgs.com/dealers/ for suggestions in your area. You can click on their world map and drill down to particular countries of interest and find authorized PCGS dealers. The last thing you need is to make a substantial investment in bullion and find out you have counterfeit coins, or bars, on your hands.

Obviously, for our friends in Europe and Japan, the price in Euros and Yen for gold could go up far more dramatically, given the issues on the table with huge debt in both lands. Various countries are in effective default in the EU and Japan has astonishing debt problems. In a Euro-collapse situation or Yen-collapse situation, gold will be among your best friends.

With chapters in this book and The $30 Trillion Heist (in both Scene Of The Crime? and Follow The Money!) dedicated to the problems of the debt of the United States and world, the Federal Reserve (and its nefarious activities) and the teetering, tottering, wobbling tower of derivatives, readers will readily understand it will not take much to have gold and silver's price shoot to the moon, once panic sets in.

The main challenge and problem with bullion is ensuring you do not receive counterfeit bars, or coins---and you don't have it confiscated by an aggressive government. There are reputable Swiss, Australian, U.S., U.K., Singaporean (Freeport) and Canadian dealers in bullion who assay their bullion holdings and store bullion privately in their non-bank vaults.

Do some internet searches for private storage facilities and services from quasi-government sponsored entities or call one of the PCGS dealers in a country of interest to you and ask them for recommendations. These authorized dealers know their local markets well.

Geographic Diversification
It would be very wise to also have geographic asset diversification to protect your bullion investments. Thus, a U.S. fund, or person, should consider Swiss, Canadian, Australian, U.K., or Singaporean bullion dealers and storage facilities, while a U.K. fund should consider those dealers and storage services outside of the U.K., etc. Just make sure you store at least half of your bullion outside of your existing country.

Gold Stocks
With the caveat you actually receive the stock certificate from those companies still issuing them, many bullion miners and funds will realize tremendous profits when bullion shoots to the moon. The major danger is the collapse of the derivatives market and the impact it will have on any company requiring DEBT to run its operations. This is the Achilles Heel of most companies in the mining industry.

Having said this, this chapter includes a list of companies with high gross margins and little, to no debt on their books, as of this writing (the companies listed and information related to them are pulled from public sources). Invest with caution and the knowledge the preferred asset to own is coin and bullion. **ALSO, CHECK WITH YOUR FINANCIAL ADVISOR, AS APPROPRIATE.**

However, given the fact D'Apocalypse™ Now! is predicting the bankers will win this battle (and ultimately lose the war), the markets will likely survive (and be revived after a shutdown). Equity investments in viable bullion companies (particularly those paying dividends) should provide handsome rewards in the future---but will undergo pain as gold finishes its correction.

These company share prices will likely DROP in price, right along with gold into 2015. JUST LIKE BULLION, please use the suggested bullion prices at the Fibonacci retracement levels and the downward sloping trend lines and channel for your entry-level timing in acquiring stock positions.

Scale in your purchase and remember they are a trade!!! Ride the wave up and be prepared to dump them as gold hits the price targets listed in the gold chart in this section of the book. With the exception of the company Rangold Resources (i.e., "GOLD,") which operates in Sub-Sahara Africa and a few of the really big operators, this list is primarily one which the author has filtered for American companies (i.e., both North AND South America).

The list in the following table was originally created on June 26, 2013 and was updated during the trading day of August 22, 2013, on October 23, 2013 and January 10th, 2014 at the end of the day. It provides the reader with an excellent snapshot of the leverage in stock prices which results, primarily, from changes in the price of gold (e.g., from $1,224.30 on June 26, 2013 to $1,375.20 on August 22, 2013, back down to $1333.40 on October 23, 2013 and $1232 on January 6, 2014), which took place during the period in which these stocks were tracked.

Given the prospect for war around the world and the coming pressures, economically, investors will likely be safer with investments in companies not subject, perhaps, to the direct onslaught of physical violence gripping the world---although, there are no guarantees.

Good Canadian companies in this sector are potentially excellent; however, the following list has many outstanding companies located primarily, in North and South America. One thing to seriously ask BEFORE you make any purchase in any bullion stock is if a particular company uses DERIVATIVES to sell its gold in the future. IF SO, abandon it like the plague. A serious investment in these companies should require a thorough reading of their 10Ks, on file with the SEC. Search specifically in the filing for information on forward sales, contracts, derivatives, etc., which should be revealed in the discussion of the company. Alternatively, pick up the phone and call investor relations and ask them if they use derivatives!

Try and pick companies which have not locked in their prices on gold (many of them may have because of the scare they received when the market dropped and gold prices collapsed during the middle of 2013). Be alert for this. If you bide your time, you can attempt to enter some of these stocks when gold trades down to between $975 and $1,150 (the "Ideal Accumulation Zone," as shown in the preceding chart), while using the downward sloping trend line as a guide in the process. **Increasing interest rates will hurt gold companies who carry even a little bit of debt**, and an expected big rally in the U.S. Dollar should also have a detrimental impact on the shiny metal, at least initially.

If you miss out on buying bullion, and/or gold stocks, and did not pull the trigger when gold was on sale, make sure you "load the boat" if you see gold prices breaking out ABOVE the upper line of the "Downward Sloping Trend Channel." This downward channel's trend lines, both upper and lower lines, are clearly labeled in the preceding "Gold Spot Prices" chart in this chapter.

REMEMBER....gold stocks are HIGHLY volatile. D'Apocalypse™ Now! expects **FURTHER drops** in the price of gold. It is very possible the bankers and elite will force it BELOW $1000/ounce. This may happen just to try and shake everyone out of their positions. The Fibonacci levels and the downward channel lines should provide excellent guides to assist you in planning entry and exit points from gold and gold stocks. Make sure by June of 2014 you own some gold. Ideally, you are buying these stocks when gold hits $1,100/ounce, or below.

The road map says gold will go sky high. It will be worth sitting on paper losses **IN GOOD COMPANIES WHICH DON'T HAVE MATERIAL DEBT AND ARE NOT USING DERIVATIVES TO SELL OUT THEIR FUTURE.**

Also, bear in mind, common stock of these companies can get sorely beaten up due to a lack of liquidity and predatory dumping (i.e. as gold drops in price, these stocks should drop---hard!). However, when gold soars, these stocks should also soar.

Finally, make sure you get the PAPER stock certificate of ownership if possible and do not store it in a safe deposit box!

Call investor relations at any company you are interested in and ask if they have direct shareholder purchase programs. This way, you could receive a stock certificate directly from the company.

INVESTORS MAKING DECISIONS TO INVEST IN ANY COMPANY SHOULD DO THEIR OWN DUE DILIGENCE AND MAKE DECISIONS WHILE CONSULTING WITH THEIR FINANCIAL ADVISORS.

Interesting Bullion Common Stocks

Gold Price

7/15/2013	8/22/2013	10/23/2013	1/10/2014
$1,224.30	$1,375.20	$1,333.40	$1,246.90

Notice Volatility In Common Stock Prices As Gold Price Moves Up And Down.

Good Gold Stocks Will Skyrocket When Gold Price Takes Off!

Ticker	$/Share 7/5/2013	$/Share 8/22/2013	$/Share 10/23/2013	$/Share 1/10/2014	$/Share 7/28/2014	Market Cap (Millions) $	Dividend Yield	Gross Margin	Operating Margin	Current Ratio	Quick Ratio	LT Debt/ Equity	Total Debt/ Equity	Profit Margin
PPP	$4.39	$5.38	$5.62	$4.62	$8.06	$534.46	2.60%	78.82%	14.75%	4.79	4.74	0.51	0.51	4.65%
AUY	$8.94	$11.65	$9.98	$9.10	$8.38	$6,850	1.80%	62.30%	35.60%	1.5	1	0.11	0.11	16.20%
GORO	$8.28	$8.53	$5.24	$4.66	$5.46	$250.10	0.90%	61.60%	29.50%	3.6	3.2	0	0	29.90%
GOLD*	$60.91	$79.24	$75.24	$61.57	$88.47	$5,680	3.25%	60.90%	43.10%	4.1	2.9	0.01	0.01	39.60%
BRD	$0.47	$0.57	$0.67	$0.80	$1.29	$185.58	0.50%	55.90%	25.90%	1.2	0.9	0.29	0.37	34.90%
NEM	$27.34	$32.63	$28.27	$23.80	$25.61	$11,850		54.40%	30.20%	2.1	1.5	0.46	0.46	17.50%
NGD	$6.46	$7.52	$6.03	$5.25	$6.53	$2,600		54.10%	30.60%	5.4	4.4	0.31	0.31	24.50%
GFI	$4.80	$5.87	$4.68	$4.05	$4.05	$2,360	2.60%	51.60%	26.40%	1.8	1.8	0.42	0.42	21.20%
AEM	$26.38	$31.50	$26.20	$26.26	$42.13	$4,740	1.20%	50.90%	24.30%	2.2	2.3	0.23	0.23	13.70%
AGI	$11.68	$16.42	$15.54	$13.28	$10.34	$1,700	3.30%	48.83%	-1.18%	1.95	1.49	1.82	1.87	-4.20%
ANY	$5.63	$4.55	$4.25	$4.01	$3.29	$416.82		47.40%	36.40%	4.2	2.5	0.86	0.92	19.80%
LODE	$1.70	$2.14	$1.71	$1.80	$1.61	$122.26		45.50%	45.50%	1.2	0.8	0.22	0.47	
GG	$23.36	$30.75	$25.88	$23.19	$28.42	$18,840	0.86%	42.20%	36.60%	2.8	2.2	0.1	0.1	31.00%
IAG	$3.89	$6.46	$5.13	$3.50	$3.81	$1,320		41.60%	30.50%	3.9	3	0.17	0.17	14.40%
AUQ	$4.34	$4.87	$4.14	$3.90	$4.24	$965.52	2.10%	39.40%	21.60%	4.3	3.5	0.08	0.09	25.80%
BVN	$14.36	$14.07	$14.26	$11.35	$11.47	$3,130	0.35%	37.50%	22.70%	1.9	1.5	0.05	0.05	37.60%
FNV	$34.09	$45.66	$44.76	$42.08	$58.34	$6,180	1.90%							
GTU	$43.15	$48.55	$46.94	$45.79	$45.79	$852.05							0	0
RGLD	$40.83	$62.35	$52.04	$50.93	$78.42	$3,330	1.65%	61.20%		34.7	34.7	0.13	0.13	27.10%

* Operates in Sub-Saharan Africa.

Information in the above table may not be accurate, please check with your financial advisor for up-to-date figures and advice.

© 2014 Robert L. Kelly

$10 Million Theoretical Bullion Portfolio

$10,000,000 Model Bullion Equity Portfolio
Recommended "Overweight" Stocks
As Originally Published January 10, 2014
Theoretical Performance Updated July 28, 2014

Price of Gold

			1/10/2014 $1,246.90	7/28/14 $1,303.50	% Increase in Gold Price 4.54%	$41,848.00

Ticker	Gold Company	Price/Share 1/10/14	Original Investment/ Even Allocation	# Shares Less 2.5% Transaction Cost	Annual Yield 1/10/14	Accumulated Dividends	Price/Share 7/28/14	Equity Position Value	Less 1% Exit Fee	Total (Net Equity Value + Dividends)	Total Theoretical % Return
PPP	Primero	$4.62	$526,316	111,073		$0	$8.06	$895,249	$886,297	$886,297	68.40%
AUY	Yamana	$9.10	$526,316	56,391	1.80%	$4,618	$8.38	$472,556	$467,831	$472,449	-10.23%
GORO	Gold Resource	$4.66	$526,316	110,120	0.90%	$2,309	$5.46	$601,254	$595,241	$597,550	13.53%
GOLD*	Rangold	$61.57	$526,316	8,335	3.25%	$8,335	$88.47	$737,357	$729,984	$738,318	40.28%
BRD	Brigus	$0.80	$526,316	642,250		$0	$1.29	$828,503	$820,218	$820,218	55.84%
NEM	Newmont	$23.80	$526,316	21,561	0.50%	$1,283	$25.61	$552,184	$546,662	$547,945	4.11%
NGD	New Gold	$5.25	$526,316	97,744		$0	$6.53	$638,271	$631,888	$631,888	20.06%
GFI	Gold Fields	$3.14	$526,316	163,426	2.60%	$6,671	$4.05	$661,876	$655,257	$661,928	25.77%
AEM	Agnico-Eagle	$26.26	$526,316	19,541	1.20%	$3,079	$42.13	$823,280	$815,043	$818,126	55.44%
AGI	Alamos	$13.28	$526,316	38,641	3.30%	$8,467	$10.34	$399,552	$395,557	$404,024	-23.24%
ANV	Allied	$4.01	$526,316	127,970		$0	$3.29	$421,020	$416,810	$416,810	-20.81%
LODE	Comstock	$1.80	$526,316	285,088		$0	$1.61	$458,991	$454,401	$454,401	-13.66%
GG	Gold Corp.	$23.19	$526,316	22,128	0.86%	$2,207	$28.42	$628,889	$622,601	$624,807	18.71%
JAG	IAMGOLD	$3.50	$526,316	146,617		$0	$3.81	$558,609	$553,023	$553,023	5.07%
AUQ	AuRico	$3.90	$526,316	131,579	2.10%	$5,388	$4.24	$557,895	$552,316	$557,704	5.96%
BVN	Compañia Buenaventu	$11.35	$526,316	45,212	0.35%	$898	$11.47	$518,583	$513,398	$514,296	-2.28%
FNV	Franco-Nevada	$42.08	$526,316	12,195	1.90%	$4,875	$58.34	$711,446	$704,331	$709,206	34.75%
GTU	Central Gold Trust	$44.15	$526,316	11,623		$0	$45.79	$532,220	$526,898	$526,898	0.11%
RGLD	Royal Gold	$50.93	$526,316	10,076	1.7%	$4,234	$78.42	$790,140	$782,239	$786,472	49.43%
TOTAL			$10,000,000			$52,363		$ 11,787,875	$ 11,669,096	$ 11,722,360	
% THEORETICAL GAIN								17.9%	16.7%	17.2%	

Information in the above table may not be accurate, please check with your financial advisor for up-to-date figures and advice.
Model portfolios are theoretical, actual results will vary.   * Operates in Sub-Saharan Africa.

At the beginning of 2014, D'Apocalypse™ Now! recommended a number of stocks, as evidenced by book proofs published in February 2014. "Bullion" and "Big Cap" $10,000,000 theoretical portfolios were created to track performance. Through July 28, 2014, the "Bullion Portfolio" beat both the Dow & S&P, significantly ("Big Cap" performance on page 319).

Performance of Theoretical Bullion Portfolio July 28, 2014 Percentages NOT annualized			
	10-Jan-14	28-Jul-14	% Gain (Loss)
Dow Jones	16437.05	16,982.59	3.32%
S&P 500	1842.37	1978.91	7.41%
Vs. D'Apocalypse™ Now! Bullion Recommendations + Dividends (Less Fees)			17.20%
Vs. D'Apocalypse™ Now! Bullion Recommendations			16.70%

No Gold Standard

Unlike most gold bugs who insist on the creation (or re-creation) of a "gold standard," this book does not suggest this, as it would be a disaster, economically speaking. A decision to move to a gold standard would cause a tremendous deflation in prices of just about everything, as gold is very scarce and is only in the hands of a few people and governments, worldwide. They hold significant quantities of it---the general population does not. They will win, the general population will lose...ergo it is a very bad idea to make it a standard!

If gold were made a standard, the price of gold would permanently skyrocket under this system---and cause everything everyone produced to DROP in price in terms of gold. This would be a disaster for the economy, but a real "gold mine" for the rich and elite who own all the gold! Gold bugs should be very careful what they wish for.

This would make gold owners extremely wealthy. They could buy much more grain, more beef, more clothes, more homes, etc. Each ounce of gold would dramatically increase in price—and it would be accepted as a CURRENCY under a "gold standard." Chapter 17, called "History Repeats Itself," in The $30 Trillion Heist---Follow The Money! has an excellent section written about the 'Coinage Act' of 1873.

This Act demonetized silver (which the U.S. had massive amounts of), while Baron de Rothschild and London bankers controlled the vast majority of gold holdings. Senator Hansbrough of North Dakota provided uncontestable evidence TO CONGRESS of the impact on grain prices because of the switch to a pure gold standard. Grain prices collapsed relative to gold and the Rothschild's grew wealthier by the minute because of America's Congressional stupidity. The Act was ultimately repealed in 1893 after causing tremendous hardship for millions of Americans.

Populations of people do not and will not generally own material amounts of gold. A pure gold standard would effectively shrink the money supply and cause billions of people to starve. There would be no work and there would be no profits for producers, as prices would drop like a rock. It would be a disaster for the poor and middle class---and another coup for the bankers and elite. While this author is not a conspiracy theorist, and prefers to look at hard facts and ask tough questions, there is at least a reasonably probability the gold supposedly owned by the United States in Fort Knox, the New York Federal Reserve Bank, etc. has been converted by fraud and is now owned by the bankers and their elite owners.
Only a full audit and assay of the gold supply will ever resolve this controversial topic.

It would be far better for the people to have our government (or any other government) fulfill its obligations under our Constitution (or theirs) and take control of monetary policy and the supply of money and institute rationale monetary policies and plans. At the same time, we should create a constitutional amendment for a balanced budget, unless in the time of war, as can only be declared by Congress. The U.S. and many Western and Eastern nations have powerful militaries. Providing a currency with the government's backing in "full faith and credit," as well as a currency's validity for the payment of taxes, is a far better system than the gold standard.

The problem today is the system has been hijacked by a bunch of sharks.

This book does not advocate a gold standard, but does advocate for a far more responsible central banking system, controlled by the people and not a bunch of private bankers who control and rob the system.

The Federal Reserve's supposed "independent" Board of Governors is anything but independent. They are all well taken care of by the banking industry when their appointed terms expire, and the most critical elements of monetary policy, including Open Market Operations, are almost entirely controlled by the New York Federal Reserve Bank.

As you may know from reading <u>The $30 Trillion Heist---Follow The Money!</u>, (Chapter 16, "Ownership of the Federal Reserve") it is directly owned by the banks and the elite.

DJIA---Bureau of Labor Statistics Inflation-Adjusted Dow

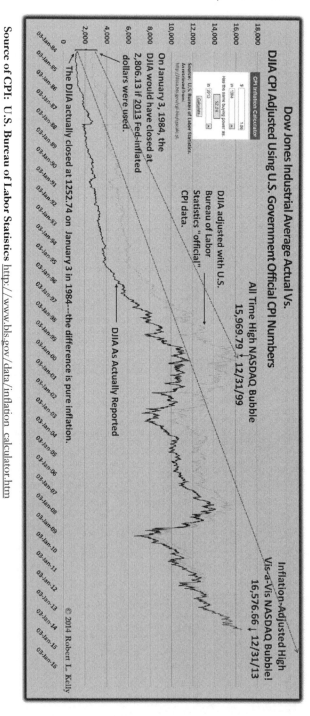

Dow Jones Industrial Average Actual Vs.
DJIA CPI Adjusted Using U.S. Government Official CPI Numbers

All Time High NASDAQ Bubble
15,969.79 ↕ 12/31/99

Inflation-Adjusted High
Vis-a-Vis NASDAQ Bubble!
16,576.66 ↓ 12/31/13

DJIA adjusted with U.S.
Bureau of Labor
Statistics "official"
CPI data.

On January 3, 1984, the
DJIA would have closed at
2,806.13 if 2013 Fed-inflated
dollars were used.

The DJIA actually closed at 1252.74 on January 3 in 1984---the difference is pure inflation.

DJIA As Actually Reported

Source: U.S. Bureau of Labor Statistics.
As retrieved from:
http://bls.bls.gov/cgi-bin/cpicalc.pl

© 2014 Robert L. Kelly

Source of CPI: U.S. Bureau of Labor Statistics http://www.bls.gov/data/inflation_calculator.htm

DJIA Equivalent Using "Real" Inflation Numbers

This chart uses different inflation assumptions than the U.S. BLS "Official" figures. DEPENDING on how you calculate inflation, "Dow Equivalent" numbers can vary, dramatically. Any projections of the Dow also vary according to the assumptions. The author's preferred projection is the Dow could nearly double from the 15,440.23 February 5, 2014 close, as we approach D'Apocalypse™. Year end 2013 close was 16,576.66.

Dow Jones Industrial Average Vs.
DJIA Adjusted With Real Inflation Assumptions

DJIA using 2013 Dollars and author's assumptions of higher "real" inflation rates than those published by U.S. Government reports.

38,558.06
12/31/99

This "crazy" inflation-adjusted uptrend line crosses 55,000 in 2015! The DJIA could explode toward this figure if sheer and utter panic gripped the Fed. This would cause them to print massive sums of money, further destroying the fortunes of the majority of Americans, in favor of those few elite who have their wealth tied up in stocks.

Target Range---Must Exit By May 2015

Break Out From Downtrend Of "Real" CPI Adjusted DJIA

Look for a "good scare" to try and fake you out of your long positions!

U.S. Government Bureau of Labor Statistics
DJIA With Adjusted CPI

15,969.79
12/31/99

11,497.12
12/31/99

Acutal DJIA As Reported

© 2014 Robert L. Kelly

Note: Author created this chart at year end 2013. Please alert yourself to the "arrow" at the far right, pointing "down." The "good scare" correction at the start of 2014 appears to be on track with the forecast—precisely as envisioned when this chart was created. Keep your eye on the ball, because this market should go on a tear, once this correction is complete. It represents a great buying opportunity.

Buy the Dow

The following graph shows you two profiles of Dow Jones Industrial Average ("DJIA") performance. The lighter colored plot line, which is the one on "top," is the DJIA's inflation-adjusted performance using "Official" U.S. Government Bureau of Labor Statistics CPI figures. Notice the theoretical "All Time High" during the NASDAQ bubble was on December 31, 1999. Recently, thanks to Assflation™, this level was exceeded by the recent rally in the markets when using government-reported inflation figures to measure Dow Performance.

The most recent high in the DJIA reached 16,576.66 on December 31, 2013, seeing the Assflation™-juiced rally finally beating the inflation-adjusted Dow during the NASDAQ bubble of 15,969.79. The darker line on the "bottom" is the actual Dow Jones Industrial Average, as reported.
The "Real" inflation number assumptions merely **confirm** what this author's forecast is and has been throughout this book. <u>Directly due to</u> <u>Assflation</u>™ and the pure hijinks of the Federal Reserve System, the banks and the elite, the Dow will go up, dramatically into 2015. Do not ever forget the banks are prepping you to be the suckers---they will froth this market and then unload everything on you at, or near, the top. They plan to completely victimize unprepared pension funds, 401Ks, IRAs, uninformed "wealth," and the regular guy on the street.

When the rally is going full force, do not be deceived by the rah-rah talking heads on TV!

While the top 20% of the world will be ecstatic because of a great rally, you will be much wiser armed with the knowledge of what will happen, before and after, D'Apocalypse™ arrives. The most inquisitive readers may wonder why the market will not "ride" the "real" inflation-adjusted DJIA graph's "upper trend line" (e.g. the previous chart titled, "Dow Jones Industrial Average Vs. DJIA Adjusted With "Real" Inflation Assumptions") to over 50,000!

As can be seen in the **table** which follows in this chapter, "Equivalent Dow Jones Industrial Average Compared With U.S. GDP 1929 Vs. 2013 Adjusted For Key Food & Products Weighted Price Changes," the **DJIA, IF ADJUSTED FOR REAL GDP GROWTH AND REAL INFLATION WOULD HAVE TO HIT A SPIKE HIGH OF 58,652.23** to equal the all-time blow off high from 1929!!!

If you look, once again at the very "top" upper trend line drawn on the preceding graph, you can see it also crosses above DJIA 55,000 in 2015!

Naturally, all inflation assumptions are subject to a great amount of interpretation, and frankly, manipulation and control. The variables of when, where and how pricing information was gathered, comparable products, services, etc. provides a great deal of room for error. This author would much rather take the "conservative" road and target prices which appear reasonable, given all the facts at hand. It is interesting, however, how these prices align with real inflation adjustments vis-à-vis the watered-down version we receive from the U.S. Government!

A line which basically "splits" the U.S. Government BLS inflation-adjusted DJIA with the "Real" inflation-adjusted DJIA created by the author, places the DJIA target in 2015 right in the middle of the target range the author is forecasting. Please see the blue, or lightly shaded (if you are reading in black and white), oval target range in the previous DJIA chart.

Do not forget the enormous debt overhang which is another huge reason why the markets may not reach the top end of the upper trend line's range. A great deal will depend on how government and the Federal Reserve respond—i.e., do they print mountains of more money, if so, in what quantities, how frequently, etc.? Another major factor will be how desperate capital is to flee an upcoming European and Japanese melt down. A finer tuning of the ultimate high will be possible later. In the meantime, enjoy the ride!!

Involuntary Seizure of Funds Coming---Must Exit By May 2015!
As stated, from the 15,440ish level, the Dow Jones Industrial Average could nearly double by September 2015. A nice ride above 20,000 should help you get prepared for D'Apocalypse™. You should be OUT of all markets by May 31, 2015—with the full knowledge you may be leaving a lot of money on the table. A problem will arise if you are still in the market when the balloon goes up, because you may never see ANY of your money, again! Any amount of money you receive after the storm hits and they reopen the banks, and/or investment banking firms, will likely be valued in a reduced currency, and/or your assets will be outright seized.

Europe is already, officially, discussing the seizure of 10% of ALL accounts if they have a crisis. Overnight, millions will see their wealth being stolen.

When considering whether to squeeze the last nickel (or even 1/3!) out of the remaining rally when you leave the markets at the end of May 2015, as this book strongly suggests, make the decision with great confidence. You will be making a very wise decision to leave the money on the table. As you can see, above, the IMF has already PUBLISHED their thoughts on SEIZING assets to pay for the banks and elite's bad bets.

This is going to happen---but not only in Europe, but also in most Western-trading nations (e.g. the U.S., Japan and Western Europe, for sure). The IMF and the Western governments KNOW a catastrophe is in the making and they are already priming the public with their "thoughts" on what will be coming. This is typical psychological conditioning. As anyone with half a brain can see, it is nothing but outright theft, but will be camouflaged in terms like "it is your patriotic duty," "we must all chip in to make sure our futures are OK," etc. All of this bologna is for the benefit of the elite---the founders of the Federal Reserve, the owners of

International Monetary Fund | October 2013   49   2. TAXING OUR WAY OUT OF---OR INTO?---TROUBLE

Box 6. A One-Off Capital Levy?

The sharp deterioration of the public finances in many countries has revived interest in a "capital levy"—a one-off tax on private wealth—as an exceptional measure to restore debt sustainability.[1] The appeal is that such a tax, if it is implemented before avoidance is possible and there is a belief that it will never be repeated, does not distort behavior (and may be seen by some as fair). There have been illustrious supporters, including Pigou, Ricardo, Schumpeter, and—until he changed his mind—Keynes. The conditions for success are strong, but also need to be weighed against the risks of the alternatives, which include repudiating public debt or inflating it away (these, in turn, are a particular form of wealth tax—on bondholders—that also falls on nonresidents).

There is a surprisingly large amount of experience to draw on, as such levies were widely adopted in Europe after World War I and in Germany and Japan after World War II. Reviewed in Eichengreen (1990), this experience suggests that more notable than any loss of credibility was a simple failure to achieve debt reduction, largely because the delay in introduction gave space for extensive avoidance and capital flight—in turn spurring inflation.

The tax rates needed to bring down public debt to precrisis levels, moreover, are sizable: reducing debt ratios to end-2007 levels would require (for a sample of 15 euro area countries) a tax rate of about 10 percent on households with positive net wealth.[2]

[2] IMF staff calculation using the Eurosystem's Household Finance and Consumption Survey (Household Finance and Consumption Network, 2013); unweighted average.

[1] As for instance in Bach (2012).

(Source: World Economic and Financial Surveys, Fiscal Monitor, Taxing Times 2013, International Monetary Fund, October 2013, as retrieved from http://www.imf.org/external/pubs/ft/fm/2013/02/pdf/fm1302.pdf).

the Federal Reserve, and its associated banks all over the world. This includes the Bank of England, controlled by the Rothschilds, the IMF, the BIS and nearly every single central bank in the West.

Politicians (in whatever country they are in) who are currently trapped by the money trust, must fight back---aggressively. The money trust needs to have the tables turned on it and ITS assets must be seized and returned to the people. As discussed previously, this should be an all-out assault on the trillions and trillions of dollars in assets taken secretly from the American Public and every other country which has been abused by this clandestine and secretive group of elites.

Julius Caesar had the right idea, where the public's debt was forgiven during an economic crisis during his day, as recounted in this book. However, because of the massive heist which has taken place, our political representatives should be doing nothing other than storming through the elite's entire system of asset and money-laundering operations and seizing THEIR assets and returning them directly to the public.

This is how the fraud can be rectified and the economy can get back on track. It is simply not possible to help all the people on unemployment when the elite have taken all the money and the futures from the non-elite standing in bread lines and barely making it on the home front. If the monies are seized, it will be up to the people, the politicians and the Attorney General from all countries to go after these elite people and organizations, criminally.

Governments who have read the section in this chapter about setting up a new and distinct International Reserve Bank have a once in a lifetime opportunity to stick it to the financial thugs who have spent the West into the grave and are non-repentant in their heisting of money from the public. This time, these sharks intend to effect an EVEN GREATER HEIST and do it "in your face," by directly seizing assets held in accounts.

Would you rather get the last nickel of the Assflation™ rally into 2015 and then wind up with a 30%, 40%, 50%, or even greater haircut, when your capital is frozen, seized and you are returned a currency worth only a fraction of what it is worth today, OR take your money and run! I think the risks and rewards are obvious and each of you can make up your own minds. This book believes taking the conservative road and getting your money off the table, while you can, is the very best thing to do.

Discretion will be the better part of valor as we approach D'Apocalypse™!

Inflation Rates Assumed in Author's Forecast of the Dow Jones

The assumptions used to formulate the author's forecast should provide the reader with compelling evidence the author is correct and the forecast of this book is reasonable and justified, even though many will think it "mad." Not only do the Fed's actions provide us with prima facie evidence of where Assflation™ is heading, but it is backed up with inflation data most people can understand. Here are the assumed inflation rates (i.e., "Real" Inflation Rates) used to create the Dow chart which shows an adjusted peak of 38,558.06 on 12/31/99 at the height of the NASDAQ bubble.

U.S. Government BLS publishes numerous tables of goods and services which show major increases in the inflation rates for most things needed to be used by the human race. Their data verifies the following "Real Inflation Rate Assumptions" formulated by the author are not "crazy" and are probably in the ball park of what reality has been. An example of such a BLS table follows. Additionally, the author has drilled down on the price increases for necessities, which also show significant inflation. Between all the data, there is really no question the author's assumptions on inflation are reasonable.

"Official" Inflation Rates				"Real" Inflation Rate Assumptions			
				(Used To Calculate 2013 Constant Dollar DJIA Chart			
U.S. Govt. Bureau of Labor Statistics				Yielding Equivalent Dec. 31, 1999 High Of 38,558.06)			
Year	Rate	Year	Rate	Year	Rate	Year	Rate
1984	4.30%	1999	2.19%	1984	5.30%	1999	8.10%
1985	3.55%	2000	3.38%	1985	4.80%	2000	9.80%
1986	1.91%	2001	2.83%	1986	4.70%	2001	9.80%
1987	3.66%	2002	1.59%	1987	2.50%	2002	7.70%
1988	4.08%	2003	2.27%	1988	5.40%	2003	8.10%
1989	4.83%	2004	2.68%	1989	6.30%	2004	8.50%
1990	5.39%	2005	3.39%	1990	7.00%	2005	9.60%
1991	4.25%	2006	3.24%	1991	8.10%	2006	10.30%
1992	3.03%	2007	2.85%	1992	5.10%	2007	10.30%
1993	2.96%	2008	3.85%	1993	5.30%	2008	12.20%
1994	2.61%	2009	-0.34%	1994	5.60%	2009	6.00%
1995	2.81%	2010	1.64%	1995	6.40%	2010	5.20%
1996	2.93%	2011	3.16%	1996	6.70%	2011	9.00%
1997	2.34%	2012	2.07%	1997	8.50%	2012	11.00%
1998	1.55%	2013	1.32%	1998	8.00%	2013	9.10%
Average BLS Inflation Rate			2.98%	Average "Real" Inflation Rate			7.74%
Which Set Of Inflation Rates Do You Believe?							
[Sources: US Government Bureau of Labor Statistics, see representative tables, below, www.ShadowStats.com and various other sources--see table "U.S. Price Changes In Key Living Costs" also, below].							© 2013 Robert L. Kelly

As you saw in the first DJIA chart titled, "Dow Jones Industrial Average, Actual Vs. CPI Adjusted, Using U.S. Government Official CPI Numbers," the purchasing power of the consumer dollar in 2013 was only $0.44 compared to 1984 (i.e., $1 ÷ $2.24), and this is based on the government's conservative estimates of inflation. The following is a sample BLS table showing changes from ONLY 2010 to 2011. They are not pretty!

Table 3A. Consumer Price Index for all Urban Consumers (CPI-U): U.S. city average, detailed expenditure categories -Continued

(1982-84=100, unless otherwise noted)

Item and Group	Annual average 2010	Annual average 2011	Percent change from 2010 to 2011
Special aggregate indexes			
All items less shelter	208.643	217.048	4.0
All items less medical care	209.689	216.325	3.2
Commodities less food	152.990	162.409	6.2
Nondurables less food	191.927	209.615	9.2
Nondurables less food and apparel	235.601	262.123	11.3
Nondurables	205.271	219.049	6.7
Apparel less footwear	113.272	116.234	2.6
Services less rent of shelter [6]	284.368	290.554	2.2
Services less medical care services	249.569	253.554	1.6
Energy	211.449	243.909	15.4
All items less energy	220.458	224.806	2.0
All items less food and energy	221.337	225.008	1.7
Commodities less food and energy commodities	143.588	145.499	1.3
Energy commodities	242.636	306.445	26.3
Services less energy services	268.278	273.057	1.8
Domestically produced farm food	221.577	232.490	4.9
Utilities and public transportation	203.061	206.541	1.7
Purchasing power of the consumer dollar (1982-84=$1.00)	$ .459	$ .445	-
Purchasing power of the consumer dollar (1967=$1.00)	$ .153	$ .148	-

[1] Special index based on a substantially smaller sample.
[2] Indexes on a December 1997=100 base.
[3] Indexes on a December 2007=100 base.
[4] Indexes on a December 2005=100 base.
[5] This index series was calculated using a Laspeyres estimator. All other item stratum index series were calculated using a geometric means estimator.
[6] Indexes on a December 1982=100 base.
[7] Indexes on a December 1986=100 base.

[8] Indexes on a December 1983=100 base.
[9] Indexes on a December 1990=100 base.
[10] Indexes on a December 2001=100 base.
[11] Indexes on a December 1993=100 base.
[12] Indexes on a December 2009=100 base.
[13] Indexes on a December 1996=100 base.
[14] Indexes on a December 1988=100 base.
- Data not available.

(Source: U.S. Government Bureau of Labor Statistics, 2011 Consumer Price Index Detailed Report Table, Annual Average Indexes 2011, page 9, Consumer Price Index for all Urban Consumers, as retrieved from http://www.bls.gov/cpi/cpid11av.pdf).

Table 24C. Historical Chained Consumer Price Index for All Urban Consumers (C-CPI-U): U. S. city average, all items

(December 1999=100, unless otherwise noted)

Year	Jan.	Feb.	Mar.	Apr.	May	June	July	Aug.	Sep.	Oct.	Nov.	Dec.	Annual avg.	Percent change from previous Dec.	Percent change from previous Annual avg.
1999	-	-	-	-	-	-	-	-	-	-	-	100.0	-	-	-
2000	100.3	100.9	101.6	101.6	101.7	102.1	102.3	102.3	102.8	102.9	102.8	102.6	102.0	2.6	-
2001	103.3	103.7	103.9	104.2	104.6	104.8	104.5	104.6	104.9	104.7	104.4	103.9	104.3	1.3	2.3
2002	104.2	104.5	105.1	105.6	105.8	105.8	105.7	106.0	106.3	106.4	106.3	106.0	105.8	2.0	1.2
2003	106.5	107.3	107.9	107.7	107.5	107.6	107.7	108.2	108.5	108.4	108.0	107.8	107.8	1.7	2.1
2004	108.5	109.1	109.7	110.0	110.6	110.8	110.7	110.7	111.0	111.6	111.6	111.2	110.5	3.2	2.5
2005	111.3	111.9	112.6	113.4	113.3	113.2	113.7	114.3	115.6	115.7	114.9	114.4	113.7	2.9	2.9
2006	115.2	115.4	116.0	116.9	117.5	117.7	118.1	118.3	117.8	117.1	116.9	117.0	117.0	2.3	2.9
2007	117.330	117.677	118.913	119.866	120.292	120.439	120.377	120.288	120.638	120.885	121.481	121.295	119.957	3.7	2.5
2008	121.867	122.250	123.323	124.116	125.171	126.307	126.918	126.594	126.551	125.500	123.044	121.557	124.433	.2	3.7
2009	122.095	122.598	122.803	123.053	123.427	124.485	124.293	124.620	124.706	124.791	124.788	124.544	123.850	2.5	-.5
2010	124.987	124.972	125.442	125.620	125.678	125.521	125.536	125.756	125.830	125.969	125.920	126.143	125.615	1.3	1.4
2011	126.700	127.286	128.353	129.062	129.548	129.531	129.636	129.974	130.196	129.997	129.856	129.586	129.144	2.7	2.8
2012	130.104	130.569	131.388	131.731	131.639	131.557	131.352	131.940	132.438	132.434	131.949	131.633	-	1.6	-

- Data not available.
Indexes for 2012 are initial estimates. Indexes for 2011 are interim adjustments. Indexes for 2010 and earlier are final.
NOTE: Index applies to a month as a whole, not to any specific date.

(Source: CPI Detailed Report, Data for December 2012, Editors Malik Crawford, Jonathan Church, Darren Rippy, page 115, as retrieved from http://www.bls.gov/cpi/cpid1212.pdf).

Sanity Check Using Real Prices of Necessities in 1929 Compared to 2013

1924 Chevrolet Utility Coupe

Sear Catalog Honor Bilt Crescent 5 rooms and a bath
Price: $2,436
Description

The Crescent
$2,436
Sears Roebuck Honor Bilt
Crescent Self Build Home From The 1920's

Here are actual prices for real products in the 1920s and today, in 2013

Price Changes
Key Living Costs

Item	1984	2013	%	2008	2013	%
Median Cost of a new home	$72,400	$249,700	345%	$221,600	$249,700	113%
Average Cost of a new home	$98,800	$295,000	299%	$290,100	$295,000	102%
Average Monthly Rent (US Avge)	$350	$735	210%	$696	$735	106%
Dodge RAM Truck	$8,995	$33,620	374%	$26,320	$33,620	128%
Median Household Income	$22,415	$52,762	235%	$50,303	$52,762	105%
Cost of a first-class stamp	$0.20	$0.46	230%	$0.42	$0.46	110%
Cost of a gallon of regular gas	$1.21	$3.69	305%	$1.87	$3.67	196%
Cost Electricity ($/500KwH)	$38.63	$68.53	177%	$65.50	$68.53	105%
Cost of a dozen eggs	$1.01	$3.89	385%	$2.39	$3.89	163%
Cost of a gallon of Milk	$2.26	$3.99	177%	$4.24	$3.99	94%
Cost of 1 lb. of Ground Beef	$1.29	$3.38	262%	$2.41	$3.38	141%
Movie Ticket	$3.36	$8.38	249%	$7.18	$8.38	117%
Gold	$329.00	$1,238.00	376%	$756.24	$1,238.00	164%

2013 Purchasing Power of Consumer Dollar Vs. 1984: $0.44(U.S.G. Bureau of Labor Statistics 1982-1984= $1.00), BLS CPI Calculator can be retrieved and calculated at: http://data.bls.gov/cgi-bin/cpicalc/pl

(Sources: http://www.theproperhistory.com/1984.html, U.S. Census Bureau 2013, http://www.peopol.com, Trader Joe's, http://1980sflashback.com/1980s/Economy.asp, 1984-30 Truck, 2013 Dodge web site, 2013-1500 Big Horn, Autotrader 2008 RAM 1500 26,320, U.S. Postal Service http://www.usps.com, US Bureau of Labor Statistics, 1984 Post Office Mojo, Variety, July 19, 2013, as retrieved from http://variety.com/2013/film/news/average-movie-ticket-price-is-highest-ever-1200556675/, gold price fix January 6, 2013 & November 2008, USA Today 4.26.08, http://usatoday30.usatoday.com/money/industries/food/2008-04-27-egg-prices_N.htm, http://money.cnn.com/2008/05/02/news/economy/milk_prices/index.htm)

© 2013 Robert L. Kelly

These kinds of comparisons are open to a great deal of scrutiny, however, from a "regular person's" perspective, a car is still a car, a home is still a home and an egg is still an egg.

This will be another good "sanity check" on the "Real" inflation figures this book is using in its analysis. We all know prices continue to creep up, and it seems like a way of life for everyone. Please notice the average 75X increase in price the necessities in the previous table have experienced since 1929. This kind of information and the assumptions one makes for actual inflation rates can have a profound impact on how you might analyze the Dow Jones Industrial Average, as well as other investments.

Using the preceding data, we can then use the "75.0787" weighted average increase in prices to see if our forecasts are in the ball park with respect to the forecast made in the chart, **"Dow Jones Industrial Average Vs. DJIA Adjusted With "Real" Inflation Assumptions"**, previously shown to you in this chapter.

Let's adjust the Dow Jones in 1929, using this inflation factor, and determine what numbers we come up with.

Let's apply the factor <u>to the blow off high in 1929 on September 3</u>, just before the great crash in October of that year, we know the Dow closed at 381.17 on this date.

> *When we apply the inflation factor of 75.0787 to 381.17, an equivalent Dow Jones close in 2013 would have to equal 28,617.75 to merely meet the blow-off high on September 3, 1929!!!*

This does not even take into consideration the 2012 GDP. When it is adjusted back down to 1929 dollars it was GREATER than the 1929 U.S. GDP by over $100 BILLION. If it is converted to 1929 dollars, it would equal $210 Billion! As you know, the U.S. GDP figure for 2013 was approximately $16 TRILLION. This staggering difference is nearly 100% attributable to the Federal Reserve and the banks printing money and debasing our currency.

When this percentage increase in the real GDP is **also** thrown into the mix, ceteris paribus and applying the percentage increase to the DJIA at the time, the Dow Jones equivalent in 1929 would have been 769.67.

Adjusting this number for inflation, with the 75.08 factor, calculates to an equivalent 2013 Dow Jones year-end number, adjusted for GDP growth and inflation (e.g. real 2013 GDP, as measured in 1929, is greater than the GDP of 1929) of 58,652.53!!

Remarkably, both these numbers, "28,617.75" (which is right in the middle of our target range for 2015 in the DJIA) and 58,652.53 (which is just above the top of the rising trend line into 2015), are potential target areas from a technical perspective.

As discussed at length, don't count on the market exceeding the blue highlighted oval target area on the chart (just above 20,000 to approximately 37,000) marking the Target Range. The debt is an enormous weight on this beast.

Exit all positions by the end of May 2015.

This is a fairly good "sanity check."

Equivalent Dow Jones Industrial Average Compared With U.S. GDP 1929 Vs. 2013 Adjusted For Key Food & Products Weighted Price Changes

$ Billions

	Nominal GDP	1929 Inflation Factor*	Adjusted GDP In 1929 $	2012 & 2013 GDP Vs. 1929 GDP Factor	Adjusted 2013 Dow Equivalent of 1929 Dow At "Blow Off" High
1929 GDP	$104				
2012 U.S. GDP	$15,776	75.08	$210.13	2.02	
2013 U.S. GDP	$16,003		$213.15	2.05	28,617.75
1929 "Blow Off Print Close" 9/3/29 Dow Jones	381.17				
Actual Print Close 12/31/13 Dow Jones	16,576.66				
Adjusted 12/31/13 Dow Jones In 1929 Using "75.08" 1929 Inflation Factor From Table, "Key Living Items"	220.79				
% the Adjusted 12/31/13 Dow Jones Trading BELOW Equivalent 1929 High On 9/3/29	42.1%				
1929 "Blow-Off Print Close Adjusted For GDP Growth	781.21				
2013 Equivalent Dow Jones Average With 75.08 Inflation Factor	58,652.53				

© 2014 Robert L. Kelly

The year-end Dec. 31, 2013 Dow Jones Industrial Average, if priced in 1929 dollars, would be trading 42.1% BELOW the 1929 blow-off high. In other words, the actual print high in 1929 would have been trading 1.72 times higher than the equivalent Dec. 31, 2013 Dow Jones Industrial Average when adjusted downward in 1929 dollars with the 75.08 1929–2013 inflation factor. This extraordinary information, based on the power of inflation (using not unreasonable assumptions—the factor is based on actual price history of similar products, all necessities in life) tells us an equivalent 2013 Dow Jones Industrial Average "Blow Off Print Close" would have to equal 28,617.75 AND IF adjusted for the real increase in GDP which has occured since 1929, the equivalent 2013 blow-off high would be 58,652.53!!!

* From previous table, "Key Living Items-Average Weighted Number Of Times Prices Increased 1920s VS. 2013"

Finally, the following are actual prices of key goods and services most people consume for the periods 1984, 2008 and 2013. You can see (even though any living being knows many, many prices have gone crazy the last several years) the written evidence of dramatic spikes in prices since the Fed began performing its secret bailouts for the banks and the elite:

Price Changes Key Living Costs						
Item	1984	2013	%	2008	2013	%
Median Cost of a new home	$72,400	$249,700	345%	$221,600	$249,700	113%
Average Cost of a new home	$98,800	$295,000	299%	$290,100	$295,000	102%
Average Monthly Rent (US Avge)	$350	$735	210%	$696	$735	106%
Dodge RAM Truck	$8,995	$33,620	374%	$26,320	$33,620	128%
Median Household Income	$22,415	$52,762	235%	$50,303	$52,762	105%
Cost of a first-class stamp	$0.20	$0.46	230%	$0.42	$0.46	110%
Cost of a gallon of regular gas	$1.21	$3.69	305%	$1.87	$3.67	196%
Cost Electricity ($/500KwH)	$38.63	$68.53	177%	$65.50	$68.53	105%
Cost of a dozen eggs	$1.01	$3.89	385%	$2.39	$3.89	163%
Cost of a gallon of Milk	$2.26	$3.99	177%	$4.24	$3.99	94%
Cost of 1 lb. of Ground Beef	$1.29	$3.38	262%	$2.41	$3.38	141%
Movie Ticket	$3.36	$8.38	249%	$7.18	$8.38	117%
Gold	$329.00	$1,238.00	376%	$756.24	$1,238.00	164%

2013 Purchasing Power of Consumer Dollar Vs. 1984: $0.44 (U.S.G. Bureau of Labor Statistics 1982-1984 = $1.00), BLS CPI Calculator can be retrieved and calculated at: http://data.bls.gov/cgi-bin/cpicalc/pi

(Sources: http://www.thepeoplehistory.com/1984.html, U.S. Census Bureau 2013, http://www.peapod.com, Trader Joe's, http://1980sflashback.com/1984/Economy.asp, 1984-50 Truck, 2013 Dodge web site, 2013- 1500 Big Horn, Autotrader 2008 RAM 1500 26,320, U.S. Postal Service http://www.usps.com, US Bureau of Labor Statistics, 1984 Box Office Mojo, Variety, July 19, 2013. as retrieved from http://variety.com/2013/film/news/average-movie-ticket-price-is-highest-ever-12005656/5/, gold price fix January 6, 2013 & November 2008, http://money.cnn.com/2008/05/02/news/economy/milk_prices/index.htm).

© 2013 Robert L. Kelly

The exact numbers and assumptions for inflation can vary, dramatically, for every person. Given the extreme disconnect seeming to exist between "Official" U.S. Government BLS reported inflation figures and the reality of families trying to live on less money, but incurring much higher costs due to constantly raising prices---the assumptions made in this book do not seem unreasonable.

However, there is certainly room for disagreement---the bottom line is the impact from Assflation™ **will** create a gigantic equity bubble in big cap stocks---you want to be on this ride while it is happening and get off the ride EARLY because of the precarious leverage involved in the derivatives markets and system, in general. It will spell disaster for most people.

Buy Big Caps With Growing Operations Carrying a Dividend
During the ride, expect the stock markets to demonstrate some dramatic volatility. The pros will do their very best to shake you out of your long positions if they can, before the end of the rally---don't let them.

Big cap stocks are the way to go, but most LIQUID equity securities will enjoy a very nice ride. <u>As discussed, any larger, well-capitalized company which has a successful business and pays a consistent DIVIDEND will likely outperform most others.</u> DO NOT INVEST in companies which merely provide you a dividend. You could get destroyed in those vehicles as interest rates increase dramatically in the next two years!!! Companies and funds designed to pay dividends, with no growth to speak of, normally trade like bonds. These will all be destroyed because of spiking interest rates. Preferred stock with a fixed dividend will also be in trouble. Avoid these kinds of investments like the plague and definitely avoid long term bonds!

The Dow is a fairly good bet because those stocks are all VERY LIQUID and thus will attract the elite's capital from all around the world. The Dow stocks are obviously comprised of successful companies and they are generally growing (at least currently) for the most part, with many providing a decent dividend yield.

It has been a long time since the Dow was the sexy index, but this is about to change in the next two years. By the way---other equities will do extremely well, also, but the Dow is highly liquid and focused on larger companies. The S&P 500 will also be exceptional, as will other equity indexes. They key is liquidity, as very big money will make it a #1 priority to invest in liquid markets.

Big money is not stupid and it can see the writing on the wall.

The following are the Dow components and some of the key oil stocks (and closing prices as of 2/5/2014). Certain stocks were recently eliminated from the DJIA and some were added. The author has kept the eliminated companies (e.g. "Eliminated") on the list and added the new companies, as well (e.g. "Added To Dow"). Stocks the author "likes" are noted with "Overweight," or "**".

Components Of The Dow Jones Industrial Average

Ticker	Name	$ Last Trade	Note
AA	Alcoa Inc.	11.04	Eliminated
AXP	American Express Company	83.72	
BA	The Boeing Company	121.40	
BAC	Bank of America Corporation	16.40	Eliminated
CAT	Caterpillar Inc.	91.96	
CSCO	Cisco Systems, Inc.	21.98	
CVX	Chevron Corporation	109.52	Overweight
DD	E. I. du Pont de Nemours and Company	61.90	Overweight
DIS	The Walt Disney Company	71.76	
GE	General Electric Company	24.52	
HD	The Home Depot, Inc.	75.26	
HPQ	Hewlett-Packard Company	28.01	Eliminated
IBM	IBM	173.29	
INTC	Intel Corporation	23.52	
JNJ	Johnson & Johnson	87.28	Overweight
JPM	JPMorgan Chase & Co.	55.21	
KO	The Coca-Cola Company	37.61	
MCD	McDonald's Corp.	93.58	
MMM	3M Company	127.36	Overweight
MRK	Merck & Co. Inc.	53.53	Overweight
MSFT	Microsoft Corporation	35.82	
PFE	Pfizer Inc.	30.65	
PG	The Procter & Gamble Company	76.45	Overweight
T	AT&T, Inc.	32.08	
TRV	The Travelers Companies, Inc.	80.44	
UNH	UnitedHealth Group Incorporated	70.82	
UTX	United Technologies Corp.	107.91	
VZ	Verizon Communications Inc.	46.69	
WMT	Wal-Mart Stores Inc.	72.87	
XOM	Exxon Mobil Corporation	88.95	Overweight
GS	Goldman Sachs	160.42	Added To Dow
NKE	Nike	70.60	Added To Dow
V	Visa	215.61	Added To Dow / Overweight

Note: Prices quoted during trading day 2/5/2014.

Quotes believed to be accurate; however, reader should recheck all information with his/her financial advisor and seek their advice before making any investment decision.

Oil stocks of the large, integrated oil companies should be excellent investments into May 2015, Exxon and Chevron (above) are "over weighted," however the NYSE "XOI" index has some excellent companies which should also be considered:

Symbol	Name	Price	Yield
APC	Anadarko Petroleum Corporation	79.13	.91%
BP	British Petroleum plc	46.04	4.76%
COP	ConocoPhillips**	63.46	4.35%
CVX	Chevron Corporation**	109.52	3.65%
HES	Hess Corporation	74.66	1.34%
MRO	Marathon Oil Corporation	32.10	2.37%
OXY	Occidental Petroleum Corporation**	87.29	2.93%
PBR	Petrobras**	10.78	2.45%
PSX	Phillips**	70.67	2.21%
TOT	Total SA**	56.75	5.59%
VLO	Valero Energy Corporation**	46.37	2.16%
XOM	Exxon**	89.58	2.81%

Note: Prices quoted during trading day 2/5/2014).

Quotes and yields believed to be accurate; however, reader should recheck all information with his/her financial advisor before making any investment decision. ** = OVERWEIGHT

Hopefully, with this road map, you can make some money to prepare for the foreboding time ahead when D'Apocalypse™ arrives. There are many index funds around the DJIA and S&P 500 and other equities which also might be excellent vehicles to participate in the rally. When you exit by June of 2015, between now and then, you should have scouted for and secured, private storage if you have to manage assets, monies, or a portfolio---preferably under as much secrecy as possible, given all the snooping the government is doing.

At the beginning of 2014, D'Apocalypse™ Now! recommended a number of stocks, as evidenced by book proofs published in February 2014. "Bullion" and "Big Cap" $10,000,000 theoretical portfolios were created to track performance. Through July 28, 2014, the theoretical portfolios beat the Dow & S&P, significantly ("Bullion" performance on page 299).

Performance of Big Cap Stocks Theoretical Portfolio July 28, 2014: Percentages NOT annualized			
	10-Jan-14	28-Jul-14	% Gain (Loss)
Dow Jones	16437.05	16,982.59	3.3%
S&P 500	1842.37	1978.91	7.4%
Vs. D'Apocalypse™ Now! Big Cap Recommendations + Dividends (Less Fees)			14.4%
Vs. D'Apocalypse™ Now! Big Cap Recommendations			14.1%

$10 Million Theoretical Big Cap Portfolio

$10,000,000 Model Portfolio Big Cap Stocks
Recommended "Overweight" Stocks
Originally Quoted January 10, 2014
Updated July 28, 2014

	Price/Share Recommended 2/5/14	Original Investment Even Allocation	# Shares Less 2.5% Transaction Cost	Annual Yield 2/5/14	Accumulated Dividends 7/28/14	Price/Share 7/28/14	Equity Position Value	Less 1% Theoretical Exit Fee	Total (Net Equity Value + Dividends) Theoretical	Total Theoretical % Return
Oil Stocks:										
CVX Chevron Corporation	$109.52	$714,286	6,359	3.65%	$12,710	$133.24	$847,262	$838,789	$851,499	19.21%
COP ConocoPhillips	$63.46	$714,286	10,974	4.35%	$15,147	$85.19	$934,900	$925,551	$940,698	31.70%
OXY Occidental Petroleum	$87.29	$714,286	7,978	2.93%	$10,203	$99.82	$796,397	$788,433	$798,636	11.81%
PBR Petrobras	$10.78	$714,286	64,604	2.45%	$8,531	$17.03	$1,100,202	$1,089,200	$1,097,731	53.68%
PSX Phillips	$70.67	$714,286	9,855	2.21%	$7,696	$82.61	$814,093	$805,952	$813,648	13.91%
TOT Total SA	$56.75	$714,286	12,272	5.59%	$19,465	$69.34	$850,931	$842,422	$861,887	20.66%
VLO Valero Energy	$46.37	$714,286	15,019	2.16%	$7,521	$49.04	$736,529	$729,164	$736,685	3.14%
XOM Exxon	$89.58	$714,286	7,774	2.81%	$9,785	$104.37	$811,412	$803,297	$813,082	13.83%
Dow Components:										
DD Du Pont	$61.90	$714,286	11,251	3.04%	$10,586	$65.32	$734,907	$727,557	$738,143	3.34%
JNJ Johnson & Johnson	$87.28	$714,286	7,979	2.70%	$9,402	$102.11	$814,761	$806,613	$816,015	14.24%
MMM 3M Company	$127.36	$714,286	5,468	2.70%	$9,402	$145.53	$795,786	$787,828	$797,229	11.61%
MRK Merck	$53.53	$714,286	13,010	3.30%	$11,491	$57.97	$754,193	$746,651	$758,142	6.14%
PG Procter & Gamble	$76.45	$714,286	9,110	3.30%	$11,491	$79.26	$722,027	$714,806	$726,297	1.68%
V Visa	$215.61	$714,286	3,230	0.70%	$2,438	$214.22	$691,939	$685,019	$687,457	-3.76%
Total		$10,000,000			$145,867		$11,405,338	$11,291,285	$11,437,152	
% THEORETICAL GAIN							14.1%	12.9%	14.4%	

© 2014 Robert L. Kelly "Overweight Stocks" as published in proof of the book, D'Apocalypse Now!—The Doomsday Cycle, in February 2014. Available at www.amazon.com.

Information in the above table may not be accurate, please check with your financial advisor for up-to-date figures and advice.

Model portfolios are theoretical, actual results WILL vary.

What to do if there is Marching in the Streets

Governments have too much debt and banks have overextended themselves in the derivatives market. On top of this, worldwide, we are seeing vast populations of people revolt against government corruption (i.e., socialism for the rich---and rugged, individual capitalism for everyone else). As is obvious, the elite have stealthily seized wealth by combining the strategies of two competing ideologies---communism and capitalism.

As the world heats up and the banks run into further trouble, change can occur at any time, and overnight. This will deliver a shock to the status quo and to depositors' money in the bank and investment accounts.

To enable a workout of a derivatives blow out governments will, or the bankers will, automatically, *steal* your deposited funds and assets. Many, many customer agreements allow these scoundrels to re-hypothecate your monies and assets on deposit with their institutions.

Like in Cypress, they will look to you, Mr. and Mrs. Depositor, to "assist" with a "workout" during the derivatives crisis. D'Apocalypse™ will see the taking of your money and assets, even if you had nothing to do with the banks' or security firms' poor business decisions and ridiculous risk taking. Don't leave anything on deposit, except for the bare minimum you need to keep the lights on in the account!

The balance in your checking account one day could be $40,000 and the next day it could be only $20,000—with $20,000 being taken to pay off "bond holders," or meet other bank obligations. You could have $20,000,000 in your corporate account and be one of the finest customers at JP Morgan Chase and overnight, you could wind up with $5,000,000---with the rest GONE.....vanished into the digital ether. You have no control over any assets which are kept, digitally speaking.

None of the big banks are safe and any reader should have their monies spread across banks with HIGH Weiss ratings (www.weissratings.com). International readers should be in smaller, regional banks with high international agency ratings. The definite preference is for PRIVATE, SECURE STORAGE of your assets *before* D'Apocalypse™ strikes. Limiting assets placed in any bank and spreading those assets around is a very, very good idea. You should start on this plan immediately.

The United States is at high risk and is bound to experience massive bank failures, and seizures unlawfully, of depositors' assets. Don't look to

Congress or the law to help you---they will have made such seizures "legal" by then.

The problems in the debt and counter-party markets will paralyze the banking system and cause its current bankrupt state to become utterly exposed. Subsequently, there will be a rush to grab money and repair the system, "for the good of everyone!" As the world's confidence in our ability to pay off our debt shatters and the derivatives casino implodes, the government, this book expects, will come apart at the seams.

The marches you see today in Spain, Greece, Italy and Brazil will be happening right in the "good old USA" and will broaden out in Europe and Japan. You should view the decaying European Union and the overextended developing countries as the "canaries in the coal mine."

Many of the developing countries have already experienced a fate where the top 1% of the wealthy and powerful, over decades and centuries, have pilfered the wealth of many of these nations. They took all the money and left everyone else with virtually nothing. This kind of tragic circumstance is common across the developing world. Powerful governments, most run by a group of elites or outright dictators, took control of the nation's resources and exclusively pandered to the rich, famous and politically connected. If this sounds like a familiar story---with eerie similarities to what is happening in America and Western Europe today, you are correct!

The men and women running the banks in America just took nearly $30 Trillion, in a $30 Trillion heist from the American taxpayer. The banks bailed themselves out of wicked trouble during the credit crisis when all the banks---and their wealthy elite owners---should have lost everything.

Now funded to the hilt, thanks to the Federal Reserve's secret bailouts at the taxpayers' expense and in full control of Assflation™, they press onward with their capital. They stand ready to pounce and strip the existing system of its wealth and prosperity. They are beyond prepared to steal additional trillions of dollars' worth of assets and companies for pennies on the dollar.

In the middle of their vicious attack, they will pivot and appear to rescue strangled governments, all of which are choking on debt, in exchange for control of monetary policy and the money supply.

They will not care how many billions of people they hurt in the process.

Chapter 10
A Special Message to Our Military and Defense Industry

Note: Reprinted from Volume II, The $30 Trillion Heist---Follow The Money Chapter 19, for those who have not read it.

Our nation needs to maintain the strongest military and defense industry on the planet. Despite this book's and the trilogy's deliberations on the Federal Reserve, the elite and the banks, the debt problem is critical. Also critical to the safety of our nation and people all over the world, is the military and defense industries of America. Until Jesus returns, their budgets should be GROWN, not slashed, with not only a focus on the defense of the nation, but a far more aggressive expansion of TECHNOLOGY into key, strategic areas which hold great promise for mankind.

The only caveat to this position is when Jesus returns, we must turn our swords into plow shares!

Until this time comes, the fight against an evil and violent world requires a just fighting force which is once again focused on God and Jesus Christ almighty---and not on the selfish impulses of bankers and politicians eager to use war as a crutch to scare the people to remain in power and enrich themselves in the process.

This means our men and women in uniform, in collaboration with their university and research partners, will need to stay the course of a just fight and provide leadership which has, historically, always led with God, duty, honor and country. For these reasons, our military has been blessed.

Our military should RESIST any demands for change from these principles and ROOT OUT the evil which is attempting to use the language of "separating church and state" to keep religion out of government and the military. Our Founding Father's tried to ensure the GOVERNMENT didn't dictate a religion *to us*---as the King of England did. They wanted to **make sure we would be free to worship as we please,** with the vast preponderance of Americans believing in Jesus Christ as our Lord and Savior.

Remembering the immortal words of Ronald Reagan:

"A state is nothing more than a reflection of its citizens: The more decent the citizens, the more decent the state. If you practice a religion, whether you're Catholic, Protestant, Jewish, or guided by some other faith, then your private life will be influenced by a sense of moral obligation, and so, too, will your public life. One affects the other. The churches of America do not exist by the grace of the State; the churches of America are not mere citizens of the State. The churches of America exist apart; they have their own vantage point, their own authority. Religion is its own realm; it makes its own claims.

We establish no religion in this country, nor will we ever. We command no worship. We mandate no belief. But we poison our society when we remove its theological underpinnings. We court corruption when we leave it bereft of belief. All are free to believe or not to believe; all are free to practice a faith or not. But those who believe must be free to speak of and act on their belief, to apply moral teaching to public questions.

I submit to you that the tolerant society is open to and encouraging of all religions. And this does not weaken us; it strengthens us; it makes us strong. You know, if we look back through history to all those great civilizations, those great nations that rose up to even world dominance and then deteriorated, declined, and fell, we find they all had one thing in common. One of the significant forerunners of their fall was their turning away from their God or gods.

Without God, there is no virtue, because there's no prompting of the conscience. Without God, we're mired in the material, that flat world that tells us only what the senses perceive. Without God, there is a coarsening of the society. And without God, democracy will not and cannot long endure. If we ever forget that we're one nation under God, then we will be a nation gone under." (Source: Ronald Reagan, President of the United States, Remarks at a Dallas Ecumenical Prayer Breakfast, delivered 23 August 1984 at Reunion Arena, Dallas, TX, as retrieved from http://www.americanrhetoric.com/ speeches/ronaldreaganecumenicalprayer.htm).

Double Military Pay

Having said this, what we pay our men and women in uniform to protect our nation is not even close to enough. A God-fearing nation with men and women in control of the military who fear God, are simply priceless gems in the eyes of a peaceful society. 99% of THESE men and women are above and beyond payoffs---and corruption is disdainful to them. The FACT most of our military believes and stands for God and His principles is the critical ingredient needed to overwhelm those who are trying to oppress others. This is why our military, historically, has been blessed.

Current Pay Marine Corps, Army, Air Force, Navy		© 2013 Robert L. Kelly
	Current Pay	**Proposed Pay**
Private, Airman, Seaman	$18,194	$36,388
Gunnery Sgt , Sgt. First Class, Master Sgt., Chief Petty Officer	$32,702	$65,404
First Lieutenant	$39,769	$79,538
Colonel , Captain	$72,778	$145,556
Brigadier General , Rear Admiral	$98,190	$196,380
	2013 Budget	**Proposed**
Total Payroll Armed Forces USA	$108,964,000,000	$217,928,000,000

For these reasons alone (aside from the fact they lay down their lives for our country and other countries when asked!), these people should have their salaries DOUBLED.

Not every reader will believe in, like, or even appreciate this perspective, but this book doesn't belong to Democrats, Republicans or Libertarians (i.e., as much as this book respects the great Ron Paul and Libertarians, most of them would mercilessly cut the military budget, which this book opposes). Our country is going to need benevolent, strong leadership to overcome the sins of the bankers and politicians. The military is the key to this endeavor, when the time comes---and push comes to shove.

This book and its sister publications in the Federal Reserve Trilogy espouse solutions to the big problems confronting our nation, while assuring the men and women in uniform---who can get us out of trouble---they are needed, loved and respected. The masses will need help from these great people to re-instill a sense of fairness and representative people-control over the system, once again, after D'Apocalypse™ strikes and it becomes clearer the bankers and the elite have made an end run around government. These people in uniform represent a tower of strength which may be capable of reversing the greed and avarice maintaining a stranglehold on the system today.

Rear Admirals and Brigadier Generals Earn Less Than 1% Of What The Four Biggest Bailed-Out Banks Paid EACH of Their Executives For 2012!

To make a point on the pay issue, imagine a Brigadier General from the Army, Marines or Air Force commanding multi-billion dollar tank forces, elite fighting capability and/or squadrons of stealth aircraft, fighters and bombers—all with nuclear arms capability or a Rear Admiral commanding an entire fleet of an advanced nuclear navy, with all of its sophisticated multi-billion dollar weaponry, earning less than 1% of what the average pay was for EACH of the executives at the secretly bailed-out 4 Horsemen of the D'Apocalypse™ (as detailed in Chapter 3 of this book, "Wall Street Profits and Compensation-How Much Are they Getting Paid?," subsection, "4 Bailed Out Horsemen of the D'Apocalypse™--$12.7 MILLION PER EXECUTIVE!"). These men and women in uniform are unbelievably underpaid.

> *The pay differential is simply outrageous between the bankers and elite who SUCK our blood and the men and women in uniform who GIVE us blood.*

People in uniform allow others to go to work and be free to earn money, have a family and enjoy a peaceful nation. Military leaders are paid a pittance compared to what other CEOs and executives are paid. The men and women underneath their commands are no less critical and vital to the protection of free people, everywhere. They should all have a HUGE pay raise!

Even the current salary (2013) for rank-and-file members of the House and Senate, most of who aren't worth anything, is $174,000 per year! Our military, along with the men and women who already served and are retired deserve more money---and just for the record, the author has never served in the military.

Among the few organizations in government which are not completely corrupt *are* the military and intelligence agencies. Unfortunately, these fine men and women are at risk because government officials, with their own agenda, take issue with many of the military's and agencies' key leaders, on a regular basis, with a clear and obvious intention of weeding out any powerful man or woman, who has a different opinion than the administration's—regardless of which administration is in power at the time.

Any of them who support and uphold the historical principles of America and its traditional stand with God are subject to direct attack and outright dismissal. We may have to ask some of the great commanders and intelligence leaders who have been dismissed or otherwise have been forced out, to return to serve their country once again, when D'Apocalypse™ strikes. Things could get really rough and we will need their leadership.

Defense Industry Must be Informed of the Plan to Eliminate the Fed

While the defense industry has a long relationship with the banking industry, at the end of the day, it is an industry filled with patriots who will support our military and traditional values. There will have to be a clear plan laid out for them, as they will need to know who will pay their bills. Once they understand Abraham Lincoln has been reincarnated through a new, non-Federal Reserve, U.S. Congress-denominated currency, backed by the full faith-and-credit of the United States Government, they will be more than happy to get rid of the leaches sucking interest payments out of government budgets which could otherwise be spent on defense and other strategic initiatives of the country.

It may indeed be the military who helps Congress deliver the new currency of the land, printed by the U.S. Congress, which shall be the new legal tender---good for the payment of all debts—both foreign and domestic.

As you know and as is described in this book, Abraham Lincoln did just this when he issued "Greenbacks" to pay for the Civil War. These kinds of currencies can even be pledged with collateral, as our U.S. Notes were backed by a gold reserve, at one point in time (but, going to a gold standard would be a very bad idea---please see Chapter 9, "Buy Bullion," subsection "No Gold Standard," of this book).

The "Greenback" and Gold-Backed Certificate

(Source: National Numismatic Collection at the Smithsonian Institution, American Bank Note Company, Smithsonian National Museum of American History, as retrieved from http://en.wikipedia.org/wiki/File:US-$10-DN-1861-Fr.7.jpg).

(Source: Antique Bank Notes retrieved from:
http://www.antiquebanknotes.com/Gold-Certificate/Series-1882.aspx)

The military and defense industry have always put their personal interests behind those of the nation. Many of them are brilliant and though not experts in the field of finance, know when a fox is running the hen house. Many of them have a profound understanding of what is being done to this country by the banks, the controlling elite and the Federal Reserve System. These fine men and women in uniform want change, also.

God-fearing men and women in both the military and defense industries, along with many others, will attempt to pick up the pieces for ALL Americans when the system goes into cardiac arrest. It will be an interesting battle of wills and power when the push is on for global control of the monetary system. Our great hope is a set of patriots can head these tyrannical megalomaniacs off at the pass and prevent the robber barons from controlling our futures. The odds are against us, but we must attempt to win this battle for the sake of hundreds of millions of souls.

After D'Apocalypse™ and the resulting power grab by the elite and their allies, many of the key people in military and the defense industry will likely be very tired of doing the un-Godlike bidding of politicians and money men. They have seen the results of wars without reason and wars without clear objectives---which by design do not allow our troops to win. They also see through the thinly veiled attempt by politicians to remain in power by creating undeclared wars to keep the United States and Western world locked up, under a cloud of fear, with the continued ability to spend profligately and unwisely.

The only real victors in these battles are the politicians currently in power, the bankers and the elite owners of the banks, as they will do anything they can to stay in power and run up the debt of any country in order to maximize their own wealth---even if it means creating a war without borders and a war without a cause, in the process.

Everyone's prayers will need to be unified and strong. We cannot allow the fear-mongering of the Federal Reserve members, the bankers, the elite and their paid-off politicians and media personalities to dissuade the country from retaking control of the Federal Reserve and the control over our nation's money supply.

The Key to Retaking Our Future

The ability of the country to control its own supply of money, rather than a cabal of elite member banks and a handful of corrupted bureaucrats, is the key to retaking our future. God's principles are required to be the

329

guiding hand of control over the men and women who have the responsibility of running our great nation and at this point in time, this writer does not believe His principles are at work. Instead, the system has been infected with greed, corruption and zest for power, existing only to serve the elite, in all directions, as far as the eye can see.

Additionally, REPUBLICANS AND DEMOCRATS have used war, violence, fear and government spending to remain in office. Working together with the Federal Reserve, many members in both parties have worked to bury our country.

While it is hoped true patriots will show up when the system fails---and this hope burns bright---right now the country's very foundations are under attack. Within the military itself, politicians are creating an environment of conflict for Americans who have traditional values who have also sworn an oath to uphold the Constitution.

They are being pressed to uphold laws and rules directly attacking the very pillars of our Christian heritage, as commemorated for thousands of years in the Old and New Testaments of <u>The Bible</u>, as well as the Pentateuch and Torah. The pillars of Christianity are founding principles of our nation and have been practiced ritually by every generation since the founding of our country.

Christians, conservatives, Tea Party members and libertarians are under political attack, seemingly, everywhere they turn. The working class and the poor are paid lip service by the Democrats and these poor do not understand they are merely cannon fodder for the elite---the elite provide them with food stamps and just barely enough to scrape by, while the bankers walk off with all the money and wealth, forever keeping the poor entombed in a new form of slavery, called poverty.

This comes full circle in and with our military, as there is intent and action to corrupt the moral code our military has maintained for CENTURIES. In fact, the situation has gotten to the point in the military where they cannot discuss their religion, they cannot disagree with the President, they cannot visit Christian-church web sites and they are being taught Catholics and Christians are potentially terrorists!

The entire system seems to be under siege from some commanding, evil force and presence which appears to be driven by a need to grab power and money without regard for any kind of principle, except the principles dictated by the wealthy, the bankers, the elite and the Federal Reserve System.

"Is it just a coincidence that the Southern Baptist website was blocked at many military installations around the nation a few weeks after a military representative labeled Roman Catholics and Evangelical Christians as extremists, according to recent articles in the Christian Post and on Fox News? Representatives of several Christian organizations said they were insulted by being lumped in with terrorist groups such as Hamas and Al-Qaeda on the military's list of dangerous cults."
(Source: The Examiner, by Edward Lane, April 29, 2013, "U.S. Army declares war on Christians BAPTISTS AND CATHOLICS LUMPED IN WITH AL QAEDA," retrieved from http://www.examiner.com/article/u-s-army-declares-war-on-christians).

The integrity of the United States military, overall, is impeccable, historically speaking. Let us all hope and pray the military (and the men and women of similar perspective and training, serving in other agencies and forces around the world in all countries) we all grew up with, dedicated to God and country, who took an oath to protect and defend the United States---from enemies both foreign and domestic---is there for all of us, when the expected grab for power begins.

They may be the only ones capable of stopping 2 Billion bullets and 2,000 tanks from what amounts to a domestic military force designed with only one purpose in mind---to use those arms against our own people on our own lands.

May God help us all.

The Unanimous Declaration of the Thirteen Colonies of the United States of America

When, in the course of human events, it becomes necessary for one people to dissolve the political bands which have connected them with another, and to assume among the powers of the earth, the separate and equal station to which the laws of nature and of nature's God entitle them, a decent respect to the opinions of mankind requires that they should declare the causes which impel them to the separation.

We hold these truths to be self-evident, that all men are created equal, that they are endowed by their Creator with certain unalienable rights, that among these are life, liberty and the pursuit of happiness. **That to secure these rights, governments are instituted among men, deriving their just powers from the consent of the governed.** *That whenever any form of government becomes destructive to these ends, it is the right of the people to alter or to abolish it, and to institute new government, laying its foundation on such principles and organizing its powers in such form, as to them shall seem most likely to effect their safety and happiness. Prudence, indeed, will dictate that governments long established should not be changed for light and transient causes; and accordingly all experience hath shown that mankind are more disposed to suffer, while evils are sufferable, than to right themselves by abolishing the forms to which they are accustomed.* **But when a long train of abuses and usurpations, pursuing invariably the same object evinces a design to reduce them under absolute despotism, it is their right, it is their duty, to throw off such government, and to provide new guards for their future security.** *--Such has been the patient sufferance of these colonies; and such is now the necessity which constrains them to alter their former systems of government. The history of the present King of Great Britain is a history of repeated injuries and usurpations, all having in direct object the establishment of an absolute tyranny over these states. To prove this, let facts be submitted to a candid world.*

He has refused his assent to laws, the most wholesome and necessary for the public good. He has forbidden his governors to pass laws of immediate and pressing importance, unless suspended in their operation till his assent should be obtained; and when so suspended, he has utterly neglected to attend to them.

He has refused to pass other laws for the accommodation of large districts of people, unless those people would relinquish the right of representation in the legislature, a right inestimable to them and formidable to tyrants only.

He has called together legislative bodies at places unusual, uncomfortable, and distant from the depository of their public records, for the sole purpose of fatiguing them into compliance with his measures.

He has dissolved representative houses repeatedly, for opposing with manly firmness his invasions on the rights of the people.

He has refused for a long time, after such dissolutions, to cause others to be elected; whereby the legislative powers, incapable of annihilation, have returned to the people at large for their exercise; the state remaining in the meantime exposed to all the dangers of invasion from without, and convulsions within.

He has endeavored to prevent the population of these states; for that purpose obstructing the laws for naturalization of foreigners; refusing to pass others to encourage their migration hither, and raising the conditions of new appropriations of lands.

He has obstructed the administration of justice, by refusing his assent to laws for establishing judiciary powers.

He has made judges dependent on his will alone, for the tenure of their offices, and the amount and payment of their salaries.

He has erected a multitude of new offices, and sent hither swarms of officers to harass our people, and eat out their substance.

He has kept among us, in times of peace, standing armies without the consent of our legislature.

He has affected to render the military independent of and superior to civil power.

He has combined with others to subject us to a jurisdiction foreign to our constitution, and unacknowledged by our laws; giving his assent to their acts of pretended legislation:

For quartering large bodies of armed troops among us:

For protecting them, by mock trial, from punishment for any murders which they should commit on the inhabitants of these states:

For cutting off our trade with all parts of the world:

For imposing taxes on us without our consent:

For depriving us in many cases, of the benefits of trial by jury:

For transporting us beyond seas to be tried for pretended offenses:

For abolishing the free system of English laws in a neighboring province, establishing therein an arbitrary government, and enlarging its boundaries so as to render it at once an example and fit instrument for introducing the same absolute rule in these colonies:

For taking away our charters, abolishing our most valuable laws, and altering fundamentally the forms of our governments:

For suspending our own legislatures, and declaring themselves invested with power to legislate for us in all cases whatsoever.

He has abdicated government here, by declaring us out of his protection and waging war against us.

He has plundered our seas, ravaged our coasts, burned our towns, and destroyed the lives of our people.

He is at this time transporting large armies of foreign mercenaries to complete the works of death, desolation and tyranny, already begun with circumstances of cruelty and perfidy scarcely paralleled in the most barbarous ages, and totally unworthy the head of a civilized nation.

He has constrained our fellow citizens taken captive on the high seas to bear arms against their country, to become the executioners of their friends and brethren, or to fall themselves by their hands.

He has excited domestic insurrections amongst us, and has endeavored to bring on the inhabitants of our frontiers, the merciless Indian savages, whose known rule of warfare, is undistinguished destruction of all ages, sexes and conditions.

In every stage of these oppressions we have petitioned for redress in the most humble terms: our repeated petitions have been answered only by repeated injury. A prince, whose character is thus marked by every act which may define a tyrant, is unfit to be the ruler of a free people.

Nor have we been wanting in attention to our British brethren. We have warned them from time to time of attempts by their legislature to extend an unwarrantable jurisdiction over us. We have reminded them of the circumstances of our emigration and settlement here. We have appealed to their native justice and magnanimity, and we have conjured them by the ties of our common kindred to disavow these usurpations, which, would inevitably interrupt our connections and correspondence. They too have been deaf to the voice of justice and of consanguinity. We must, therefore, acquiesce in the necessity, which denounces our separation, and hold them, as we hold the rest of mankind, enemies in war, in peace friends.

*We, therefore, the representatives of the United States of America, in General Congress, assembled, <u>appealing to the Supreme Judge of the world</u> for the rectitude of our intentions, do, in the name, and by <u>colonies are, and of right ought to be free and independent states; that they are absolved from all allegiance to the British Crown, and that all political connection between them and the state of Great Britain, is and ought to be totally dissolved; and that as free and independent states, they have full power to levy war, conclude peace, contract alliances, establish commerce, and to do all other acts and things which independent states may of right do. And for the support of this declaration, with a firm reliance on the protection of Divine Providence,</u> **we mutually pledge to each other our lives, our fortunes and our sacred honor.**

(Image credit: Wikipedia, as retrieved from
http://upload.wikimedia.org/wikipedia/commons/b/b6/Us_declaration_independence_signatures.jpg).

New Hampshire: Josiah Bartlett, William Whipple, Matthew Thornton
Massachusetts: John Hancock, Samuel Adams, John Adams, Robert Treat Paine, Elbridge Gerry
Rhode Island: Stephen Hopkins, William Ellery
Connecticut: Roger Sherman, Samuel Huntington, William Williams, Oliver Wolcott
New York: William Floyd, Philip Livingston, Francis Lewis, Lewis Morris
New Jersey: Richard Stockton, John Witherspoon, Francis Hopkinson, John Hart, Abraham Clark
Pennsylvania: Robert Morris, Benjamin Rush, Benjamin Franklin, John Morton, George Clymer, James Smith, George Taylor, James Wilson, George Ross
Delaware: Caesar Rodney, George Read, Thomas McKean
Maryland: Samuel Chase, William Paca, Thomas Stone, Charles Carroll of Carrollton
Virginia: George Wythe, Richard Henry Lee, Thomas Jefferson, Benjamin Harrison, Thomas Nelson, Jr., Francis Lightfoot Lee, Carter Braxton
North Carolina: William Hooper, Joseph Hewes, John Penn
South Carolina: Edward Rutledge, Thomas Heyward, Jr., Thomas Lynch, Jr., Arthur Middleton
Georgia: Button Gwinnett, Lyman Hall, George Walton

(Source: The Declaration of Independence, July 4, 1776, signed by the 56 delegates at the Second Continental Congress in Philadelphia, as retrieved from http://www.archives.gov/exhibits/charters/declaration_transcript.html).

Epilogue
Author's Personal Note & Invitation to Make a Commitment

Please note: if you have read either Volume I or II of The $30 Trillion Heist---Scene Of The Crime? or Follow The Money!, this Epilogue is repeated as the author's personal note and invitation to the reader.

The trilogy of The $30 Trillion Heist, Volume I, Scene of the Crime? and Volume II Follow The Money!, along with D'Apocalypse™ Now!---The Doomsday Cycle, tells three very important interrelated stories. The author incorporated a few important sections of The $30 Trillion Heist into D'Apocalypse™ Now! to provide continuity and perspective for new readers of the author's work---just in case a person hadn't read either Volume I, or Volume II of The $30 Trillion Heist. Each book of the trilogy has a unique message and is distinct. Together, they may be vital to any person seeking to discover the truth and become prepared for the dangers heading our way.

Without a proper understanding of the Federal Reserve, readers may find it difficult to understand why America has changed dramatically---in seemingly dastardly ways, at all points of the compass. Understanding the fact the Federal Reserve is **the problem** is critical to the reader's ability to educate Congressmen, Senators, neighbors and friends. It is only through this process of education can real reform be accomplished.

It is hoped these works will help all Americans in their quest for justice against the elite, the banks and the Federal Reserve System in the aftermath of the great D'Apocalypse™. They have heisted trillions from future generations of Americans---and we need to recover these assets if our children and our children's children have any chance for recovery.

Attempting such a work against such powerful people and organizations is a daunting task. When you read these words, thoughts and theories from The Federal Reserve Trilogy, please remember these words were written by a mere man applying his worldly knowledge to facts he uncovered and events he foresees from a Christian's and businessman's perspective.

If I am wrong with respect to any outcome prognosticated or reported in these works, don't blame God.

Just blame it on a mortal man who was doing the best job he could to interpret events and evidence the best *way* he could, while turning to God in prayer. Personally, I hope I am wrong with events I expect to unfold and a miracle does happen, because the D'Apocalypse™ expected is extremely severe and extremely traumatic; hundreds of millions of people will suffer unbelievably as a result.

> Real, global war will VERY LIKELY begin in and around D'Apocalypse™, but with near certainty by 2019, as there has never been a collapse of this nature before in history---and nearly all historic collapses which create massive economic hardship have led to great wars, as one economic tribe battles another to maintain control, feed its people and attempt to spark economic recovery.

When Life Isn't Easy
As you might have guessed by now, despite the ability to look ahead of the curve, nothing in my life has ever come easy. I did not grow up with a silver spoon in my mouth and it seems God has always been testing me and my faith. The funny part of it is each and every time I thought there was just too much pressure—the Holy Spirit somehow provided relief and a solution for me to follow; and I can promise you, the Holy Spirit has sustained me throughout significant trials in my life.

If you have found yourself in a similar position, where you may have been challenged, are under duress, are having a tough time, or otherwise find yourself at wits end, just read the book of Job (or even sections of it) from The Bible and you will see how truly blessed we all are.

When the roof feels like it is caving in and financially you feel like a train wreck, just look on the Internet, or on TV (CNN International, or the BBC, for example) and witness the absolute poverty which abounds outside of the confines of the United States and Western Europe. You will see it, but will not probably fully appreciate it, as you cannot smell rotting stench through television, or through the computer screen. Nevertheless, reminding ourselves of how fortunate we are, compared to many billions of other people, will lend some perspective and help you stop worrying, while keeping you strong in your faith and convictions. This will allow you to focus on the positives, which is what you need to do to survive what is lying dead ahead during the firestorm of D'Apocalypse™.

If the words written in this book touch you, or make sense and you are convinced of the evidence presented within these pages, then immediately take to heart some of the advice and get prepared for a complete meltdown in the financial markets and economic structure of society---it is coming and soon.

Then, if you don't know Jesus Christ and you are led by the Holy Spirit, pray to Jesus for your salvation and watch the miracle of a changed life begin to take place. You will no longer fear for the future, but will find you are now in the army of God and one of His confident foot soldiers who KNOWS they will be victorious in the end.

At any time when you read this book, depending on who you are, I leave three, and only three, decision boxes to help you open your heart to the Lord our God, Jesus Christ His son and the Holy Spirit.

God Bless You in your new walk with the Lord! He is mighty, indeed!!

1)   FOREVER CHANGE YOUR LIFE!

"Dear God, the sole God for all eternity, I pray in your son's name, Jesus Christ, to please forgive my sins and hear my prayer. I accept Jesus Christ as my Lord and personal savior and believe you sent Him from heaven to earth, where He was born of the Virgin Mary. I believe in His life, His teachings, His horrible death and the sacrifice He made for my sins---and all mankind's sins. I KNOW AND BELIEVE HIS RESURRECTION IS TRUE AND I KNOW AND BELIEVE HE ASCENDED INTO HEAVEN AND SITS AT THE RIGHT HAND OF THE FATHER. I accept your gift and promise of eternal life through faith in Jesus Christ, for you have promised us by your grace, the grace of the one and only eternal God, I can be saved through the gift of faith. I also know my earthly works will not get me into your heavenly kingdom, as you don't want any man to boast, but I know we are created in Jesus to do good works out of the love and gratefulness we have for your mercy, power and gift of eternal life through the sacrifice made for us by Jesus Christ, your son and savior. AMEN"

"For it is by grace you have been saved, through faith—and this is not from yourselves, it is the gift of God—not by works, so that no one can boast. For we are God's handiwork, <u>created in Christ Jesus to do good works,</u> which <u>God prepared in advance for us to do</u>."
(Source: <u>The Bible, Ephesians 2:8-10</u>, New International Version).

"For God so loved the world that He gave His only begotten son, that whosoever believeth in Him should not perish, but have eternal life." (Source: <u>The Bible, John 3:16</u>, King James Version)

If you pray this prayer, or a form of prayer accepting Jesus Christ as your Lord and Savior, I urge you to find brothers and sisters in Christ to nurture your walk with God. The Holy Spirit will guide you and you will notice a difference in the way you walk and talk through life…..you will see differences in your attitudes and actions. Embrace these, read and study His Holy Word, <u>The Bible</u>, and REPENT of your sins. Your heart will naturally want to do good works, because you realize what an amazing *free* gift has been given to you---ETERNAL LIFE!

In today's hurry-up world, it is becoming even more important to immediately embrace Jesus Christ as your savior, <u>as God gave us Jesus to allow us to enter heaven.</u> The Quickening is upon us all…he who has ears, let him hear….he or she who has heart, let them give it to the Lord our God—the one God of eternity. In the name of the Father, the Son and the Holy Spirit, AMEN!

Finally, after all the reading, studying, successes, failures, sacrifices and opportunities in life---there is only one thing which matters.

Jesus.

For those of you who are trapped in the sleek corporate confines of our banks and the thousands of companies thirsting for profits, worldwide, this book is especially for you. It is written to those living in comfort in the most American and Western-European sense of the word, with children and young adults honey-stuck to their smart phones and video games, while Mom and Dad are living, eating and drinking like kings and queens, with everyone engrossed in the TV set. Unfortunately for one all, they are completely ignoring the dark, ominous clouds on the horizon foreshadowing their very own deaths. Without Jesus you are doomed.

To any and all backsliders who are out there—I urge you to read the Holy Scripture and take heed and warning…! Take up the courage of conviction and KNOW <u>The Bible</u> is TRUE!! The evidence is overwhelming…pray for the strength to overcome evil with good….AND DO SO!!

2) THE BACKSLIDER'S MAKE, OR BREAK TIME!

> **"What good is it, my brothers and sisters, if someone claims to have faith but has no deeds? Can such faith save them? Suppose a brother or a sister is without clothes and daily food. If one of you says to them, "Go in peace; keep warm and well fed," but does nothing about their physical needs, what good is it? In the same way, faith by itself, if it is not accompanied by action, is dead.**

> But someone will say, "You have faith; I have deeds."
>
> Show me your faith without deeds, and I will show you my faith by my deeds. You believe that there is one God. Good! Even the demons believe that—and shudder.
>
> You foolish person, do you want evidence that faith without deeds is useless? Was not our father Abraham considered righteous for what he did when he offered his son Isaac on the altar? You see that his faith and his actions were working together, and his faith was made complete by what he did. And the scripture was fulfilled that says, "Abraham believed God, and it was credited to him as righteousness," and he was called God's friend. You see that a person is considered righteous by what they do and not by faith alone.
>
> In the same way, was not even Rahab the prostitute considered righteous for what she did when she gave lodging to the spies and sent them off in a different direction? As the body without the spirit is dead, so faith without deeds is dead."
>
> (Source: The Bible, James 2:14-24, New International Version).

Sadly, there are millions of souls who believe in Jesus, but go back to their old ways of sin after they have received Jesus as their savior and don't do any good works. The Holy Scripture is very clear on this topic....FAITH WITHOUT WORKS IS DEAD.

As even the History Channel recounts the story of Abraham being obedient to God---The Bible---in both the Old and New Testaments--- informed us of God's principle of obedience long before it streamed into our living rooms courtesy of your cable provider. If you truly have given your heart and life to Jesus Christ, your natural desire---and your own predetermined destiny, is to do good deeds!

Backsliders, one and all, you must believe in the imminence of His arrival and I implore you to make a different, real change in your life.

Remember... *"Even the demons believe...and they shudder."*

It is not enough to just "believe." Make a difference in the life around you---just as Jesus and the disciples did, and "do" for other people. Help them, pray for them, feed them, cloth them, return to a simpler life (e.g., Jesus and His disciples didn't have any worldly possessions). Do not go down the slippery slope of, "Well, the Lord blessed me with this, so it is all OK...."

We probably all know numbers of wealthy Christians who have been blessed with much---but have done very little for other people in relation to what was given to them. To these people, I implore you to remember what Jesus said:

"It is easier for a camel to go through the eye of a needle, than for a rich man to enter into the kingdom of God."
(Source: The Bible, Matthew 19:23-24, King James Version).

Of course, the wealthy will go on to the next words of Jesus when the disciples asked Him who can be saved and Jesus replied all things are possible for God.

The admonition is clear, however, the wealthy shall be scrutinized very carefully by our heavenly and just God.

The disciples themselves gave up EVERYTHING THEY HAD TO FOLLOW JESUS. They all changed. They were all afraid at His death and went into hiding (fearful the Romans and the Jews would crucify them, just as they had Jesus), but they became ferocious and vociferous zealots for Christ---brandishing the helmet of salvation, the shield of faith, while swinging with all of their might, the sword of the Holy Spirit---and they died martyrs' deaths, with one spared to write the Book of Revelation---the Book of the Apocalypse, who of course was the Apostle John.

It was quite a change for a small group of men---all once terrified and in hiding and all unafraid to die for Christ. I don't know of a single case in history where any person, let alone an entire group of people (except John, spared to write the Book of Revelation, the Book of the Apocalypse) would die for a lie when they could have just walked away if they had just chosen to denounce Jesus Christ as their Lord and Savior!

These men are as relevant to us today more than ever before in history.

If you have ears to hear, then listen; if you have eyes to see, then read:

3)   THE MOST DANGEROUS ROUTE TO HELL IS BEING TOO COMFORTABLE!

> "Then Peter said to Him, 'Behold, we have left everything and followed You; what then will there be for us?' And Jesus said to them, 'Truly I say to you, that you who have followed Me, in the regeneration when the Son of Man will sit on His glorious throne, you also shall sit upon twelve thrones, judging the twelve tribes of Israel. And everyone who has left houses or brothers or sisters or father or mother or children or farms for My name's sake, will receive many times as much, and will inherit eternal life. But many who are first will be last; and the last, first.'"
>
> (Source: The Bible, Matthew 19:27-30, New American Standard Version).

The author, Robert Lyman Peter Kelly (as a boy, I chose "Peter" as my confirmation name), just like you, the reader, and just like the Apostle Peter, is a sinner and the words I write are only possible because I have been forgiven by the grace of God through the faith I have in the sacrifice and resurrection of the son of God, Jesus Christ. I know He shed His blood for me and for all mankind. He was born of the Virgin Mary and Jesus truly lived, taught, breathed, witnessed, suffered, died, buried, was resurrected AND ascended into heaven in front of many, many witnesses--all in fulfillment of the scriptures. He performed (and performs today) many miracles for the living while He walked among the disciples—and continues to perform those miracles after His earthly death.

The biggest miracle Jesus gives us ALL is the miraculous change He brings to those who truly give themselves to Him. This is the miracle of a changed life.   If you are not saved through the blood of Christ and your absolute faith in His resurrection and teachings, pray to God as you have been led by the Holy Spirit in one of the DECISION BOXES of this book, above, or otherwise. Ask for His forgiveness in His son's name, Jesus Christ, and commit your life to Him.   SEEK other like-minded individuals who can help you learn more about your new walk and birth in Jesus.   This is what Jesus meant when He said you cannot enter the Kingdom of Heaven---UNLESS YOU ARE BORN AGAIN!!

Finally, for all you backsliders out there, whether RICH, or POOR, **Jesus did not put a limit on how many times you can ask for, AND RECEIVE, complete forgiveness and thus eternal life in Heaven.**

With your new life, you have a new beginning. Make the most of it for His glory and not your own. When the disaster of D'Apocalypse™ strikes, remain calm and KNOW the Lord is our God and has complete control of EVERYTHING. This is part of the battle which must be fought before Jesus returns to earth.

I hope and pray you choose the side of might for right.

To this, the people said, in Jesus name,

Amen!

Christian Cross at the Roman Coliseum
© 2010 Robert L. Kelly

Made in the USA
Middletown, DE
15 December 2016